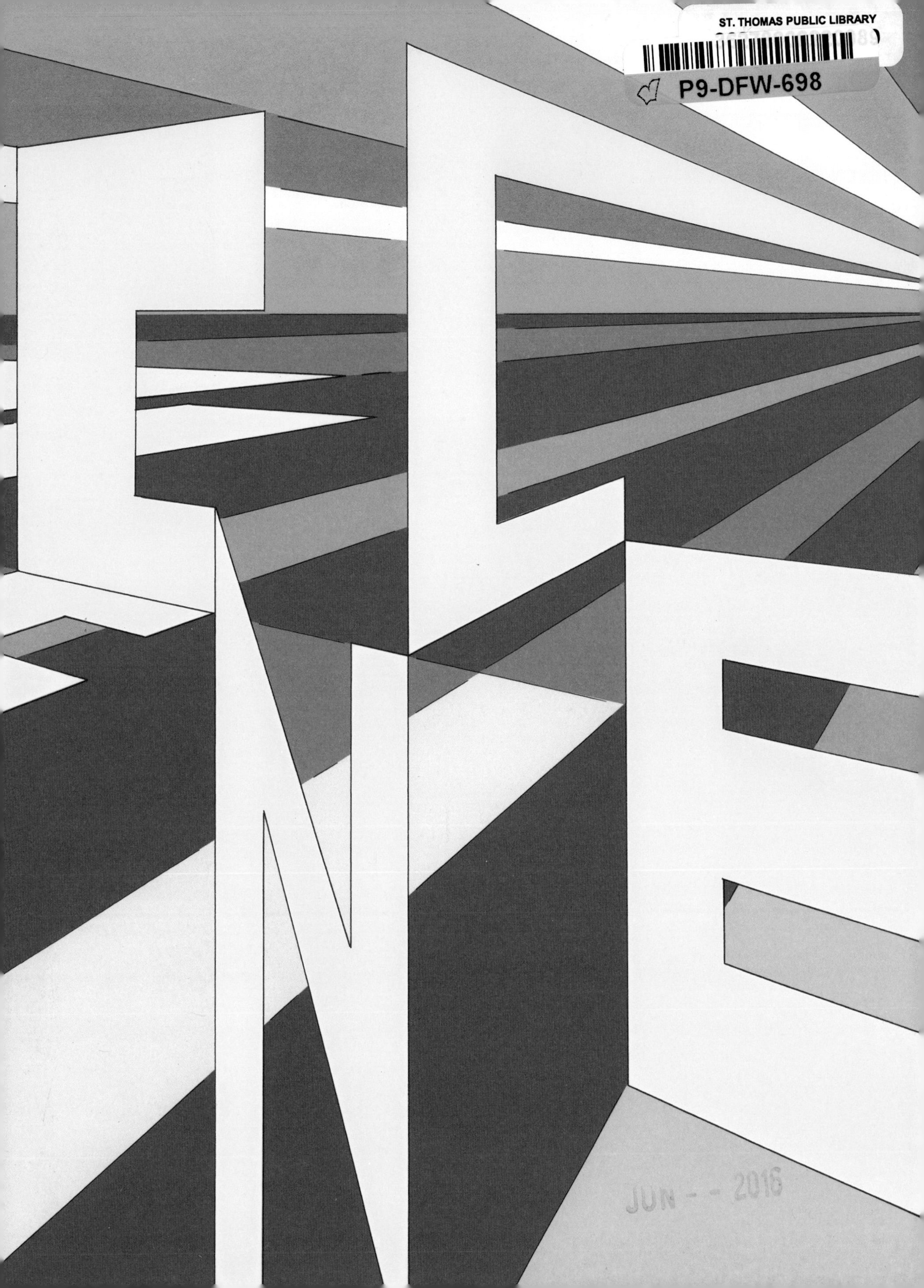

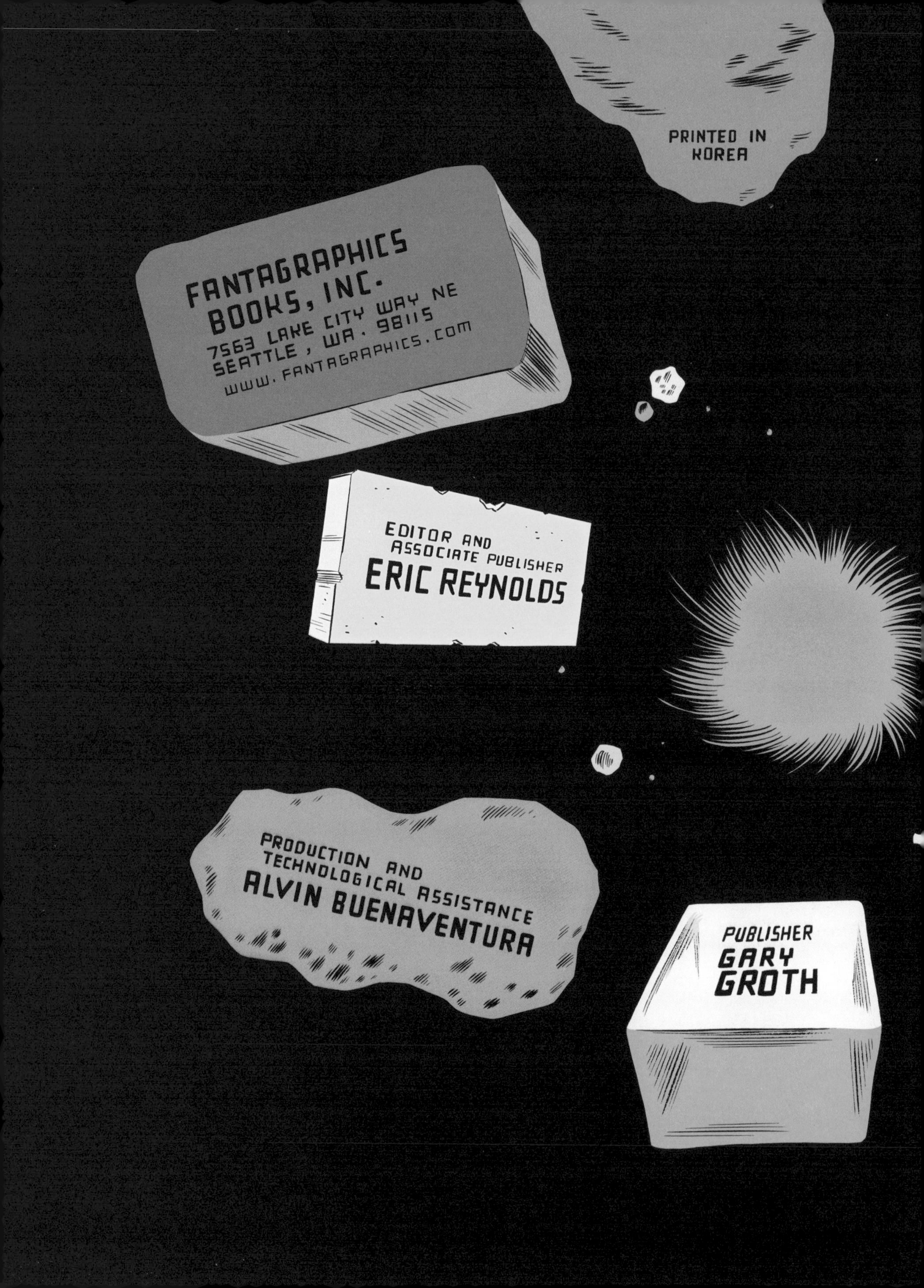
PRINTED IN KOREA
FANTAGRAPHICS BOOKS, INC.
7563 LAKE CITY WAY NE
SEATTLE, WA. 98115
WWW.FANTAGRAPHICS.COM
EDITOR AND ASSOCIATE PUBLISHER
ERIC REYNOLDS
PRODUCTION AND TECHNOLOGICAL ASSISTANCE
ALVIN BUENAVENTURA
PUBLISHER
GARY GROTH

FIRST PRINTING
MARCH 2016

FOR ERIKA

ISBN: 978-1-60699-905-9
LIBRARY OF CONGRESS CONTROL NUMBER: 2015953161

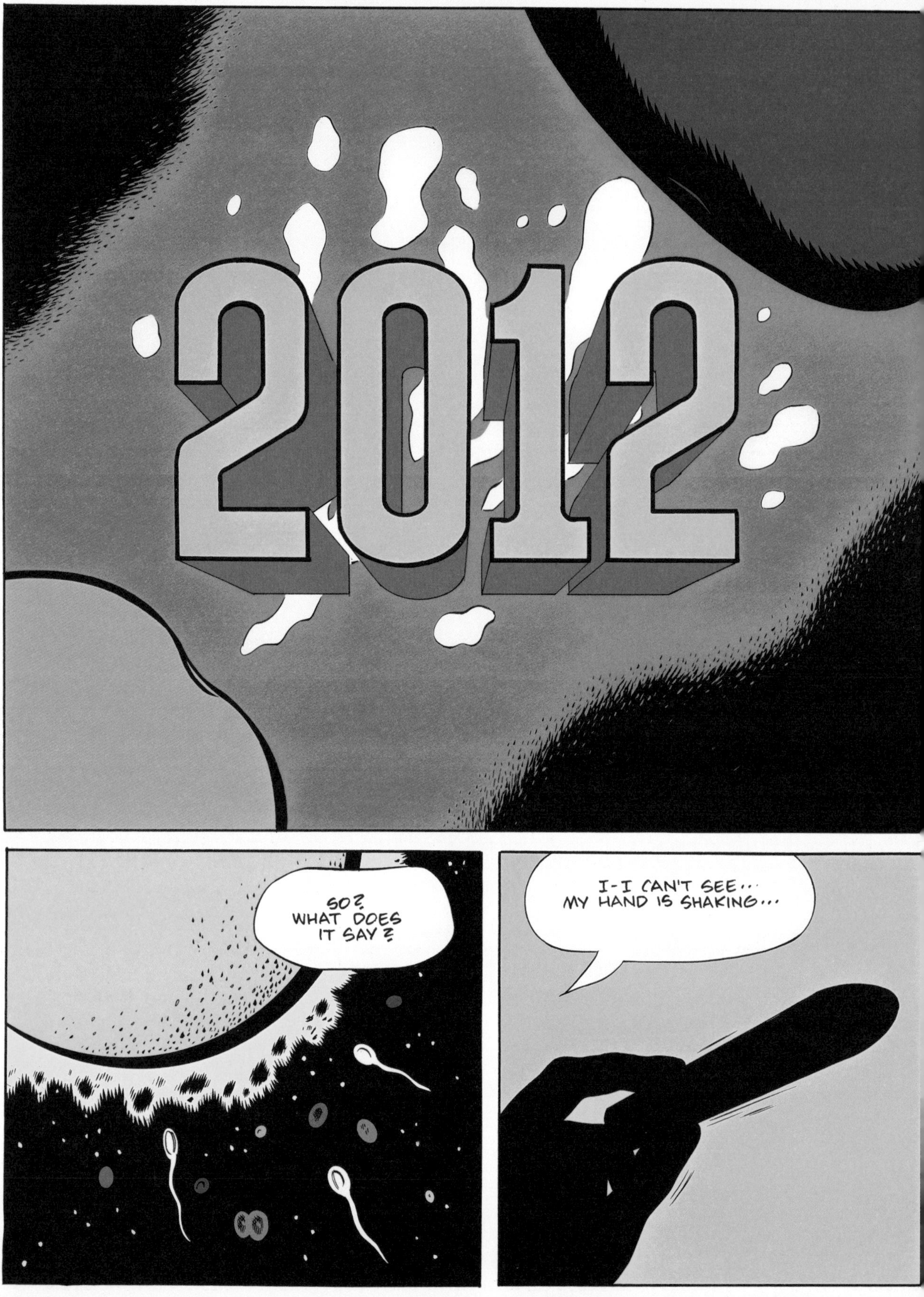
2012
SO? WHAT DOES IT SAY?
I-I CAN'T SEE... MY HAND IS SHAKING...

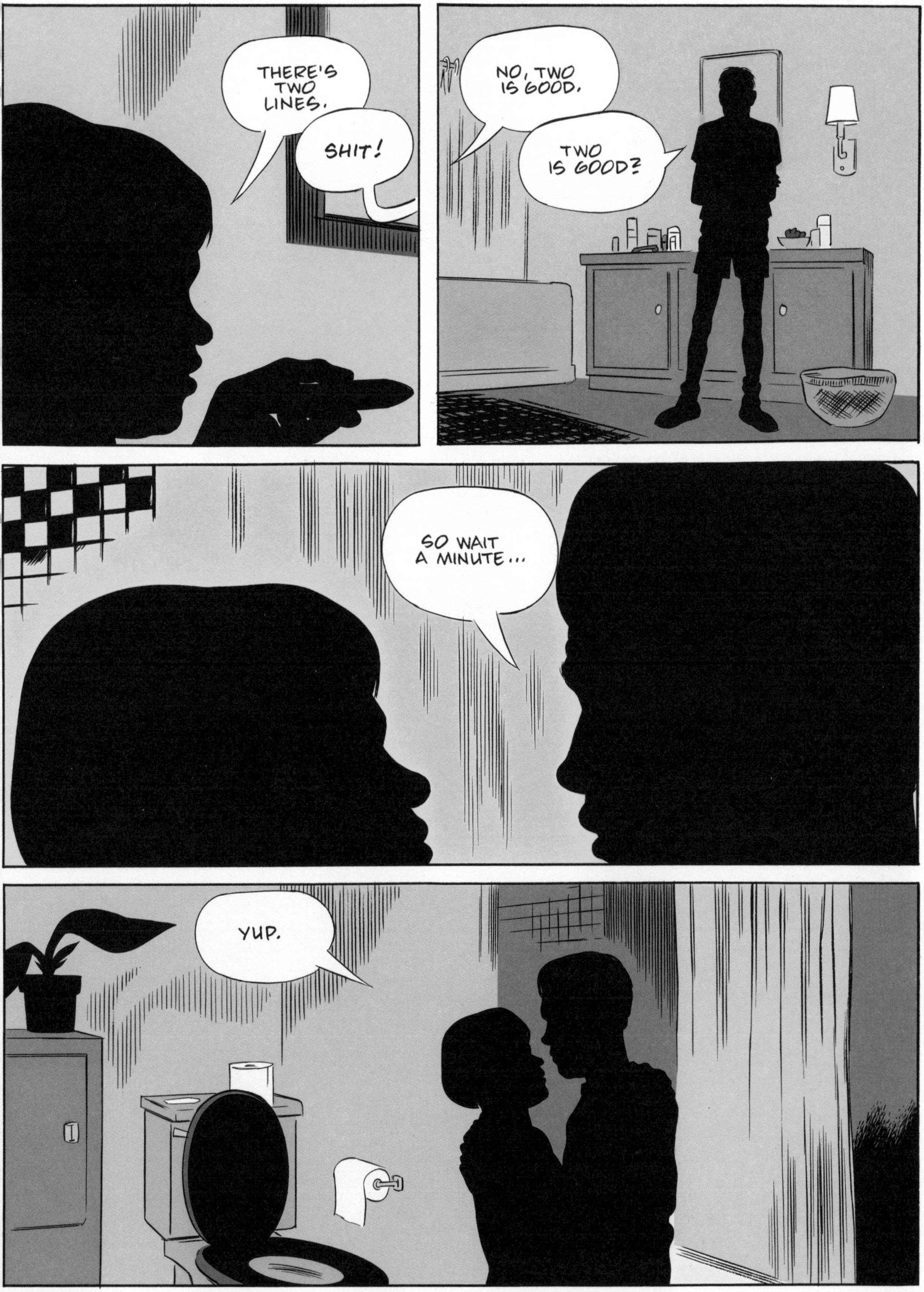
THERE'S TWO LINES.
SHIT!
NO, TWO IS GOOD.
TWO IS GOOD?
SO WAIT A MINUTE...
YUP.

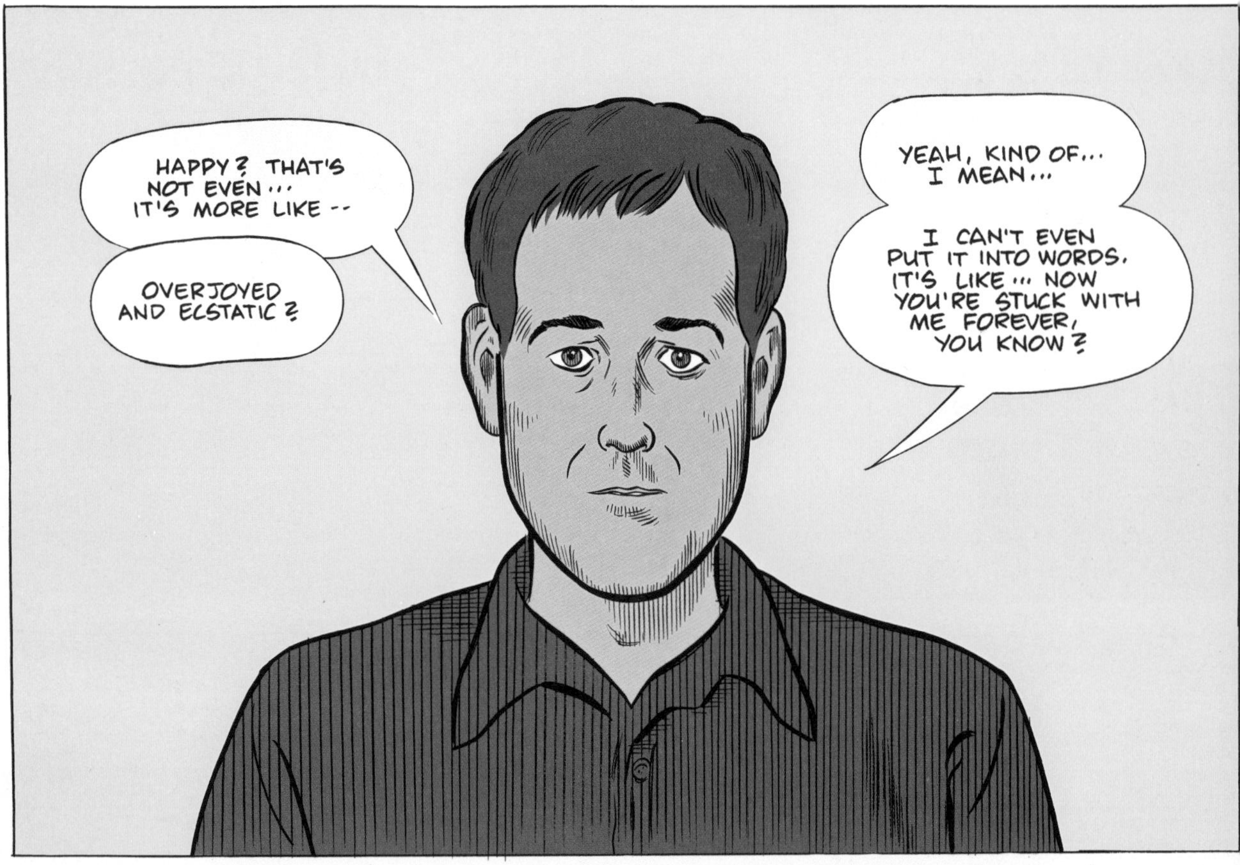
HAPPY? THAT'S NOT EVEN... IT'S MORE LIKE --
OVERJOYED AND ECSTATIC?
YEAH, KIND OF... I MEAN...
I CAN'T EVEN PUT IT INTO WORDS. IT'S LIKE... NOW YOU'RE STUCK WITH ME FOREVER, YOU KNOW?

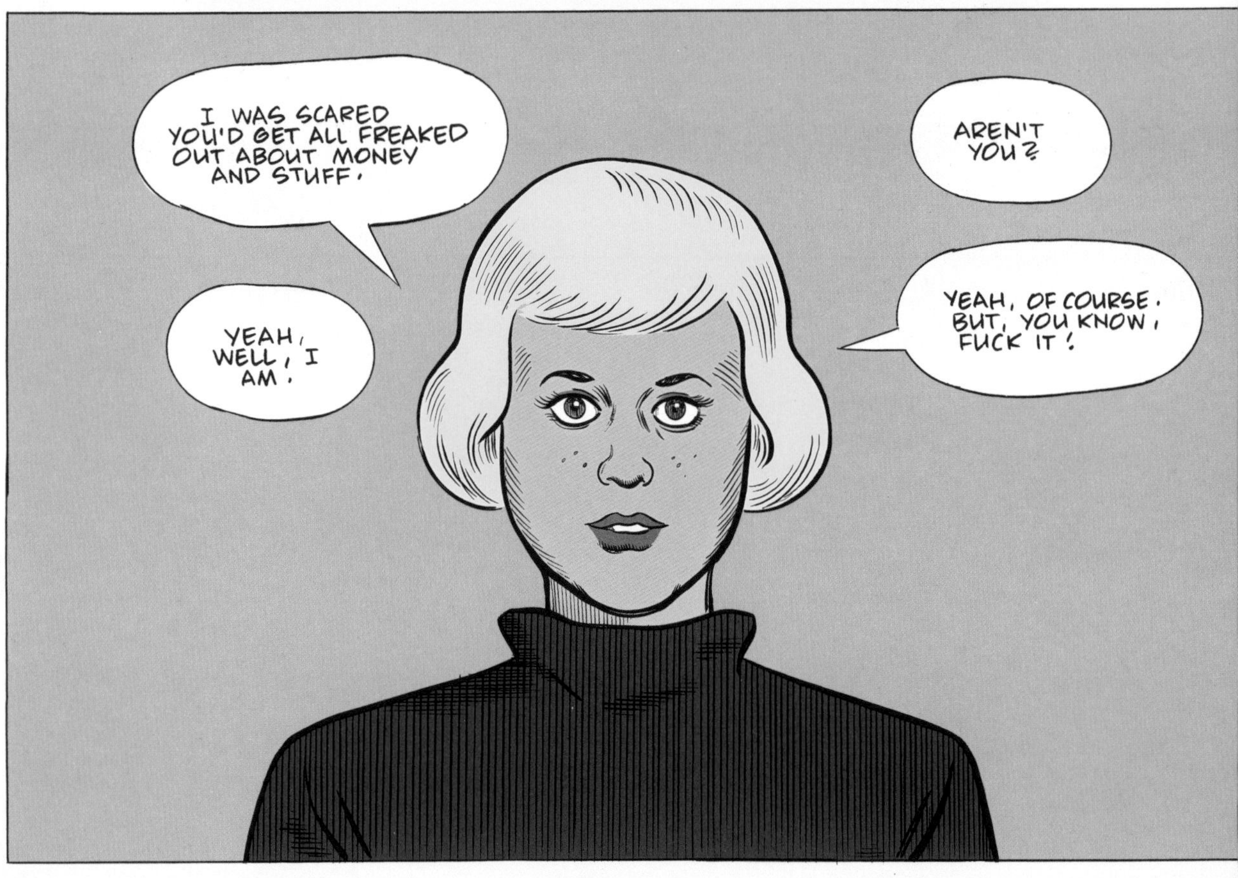
I WAS SCARED YOU'D GET ALL FREAKED OUT ABOUT MONEY AND STUFF.
YEAH, WELL, I AM.
AREN'T YOU?
YEAH, OF COURSE. BUT, YOU KNOW, FUCK IT!

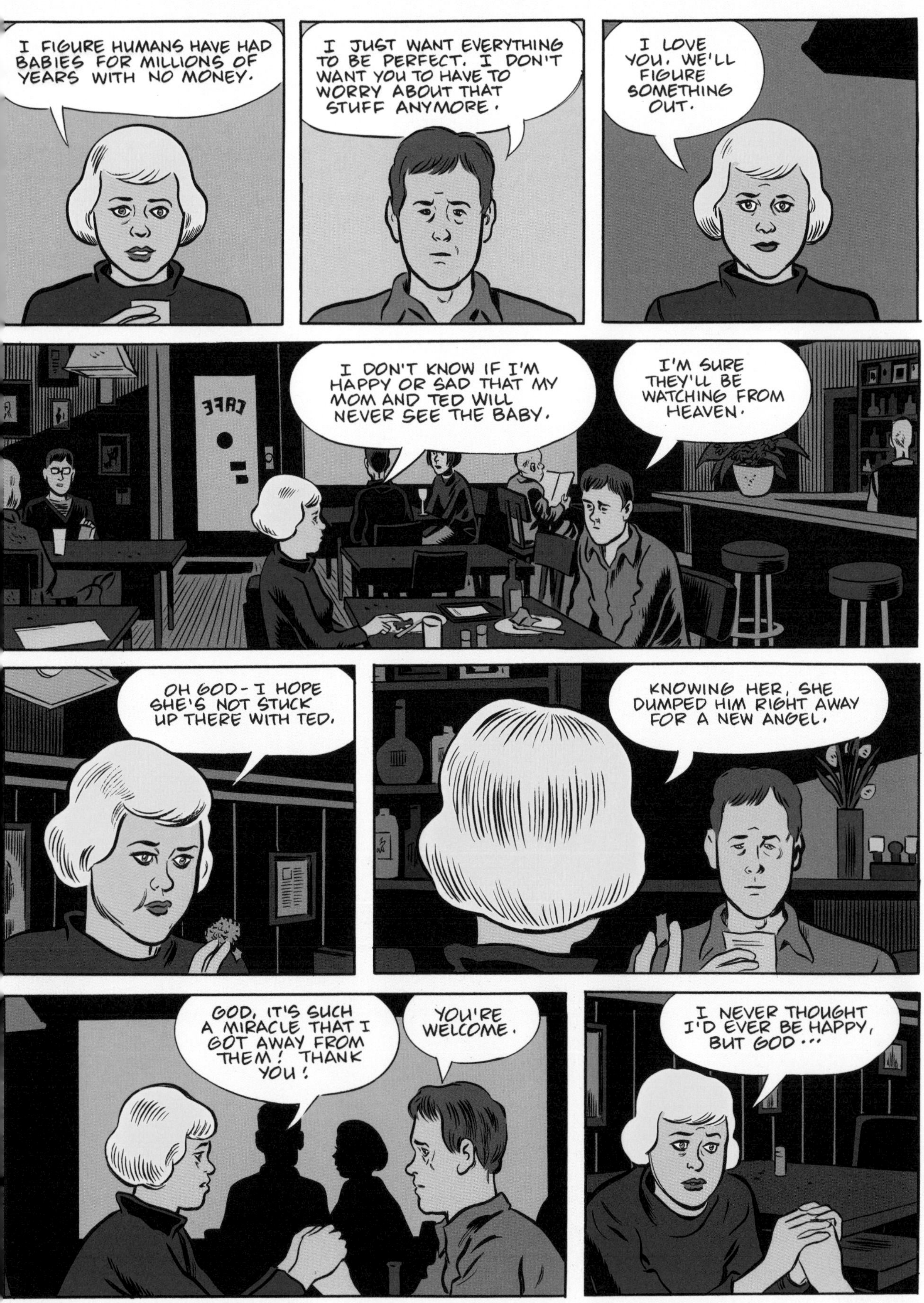
I FIGURE HUMANS HAVE HAD BABIES FOR MILLIONS OF YEARS WITH NO MONEY.
I JUST WANT EVERYTHING TO BE PERFECT. I DON'T WANT YOU TO HAVE TO WORRY ABOUT THAT STUFF ANYMORE.
I LOVE YOU. WE'LL FIGURE SOMETHING OUT.
CAFE
I DON'T KNOW IF I'M HAPPY OR SAD THAT MY MOM AND TED WILL NEVER SEE THE BABY.
I'M SURE THEY'LL BE WATCHING FROM HEAVEN.
OH GOD - I HOPE SHE'S NOT STUCK UP THERE WITH TED.
KNOWING HER, SHE DUMPED HIM RIGHT AWAY FOR A NEW ANGEL.
GOD, IT'S SUCH A MIRACLE THAT I GOT AWAY FROM THEM! THANK YOU!
YOU'RE WELCOME.
I NEVER THOUGHT I'D EVER BE HAPPY, BUT GOD...

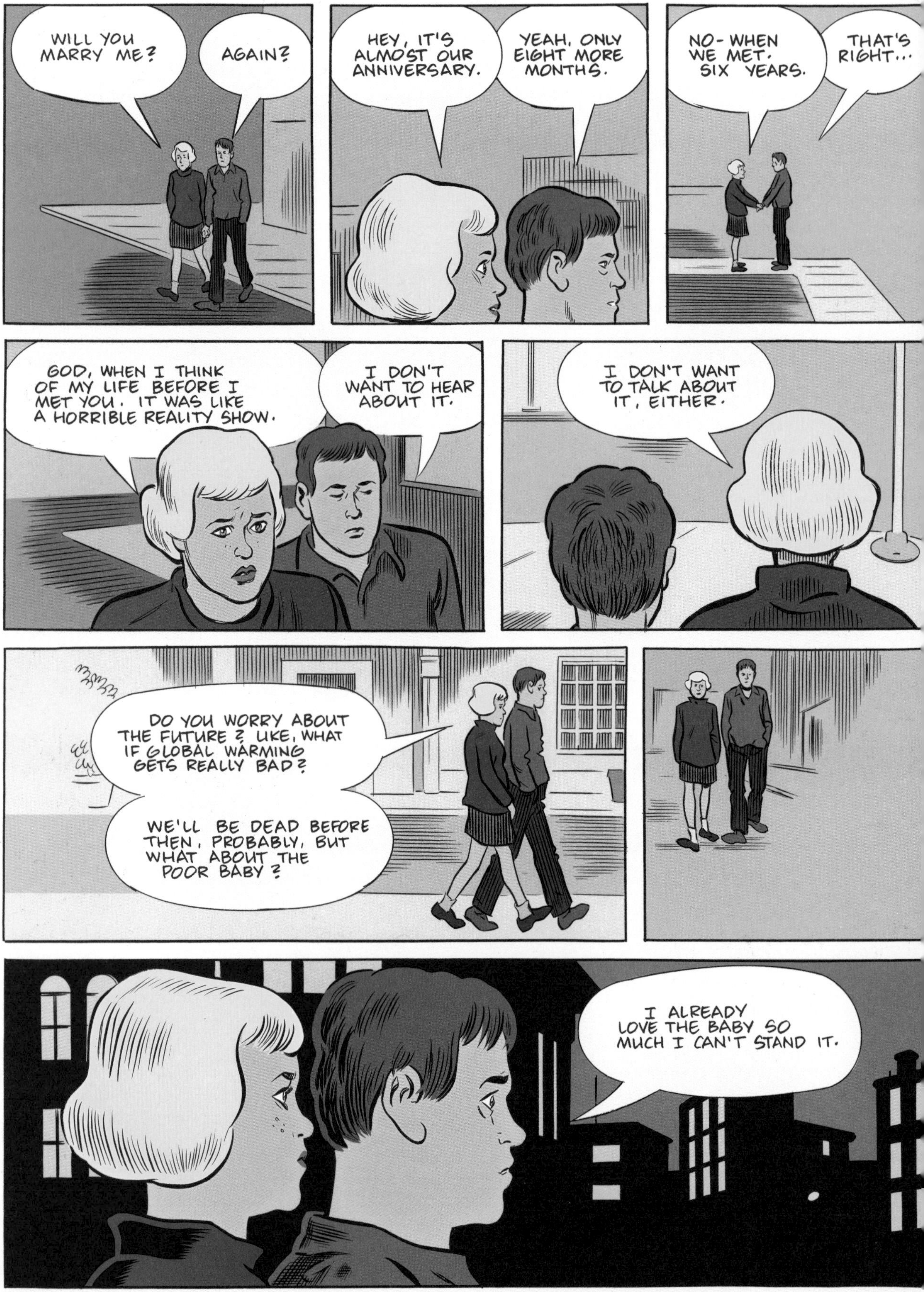
WILL YOU MARRY ME?
AGAIN?
HEY, IT'S ALMOST OUR ANNIVERSARY.
YEAH, ONLY EIGHT MORE MONTHS.
NO- WHEN WE MET. SIX YEARS.
THAT'S RIGHT...
GOD, WHEN I THINK OF MY LIFE BEFORE I MET YOU. IT WAS LIKE A HORRIBLE REALITY SHOW.
I DON'T WANT TO HEAR ABOUT IT.
I DON'T WANT TO TALK ABOUT IT, EITHER.
DO YOU WORRY ABOUT THE FUTURE? LIKE, WHAT IF GLOBAL WARMING GETS REALLY BAD?
WE'LL BE DEAD BEFORE THEN, PROBABLY, BUT WHAT ABOUT THE POOR BABY?
I ALREADY LOVE THE BABY SO MUCH I CAN'T STAND IT.

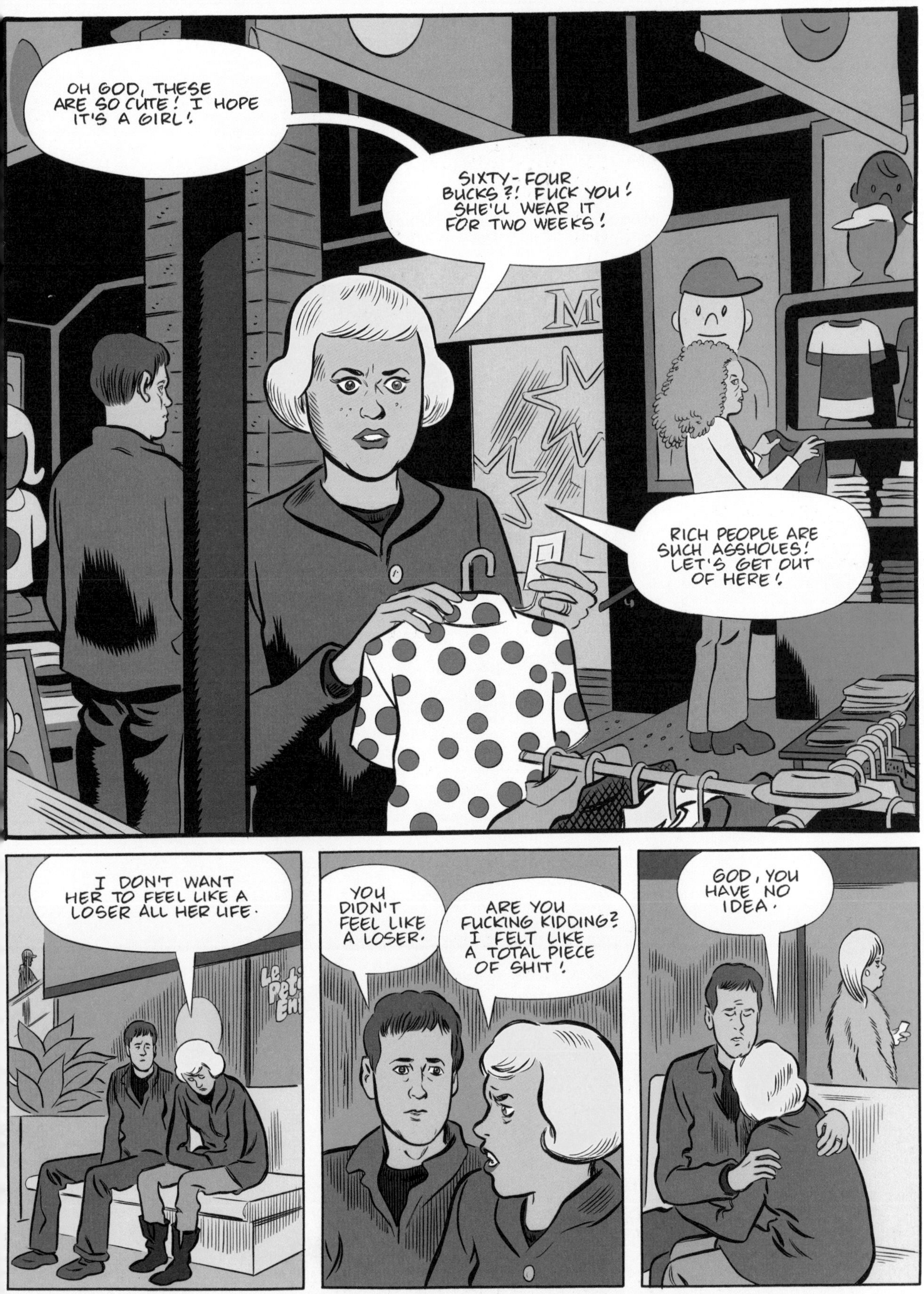

OH GOD, THESE ARE SO CUTE! I HOPE IT'S A GIRL!
SIXTY-FOUR BUCKS?! FUCK YOU! SHE'LL WEAR IT FOR TWO WEEKS!
RICH PEOPLE ARE SUCH ASSHOLES! LET'S GET OUT OF HERE!
I DON'T WANT HER TO FEEL LIKE A LOSER ALL HER LIFE.
YOU DIDN'T FEEL LIKE A LOSER.
ARE YOU FUCKING KIDDING? I FELT LIKE A TOTAL PIECE OF SHIT!
GOD, YOU HAVE NO IDEA.

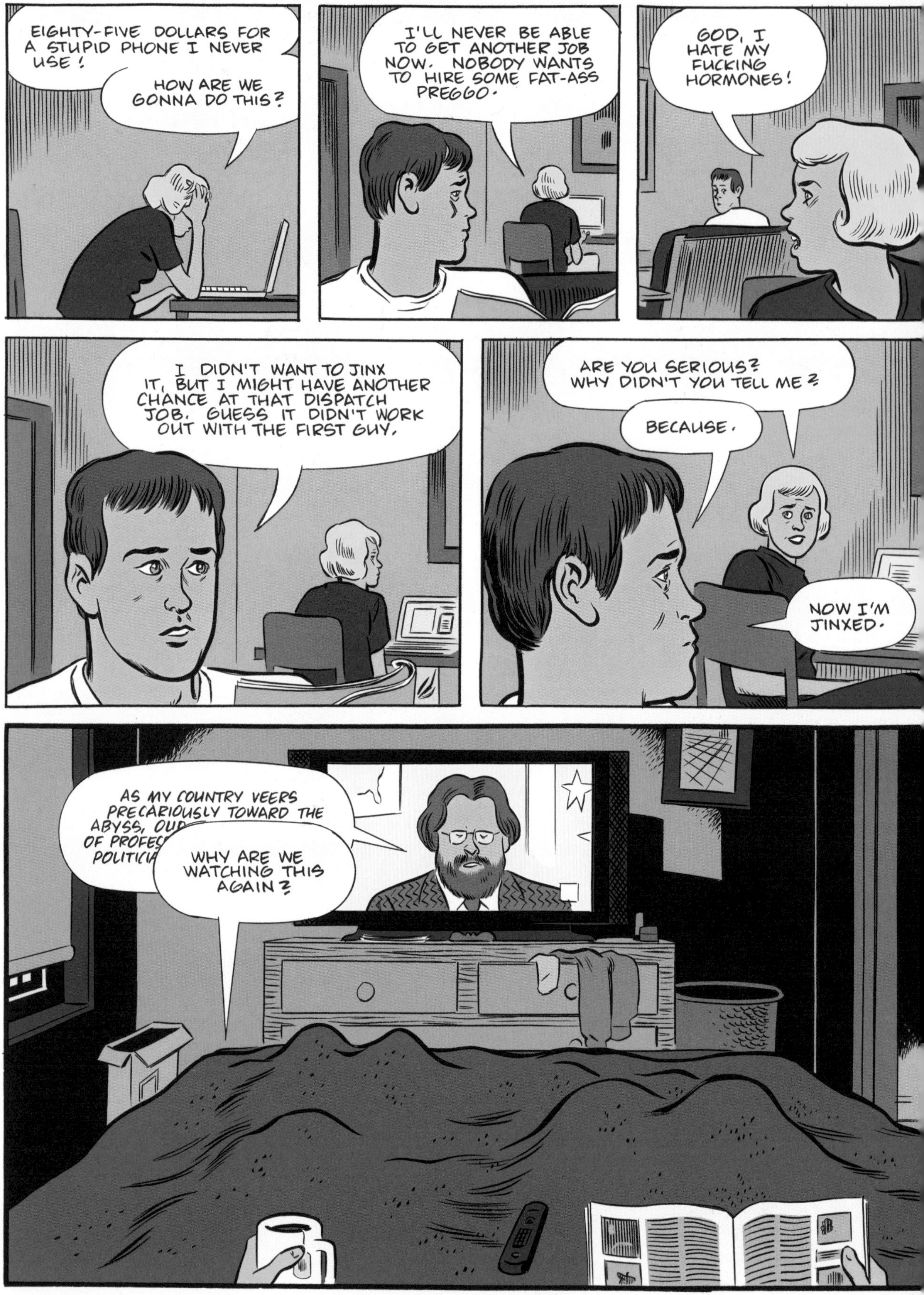
EIGHTY-FIVE DOLLARS FOR A STUPID PHONE I NEVER USE!
HOW ARE WE GONNA DO THIS?
I'LL NEVER BE ABLE TO GET ANOTHER JOB NOW. NOBODY WANTS TO HIRE SOME FAT-ASS PREGGO.
GOD, I HATE MY FUCKING HORMONES!
I DIDN'T WANT TO JINX IT, BUT I MIGHT HAVE ANOTHER CHANCE AT THAT DISPATCH JOB. GUESS IT DIDN'T WORK OUT WITH THE FIRST GUY.
ARE YOU SERIOUS? WHY DIDN'T YOU TELL ME?
BECAUSE.
NOW I'M JINXED.
AS MY COUNTRY VEERS PRECARIOUSLY TOWARD THE ABYSS, OUR
WHY ARE WE WATCHING THIS AGAIN?

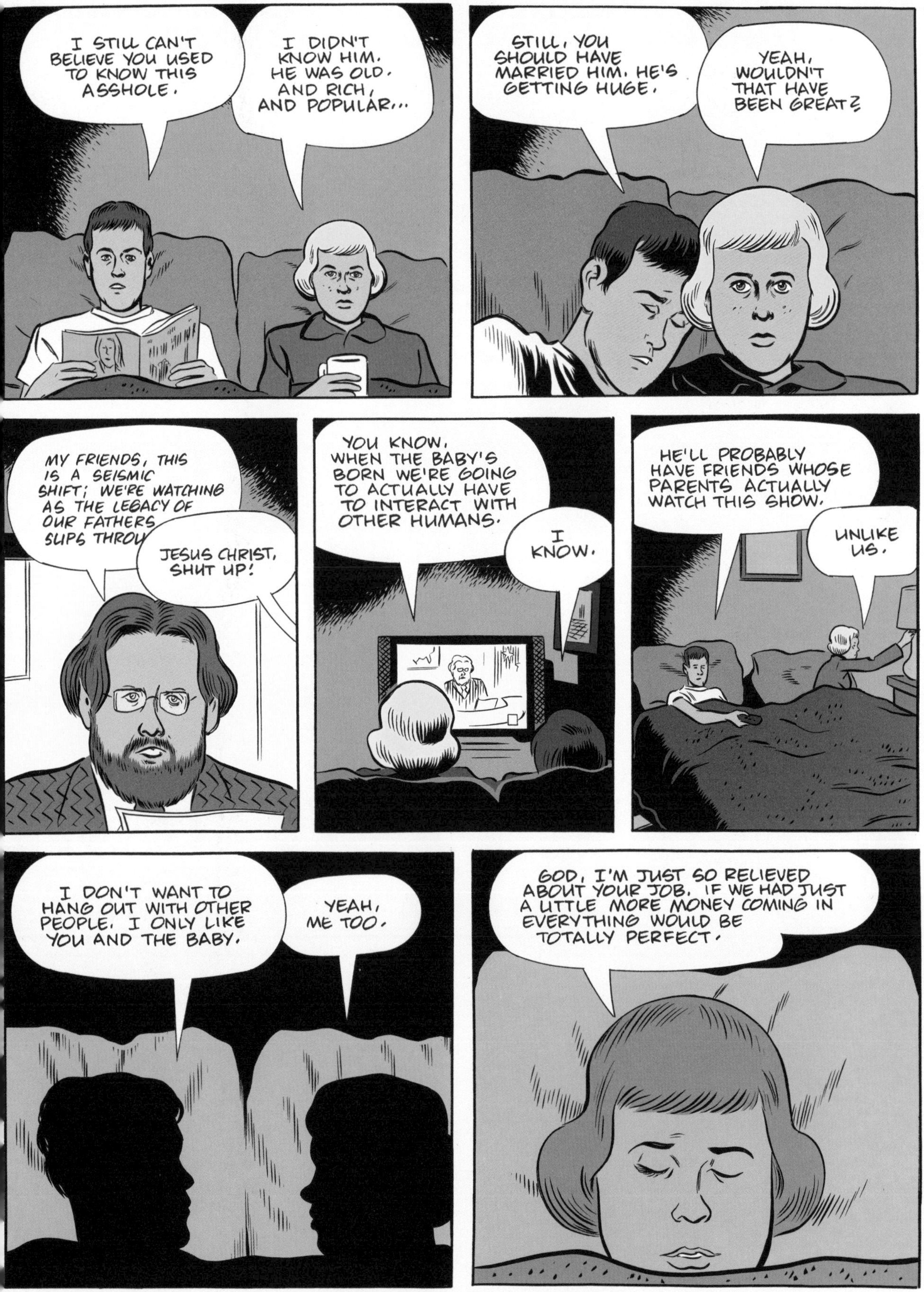
I STILL CAN'T BELIEVE YOU USED TO KNOW THIS ASSHOLE.
I DIDN'T KNOW HIM. HE WAS OLD, AND RICH, AND POPULAR...
STILL, YOU SHOULD HAVE MARRIED HIM. HE'S GETTING HUGE.
YEAH, WOULDN'T THAT HAVE BEEN GREAT?
MY FRIENDS, THIS IS A SEISMIC SHIFT; WE'RE WATCHING AS THE LEGACY OF OUR FATHERS SLIPS THROU
JESUS CHRIST, SHUT UP!
YOU KNOW, WHEN THE BABY'S BORN WE'RE GOING TO ACTUALLY HAVE TO INTERACT WITH OTHER HUMANS.
I KNOW.
HE'LL PROBABLY HAVE FRIENDS WHOSE PARENTS ACTUALLY WATCH THIS SHOW.
UNLIKE US.
I DON'T WANT TO HANG OUT WITH OTHER PEOPLE. I ONLY LIKE YOU AND THE BABY.
YEAH, ME TOO.
GOD, I'M JUST SO RELIEVED ABOUT YOUR JOB. IF WE HAD JUST A LITTLE MORE MONEY COMING IN EVERYTHING WOULD BE TOTALLY PERFECT.

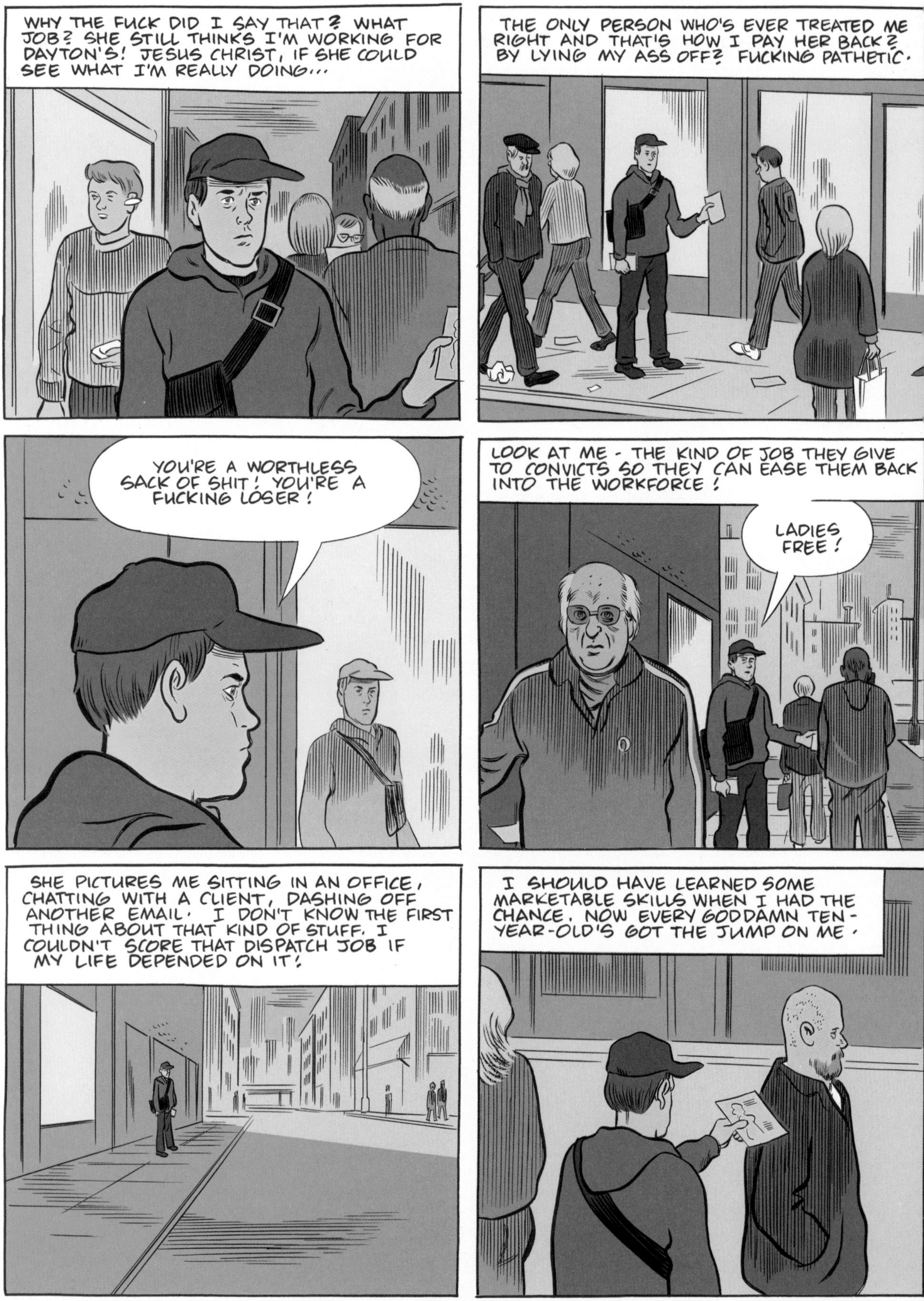
WHY THE FUCK DID I SAY THAT? WHAT JOB? SHE STILL THINKS I'M WORKING FOR DAYTON'S! JESUS CHRIST, IF SHE COULD SEE WHAT I'M REALLY DOING...
THE ONLY PERSON WHO'S EVER TREATED ME RIGHT AND THAT'S HOW I PAY HER BACK? BY LYING MY ASS OFF? FUCKING PATHETIC.
YOU'RE A WORTHLESS SACK OF SHIT! YOU'RE A FUCKING LOSER!
LOOK AT ME - THE KIND OF JOB THEY GIVE TO CONVICTS SO THEY CAN EASE THEM BACK INTO THE WORKFORCE!
LADIES FREE!
SHE PICTURES ME SITTING IN AN OFFICE, CHATTING WITH A CLIENT, DASHING OFF ANOTHER EMAIL. I DON'T KNOW THE FIRST THING ABOUT THAT KIND OF STUFF. I COULDN'T SCORE THAT DISPATCH JOB IF MY LIFE DEPENDED ON IT!
I SHOULD HAVE LEARNED SOME MARKETABLE SKILLS WHEN I HAD THE CHANCE. NOW EVERY GODDAMN TEN-YEAR-OLD'S GOT THE JUMP ON ME.

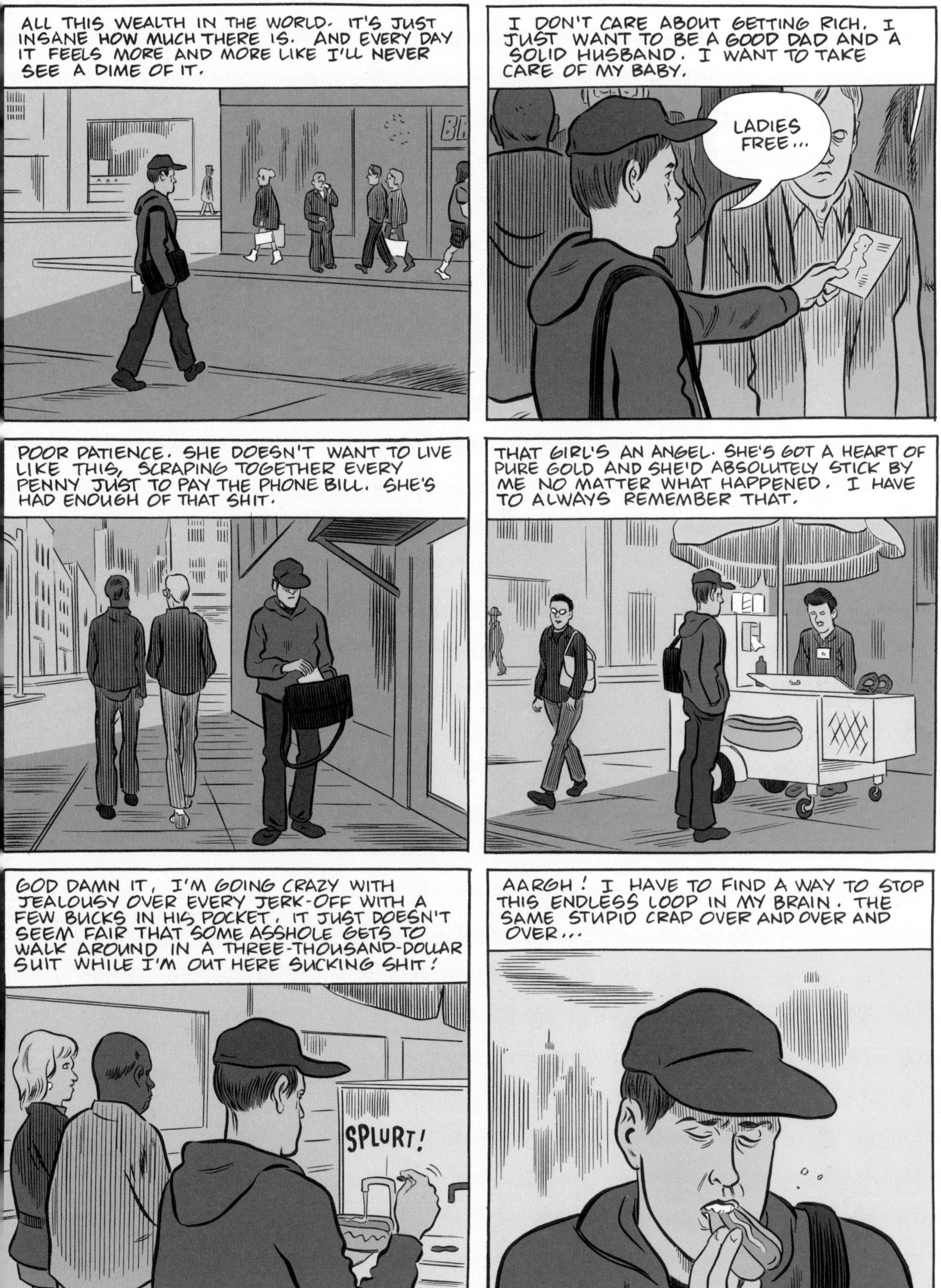
ALL THIS WEALTH IN THE WORLD. IT'S JUST INSANE HOW MUCH THERE IS. AND EVERY DAY IT FEELS MORE AND MORE LIKE I'LL NEVER SEE A DIME OF IT.
I DON'T CARE ABOUT GETTING RICH. I JUST WANT TO BE A GOOD DAD AND A SOLID HUSBAND. I WANT TO TAKE CARE OF MY BABY.
LADIES FREE...
POOR PATIENCE. SHE DOESN'T WANT TO LIVE LIKE THIS, SCRAPING TOGETHER EVERY PENNY JUST TO PAY THE PHONE BILL. SHE'S HAD ENOUGH OF THAT SHIT.
THAT GIRL'S AN ANGEL. SHE'S GOT A HEART OF PURE GOLD AND SHE'D ABSOLUTELY STICK BY ME NO MATTER WHAT HAPPENED. I HAVE TO ALWAYS REMEMBER THAT.
GOD DAMN IT, I'M GOING CRAZY WITH JEALOUSY OVER EVERY JERK-OFF WITH A FEW BUCKS IN HIS POCKET. IT JUST DOESN'T SEEM FAIR THAT SOME ASSHOLE GETS TO WALK AROUND IN A THREE-THOUSAND-DOLLAR SUIT WHILE I'M OUT HERE SUCKING SHIT!
SPLURT!
AARGH! I HAVE TO FIND A WAY TO STOP THIS ENDLESS LOOP IN MY BRAIN. THE SAME STUPID CRAP OVER AND OVER AND OVER...

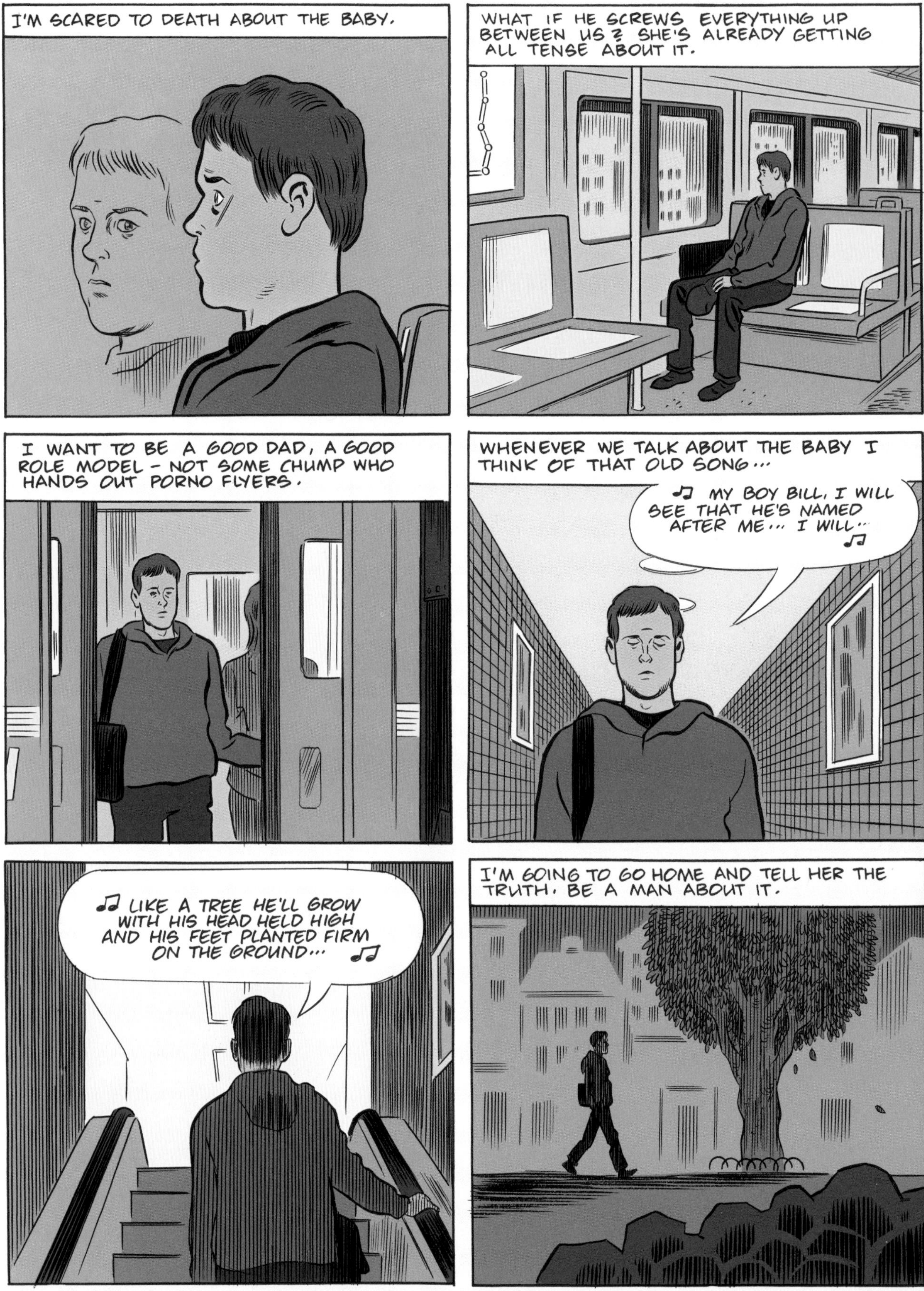
I'M SCARED TO DEATH ABOUT THE BABY.
WHAT IF HE SCREWS EVERYTHING UP BETWEEN US? SHE'S ALREADY GETTING ALL TENSE ABOUT IT.
I WANT TO BE A GOOD DAD, A GOOD ROLE MODEL - NOT SOME CHUMP WHO HANDS OUT PORNO FLYERS.
WHENEVER WE TALK ABOUT THE BABY I THINK OF THAT OLD SONG...
♫ MY BOY BILL, I WILL SEE THAT HE'S NAMED AFTER ME... I WILL... ♫
♫ LIKE A TREE HE'LL GROW WITH HIS HEAD HELD HIGH AND HIS FEET PLANTED FIRM ON THE GROUND... ♫
I'M GOING TO GO HOME AND TELL HER THE TRUTH. BE A MAN ABOUT IT.

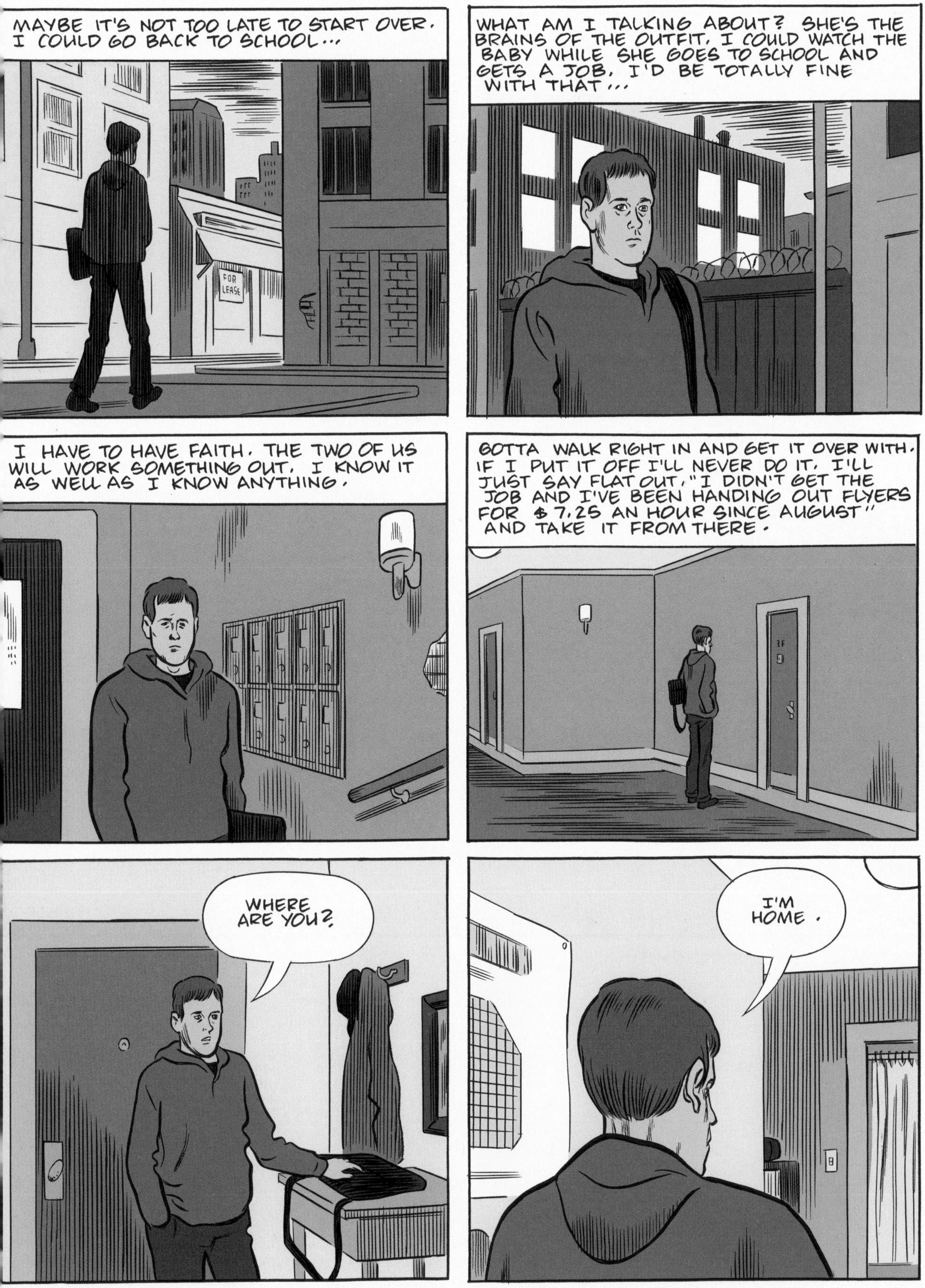
MAYBE IT'S NOT TOO LATE TO START OVER. I COULD GO BACK TO SCHOOL...
FOR LEASE
WHAT AM I TALKING ABOUT? SHE'S THE BRAINS OF THE OUTFIT. I COULD WATCH THE BABY WHILE SHE GOES TO SCHOOL AND GETS A JOB. I'D BE TOTALLY FINE WITH THAT...
I HAVE TO HAVE FAITH. THE TWO OF US WILL WORK SOMETHING OUT. I KNOW IT AS WELL AS I KNOW ANYTHING.
GOTTA WALK RIGHT IN AND GET IT OVER WITH. IF I PUT IT OFF I'LL NEVER DO IT. I'LL JUST SAY FLAT OUT, "I DIDN'T GET THE JOB AND I'VE BEEN HANDING OUT FLYERS FOR $7.25 AN HOUR SINCE AUGUST" AND TAKE IT FROM THERE.
WHERE ARE YOU?
I'M HOME.

AND THIS IS WHERE MY STORY BEGINS.

THE PAIN WAS BEYOND ANYTHING YOU COULD IMAGINE, A FUCKING CANNON HOLE IN THE CHEST.

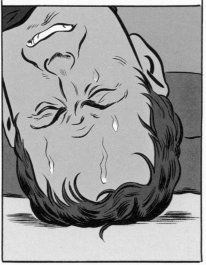

I COULDN'T MOVE FOR WHAT SEEMED LIKE HOURS, LIKE I WAS STUCK IN DRYING CONCRETE. PROBABLY JUST A TRICK BY MY DNA TO KEEP ME FROM BASHING MY BRAINS IN.

THE FACT IS, I DIDN'T WANT TO KILL MYSELF. MY MEMORIES WERE ALL THAT WAS LEFT OF HER. I COULDN'T BEAR TO SNUFF THOSE OUT TOO.

YOU SHOULD HAVE HEARD THE SOUND I MADE: LIKE A BEAGLE STUCK IN A BEAR-TRAP.

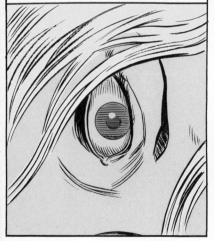

AND EVEN THOUGH THIS EVENT HAD DEMONSTRATED THE TOTAL ABSENCE OF ORDER IN THE UNIVERSE, I COULDN'T STAND TO THINK OF SOME INHUMAN DEMON WALKING FREE WHILE THE COPS PINNED THE WHOLE THING ON ME.

BUT I'LL BE FUCKED IF THAT ISN'T EXACTLY WHAT HAPPENED.

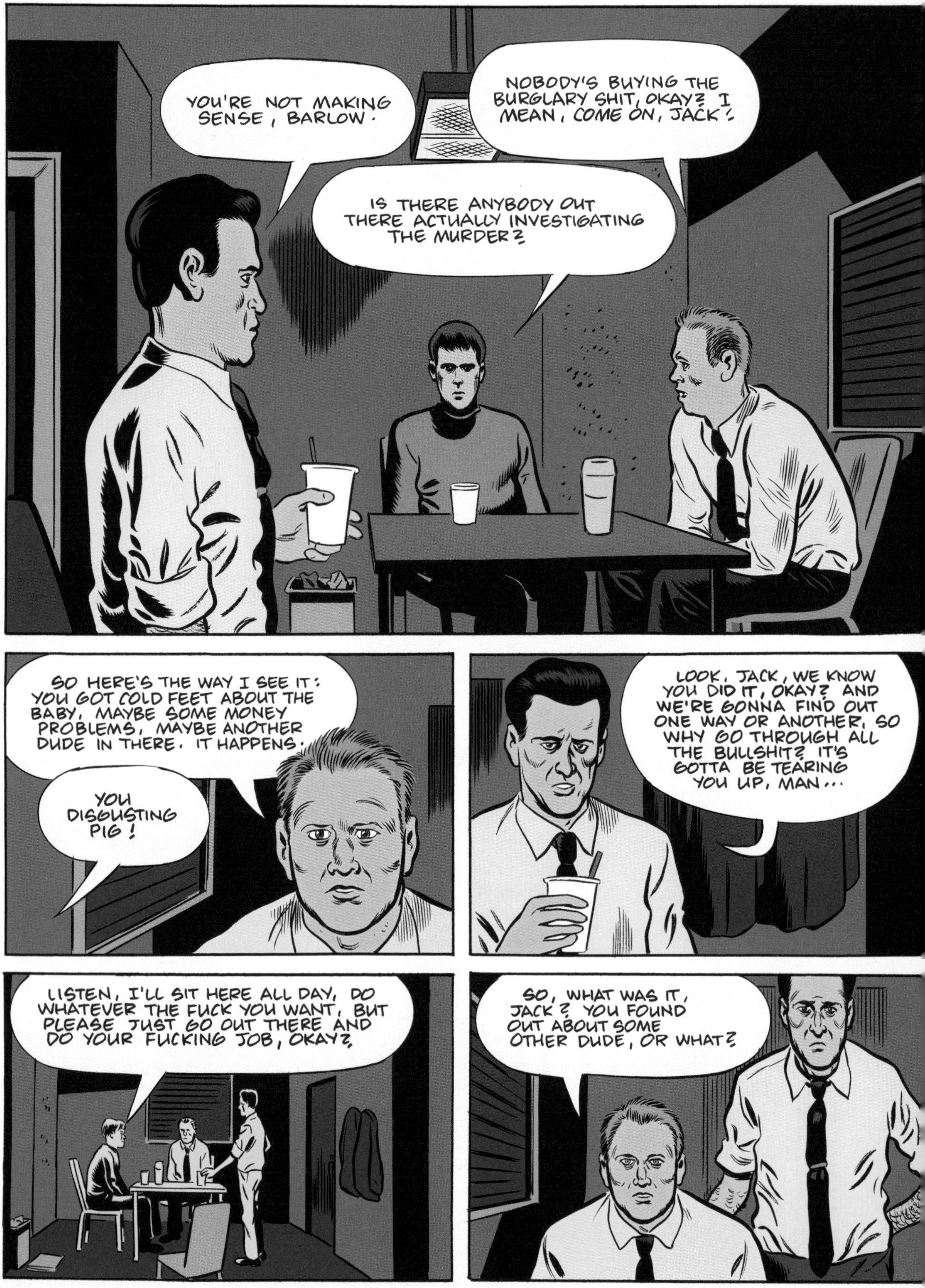
YOU'RE NOT MAKING SENSE, BARLOW.
NOBODY'S BUYING THE BURGLARY SHIT, OKAY? I MEAN, COME ON, JACK!
IS THERE ANYBODY OUT THERE ACTUALLY INVESTIGATING THE MURDER?
SO HERE'S THE WAY I SEE IT: YOU GOT COLD FEET ABOUT THE BABY, MAYBE SOME MONEY PROBLEMS, MAYBE ANOTHER DUDE IN THERE. IT HAPPENS.
YOU DISGUSTING PIG!
LOOK, JACK, WE KNOW YOU DID IT, OKAY? AND WE'RE GONNA FIND OUT ONE WAY OR ANOTHER, SO WHY GO THROUGH ALL THE BULLSHIT? IT'S GOTTA BE TEARING YOU UP, MAN...
LISTEN, I'LL SIT HERE ALL DAY, DO WHATEVER THE FUCK YOU WANT, BUT PLEASE JUST GO OUT THERE AND DO YOUR FUCKING JOB, OKAY?
SO, WHAT WAS IT, JACK? YOU FOUND OUT ABOUT SOME OTHER DUDE, OR WHAT?

AND SO THEY PUT ME IN THE COUNTY JAIL. NO BAIL. ASSHOLE PUBLIC DEFENDER THINKS I'M GUILTY, BUT STARTS GIVING IT A SHOT WHEN I MAKE THE NEWS.

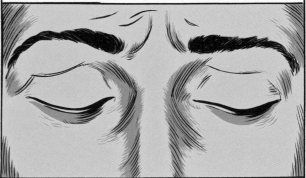

HE TELLS ME TO KEEP MY MOUTH SHUT AND I DO IT. GOOD ADVICE FOR ONCE.

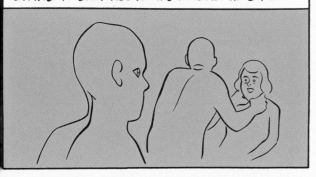

OF COURSE THAT MAKES ME LOOK EVEN MORE GUILTY, BUT SO WHAT? I STOPPED GIVING A SHIT ABOUT ME A LONG TIME AGO.

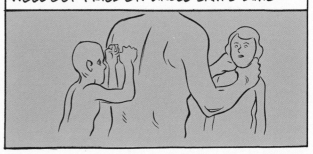

I ALWAYS USED TO WONDER WHY, IF SOME GUY GETS ACCUSED OF KILLING HIS FAMILY, HE EVEN BOTHERS TO FIGHT FOR HIS INNOCENCE. I MEAN, YOUR LIFE IS OVER, RIGHT? MAY AS WELL GET FRIED ON UNCLE SAM'S DIME.

BUT NOW I KINDA GET IT. IT'S NOT JUST YOU THEY'RE DISMISSING BUT THE VICTIM, TOO. "SHE MARRIED SOME ASSHOLE HOTHEAD, SHE WAS A TOTAL MESS - GOOD RIDDANCE!"

TEN MONTHS LATER AND I'M STILL FUCKIN' HERE!

AND THEN ONE DAY, LAWYER #3 TELLS ME THERE'S ALL THIS EVIDENCE - FIBERS, DNA - THAT DOESN'T MATCH ME AT ALL. PLUS, THEY FINALLY DECIDED I WAS REALLY WHERE I SAID I WAS WHEN IT HAPPENED. GUESS THEY'VE KNOWN THIS FOR MONTHS BUT ONLY JUST NOW DECIDED TO LET ME IN ON IT.

AND THEN THAT'S IT. NO APOLOGY, NOTHING. JUST SEE YA LATER, ASSHOLE.

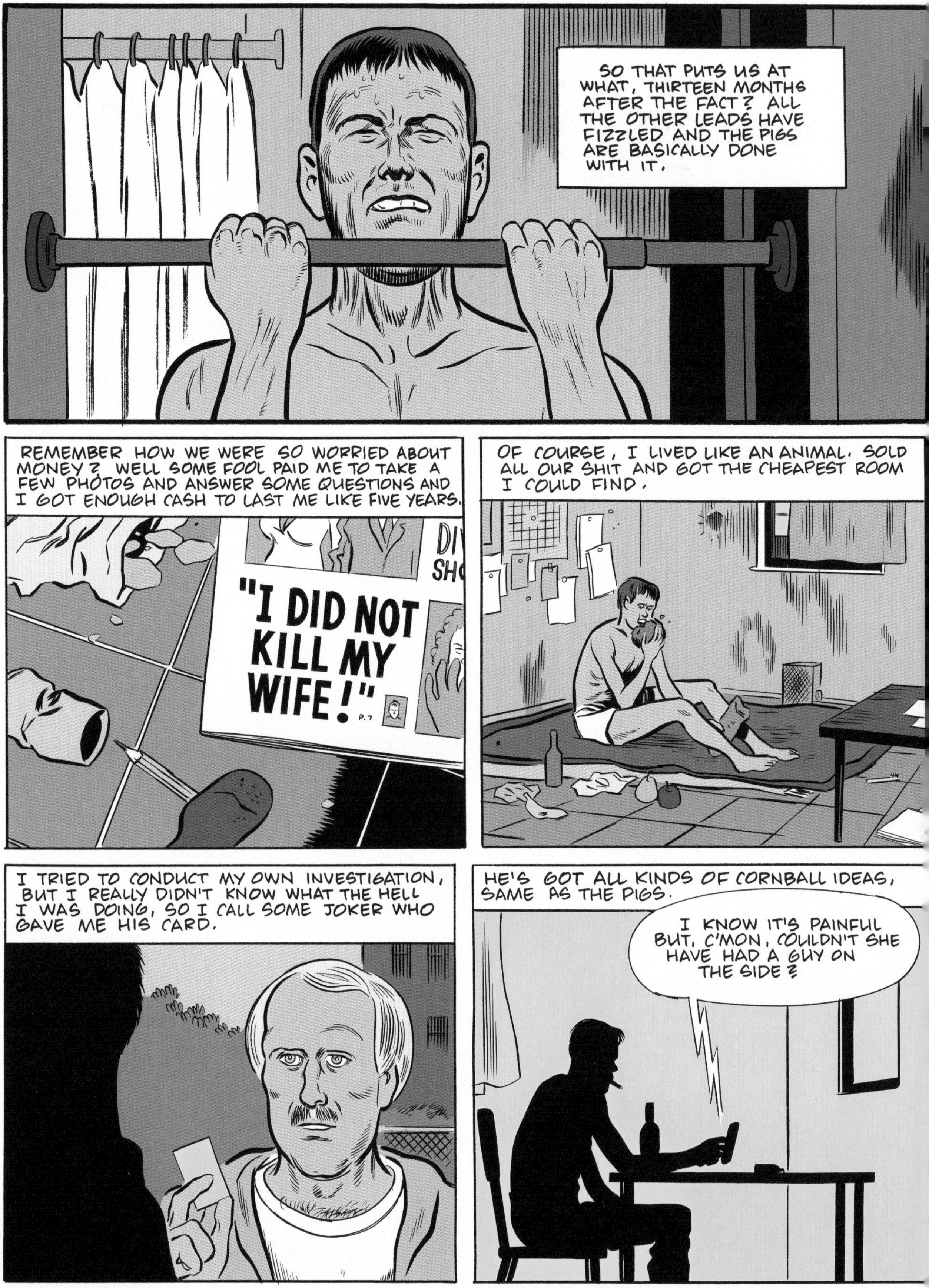
SO THAT PUTS US AT WHAT, THIRTEEN MONTHS AFTER THE FACT? ALL THE OTHER LEADS HAVE FIZZLED AND THE PIGS ARE BASICALLY DONE WITH IT.
REMEMBER HOW WE WERE SO WORRIED ABOUT MONEY? WELL SOME FOOL PAID ME TO TAKE A FEW PHOTOS AND ANSWER SOME QUESTIONS AND I GOT ENOUGH CASH TO LAST ME LIKE FIVE YEARS.
"I DID NOT KILL MY WIFE!"
P.7
OF COURSE, I LIVED LIKE AN ANIMAL. SOLD ALL OUR SHIT AND GOT THE CHEAPEST ROOM I COULD FIND.
I TRIED TO CONDUCT MY OWN INVESTIGATION, BUT I REALLY DIDN'T KNOW WHAT THE HELL I WAS DOING, SO I CALL SOME JOKER WHO GAVE ME HIS CARD.
HE'S GOT ALL KINDS OF CORNBALL IDEAS, SAME AS THE PIGS.
I KNOW IT'S PAINFUL BUT, C'MON, COULDN'T SHE HAVE HAD A GUY ON THE SIDE?

SO HE JERKS ME AROUND FOR A WHILE AND THEN ONE DAY, BOOM.

...HE STOOD TRIAL FOR RAPE TWICE, DID TIME FOR ASSAULT, BUT THAT'S LIKE ONE PERCENT OF IT. GUESS WHERE HE WAS LIVING ON OCTOBER ELEVENTH?

RIGHT ACROSS THE STREET, THAT'S WHERE.

WE DREDGE UP A TON OF SHIT ON THIS CLOWN. BASICALLY, HE'S A FUCKING MANIAC WHO SOMEHOW SLIPPED THROUGH THE CRACKS. NICE WORK, PIGS!

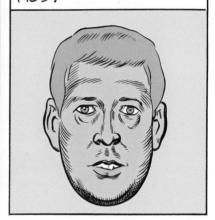

MY GUY'S ALL READY TO TURN OVER THE FILE AND CASH HIS CHECK, BUT I SAID FUCK THAT.

NO WAY. I'M DOING IT MYSELF.

I HAVE THIS WHOLE PLAN I CAME UP WITH IN JAIL. NOT SOMETHING I'M PROUD OF EXACTLY, BUT IT FEELS RIGHT.

OBVIOUSLY, I WANT TO MAKE SURE IT'S THE REAL GUY, SINCE I'LL DEFINITELY FRY FOR WHAT I'VE GOT IN MIND.

I'M ALL READY TO MAKE MY MOVE, SCOPING THE GUY OUT ONE LAST TIME, WHEN ALL OF A SUDDEN, HERE COME THE PIGS TO HAUL HIM OFF.

SO I'M LIKE GREAT, THEY GOT HIM; I'LL TAKE IT. AND SURE ENOUGH, WE GET WORD HE'S BOOKED FOR A HOMICIDE ON OCTOBER 11. UNDISCLOSED FEMALE.

I CAN'T SAY IT MADE ME FEEL BETTER - WHAT COULD? - BUT IT WAS SOMETHING. AND THEN, GET THIS:

THE MURDER TOOK PLACE DOWN IN FERNDALE. 60-YEAR-OLD HOUSEWIFE. HE COULDN'T BE THE GUY. SAME FUCKING DAY, CAN YOU BELIEVE IT?

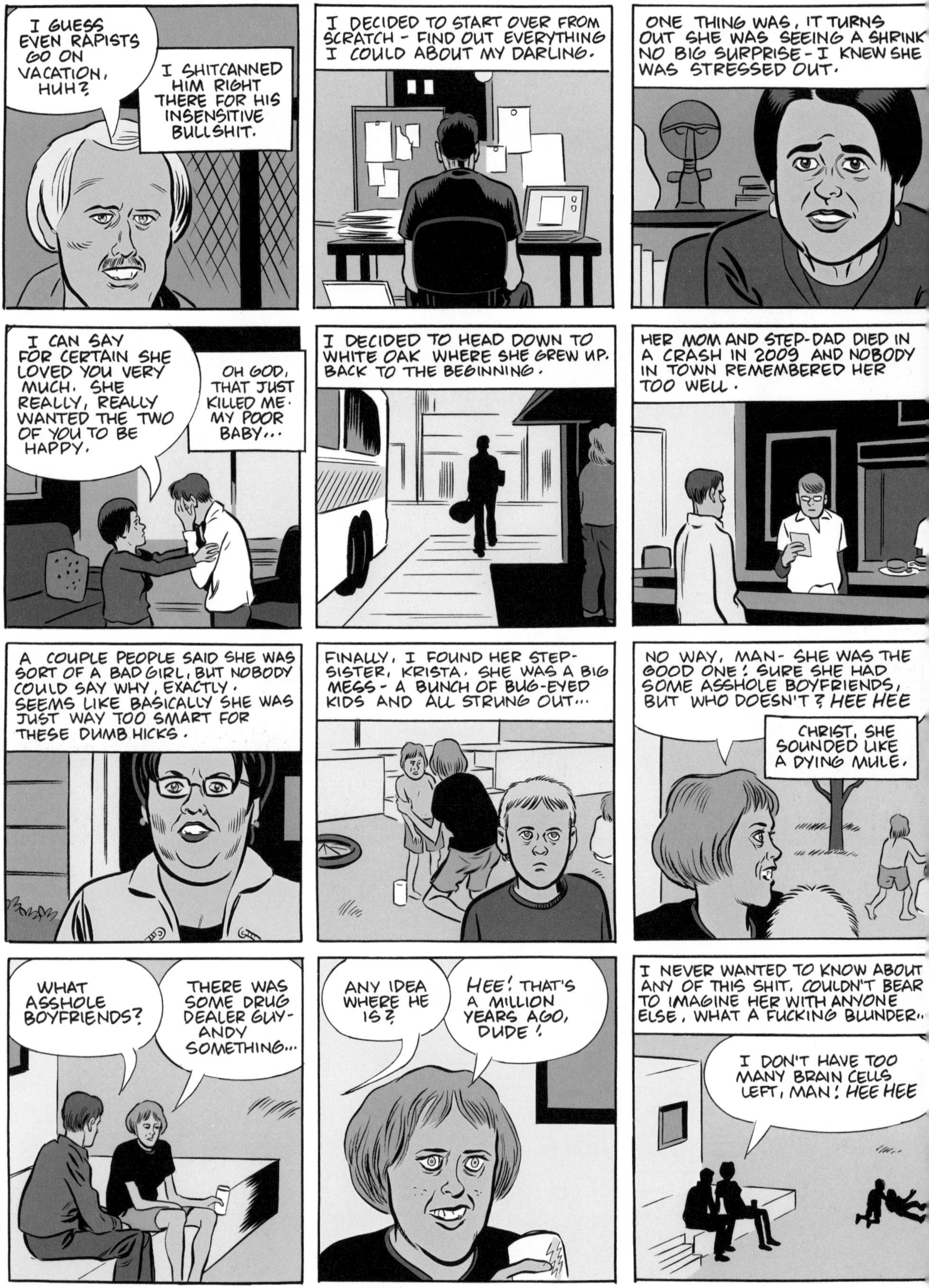
I GUESS EVEN RAPISTS GO ON VACATION, HUH?
I SHITCANNED HIM RIGHT THERE FOR HIS INSENSITIVE BULLSHIT.
I DECIDED TO START OVER FROM SCRATCH - FIND OUT EVERYTHING I COULD ABOUT MY DARLING.
ONE THING WAS, IT TURNS OUT SHE WAS SEEING A SHRINK NO BIG SURPRISE - I KNEW SHE WAS STRESSED OUT.
I CAN SAY FOR CERTAIN SHE LOVED YOU VERY MUCH. SHE REALLY, REALLY WANTED THE TWO OF YOU TO BE HAPPY.
OH GOD, THAT JUST KILLED ME. MY POOR BABY...
I DECIDED TO HEAD DOWN TO WHITE OAK WHERE SHE GREW UP. BACK TO THE BEGINNING.
HER MOM AND STEP-DAD DIED IN A CRASH IN 2009 AND NOBODY IN TOWN REMEMBERED HER TOO WELL.
A COUPLE PEOPLE SAID SHE WAS SORT OF A BAD GIRL, BUT NOBODY COULD SAY WHY, EXACTLY. SEEMS LIKE BASICALLY SHE WAS JUST WAY TOO SMART FOR THESE DUMB HICKS.
FINALLY, I FOUND HER STEP-SISTER, KRISTA. SHE WAS A BIG MESS - A BUNCH OF BUG-EYED KIDS AND ALL STRUNG OUT...
NO WAY, MAN- SHE WAS THE GOOD ONE! SURE SHE HAD SOME ASSHOLE BOYFRIENDS, BUT WHO DOESN'T? HEE HEE
CHRIST, SHE SOUNDED LIKE A DYING MULE.
WHAT ASSHOLE BOYFRIENDS?
THERE WAS SOME DRUG DEALER GUY- ANDY SOMETHING...
ANY IDEA WHERE HE IS?
HEE! THAT'S A MILLION YEARS AGO, DUDE!
I NEVER WANTED TO KNOW ABOUT ANY OF THIS SHIT. COULDN'T BEAR TO IMAGINE HER WITH ANYONE ELSE. WHAT A FUCKING BLUNDER...
I DON'T HAVE TOO MANY BRAIN CELLS LEFT, MAN! HEE HEE

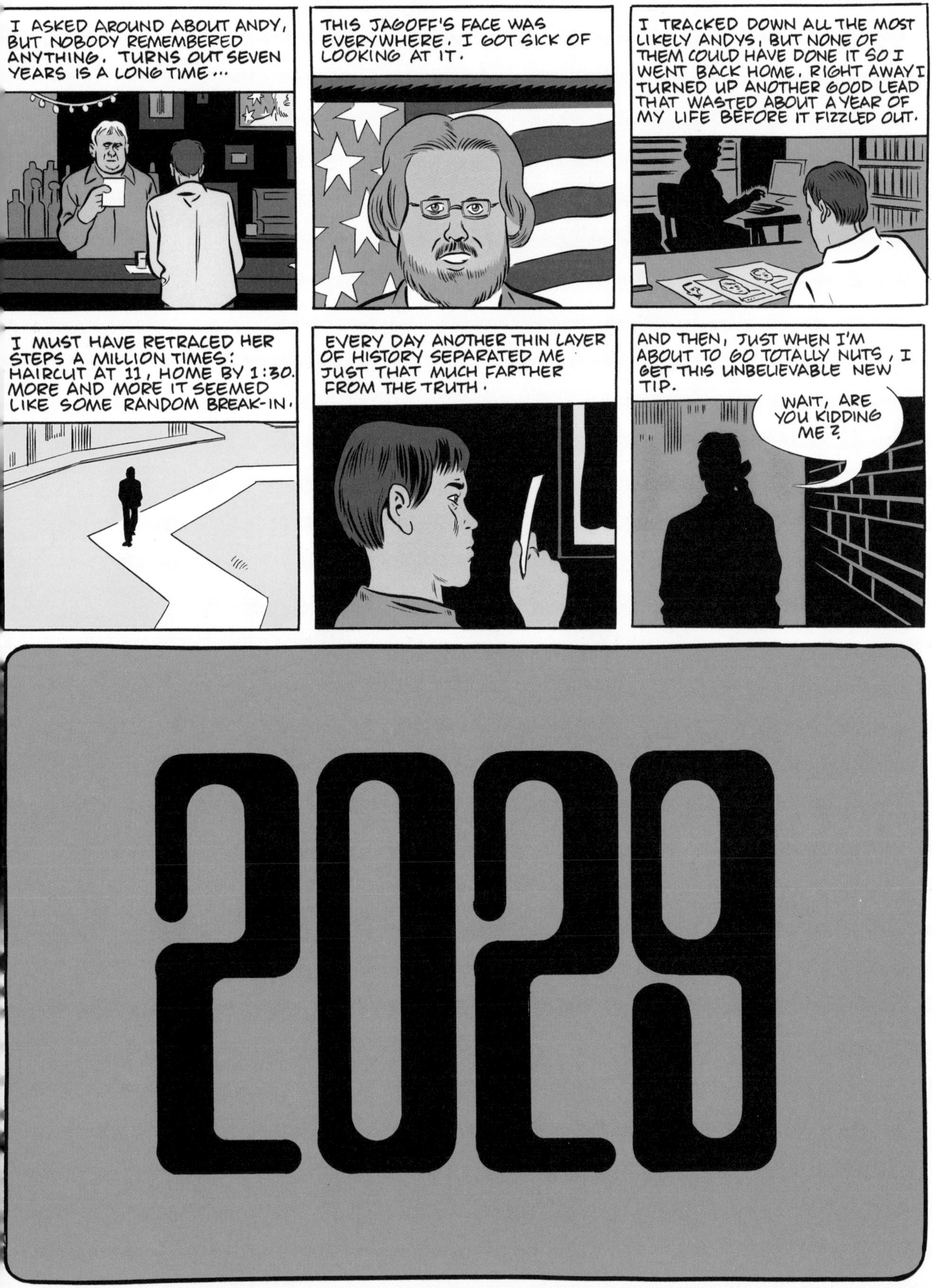
I ASKED AROUND ABOUT ANDY, BUT NOBODY REMEMBERED ANYTHING. TURNS OUT SEVEN YEARS IS A LONG TIME...
THIS JAGOFF'S FACE WAS EVERYWHERE. I GOT SICK OF LOOKING AT IT.
I TRACKED DOWN ALL THE MOST LIKELY ANDYS, BUT NONE OF THEM COULD HAVE DONE IT SO I WENT BACK HOME. RIGHT AWAY I TURNED UP ANOTHER GOOD LEAD THAT WASTED ABOUT A YEAR OF MY LIFE BEFORE IT FIZZLED OUT.
I MUST HAVE RETRACED HER STEPS A MILLION TIMES: HAIRCUT AT 11, HOME BY 1:30. MORE AND MORE IT SEEMED LIKE SOME RANDOM BREAK-IN.
EVERY DAY ANOTHER THIN LAYER OF HISTORY SEPARATED ME JUST THAT MUCH FARTHER FROM THE TRUTH.
AND THEN, JUST WHEN I'M ABOUT TO GO TOTALLY NUTS, I GET THIS UNBELIEVABLE NEW TIP.
WAIT, ARE YOU KIDDING ME?
2029

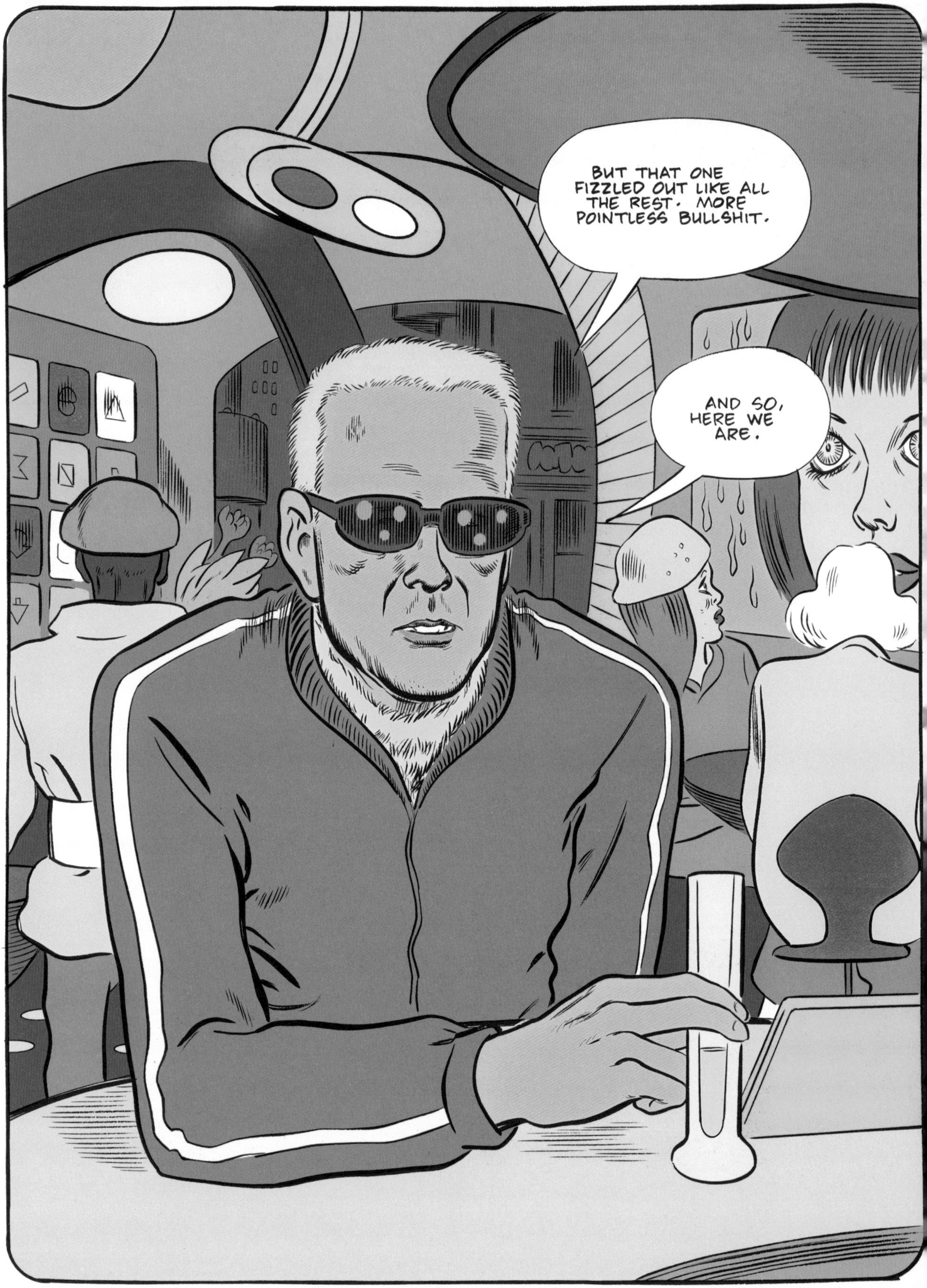
BUT THAT ONE FIZZLED OUT LIKE ALL THE REST. MORE POINTLESS BULLSHIT.
AND SO, HERE WE ARE.

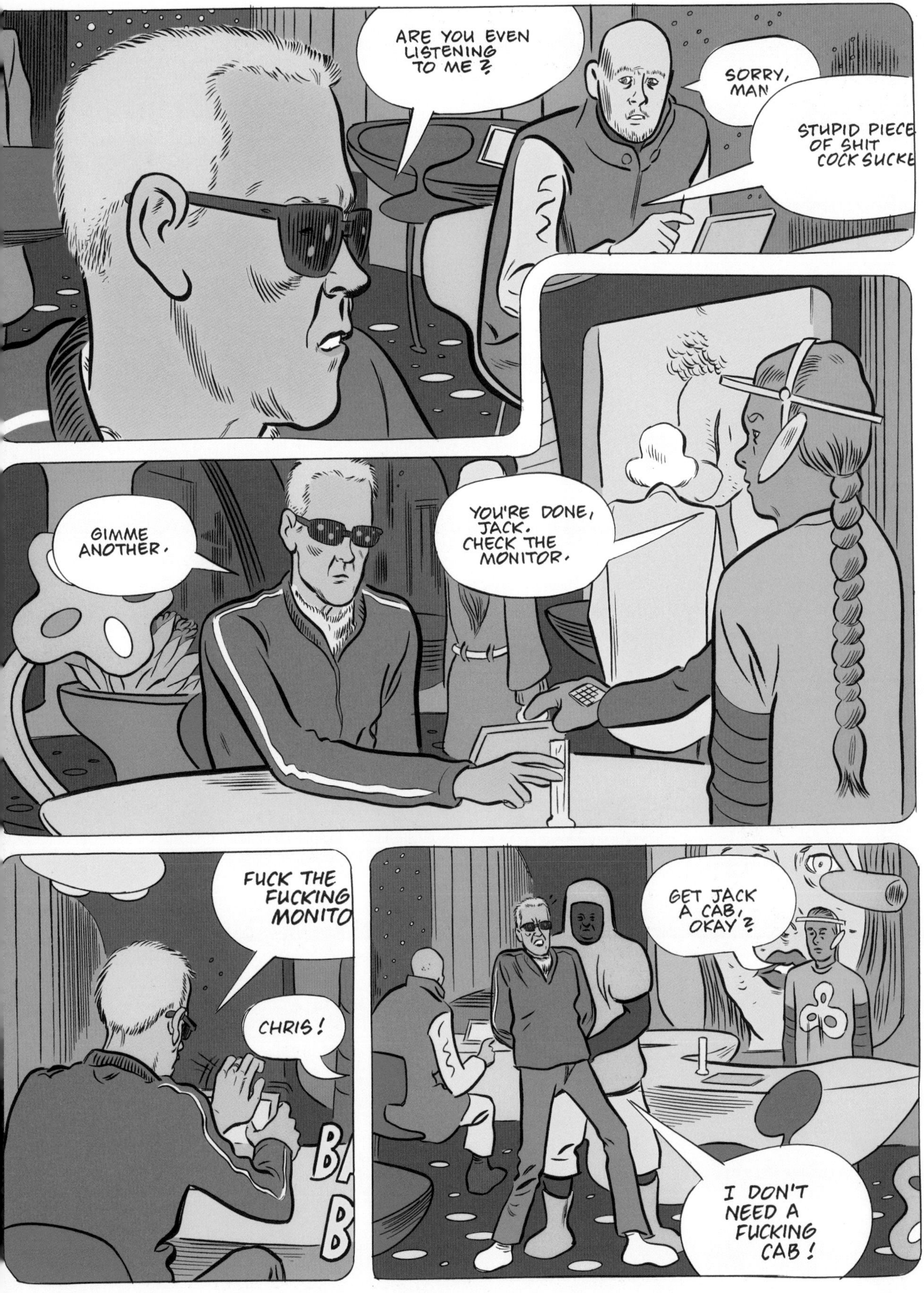

ARE YOU EVEN LISTENING TO ME?
SORRY, MAN
STUPID PIECE OF SHIT COCKSUCKE
GIMME ANOTHER.
YOU'RE DONE, JACK. CHECK THE MONITOR.
FUCK THE FUCKING MONITO
CHRIS!
GET JACK A CAB, OKAY?
I DON'T NEED A FUCKING CAB!

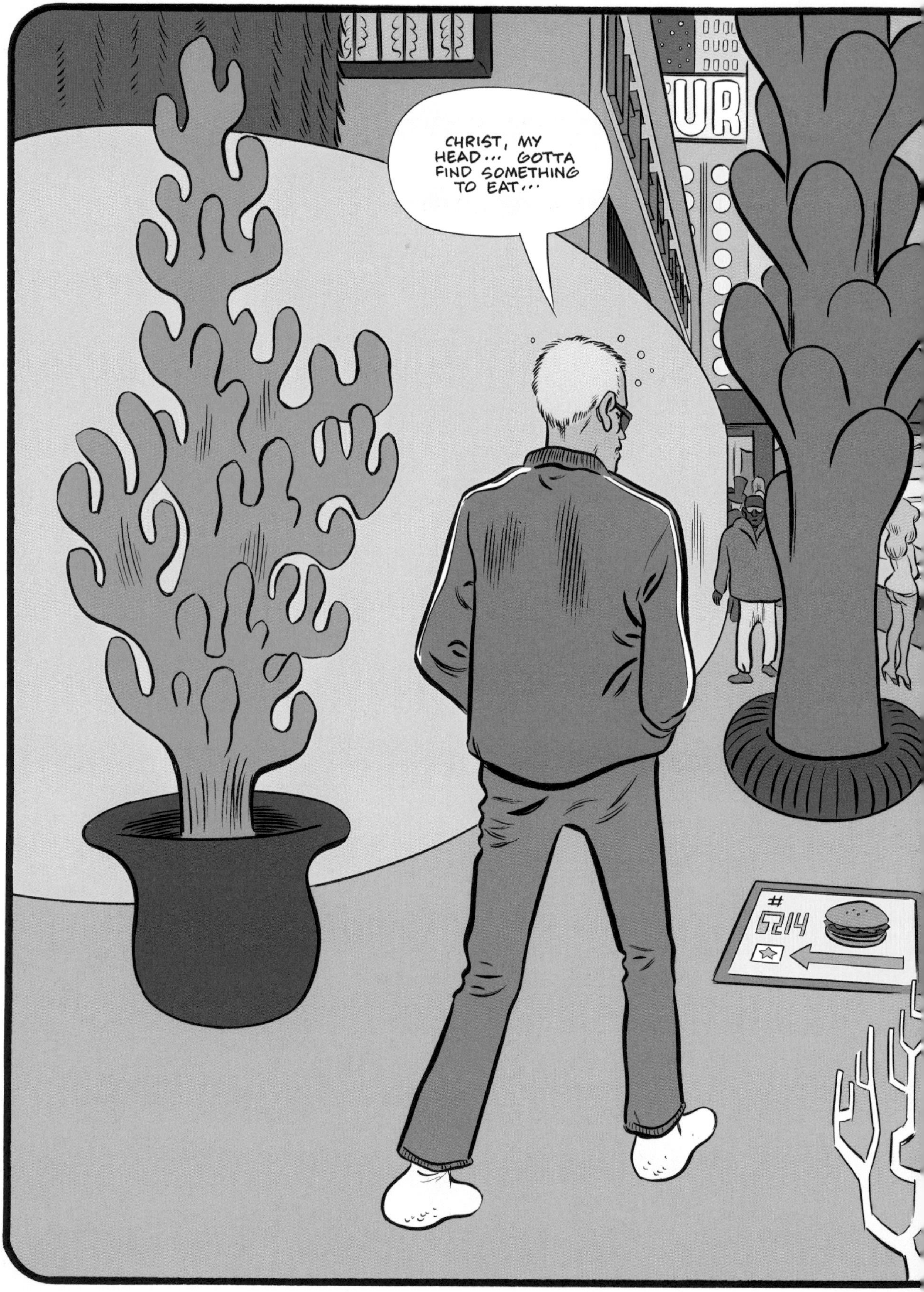
CHRIST, MY HEAD... GOTTA FIND SOMETHING TO EAT...
UR
#
G214

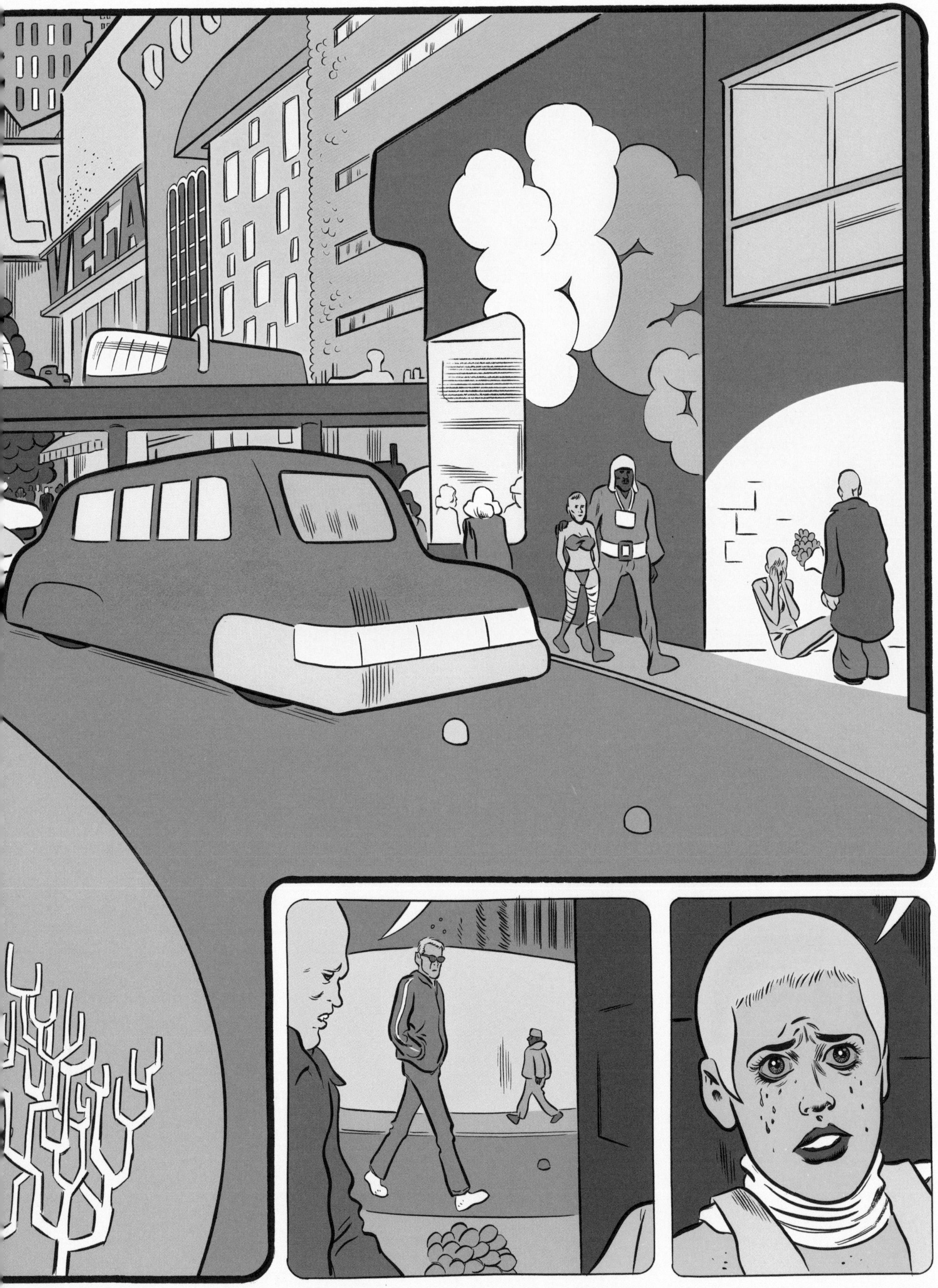
VEGA

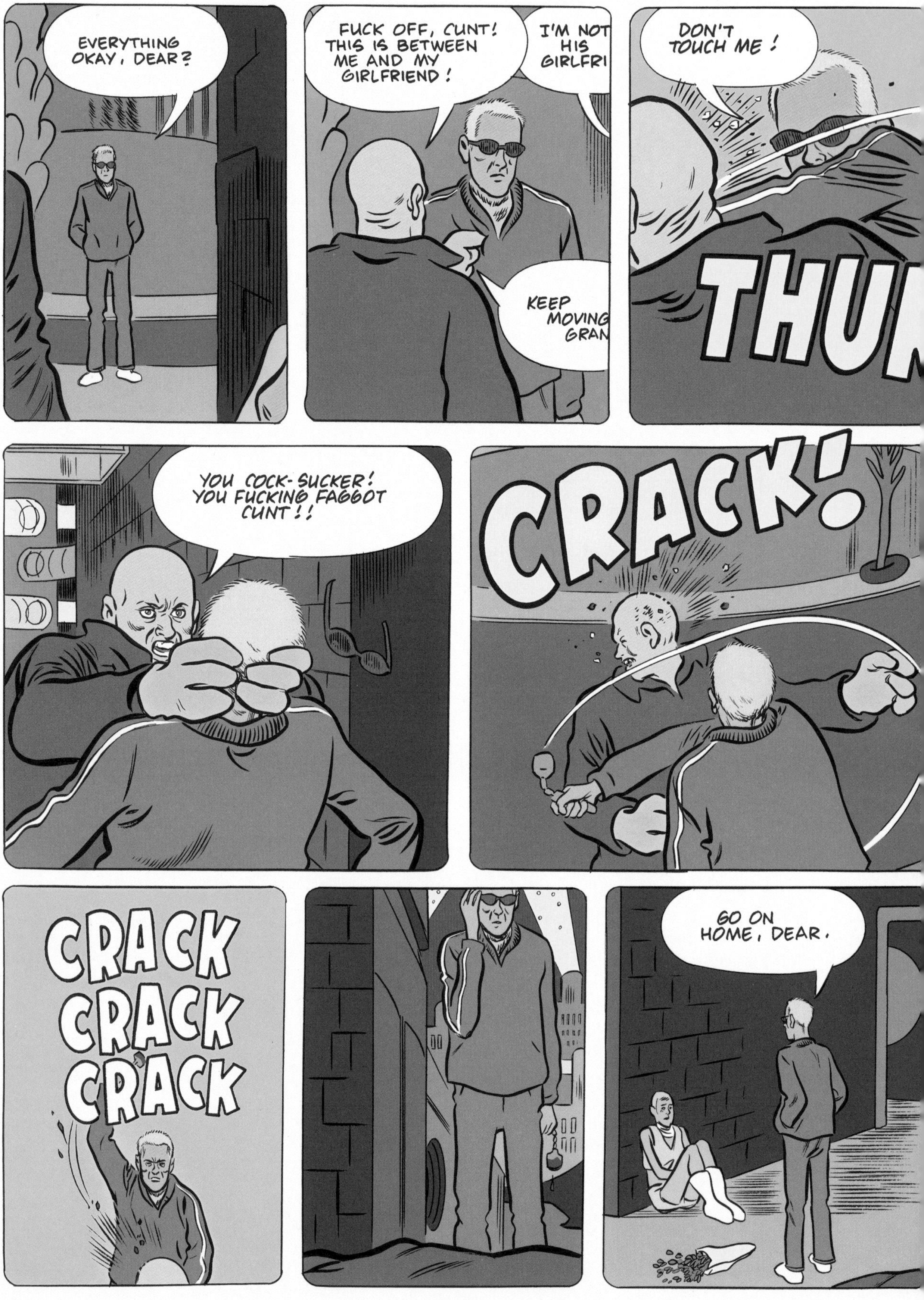

EVERYTHING OKAY, DEAR?
FUCK OFF, CUNT! THIS IS BETWEEN ME AND MY GIRLFRIEND!
I'M NOT HIS GIRLFRI
KEEP MOVING GRAN
DON'T TOUCH ME!
THUN
YOU COCK-SUCKER! YOU FUCKING FAGGOT CUNT!!
CRACK!
CRACK
CRACK
CRACK
GO ON HOME, DEAR.

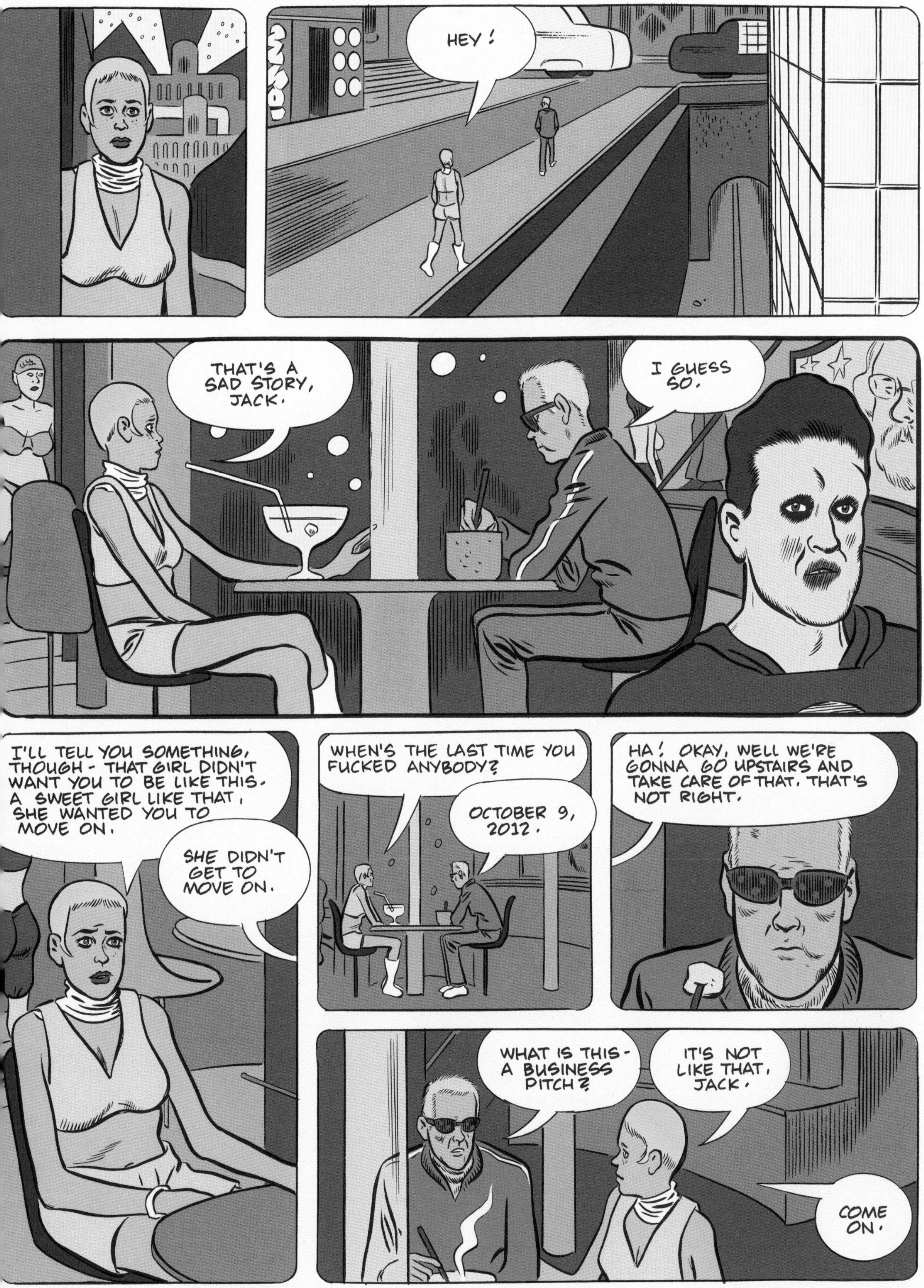
HEY!
THAT'S A SAD STORY, JACK.
I GUESS SO.
I'LL TELL YOU SOMETHING, THOUGH - THAT GIRL DIDN'T WANT YOU TO BE LIKE THIS. A SWEET GIRL LIKE THAT, SHE WANTED YOU TO MOVE ON.
SHE DIDN'T GET TO MOVE ON.
WHEN'S THE LAST TIME YOU FUCKED ANYBODY?
OCTOBER 9, 2012.
HA! OKAY, WELL WE'RE GONNA GO UPSTAIRS AND TAKE CARE OF THAT. THAT'S NOT RIGHT.
WHAT IS THIS - A BUSINESS PITCH?
IT'S NOT LIKE THAT, JACK.
COME ON.

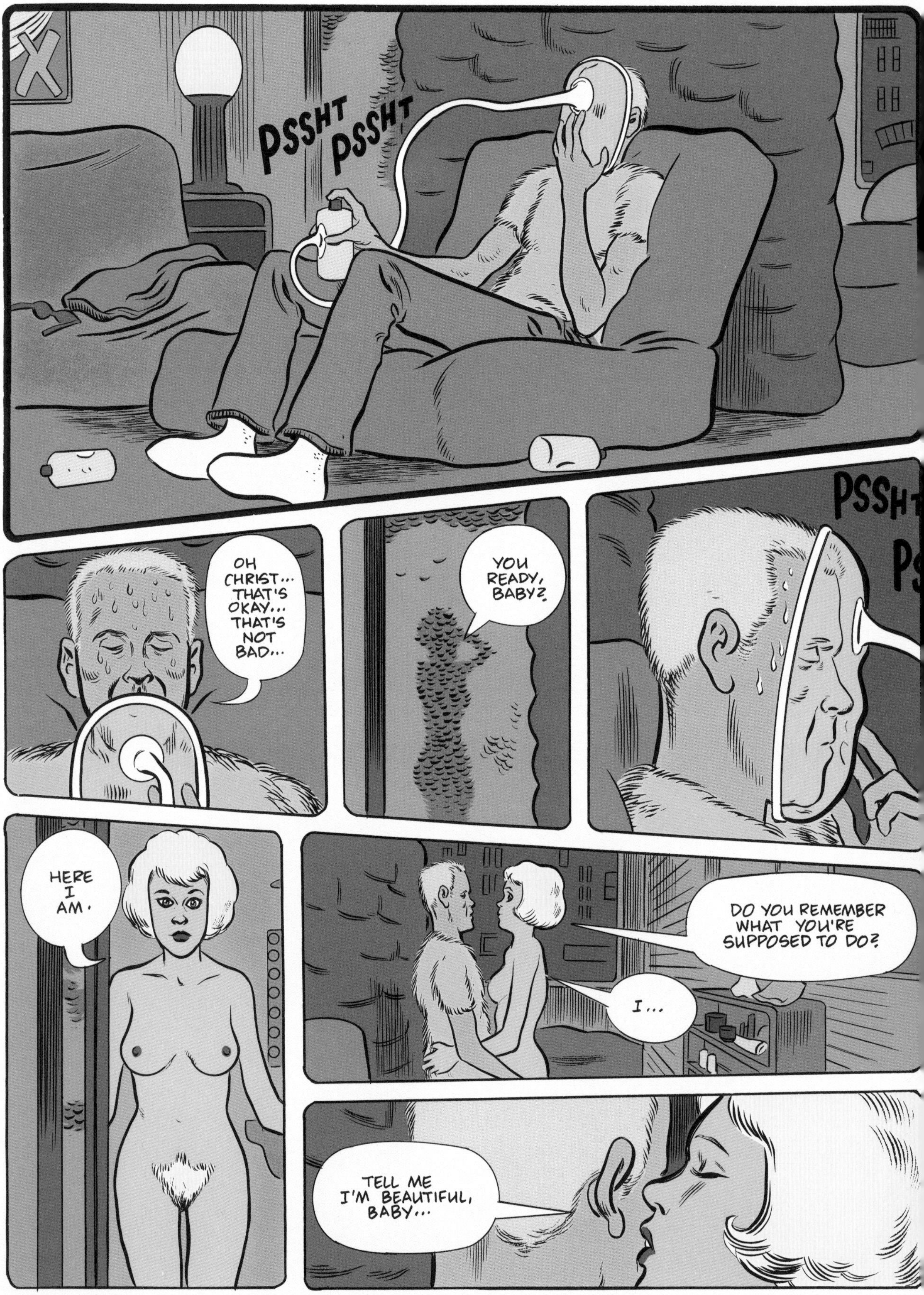
PSSHT PSSHT
OH CHRIST... THAT'S OKAY... THAT'S NOT BAD...
YOU READY, BABY?
PSSHT
HERE I AM.
DO YOU REMEMBER WHAT YOU'RE SUPPOSED TO DO?
I...
TELL ME I'M BEAUTIFUL, BABY...

SAY IT, BABY...

YOU READY FOR ME?

GET THE FUCK OFF!

FUCKING WHORE! DON'T TOUCH ME!

OH FUCK FUCK FUCK...

I'M SORRY.

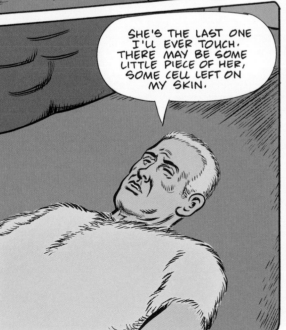

SHE'S THE LAST ONE I'LL EVER TOUCH. THERE MAY BE SOME LITTLE PIECE OF HER, SOME CELL LEFT ON MY SKIN.

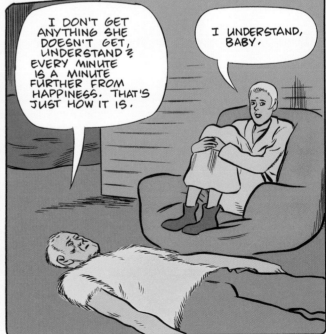

I DON'T GET ANYTHING SHE DOESN'T GET, UNDERSTAND? EVERY MINUTE IS A MINUTE FURTHER FROM HAPPINESS. THAT'S JUST HOW IT IS.

I UNDERSTAND, BABY.

I HAVEN'T WATCHED THIS SHIT IN YEARS.

SO BABY, I'M GONNA HAVE TO ASK YOU TO LEAVE PRETTY SOON.

HOW ABOUT I STAY THE NIGHT? I CAN PAY.

WHAT KINDA CARD YOU GOT?

OKAY, BABY.

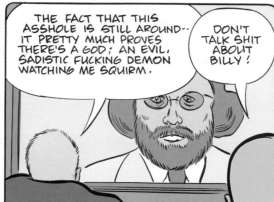

THE FACT THAT THIS ASSHOLE IS STILL AROUND-- IT PRETTY MUCH PROVES THERE'S A GOD; AN EVIL, SADISTIC FUCKING DEMON WATCHING ME SQUIRM.

DON'T TALK SHIT ABOUT BILLY!

PFFT.

DON'T YOU THINK HE'S DONE A GOOD JOB?

SO THE WORLD'S A LITTLE BETTER THAN THE SHITHOLE WE LIVED IN TWENTY YEARS AGO. WHO GIVES A FUCK?

SHE WAS ALWAYS SO WORRIED ABOUT THE STUFF THAT WAS HAPPENING. IT DIDN'T TAKE MUCH TO MAKE HER THINK IT WAS ALL GONNA COME CRASHING DOWN.

IF I COULD JUST GO BACK TO THE DAY WE MET AND TELL HER EVERYTHING WAS GONNA BE ALL RIGHT WITH THE WORLD...LET HER HAVE A FEW YEARS OF PEACE...

YOU'RE SOUNDING MORE AND MORE LIKE BERNIE.

ONE OF MY GUYS DECIDED INSTEAD OF DEALING WITH HIS SHIT HE WAS JUST GONNA INVENT A TIME MACHINE AND GO BACK TO WHEN HE WAS HAPPY. PROBLEM SOLVED!

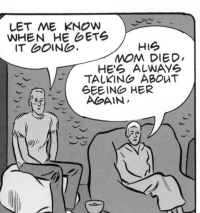

LET ME KNOW WHEN HE GETS IT GOING.

HIS MOM DIED. HE'S ALWAYS TALKING ABOUT SEEING HER AGAIN.

I KNOW HOW IT IS. BELIEVE ME, I'VE PLAYED IT OVER SO MANY TIMES... WHAT IF I COULD GO BACK FOR FIVE MINUTES? WHAT WOULD I DO?

YOU AND BERNIE WOULD BE GOOD FRIENDS.

THE REALLY SICK THING -- IF I HAD THE CHOICE TO EITHER GO BACK AND BE WITH HER, OR TO FIND OUT WHO DID IT AND KILL THEM, I HONESTLY DON'T KNOW WHICH I'D CHOOSE.

I'M NOT THE SAME GUY I WAS. UNLESS I COULD ERASE THE PAST...

I GOTTA GET TO SLEEP, BABY.

... AND WITH THE FULL APPROVAL OF BOTH HOUSES OF...

.. FUCKING ASSHOLE ...

CHRIST. PATHETIC.

BERNI
0048140
AE6470P

MAGE
0046808

30

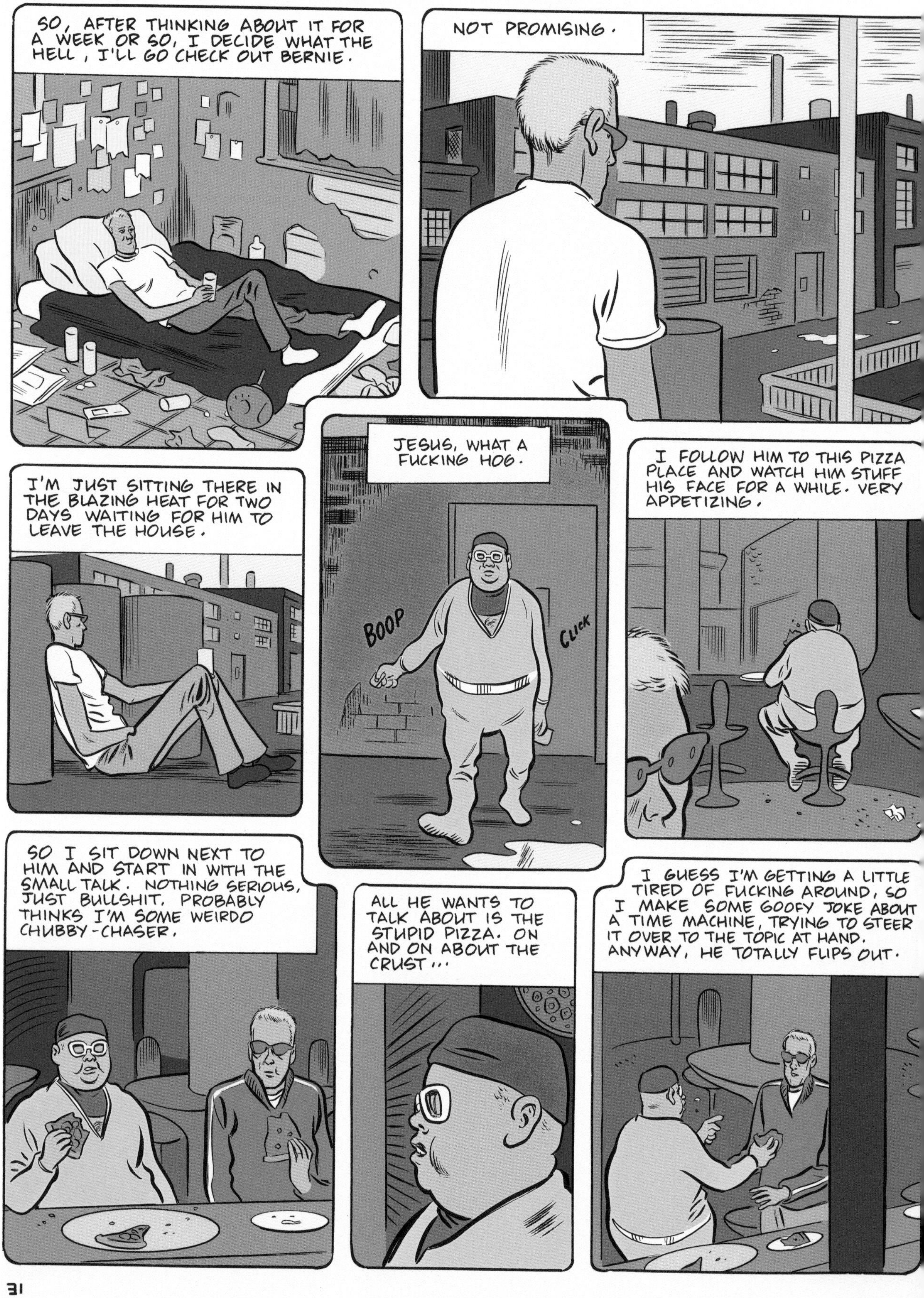
SO, AFTER THINKING ABOUT IT FOR A WEEK OR SO, I DECIDE WHAT THE HELL, I'LL GO CHECK OUT BERNIE.
NOT PROMISING.
I'M JUST SITTING THERE IN THE BLAZING HEAT FOR TWO DAYS WAITING FOR HIM TO LEAVE THE HOUSE.
JESUS, WHAT A FUCKING HOG.
BOOP
CLICK
I FOLLOW HIM TO THIS PIZZA PLACE AND WATCH HIM STUFF HIS FACE FOR A WHILE. VERY APPETIZING.
SO I SIT DOWN NEXT TO HIM AND START IN WITH THE SMALL TALK. NOTHING SERIOUS, JUST BULLSHIT. PROBABLY THINKS I'M SOME WEIRDO CHUBBY-CHASER.
ALL HE WANTS TO TALK ABOUT IS THE STUPID PIZZA. ON AND ON ABOUT THE CRUST...
I GUESS I'M GETTING A LITTLE TIRED OF FUCKING AROUND, SO I MAKE SOME GOOFY JOKE ABOUT A TIME MACHINE, TRYING TO STEER IT OVER TO THE TOPIC AT HAND. ANYWAY, HE TOTALLY FLIPS OUT.

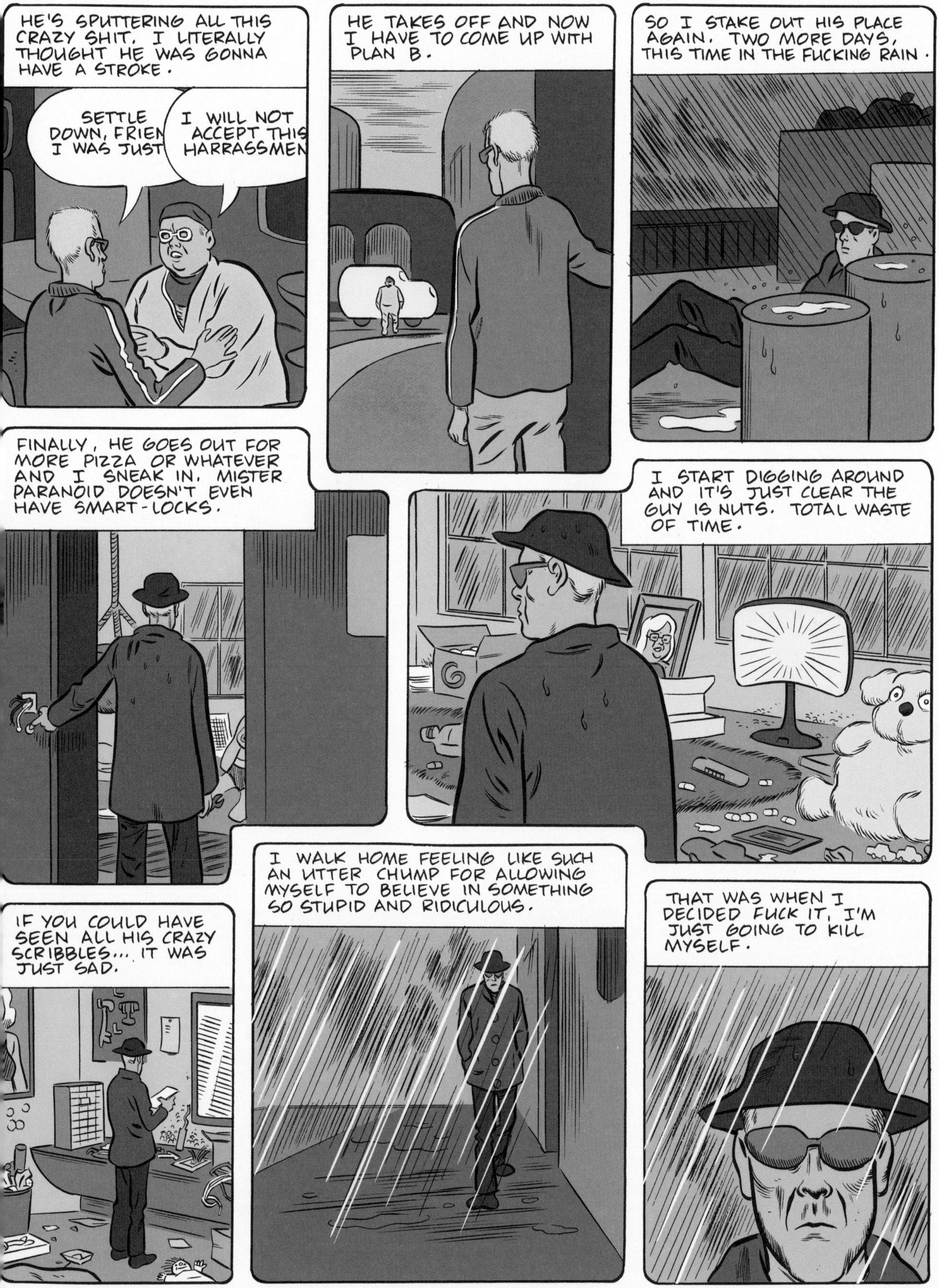
HE'S SPUTTERING ALL THIS CRAZY SHIT. I LITERALLY THOUGHT HE WAS GONNA HAVE A STROKE.
SETTLE DOWN, FRIEN I WAS JUST
I WILL NOT ACCEPT THIS HARRASSMEN
HE TAKES OFF AND NOW I HAVE TO COME UP WITH PLAN B.
SO I STAKE OUT HIS PLACE AGAIN. TWO MORE DAYS, THIS TIME IN THE FUCKING RAIN.
FINALLY, HE GOES OUT FOR MORE PIZZA OR WHATEVER AND I SNEAK IN. MISTER PARANOID DOESN'T EVEN HAVE SMART-LOCKS.
I START DIGGING AROUND AND IT'S JUST CLEAR THE GUY IS NUTS. TOTAL WASTE OF TIME.
IF YOU COULD HAVE SEEN ALL HIS CRAZY SCRIBBLES... IT WAS JUST SAD.
I WALK HOME FEELING LIKE SUCH AN UTTER CHUMP FOR ALLOWING MYSELF TO BELIEVE IN SOMETHING SO STUPID AND RIDICULOUS.
THAT WAS WHEN I DECIDED FUCK IT, I'M JUST GOING TO KILL MYSELF.

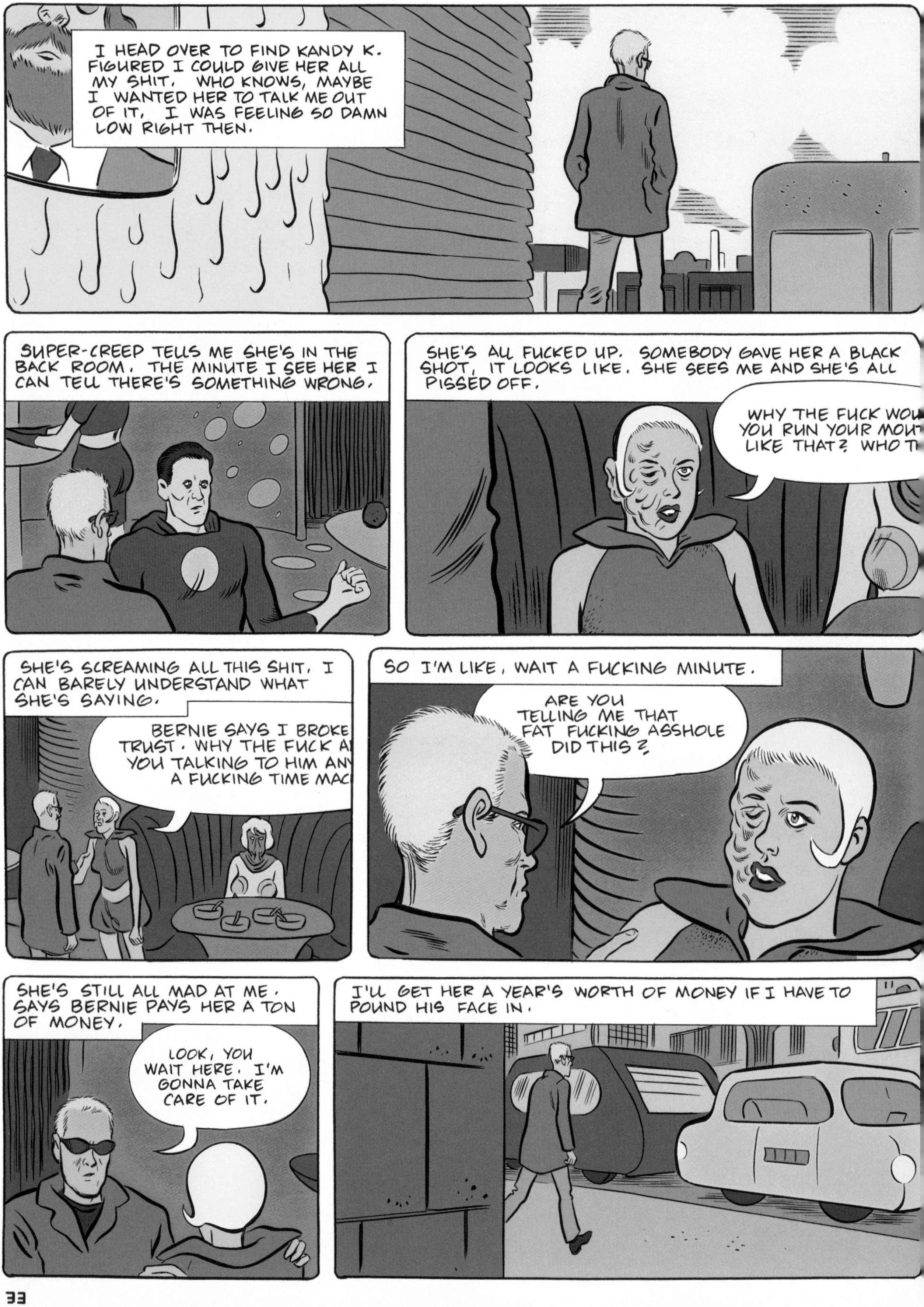
I HEAD OVER TO FIND KANDY K. FIGURED I COULD GIVE HER ALL MY SHIT. WHO KNOWS, MAYBE I WANTED HER TO TALK ME OUT OF IT, I WAS FEELING SO DAMN LOW RIGHT THEN.
SUPER-CREEP TELLS ME SHE'S IN THE BACK ROOM. THE MINUTE I SEE HER I CAN TELL THERE'S SOMETHING WRONG.
SHE'S ALL FUCKED UP. SOMEBODY GAVE HER A BLACK SHOT, IT LOOKS LIKE. SHE SEES ME AND SHE'S ALL PISSED OFF.
WHY THE FUCK WOU YOU RUN YOUR MOUT LIKE THAT? WHO T
SHE'S SCREAMING ALL THIS SHIT. I CAN BARELY UNDERSTAND WHAT SHE'S SAYING.
BERNIE SAYS I BROKE TRUST. WHY THE FUCK A YOU TALKING TO HIM ANY A FUCKING TIME MAC
SO I'M LIKE, WAIT A FUCKING MINUTE.
ARE YOU TELLING ME THAT FAT FUCKING ASSHOLE DID THIS?
SHE'S STILL ALL MAD AT ME. SAYS BERNIE PAYS HER A TON OF MONEY.
LOOK, YOU WAIT HERE. I'M GONNA TAKE CARE OF IT.
I'LL GET HER A YEAR'S WORTH OF MONEY IF I HAVE TO POUND HIS FACE IN.

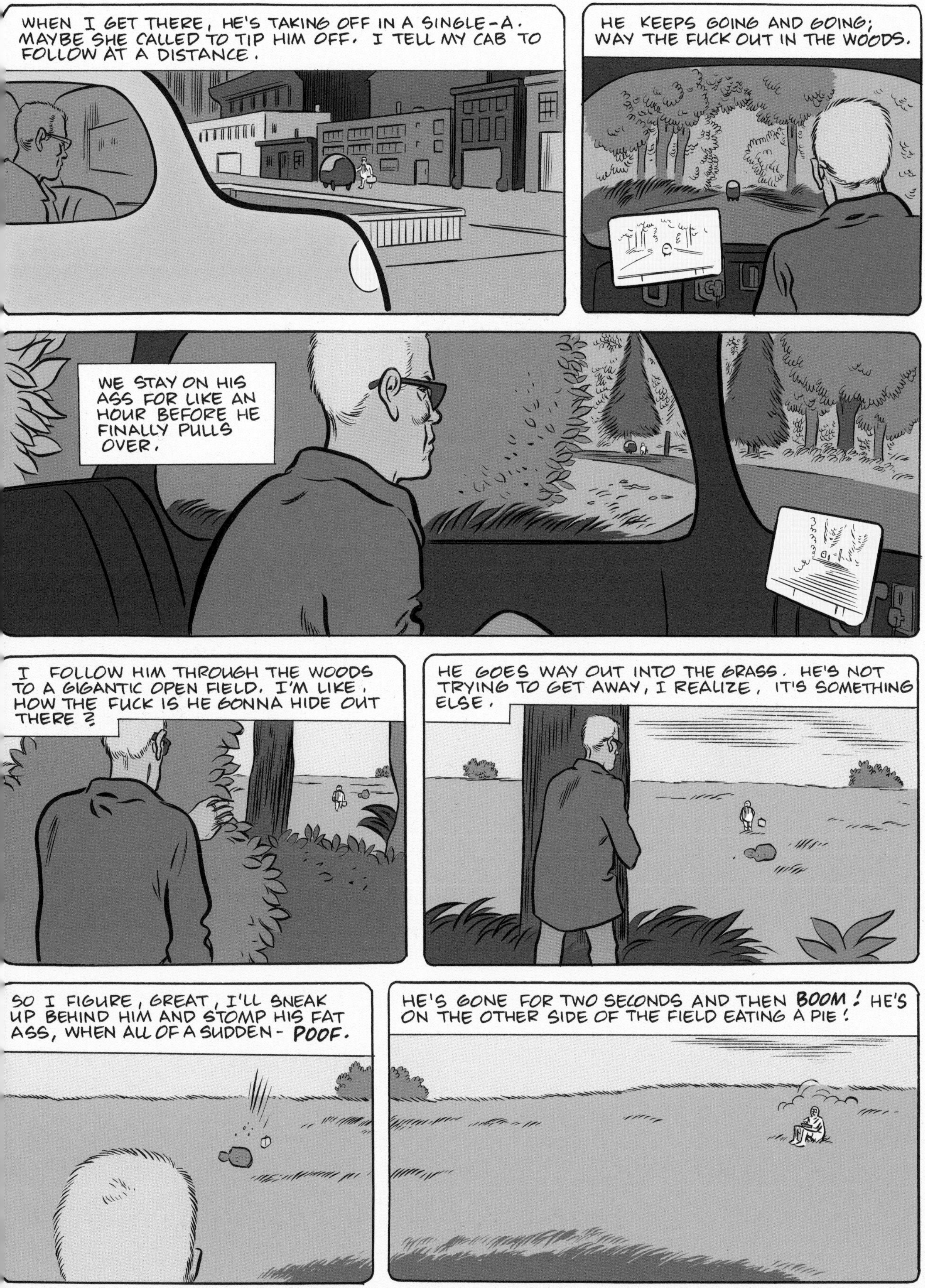
WHEN I GET THERE, HE'S TAKING OFF IN A SINGLE-A. MAYBE SHE CALLED TO TIP HIM OFF. I TELL MY CAB TO FOLLOW AT A DISTANCE.
HE KEEPS GOING AND GOING; WAY THE FUCK OUT IN THE WOODS.
WE STAY ON HIS ASS FOR LIKE AN HOUR BEFORE HE FINALLY PULLS OVER.
I FOLLOW HIM THROUGH THE WOODS TO A GIGANTIC OPEN FIELD. I'M LIKE, HOW THE FUCK IS HE GONNA HIDE OUT THERE?
HE GOES WAY OUT INTO THE GRASS. HE'S NOT TRYING TO GET AWAY, I REALIZE, IT'S SOMETHING ELSE.
SO I FIGURE, GREAT, I'LL SNEAK UP BEHIND HIM AND STOMP HIS FAT ASS, WHEN ALL OF A SUDDEN- **POOF**.
HE'S GONE FOR TWO SECONDS AND THEN **BOOM**! HE'S ON THE OTHER SIDE OF THE FIELD EATING A PIE!

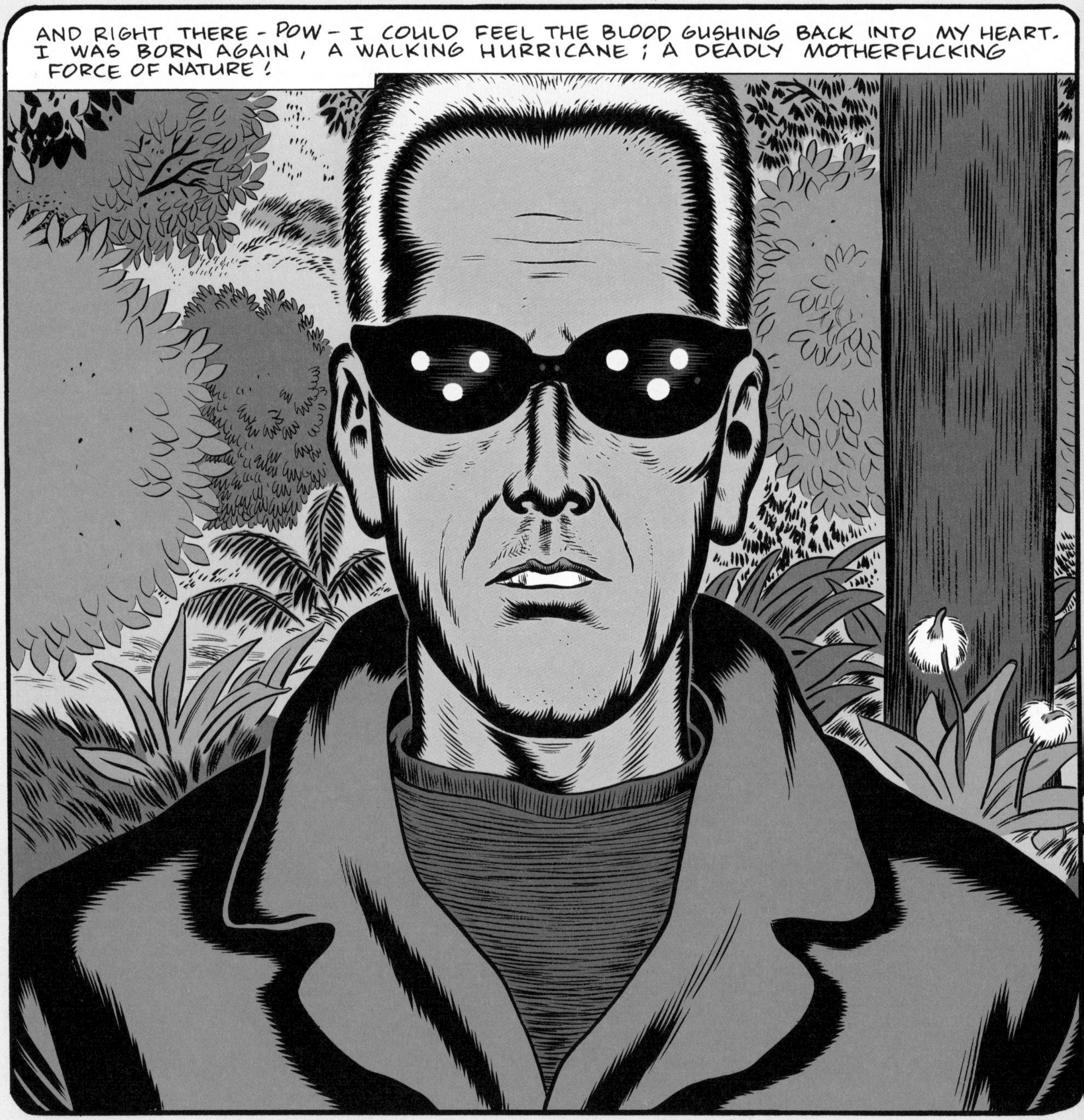
AND RIGHT THERE - POW - I COULD FEEL THE BLOOD GUSHING BACK INTO MY HEART. I WAS BORN AGAIN , A WALKING HURRICANE ; A DEADLY MOTHERFUCKING FORCE OF NATURE !

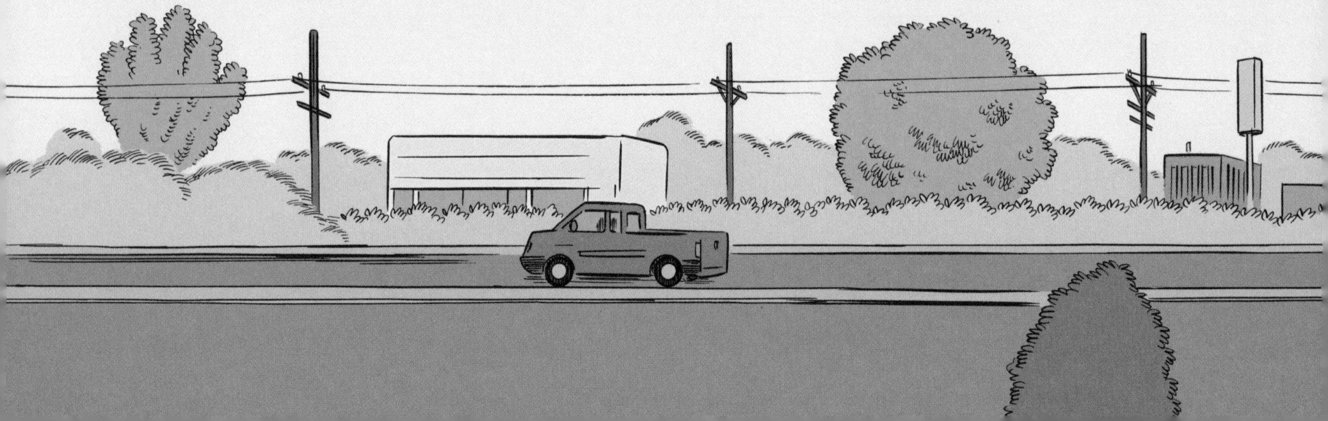

2006

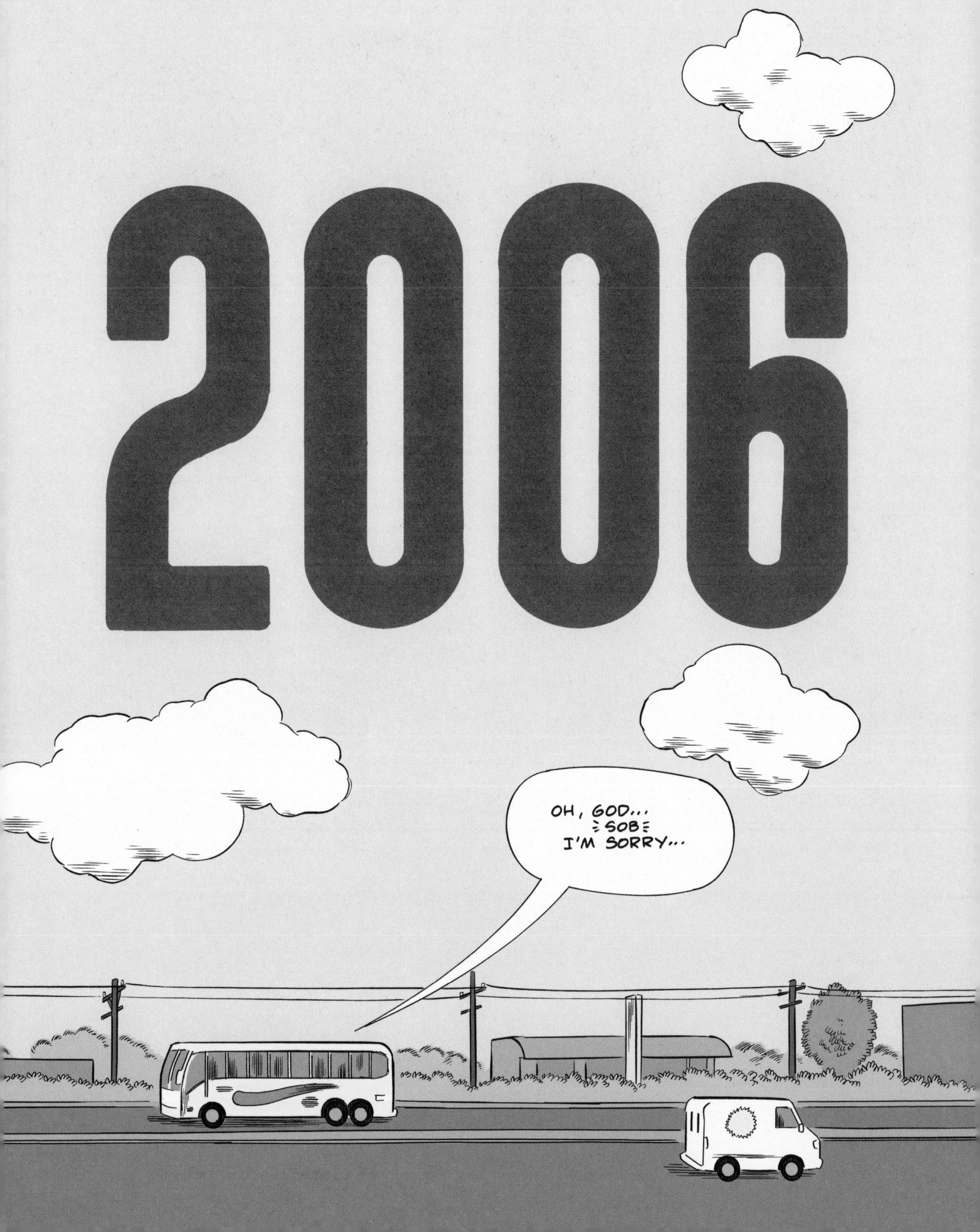
OH, GOD...
SOB
I'M SORRY...

≥ SNUKK ≥ I'M JUST... I'M REALLY GOING THROUGH A HARD TIME... ≥ SNIFF ≥

GOD, YOU'RE PROBABLY LIKE, "WHY DID I GET STUCK NEXT TO THIS ANNOYING BITCH ?!" ≥ SNIFF ≥

I WAS GETTING TOTAL A'S! LIKE! A FUCKING 3.9! WHAT THE FUCK MORE DO THEY WANT?

THEY PROMISE YOU A SCHOLARSHIP AND THEN POOF, THEY'RE LIKE, "THAT'LL BE 25 GRAND, BITCH! PAY THE FUCK UP!"

YOU GOING OFF TO SCHOOL?

NO. THAT'S WHAT I'M SAYING: I'M PRETTY MUCH DOING THE EXACT OPPOSITE OF THAT.

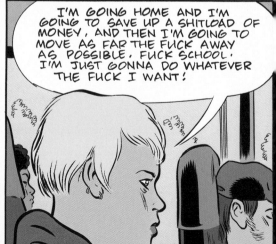

I'M GOING HOME AND I'M GOING TO SAVE UP A SHITLOAD OF MONEY, AND THEN I'M GOING TO MOVE AS FAR THE FUCK AWAY AS POSSIBLE. FUCK SCHOOL. I'M JUST GONNA DO WHATEVER THE FUCK I WANT!

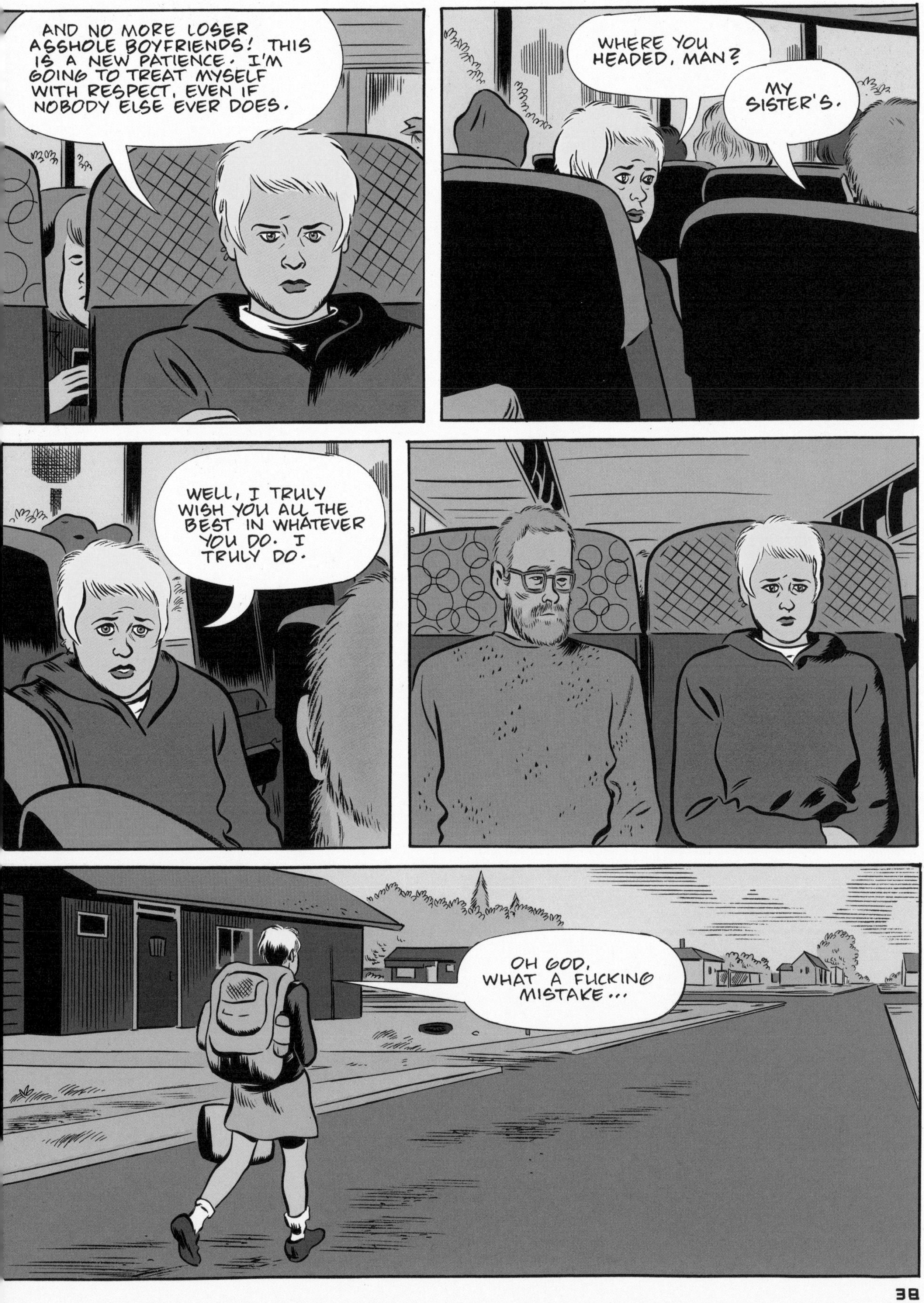
AND NO MORE LOSER ASSHOLE BOYFRIENDS! THIS IS A NEW PATIENCE. I'M GOING TO TREAT MYSELF WITH RESPECT, EVEN IF NOBODY ELSE EVER DOES.
WHERE YOU HEADED, MAN?
MY SISTER'S.
WELL, I TRULY WISH YOU ALL THE BEST IN WHATEVER YOU DO. I TRULY DO.
OH GOD, WHAT A FUCKING MISTAKE...

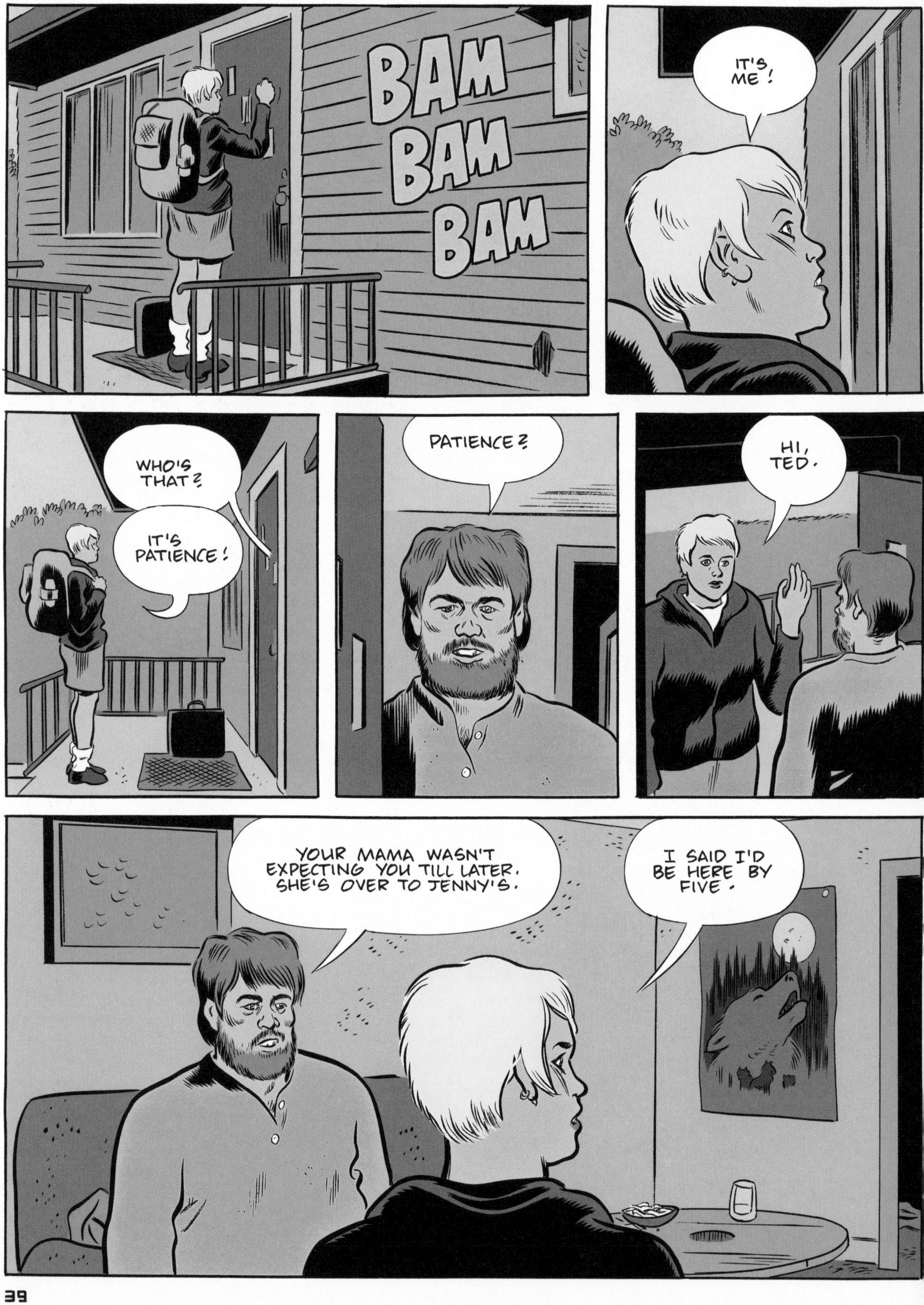

BAM
BAM
BAM
IT'S ME!
WHO'S THAT?
IT'S PATIENCE!
PATIENCE?
HI, TED.
YOUR MAMA WASN'T EXPECTING YOU TILL LATER. SHE'S OVER TO JENNY'S.
I SAID I'D BE HERE BY FIVE.

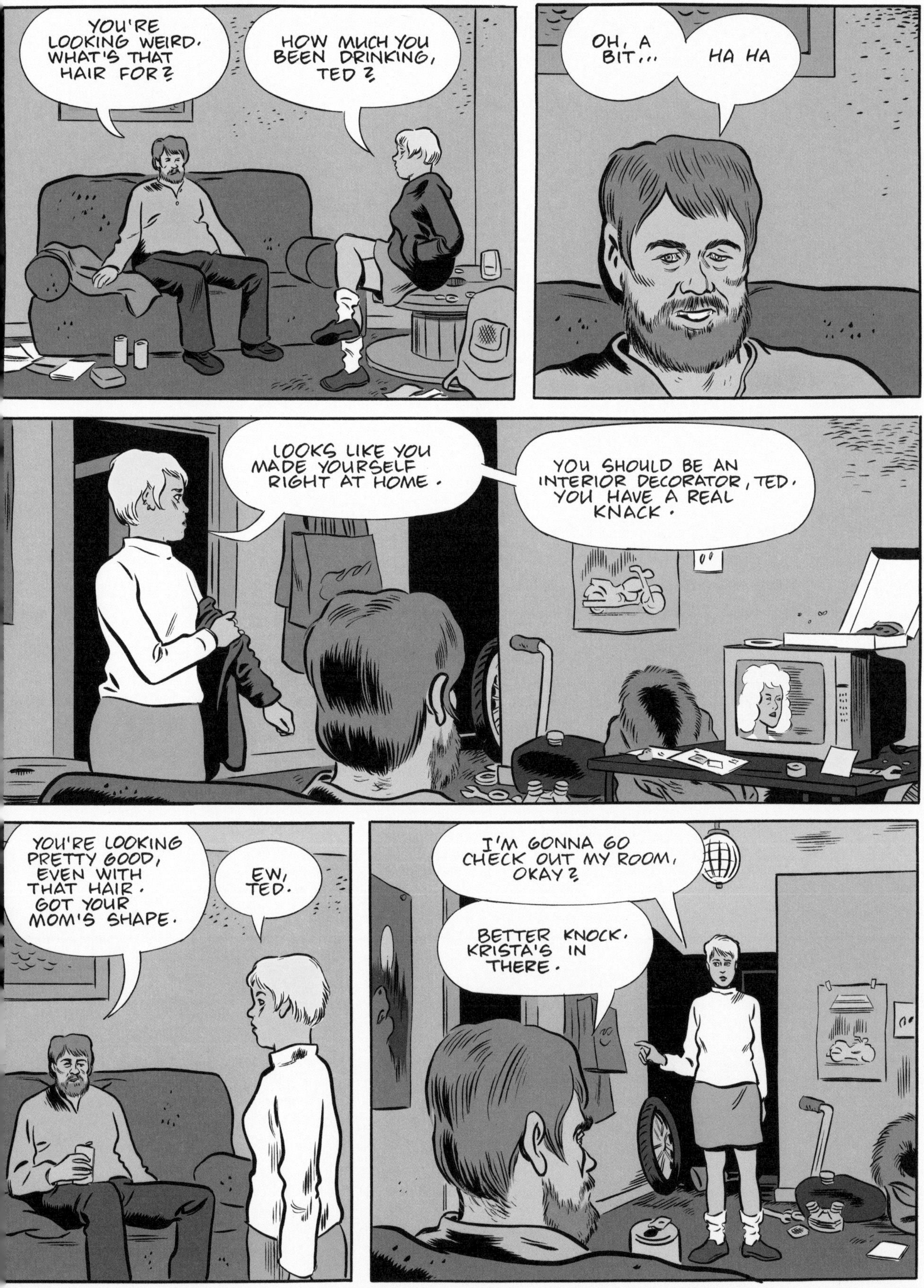
YOU'RE LOOKING WEIRD. WHAT'S THAT HAIR FOR?
HOW MUCH YOU BEEN DRINKING, TED?
OH, A BIT...
HA HA
LOOKS LIKE YOU MADE YOURSELF RIGHT AT HOME.
YOU SHOULD BE AN INTERIOR DECORATOR, TED. YOU HAVE A REAL KNACK.
YOU'RE LOOKING PRETTY GOOD, EVEN WITH THAT HAIR. GOT YOUR MOM'S SHAPE.
EW, TED.
I'M GONNA GO CHECK OUT MY ROOM, OKAY?
BETTER KNOCK. KRISTA'S IN THERE.

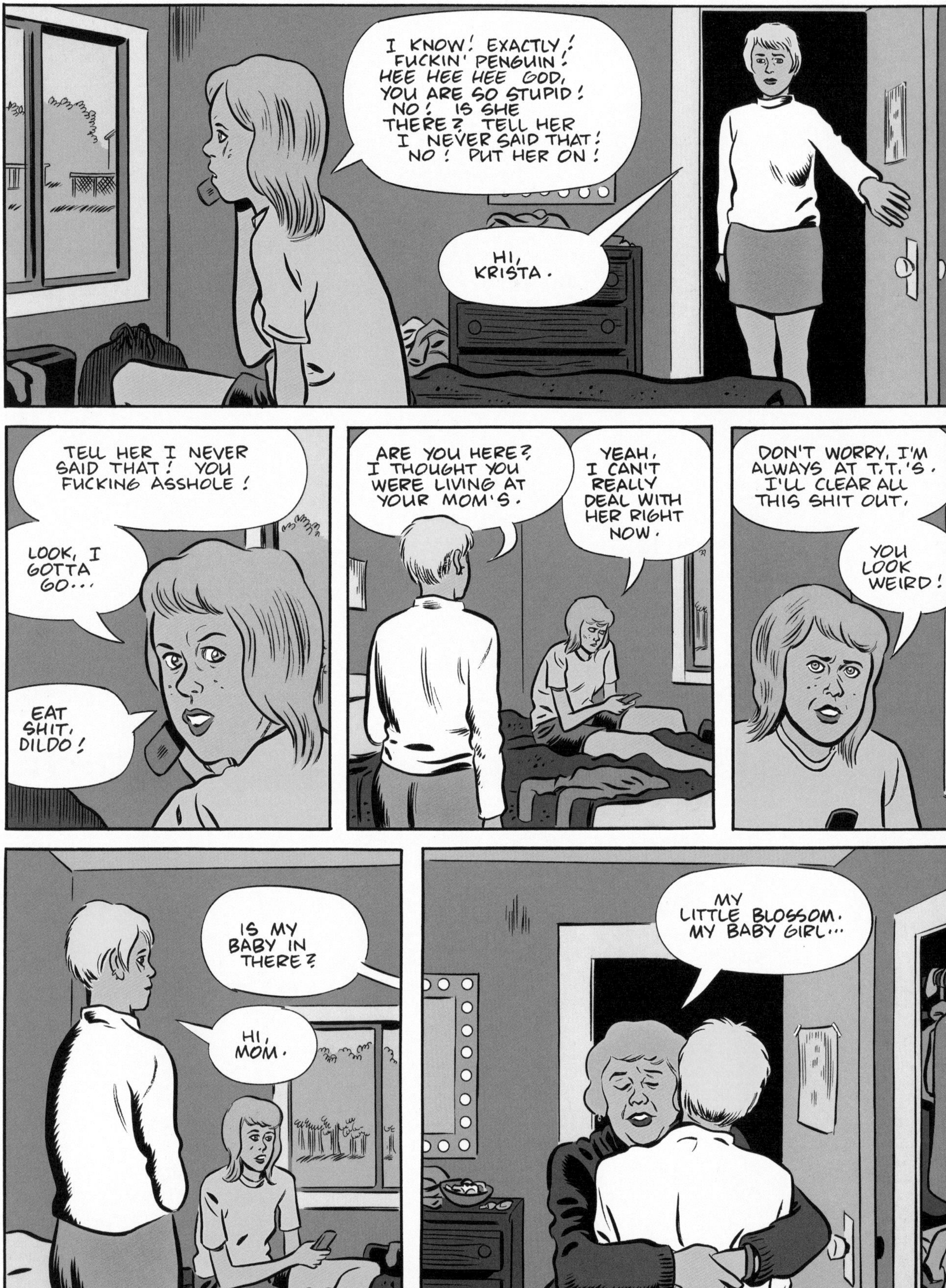

I KNOW! EXACTLY! FUCKIN' PENGUIN! HEE HEE HEE GOD, YOU ARE SO STUPID! NO! IS SHE THERE? TELL HER I NEVER SAID THAT! NO! PUT HER ON!
HI, KRISTA.
TELL HER I NEVER SAID THAT! YOU FUCKING ASSHOLE!
LOOK, I GOTTA GO...
EAT SHIT, DILDO!
ARE YOU HERE? I THOUGHT YOU WERE LIVING AT YOUR MOM'S.
YEAH, I CAN'T REALLY DEAL WITH HER RIGHT NOW.
DON'T WORRY, I'M ALWAYS AT T.T.'S. I'LL CLEAR ALL THIS SHIT OUT.
YOU LOOK WEIRD!
IS MY BABY IN THERE?
HI, MOM.
MY LITTLE BLOSSOM. MY BABY GIRL...

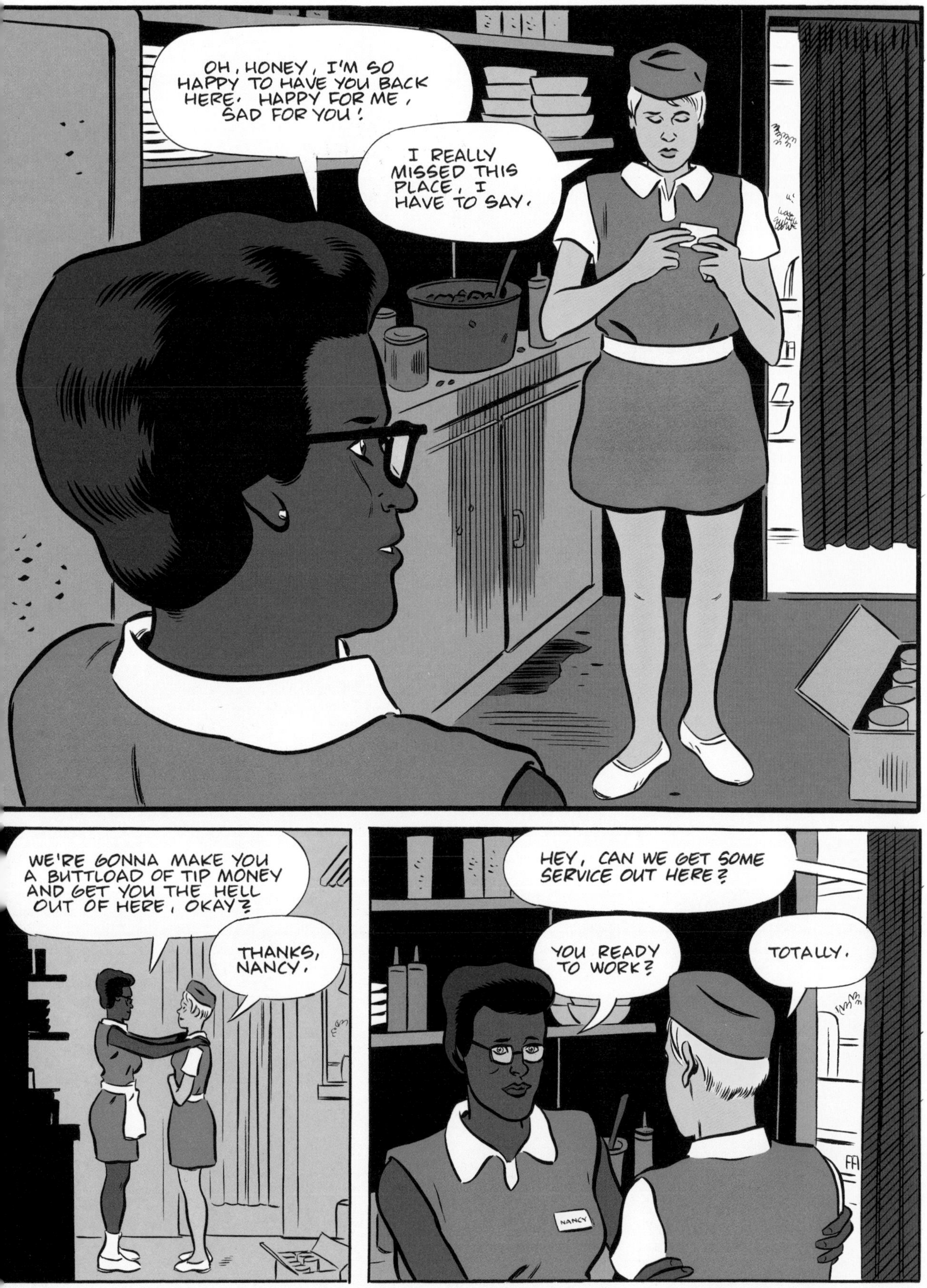
OH, HONEY, I'M SO HAPPY TO HAVE YOU BACK HERE. HAPPY FOR ME, SAD FOR YOU!
I REALLY MISSED THIS PLACE, I HAVE TO SAY.
WE'RE GONNA MAKE YOU A BUTTLOAD OF TIP MONEY AND GET YOU THE HELL OUT OF HERE, OKAY?
THANKS, NANCY.
HEY, CAN WE GET SOME SERVICE OUT HERE?
YOU READY TO WORK?
TOTALLY.
NANCY

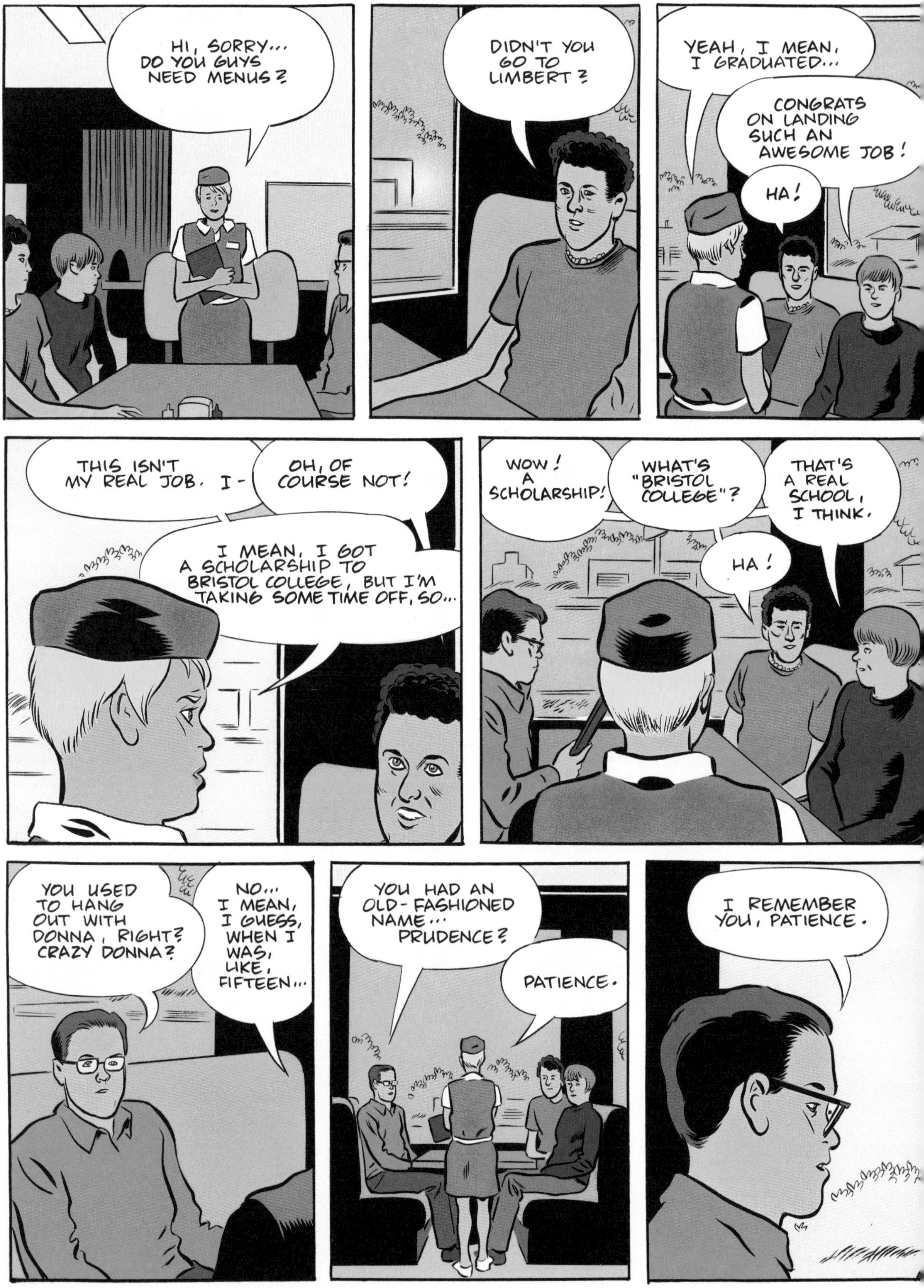
HI, SORRY... DO YOU GUYS NEED MENUS?
DIDN'T YOU GO TO LIMBERT?
YEAH, I MEAN, I GRADUATED...
CONGRATS ON LANDING SUCH AN AWESOME JOB!
HA!
THIS ISN'T MY REAL JOB. I-
OH, OF COURSE NOT!
I MEAN, I GOT A SCHOLARSHIP TO BRISTOL COLLEGE, BUT I'M TAKING SOME TIME OFF, SO...
WOW! A SCHOLARSHIP!
WHAT'S "BRISTOL COLLEGE"?
THAT'S A REAL SCHOOL, I THINK.
HA!
YOU USED TO HANG OUT WITH DONNA, RIGHT? CRAZY DONNA?
NO... I MEAN, I GUESS, WHEN I WAS, LIKE, FIFTEEN...
YOU HAD AN OLD-FASHIONED NAME... PRUDENCE?
PATIENCE.
I REMEMBER YOU, PATIENCE.

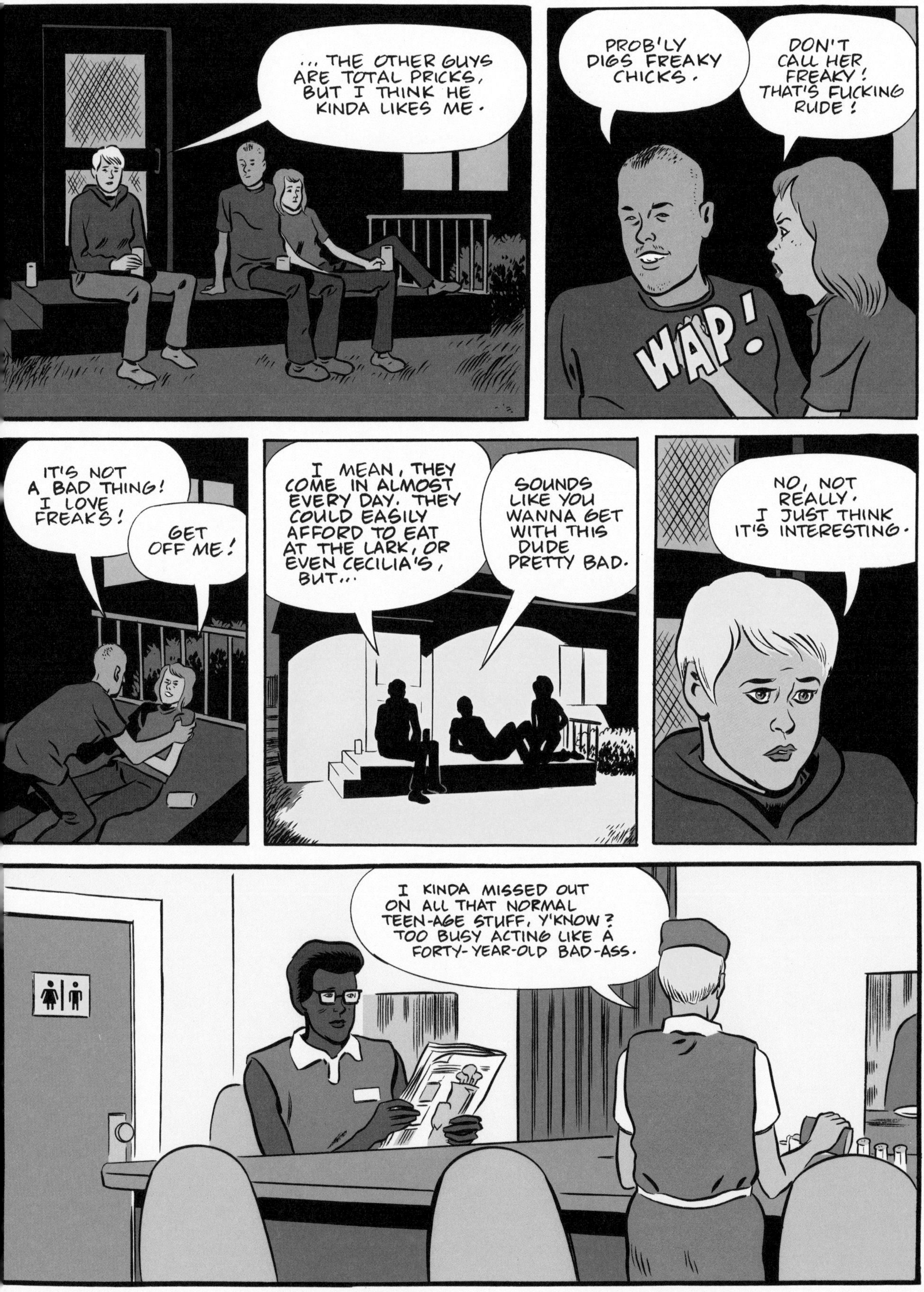

... THE OTHER GUYS ARE TOTAL PRICKS, BUT I THINK HE KINDA LIKES ME.
PROB'LY DIGS FREAKY CHICKS.
DON'T CALL HER FREAKY! THAT'S FUCKING RUDE!
WAP!
IT'S NOT A BAD THING! I LOVE FREAKS!
GET OFF ME!
I MEAN, THEY COME IN ALMOST EVERY DAY. THEY COULD EASILY AFFORD TO EAT AT THE LARK, OR EVEN CECILIA'S, BUT...
SOUNDS LIKE YOU WANNA GET WITH THIS DUDE PRETTY BAD.
NO, NOT REALLY. I JUST THINK IT'S INTERESTING.
I KINDA MISSED OUT ON ALL THAT NORMAL TEEN-AGE STUFF, Y'KNOW? TOO BUSY ACTING LIKE A FORTY-YEAR-OLD BAD-ASS.

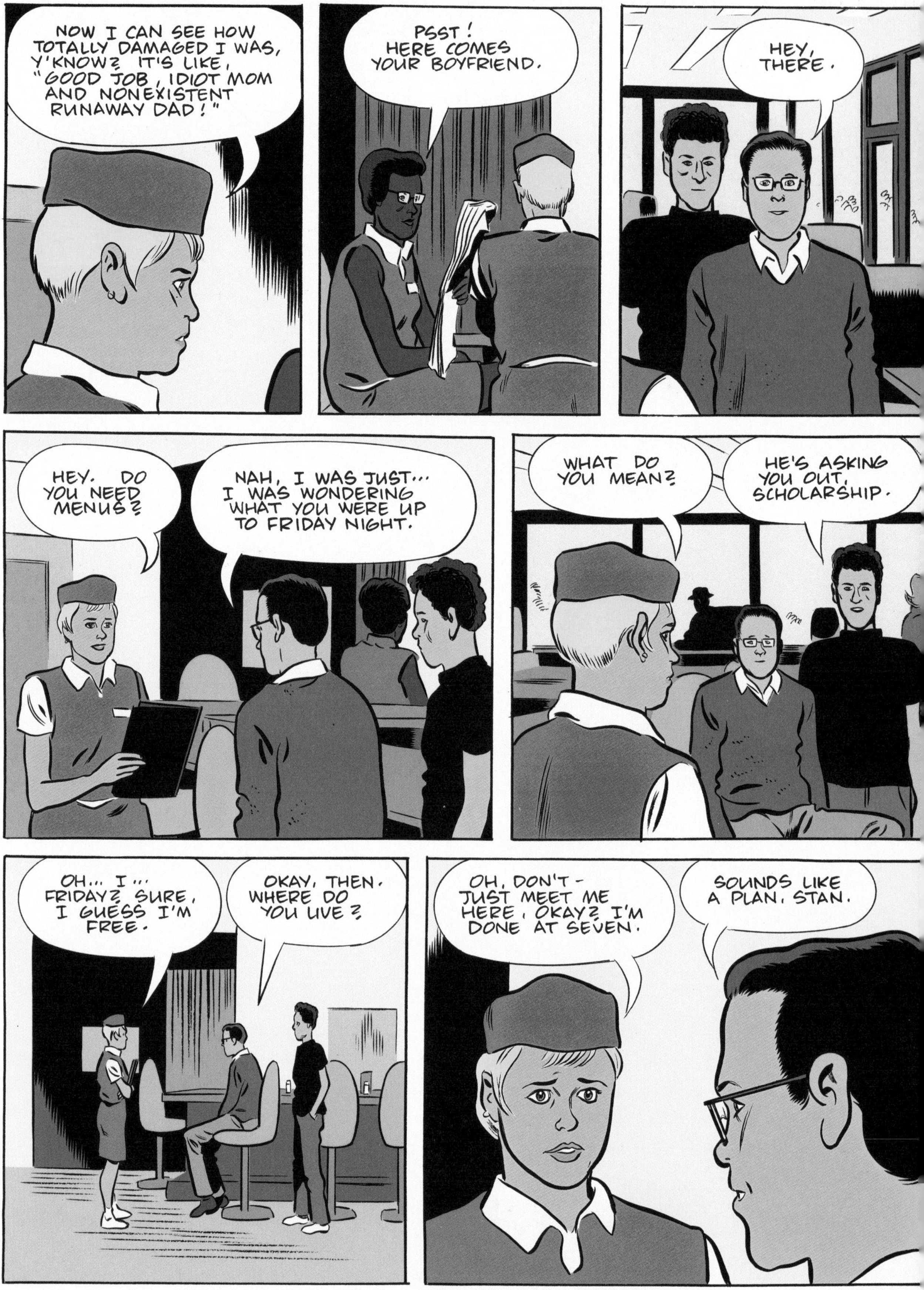
NOW I CAN SEE HOW TOTALLY DAMAGED I WAS, Y'KNOW? IT'S LIKE, "GOOD JOB, IDIOT MOM AND NONEXISTENT RUNAWAY DAD!"
PSST! HERE COMES YOUR BOYFRIEND.
HEY, THERE.
HEY. DO YOU NEED MENUS?
NAH, I WAS JUST... I WAS WONDERING WHAT YOU WERE UP TO FRIDAY NIGHT.
WHAT DO YOU MEAN?
HE'S ASKING YOU OUT, SCHOLARSHIP.
OH... I... FRIDAY? SURE, I GUESS I'M FREE.
OKAY, THEN. WHERE DO YOU LIVE?
OH, DON'T - JUST MEET ME HERE, OKAY? I'M DONE AT SEVEN.
SOUNDS LIKE A PLAN, STAN.

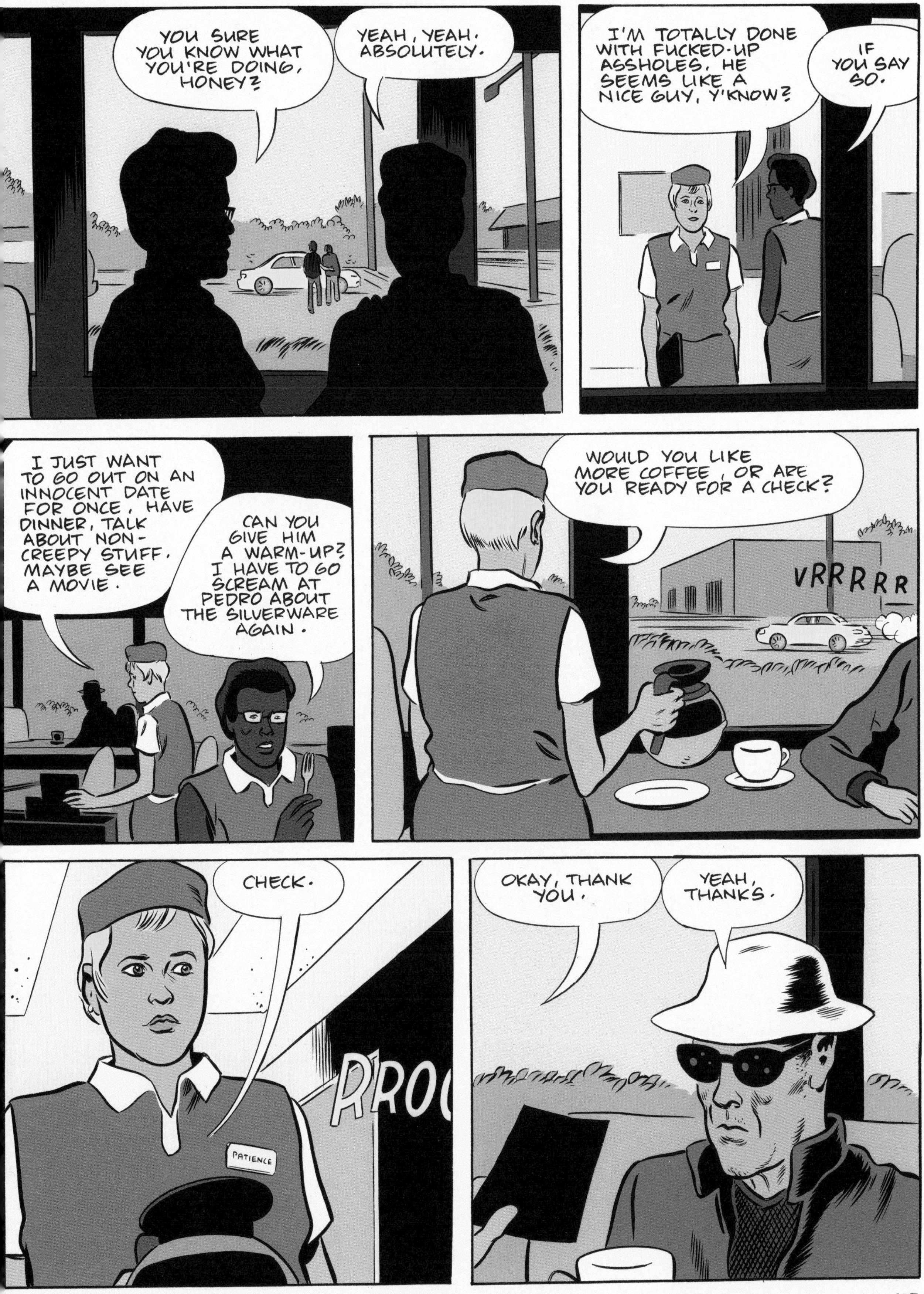

YOU SURE YOU KNOW WHAT YOU'RE DOING, HONEY?
YEAH, YEAH. ABSOLUTELY.
I'M TOTALLY DONE WITH FUCKED-UP ASSHOLES. HE SEEMS LIKE A NICE GUY, Y'KNOW?
IF YOU SAY SO.
I JUST WANT TO GO OUT ON AN INNOCENT DATE FOR ONCE. HAVE DINNER, TALK ABOUT NON-CREEPY STUFF. MAYBE SEE A MOVIE.
CAN YOU GIVE HIM A WARM-UP? I HAVE TO GO SCREAM AT PEDRO ABOUT THE SILVERWARE AGAIN.
WOULD YOU LIKE MORE COFFEE, OR ARE YOU READY FOR A CHECK?
VRRRRRR
CHECK.
PATIENCE
RROO
OKAY, THANK YOU.
YEAH, THANKS.

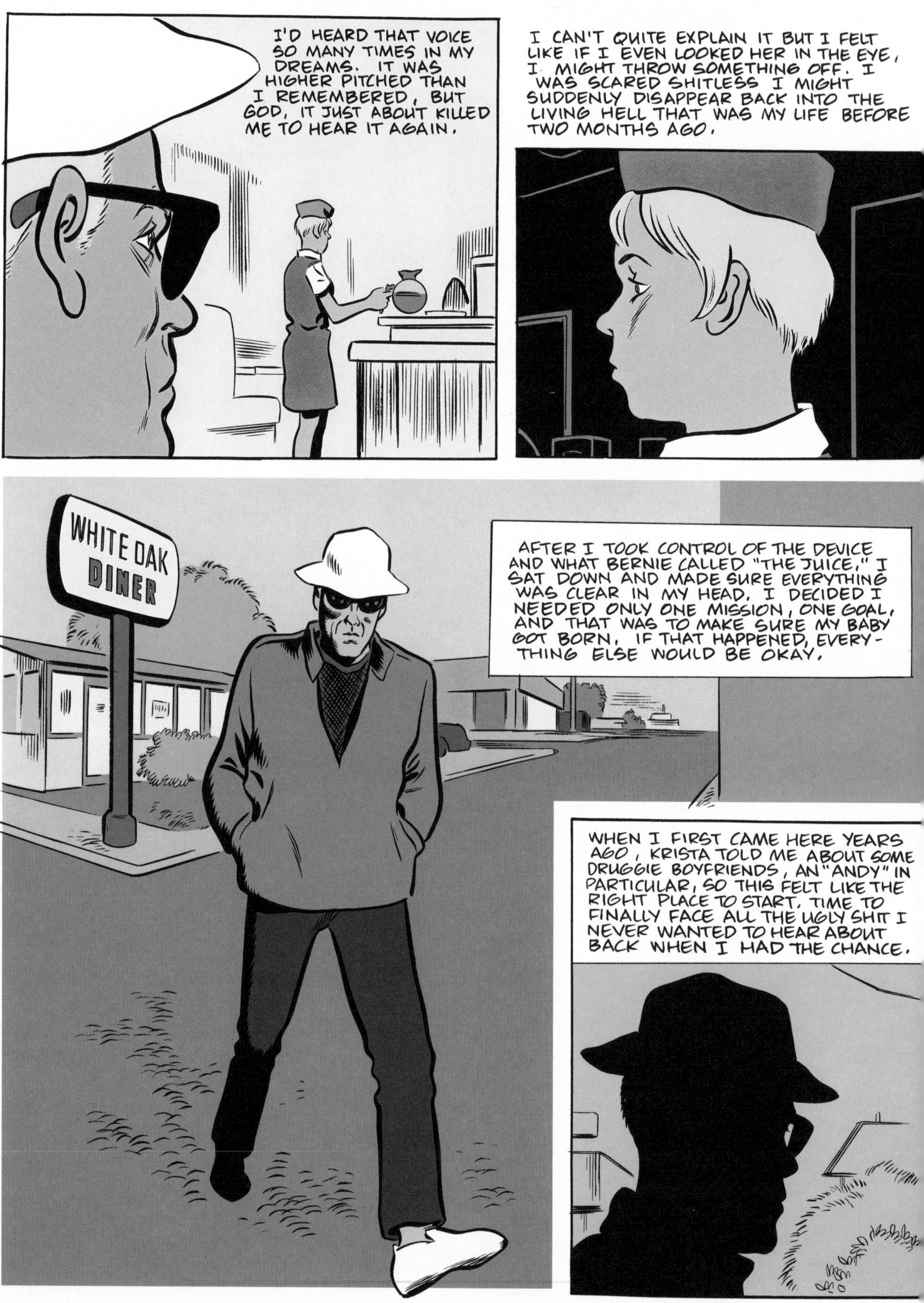
I'D HEARD THAT VOICE SO MANY TIMES IN MY DREAMS. IT WAS HIGHER PITCHED THAN I REMEMBERED, BUT GOD, IT JUST ABOUT KILLED ME TO HEAR IT AGAIN.
I CAN'T QUITE EXPLAIN IT BUT I FELT LIKE IF I EVEN LOOKED HER IN THE EYE, I MIGHT THROW SOMETHING OFF. I WAS SCARED SHITLESS I MIGHT SUDDENLY DISAPPEAR BACK INTO THE LIVING HELL THAT WAS MY LIFE BEFORE TWO MONTHS AGO.
WHITE OAK DINER
AFTER I TOOK CONTROL OF THE DEVICE AND WHAT BERNIE CALLED "THE JUICE," I SAT DOWN AND MADE SURE EVERYTHING WAS CLEAR IN MY HEAD. I DECIDED I NEEDED ONLY ONE MISSION, ONE GOAL, AND THAT WAS TO MAKE SURE MY BABY GOT BORN. IF THAT HAPPENED, EVERYTHING ELSE WOULD BE OKAY.
WHEN I FIRST CAME HERE YEARS AGO, KRISTA TOLD ME ABOUT SOME DRUGGIE BOYFRIENDS, AN "ANDY" IN PARTICULAR, SO THIS FELT LIKE THE RIGHT PLACE TO START. TIME TO FINALLY FACE ALL THE UGLY SHIT I NEVER WANTED TO HEAR ABOUT BACK WHEN I HAD THE CHANCE.

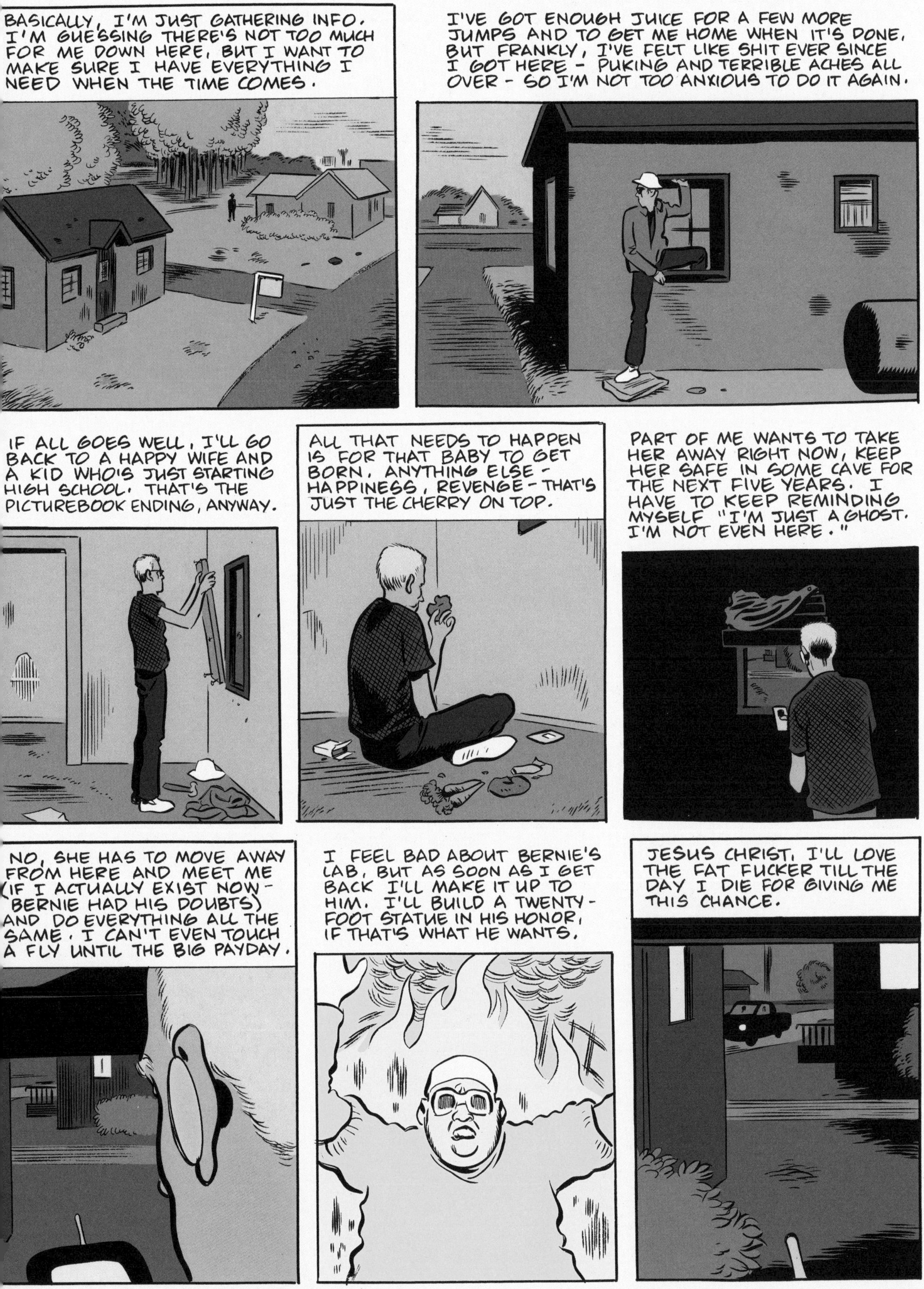
BASICALLY, I'M JUST GATHERING INFO. I'M GUESSING THERE'S NOT TOO MUCH FOR ME DOWN HERE, BUT I WANT TO MAKE SURE I HAVE EVERYTHING I NEED WHEN THE TIME COMES.
I'VE GOT ENOUGH JUICE FOR A FEW MORE JUMPS AND TO GET ME HOME WHEN IT'S DONE, BUT FRANKLY, I'VE FELT LIKE SHIT EVER SINCE I GOT HERE - PUKING AND TERRIBLE ACHES ALL OVER - SO I'M NOT TOO ANXIOUS TO DO IT AGAIN.
IF ALL GOES WELL, I'LL GO BACK TO A HAPPY WIFE AND A KID WHO'S JUST STARTING HIGH SCHOOL. THAT'S THE PICTUREBOOK ENDING, ANYWAY.
ALL THAT NEEDS TO HAPPEN IS FOR THAT BABY TO GET BORN. ANYTHING ELSE - HAPPINESS, REVENGE - THAT'S JUST THE CHERRY ON TOP.
PART OF ME WANTS TO TAKE HER AWAY RIGHT NOW, KEEP HER SAFE IN SOME CAVE FOR THE NEXT FIVE YEARS. I HAVE TO KEEP REMINDING MYSELF "I'M JUST A GHOST. I'M NOT EVEN HERE."
NO, SHE HAS TO MOVE AWAY FROM HERE AND MEET ME (IF I ACTUALLY EXIST NOW - BERNIE HAD HIS DOUBTS) AND DO EVERYTHING ALL THE SAME. I CAN'T EVEN TOUCH A FLY UNTIL THE BIG PAYDAY.
I FEEL BAD ABOUT BERNIE'S LAB, BUT AS SOON AS I GET BACK I'LL MAKE IT UP TO HIM. I'LL BUILD A TWENTY-FOOT STATUE IN HIS HONOR, IF THAT'S WHAT HE WANTS.
JESUS CHRIST. I'LL LOVE THE FAT FUCKER TILL THE DAY I DIE FOR GIVING ME THIS CHANCE.

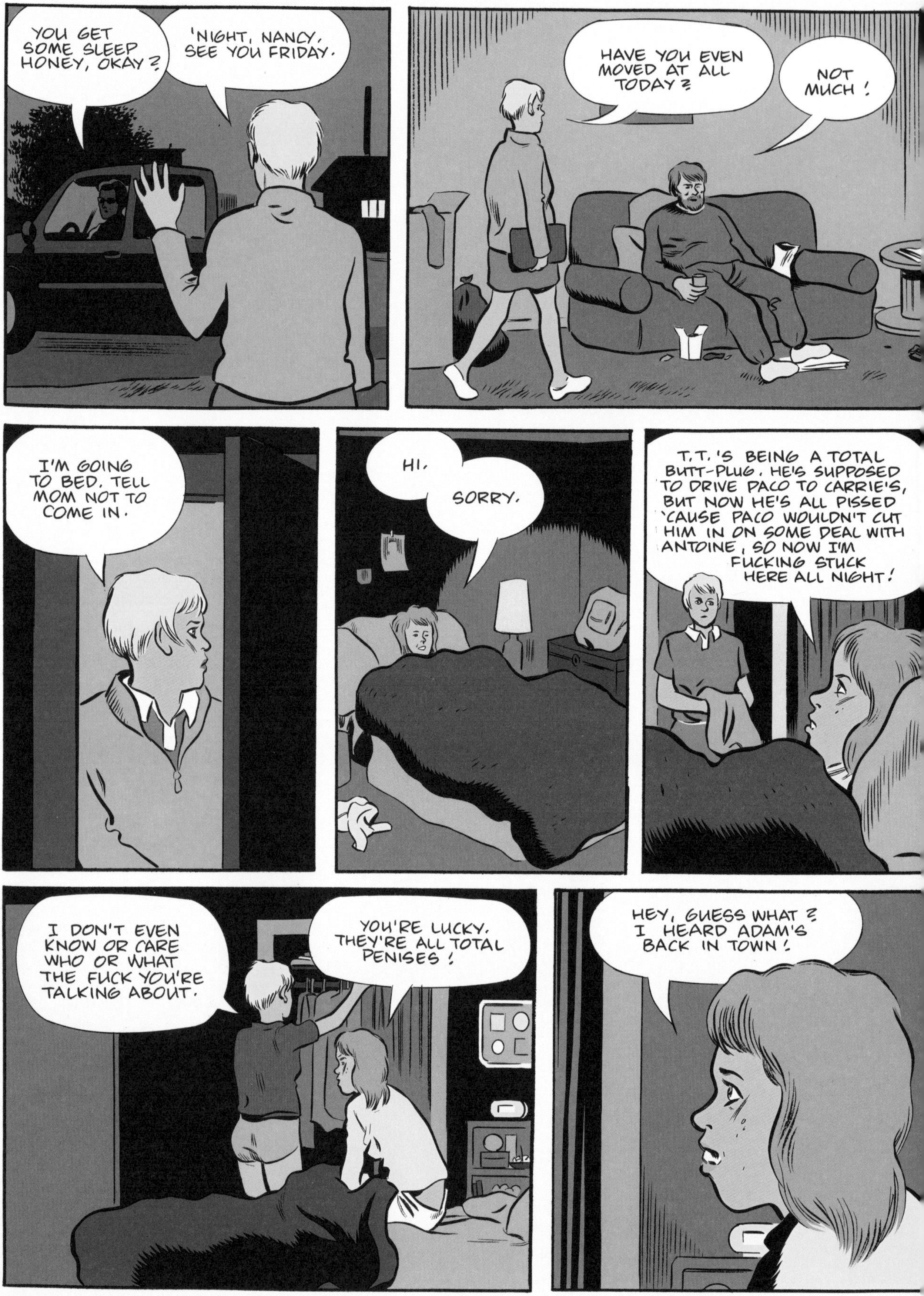
YOU GET SOME SLEEP HONEY, OKAY?
'NIGHT, NANCY, SEE YOU FRIDAY.
HAVE YOU EVEN MOVED AT ALL TODAY?
NOT MUCH!
I'M GOING TO BED. TELL MOM NOT TO COME IN.
HI.
SORRY.
T.T.'S BEING A TOTAL BUTT-PLUG. HE'S SUPPOSED TO DRIVE PACO TO CARRIE'S, BUT NOW HE'S ALL PISSED 'CAUSE PACO WOULDN'T CUT HIM IN ON SOME DEAL WITH ANTOINE, SO NOW I'M FUCKING STUCK HERE ALL NIGHT!
I DON'T EVEN KNOW OR CARE WHO OR WHAT THE FUCK YOU'RE TALKING ABOUT.
YOU'RE LUCKY. THEY'RE ALL TOTAL PENISES!
HEY, GUESS WHAT? I HEARD ADAM'S BACK IN TOWN!

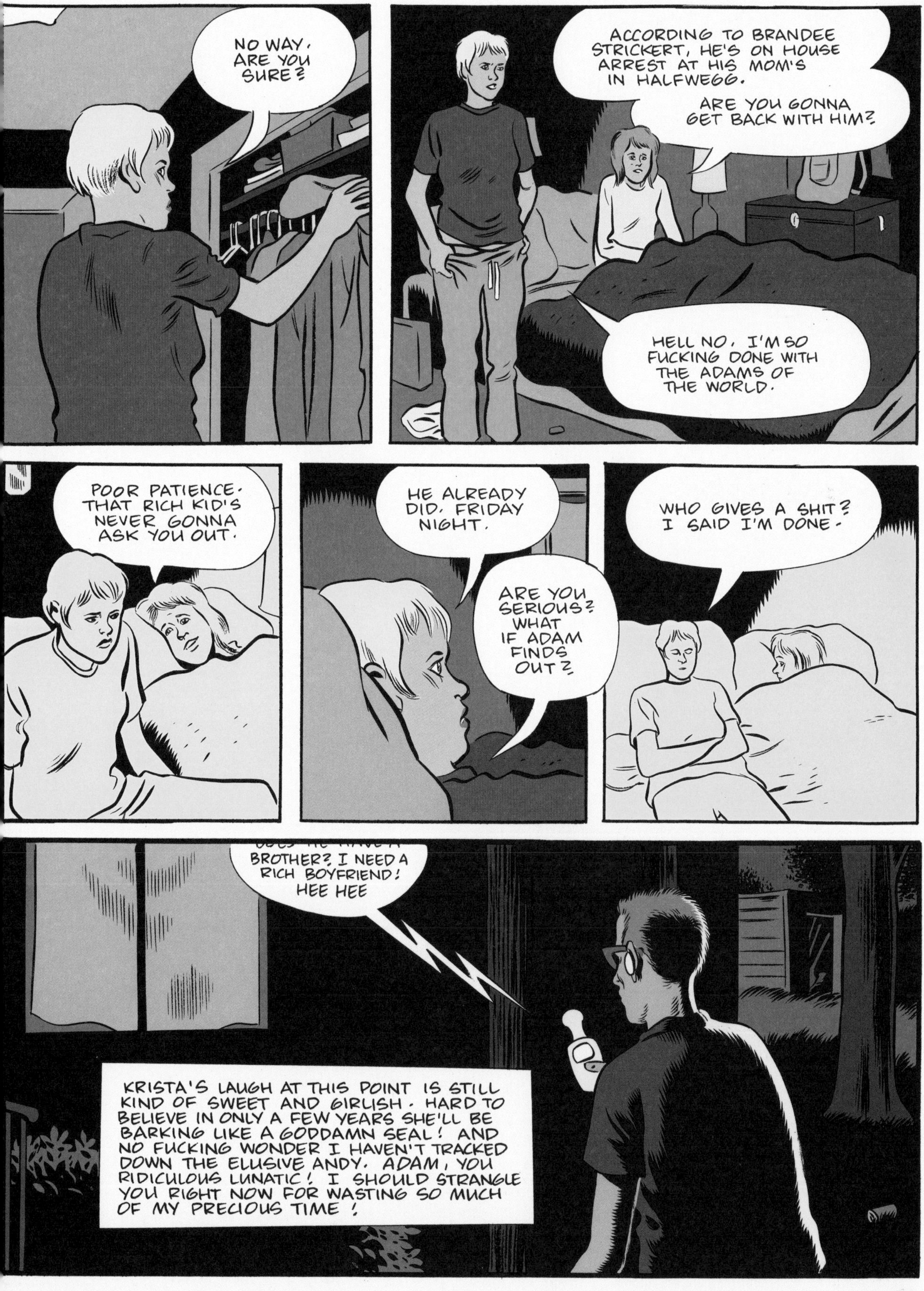
NO WAY. ARE YOU SURE?
ACCORDING TO BRANDEE STRICKERT, HE'S ON HOUSE ARREST AT HIS MOM'S IN HALFWEGG.
ARE YOU GONNA GET BACK WITH HIM?
HELL NO. I'M SO FUCKING DONE WITH THE ADAMS OF THE WORLD.
POOR PATIENCE. THAT RICH KID'S NEVER GONNA ASK YOU OUT.
HE ALREADY DID. FRIDAY NIGHT.
ARE YOU SERIOUS? WHAT IF ADAM FINDS OUT?
WHO GIVES A SHIT? I SAID I'M DONE.
BROTHER? I NEED A RICH BOYFRIEND! HEE HEE
KRISTA'S LAUGH AT THIS POINT IS STILL KIND OF SWEET AND GIRLISH. HARD TO BELIEVE IN ONLY A FEW YEARS SHE'LL BE BARKING LIKE A GODDAMN SEAL! AND NO FUCKING WONDER I HAVEN'T TRACKED DOWN THE ELUSIVE ANDY. ADAM, YOU RIDICULOUS LUNATIC! I SHOULD STRANGLE YOU RIGHT NOW FOR WASTING SO MUCH OF MY PRECIOUS TIME!

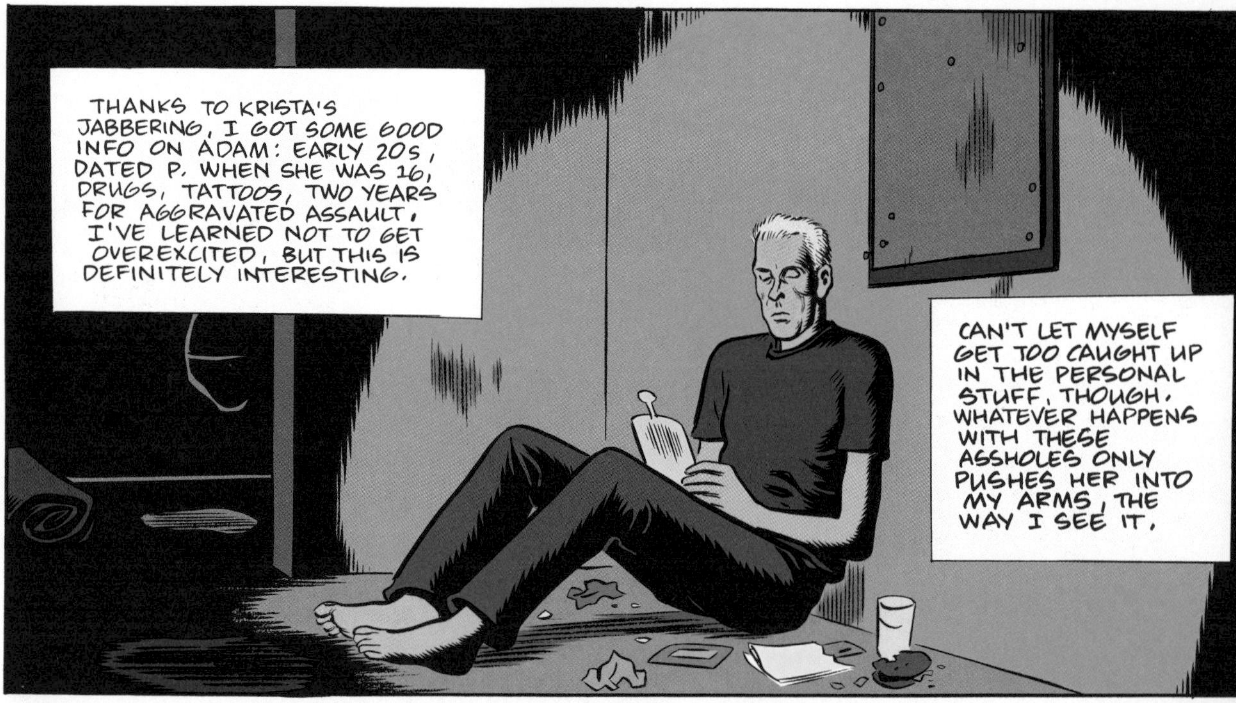
THANKS TO KRISTA'S JABBERING, I GOT SOME GOOD INFO ON ADAM: EARLY 20s, DATED P. WHEN SHE WAS 16, DRUGS, TATTOOS, TWO YEARS FOR AGGRAVATED ASSAULT. I'VE LEARNED NOT TO GET OVEREXCITED, BUT THIS IS DEFINITELY INTERESTING.
CAN'T LET MYSELF GET TOO CAUGHT UP IN THE PERSONAL STUFF, THOUGH. WHATEVER HAPPENS WITH THESE ASSHOLES ONLY PUSHES HER INTO MY ARMS, THE WAY I SEE IT.

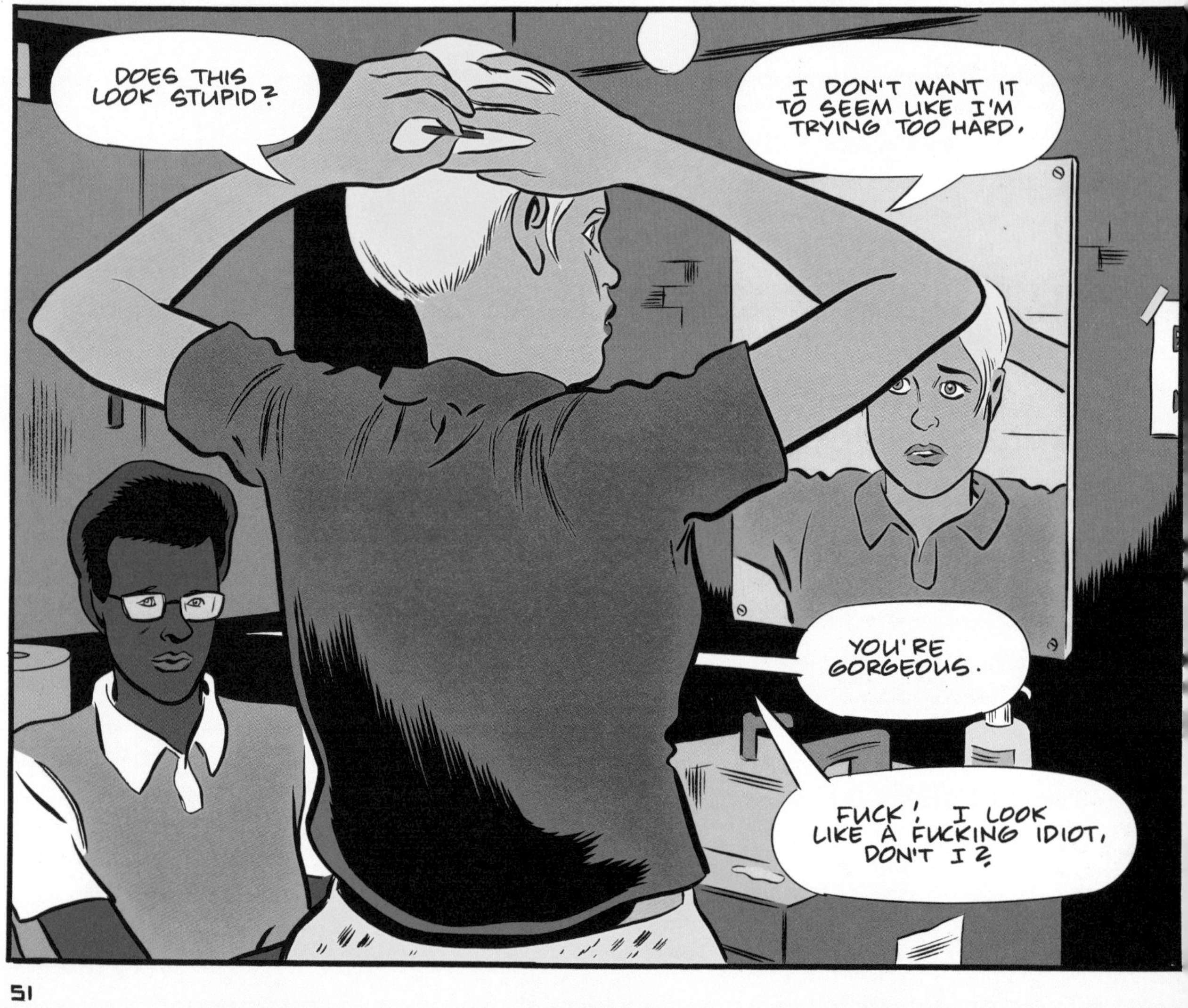
DOES THIS LOOK STUPID?
I DON'T WANT IT TO SEEM LIKE I'M TRYING TOO HARD.
YOU'RE GORGEOUS.
FUCK! I LOOK LIKE A FUCKING IDIOT, DON'T I?

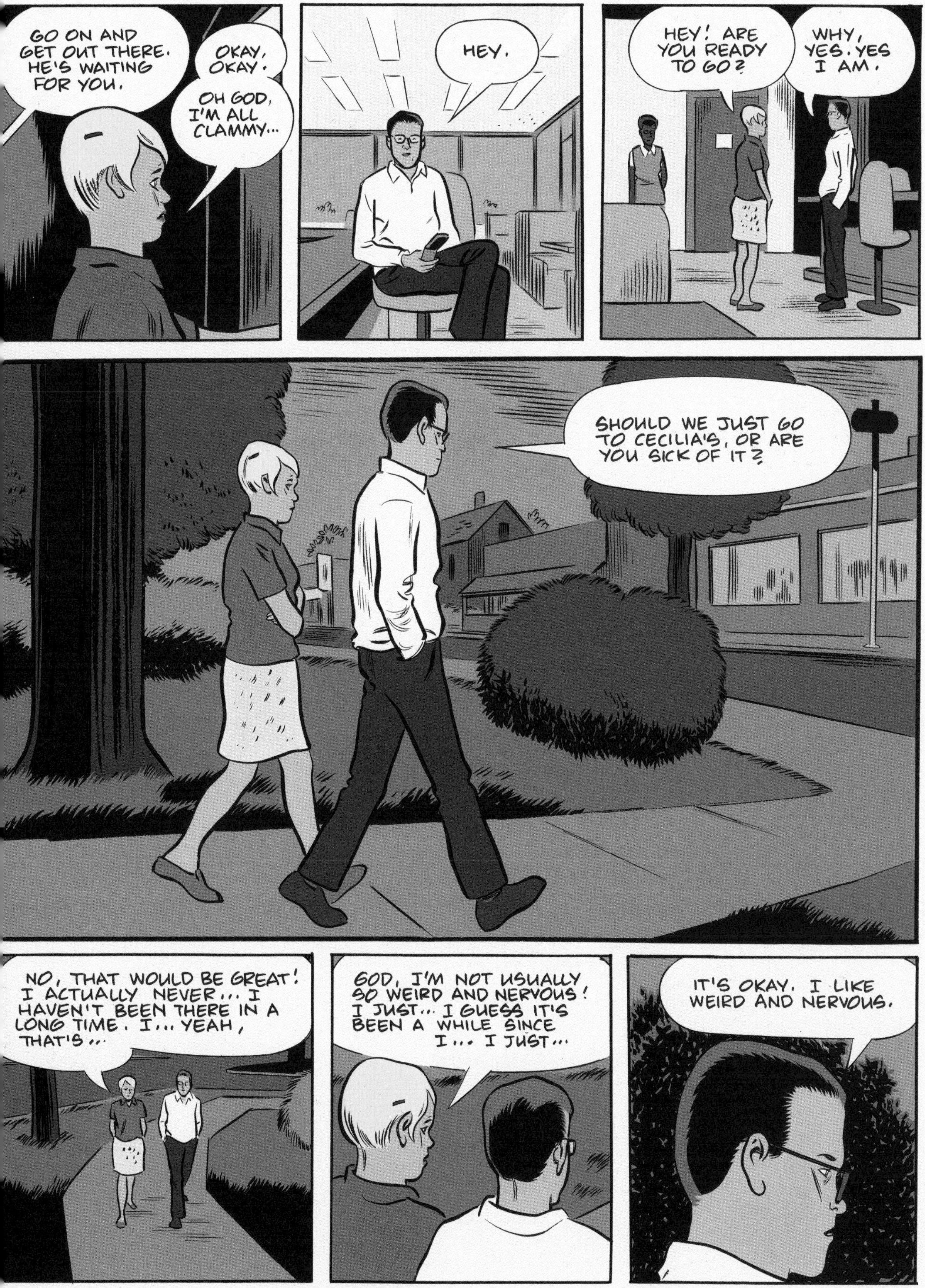
GO ON AND GET OUT THERE. HE'S WAITING FOR YOU.
OKAY, OKAY.
OH GOD, I'M ALL CLAMMY...
HEY.
HEY! ARE YOU READY TO GO?
WHY, YES. YES I AM.
SHOULD WE JUST GO TO CECILIA'S, OR ARE YOU SICK OF IT?
NO, THAT WOULD BE GREAT! I ACTUALLY NEVER... I HAVEN'T BEEN THERE IN A LONG TIME. I... YEAH, THAT'S...
GOD, I'M NOT USUALLY SO WEIRD AND NERVOUS! I JUST... I GUESS IT'S BEEN A WHILE SINCE I... I JUST...
IT'S OKAY. I LIKE WEIRD AND NERVOUS.

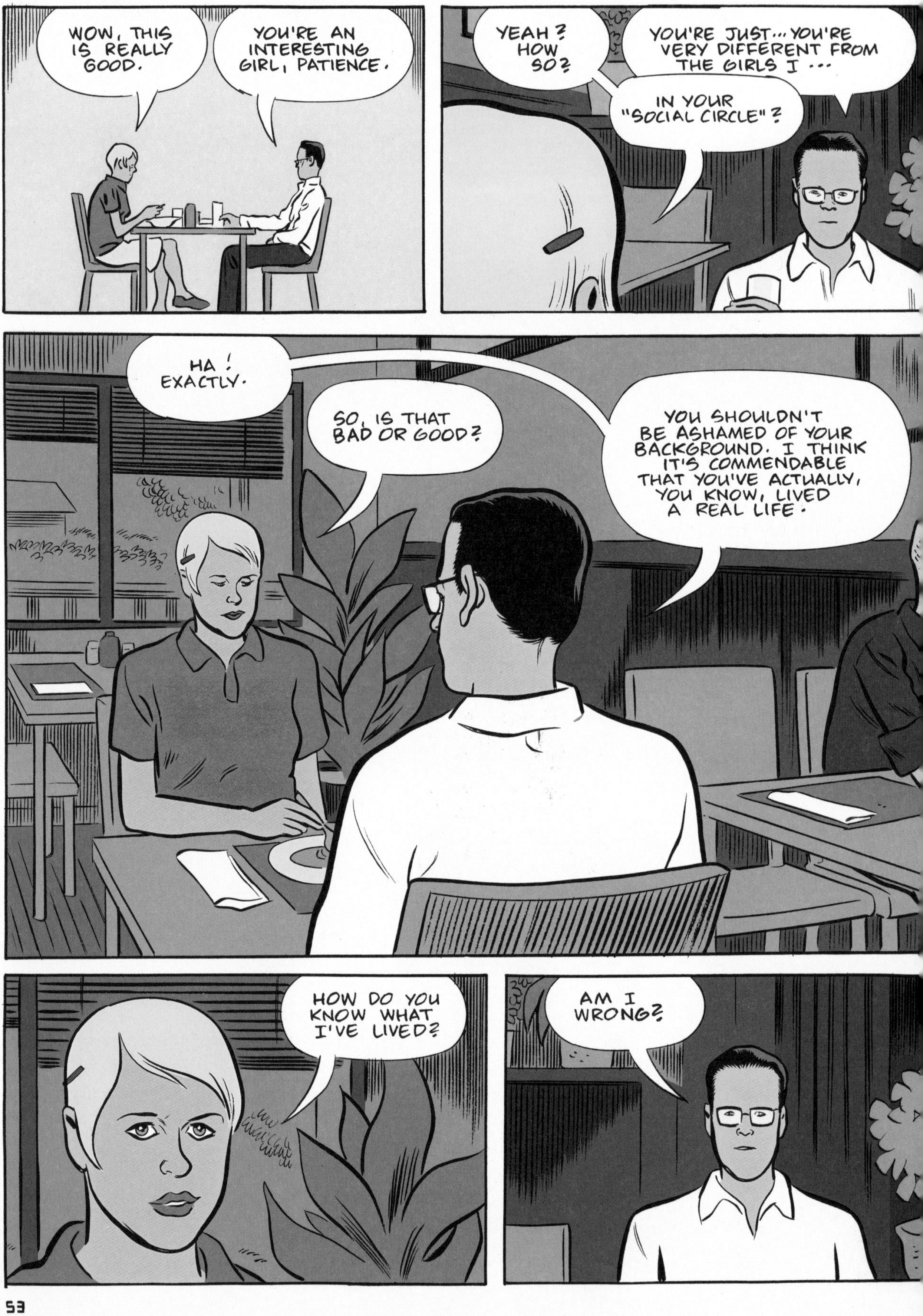
WOW, THIS IS REALLY GOOD.
YOU'RE AN INTERESTING GIRL, PATIENCE.
YEAH? HOW SO?
YOU'RE JUST... YOU'RE VERY DIFFERENT FROM THE GIRLS I...
IN YOUR "SOCIAL CIRCLE"?
HA! EXACTLY.
SO, IS THAT BAD OR GOOD?
YOU SHOULDN'T BE ASHAMED OF YOUR BACKGROUND. I THINK IT'S COMMENDABLE THAT YOU'VE ACTUALLY, YOU KNOW, LIVED A REAL LIFE.
HOW DO YOU KNOW WHAT I'VE LIVED?
AM I WRONG?

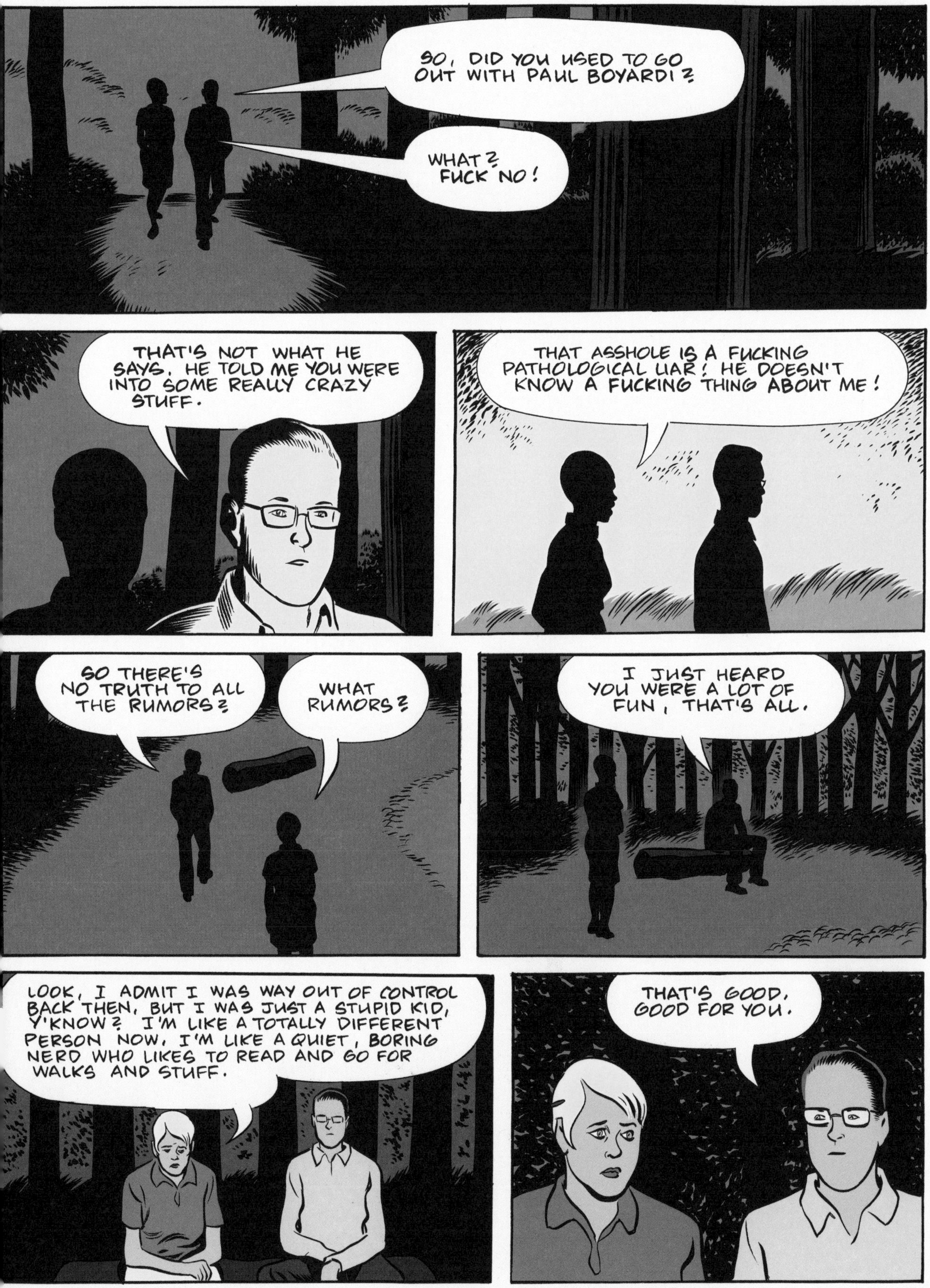
SO, DID YOU USED TO GO OUT WITH PAUL BOYARDI?
WHAT? FUCK NO!
THAT'S NOT WHAT HE SAYS. HE TOLD ME YOU WERE INTO SOME REALLY CRAZY STUFF.
THAT ASSHOLE IS A FUCKING PATHOLOGICAL LIAR! HE DOESN'T KNOW A FUCKING THING ABOUT ME!
SO THERE'S NO TRUTH TO ALL THE RUMORS?
WHAT RUMORS?
I JUST HEARD YOU WERE A LOT OF FUN, THAT'S ALL.
LOOK, I ADMIT I WAS WAY OUT OF CONTROL BACK THEN, BUT I WAS JUST A STUPID KID, Y'KNOW? I'M LIKE A TOTALLY DIFFERENT PERSON NOW, I'M LIKE A QUIET, BORING NERD WHO LIKES TO READ AND GO FOR WALKS AND STUFF.
THAT'S GOOD. GOOD FOR YOU.

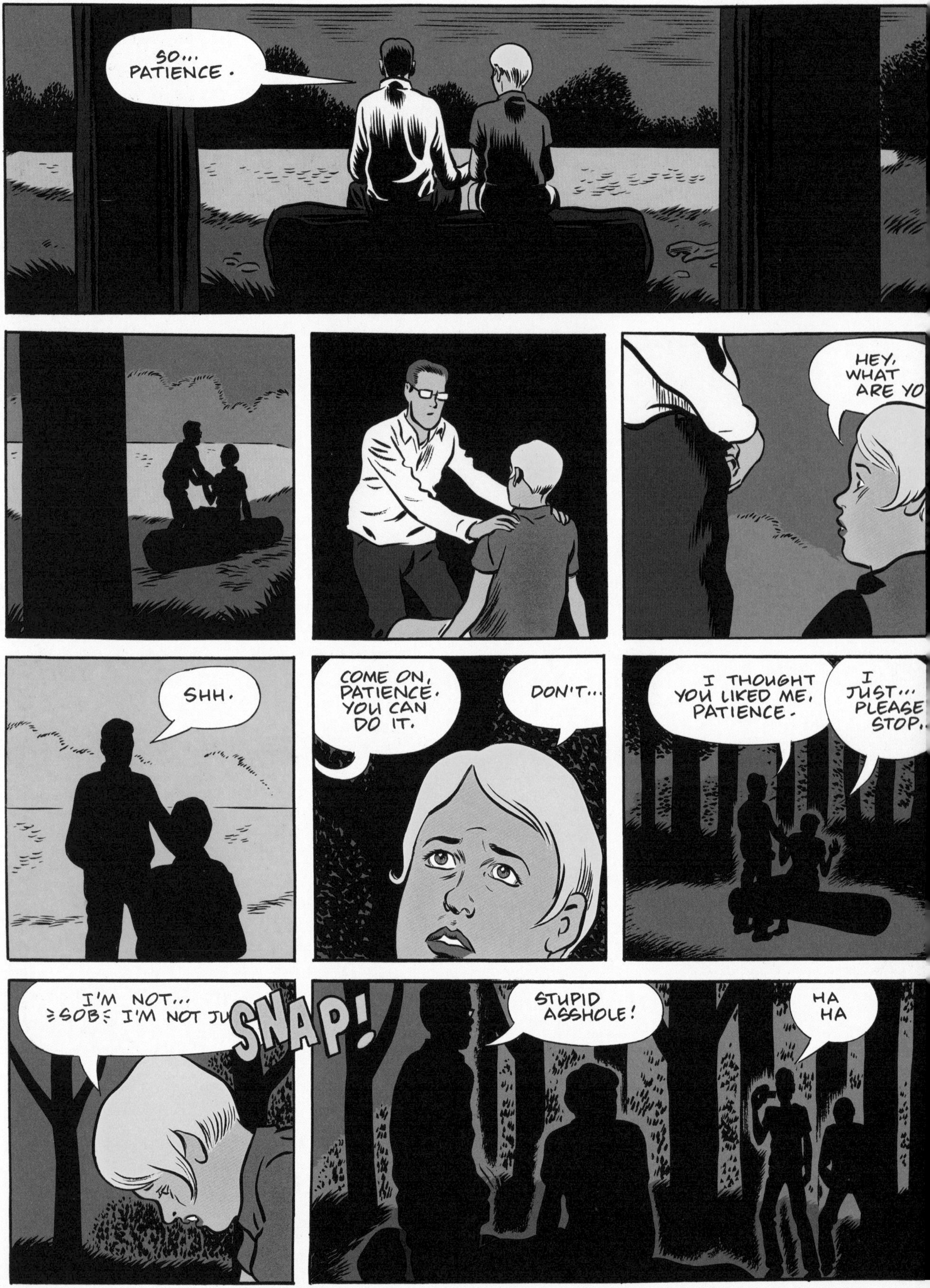
SO... PATIENCE.
HEY, WHAT ARE YO
SHH.
COME ON, PATIENCE. YOU CAN DO IT.
DON'T...
I THOUGHT YOU LIKED ME, PATIENCE.
I JUST... PLEASE STOP...
I'M NOT... ≶SOB≶ I'M NOT JU
SNAP!
STUPID ASSHOLE!
HA HA

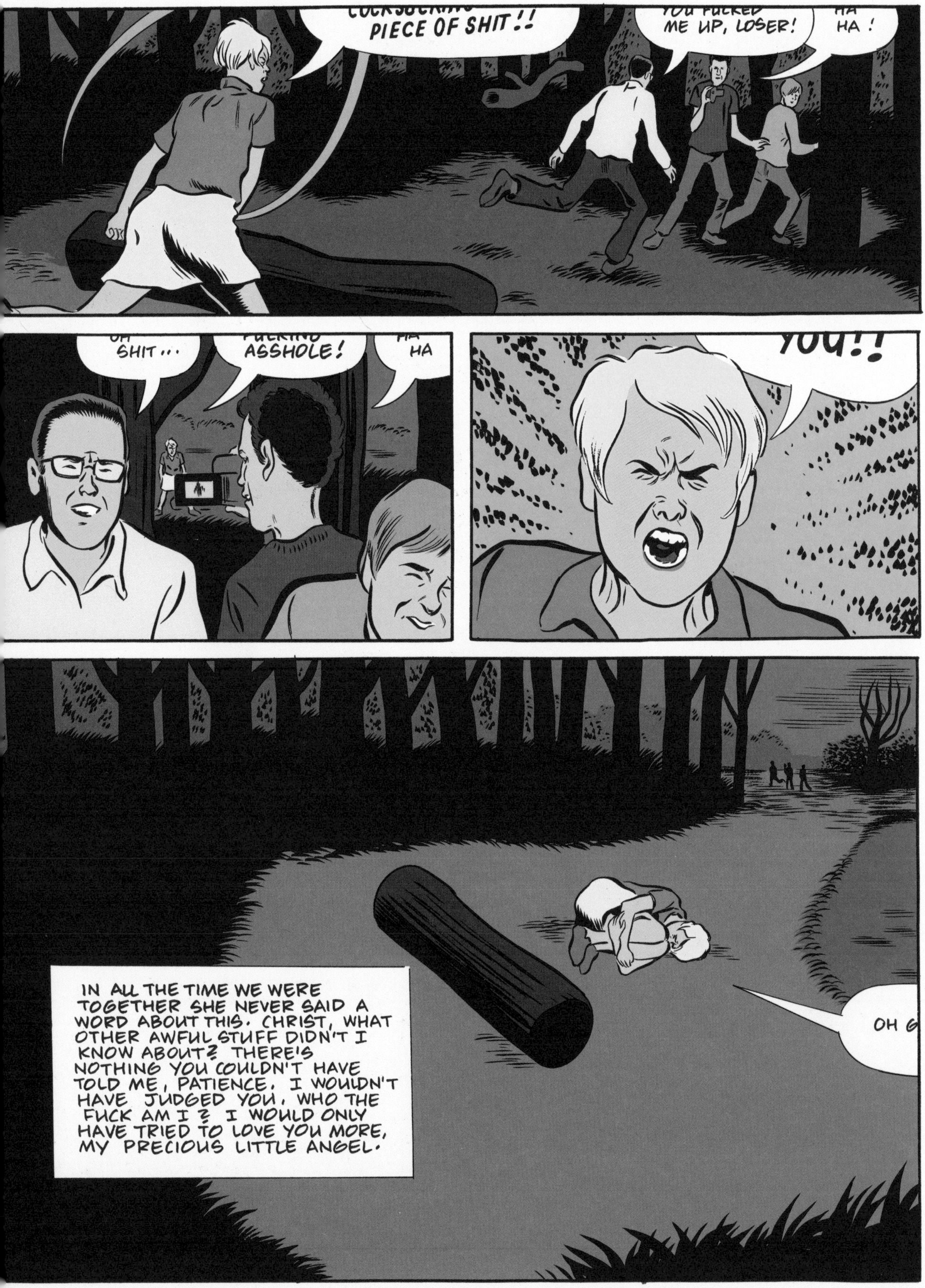
PIECE OF SHIT!!
ME UP, LOSER!
HA !
SHIT...
ASSHOLE!
HA
YOU!!
IN ALL THE TIME WE WERE TOGETHER SHE NEVER SAID A WORD ABOUT THIS. CHRIST, WHAT OTHER AWFUL STUFF DIDN'T I KNOW ABOUT? THERE'S NOTHING YOU COULDN'T HAVE TOLD ME, PATIENCE. I WOULDN'T HAVE JUDGED YOU. WHO THE FUCK AM I? I WOULD ONLY HAVE TRIED TO LOVE YOU MORE, MY PRECIOUS LITTLE ANGEL.
OH

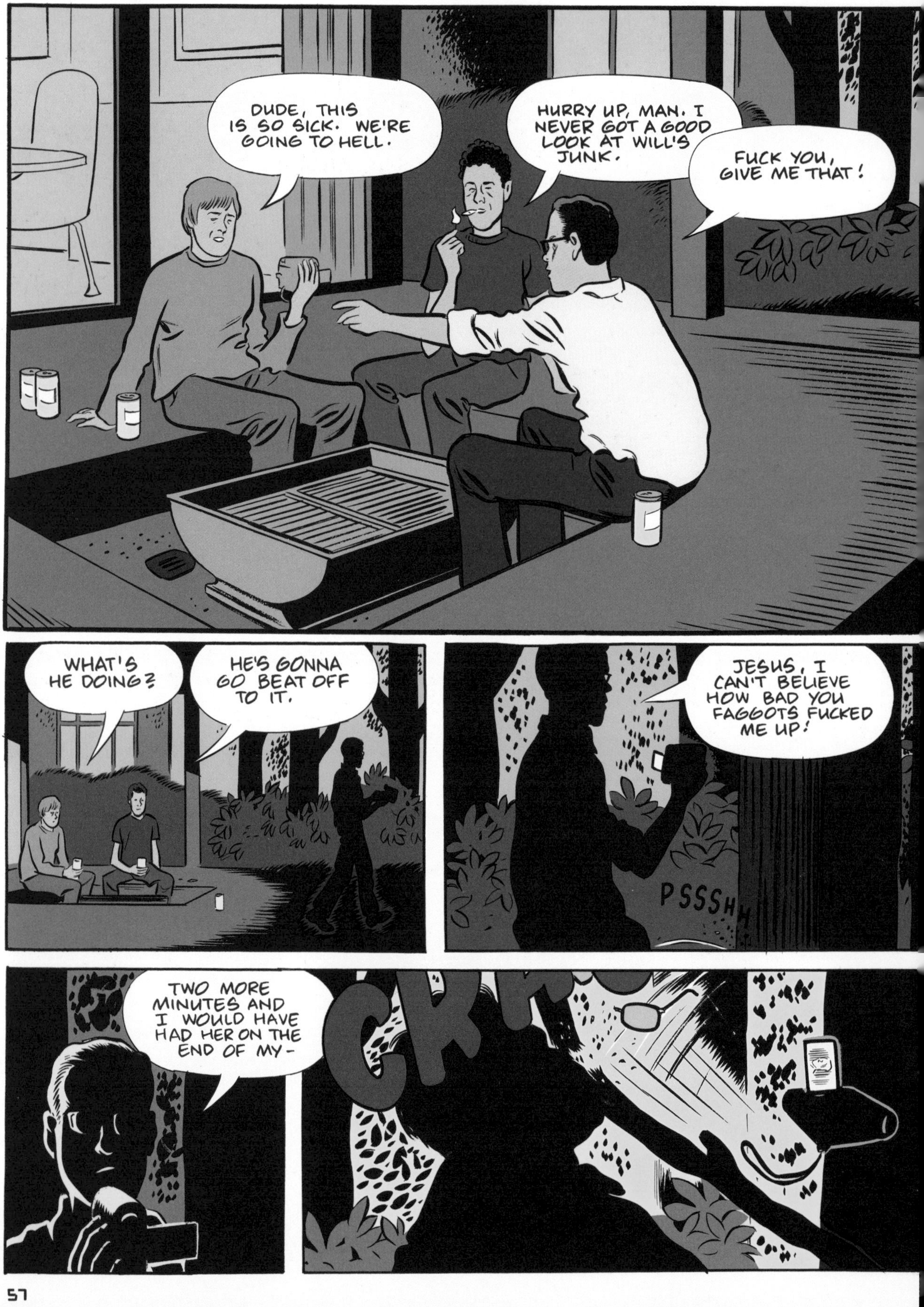
DUDE, THIS IS SO SICK. WE'RE GOING TO HELL.
HURRY UP, MAN. I NEVER GOT A GOOD LOOK AT WILL'S JUNK.
FUCK YOU, GIVE ME THAT!
WHAT'S HE DOING?
HE'S GONNA GO BEAT OFF TO IT.
JESUS, I CAN'T BELIEVE HOW BAD YOU FAGGOTS FUCKED ME UP!
PSSSHH
TWO MORE MINUTES AND I WOULD HAVE HAD HER ON THE END OF MY-

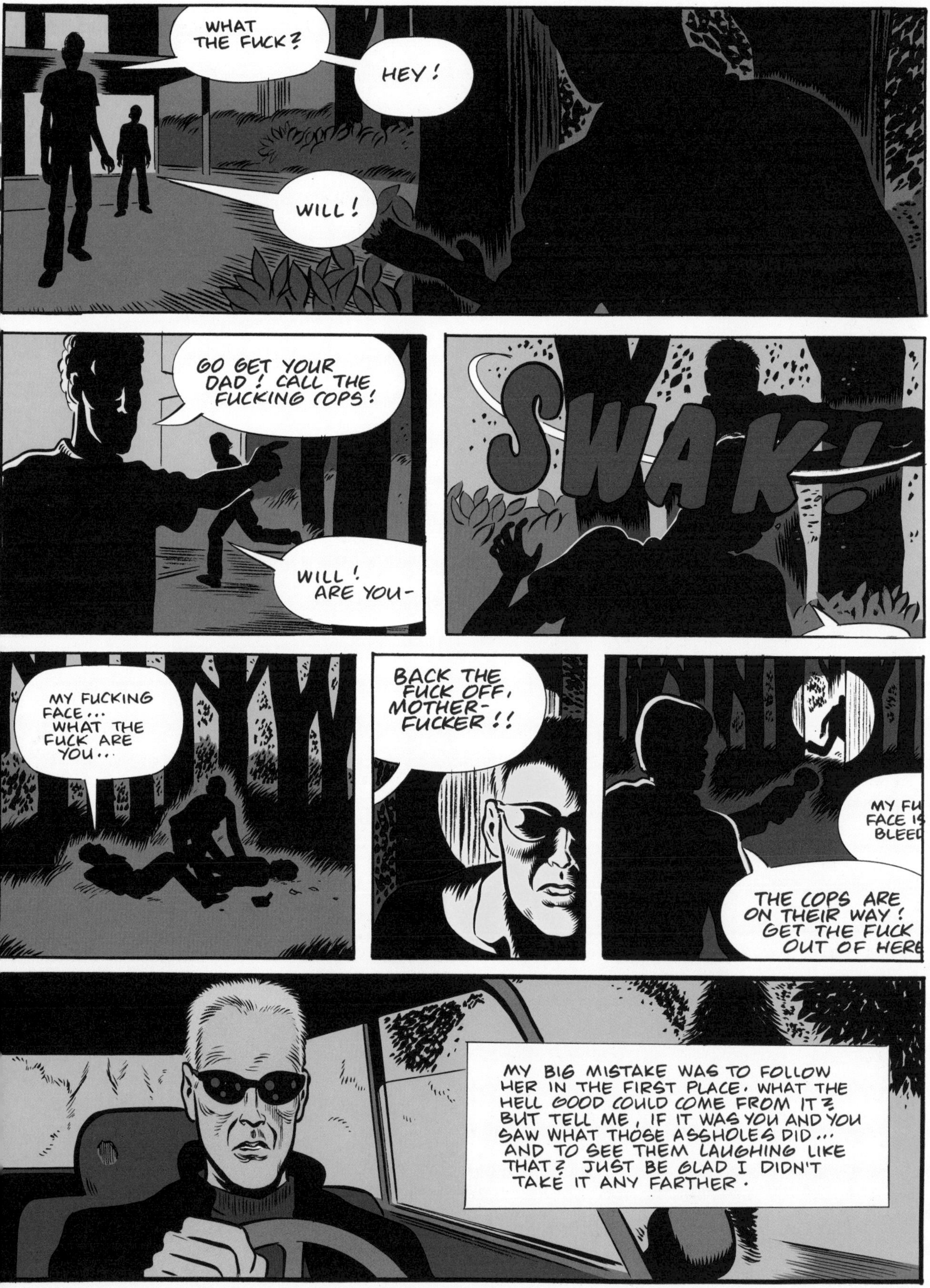
WHAT THE FUCK?
HEY!
WILL!
GO GET YOUR DAD! CALL THE FUCKING COPS!
WILL! ARE YOU-
SWAK!
MY FUCKING FACE... WHAT THE FUCK ARE YOU...
BACK THE FUCK OFF, MOTHER-FUCKER!!
MY FU FACE IS BLEED
THE COPS ARE ON THEIR WAY! GET THE FUCK OUT OF HERE
MY BIG MISTAKE WAS TO FOLLOW HER IN THE FIRST PLACE. WHAT THE HELL GOOD COULD COME FROM IT? BUT TELL ME, IF IT WAS YOU AND YOU SAW WHAT THOSE ASSHOLES DID... AND TO SEE THEM LAUGHING LIKE THAT? JUST BE GLAD I DIDN'T TAKE IT ANY FARTHER.

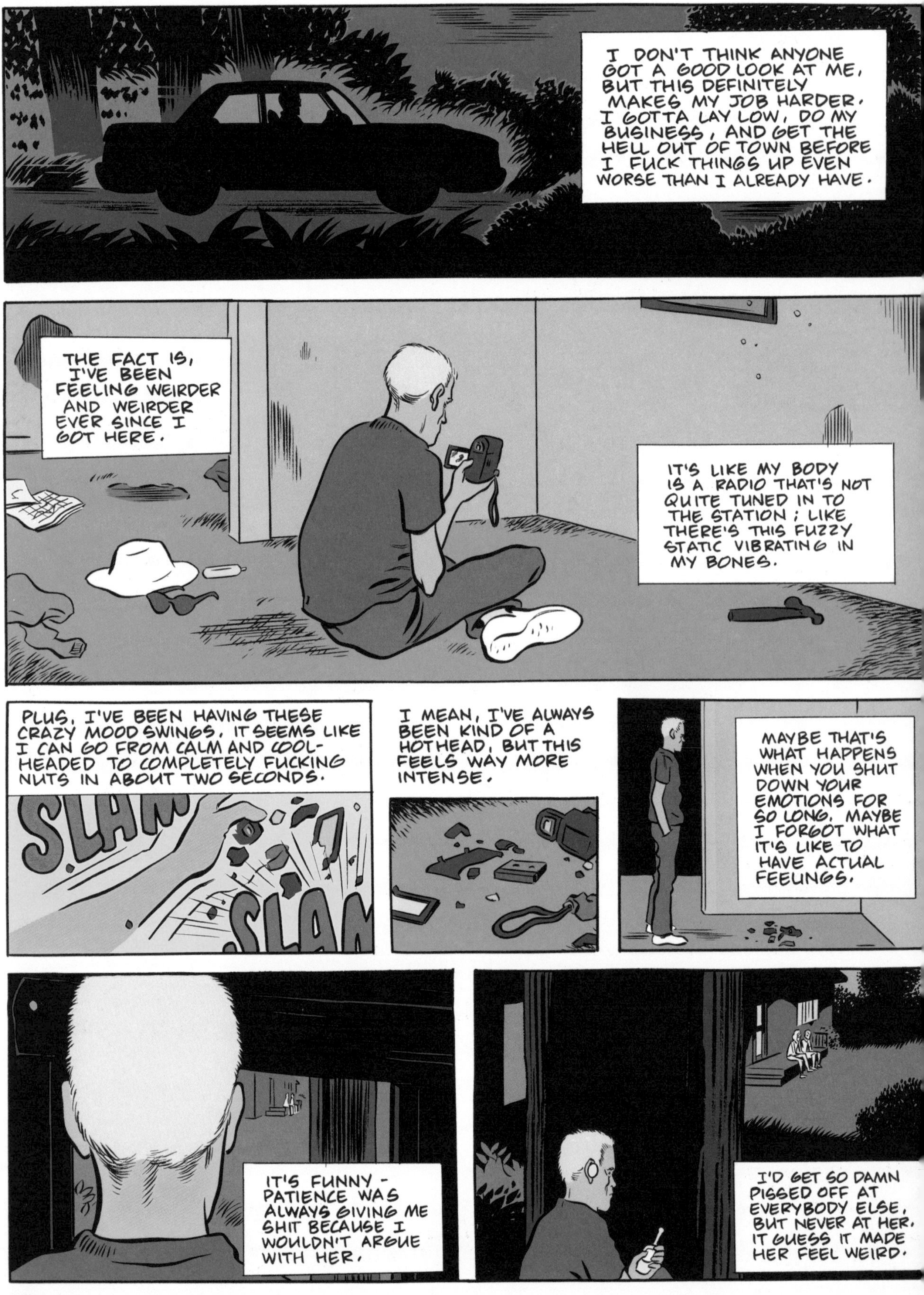
I DON'T THINK ANYONE GOT A GOOD LOOK AT ME, BUT THIS DEFINITELY MAKES MY JOB HARDER. I GOTTA LAY LOW, DO MY BUSINESS, AND GET THE HELL OUT OF TOWN BEFORE I FUCK THINGS UP EVEN WORSE THAN I ALREADY HAVE.
THE FACT IS, I'VE BEEN FEELING WEIRDER AND WEIRDER EVER SINCE I GOT HERE.
IT'S LIKE MY BODY IS A RADIO THAT'S NOT QUITE TUNED IN TO THE STATION; LIKE THERE'S THIS FUZZY STATIC VIBRATING IN MY BONES.
PLUS, I'VE BEEN HAVING THESE CRAZY MOOD SWINGS. IT SEEMS LIKE I CAN GO FROM CALM AND COOL-HEADED TO COMPLETELY FUCKING NUTS IN ABOUT TWO SECONDS.
SLAM
SLAM
I MEAN, I'VE ALWAYS BEEN KIND OF A HOTHEAD, BUT THIS FEELS WAY MORE INTENSE.
MAYBE THAT'S WHAT HAPPENS WHEN YOU SHUT DOWN YOUR EMOTIONS FOR SO LONG. MAYBE I FORGOT WHAT IT'S LIKE TO HAVE ACTUAL FEELINGS.
IT'S FUNNY - PATIENCE WAS ALWAYS GIVING ME SHIT BECAUSE I WOULDN'T ARGUE WITH HER.
I'D GET SO DAMN PISSED OFF AT EVERYBODY ELSE, BUT NEVER AT HER. IT GUESS IT MADE HER FEEL WEIRD.

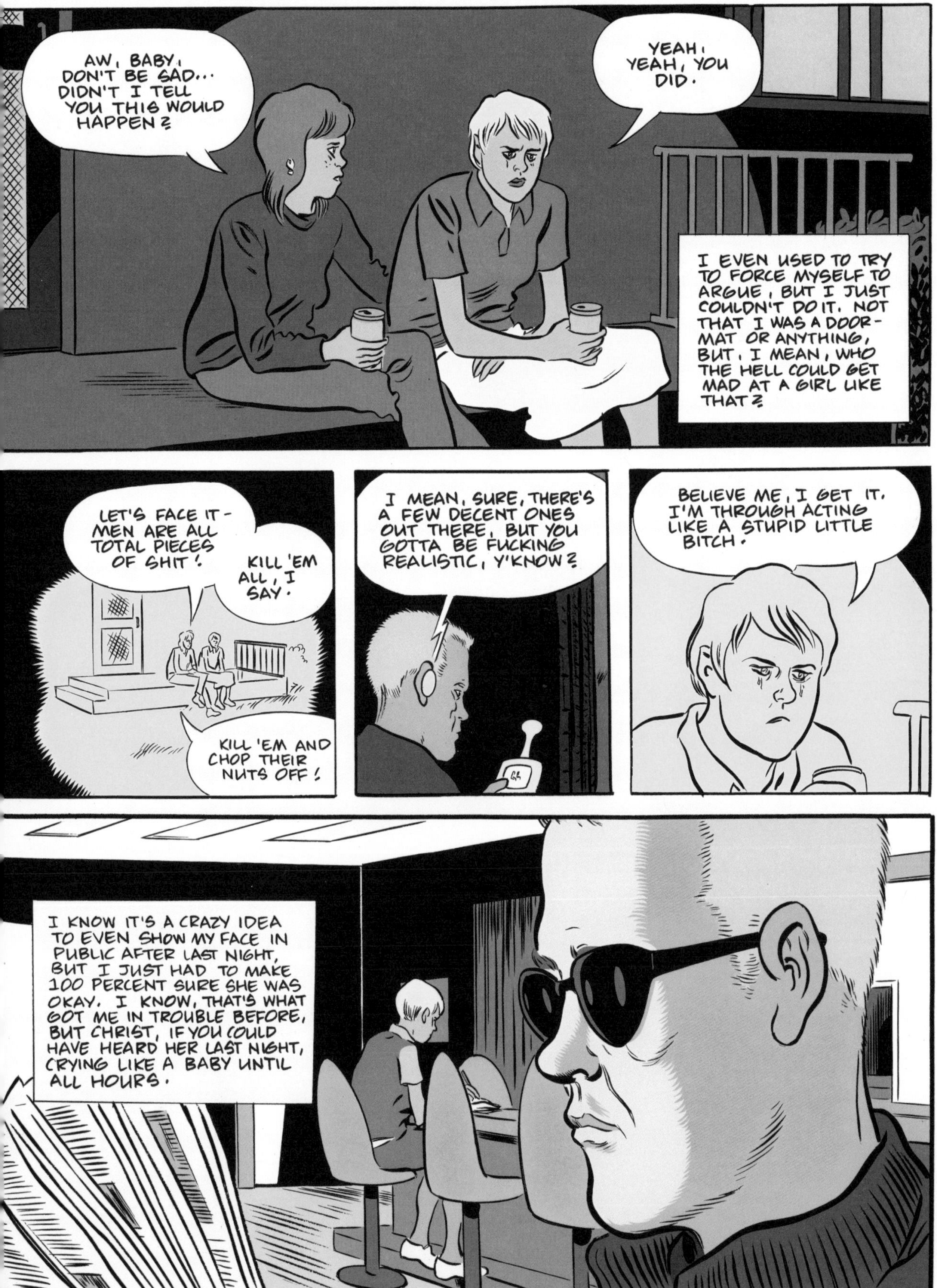
AW, BABY, DON'T BE SAD... DIDN'T I TELL YOU THIS WOULD HAPPEN?
YEAH, YEAH, YOU DID.
I EVEN USED TO TRY TO FORCE MYSELF TO ARGUE, BUT I JUST COULDN'T DO IT. NOT THAT I WAS A DOOR-MAT OR ANYTHING, BUT, I MEAN, WHO THE HELL COULD GET MAD AT A GIRL LIKE THAT?
LET'S FACE IT- MEN ARE ALL TOTAL PIECES OF SHIT!
KILL 'EM ALL, I SAY.
KILL 'EM AND CHOP THEIR NUTS OFF!
I MEAN, SURE, THERE'S A FEW DECENT ONES OUT THERE, BUT YOU GOTTA BE FUCKING REALISTIC, Y'KNOW?
BELIEVE ME, I GET IT. I'M THROUGH ACTING LIKE A STUPID LITTLE BITCH.
I KNOW IT'S A CRAZY IDEA TO EVEN SHOW MY FACE IN PUBLIC AFTER LAST NIGHT, BUT I JUST HAD TO MAKE 100 PERCENT SURE SHE WAS OKAY. I KNOW, THAT'S WHAT GOT ME IN TROUBLE BEFORE, BUT CHRIST, IF YOU COULD HAVE HEARD HER LAST NIGHT, CRYING LIKE A BABY UNTIL ALL HOURS.

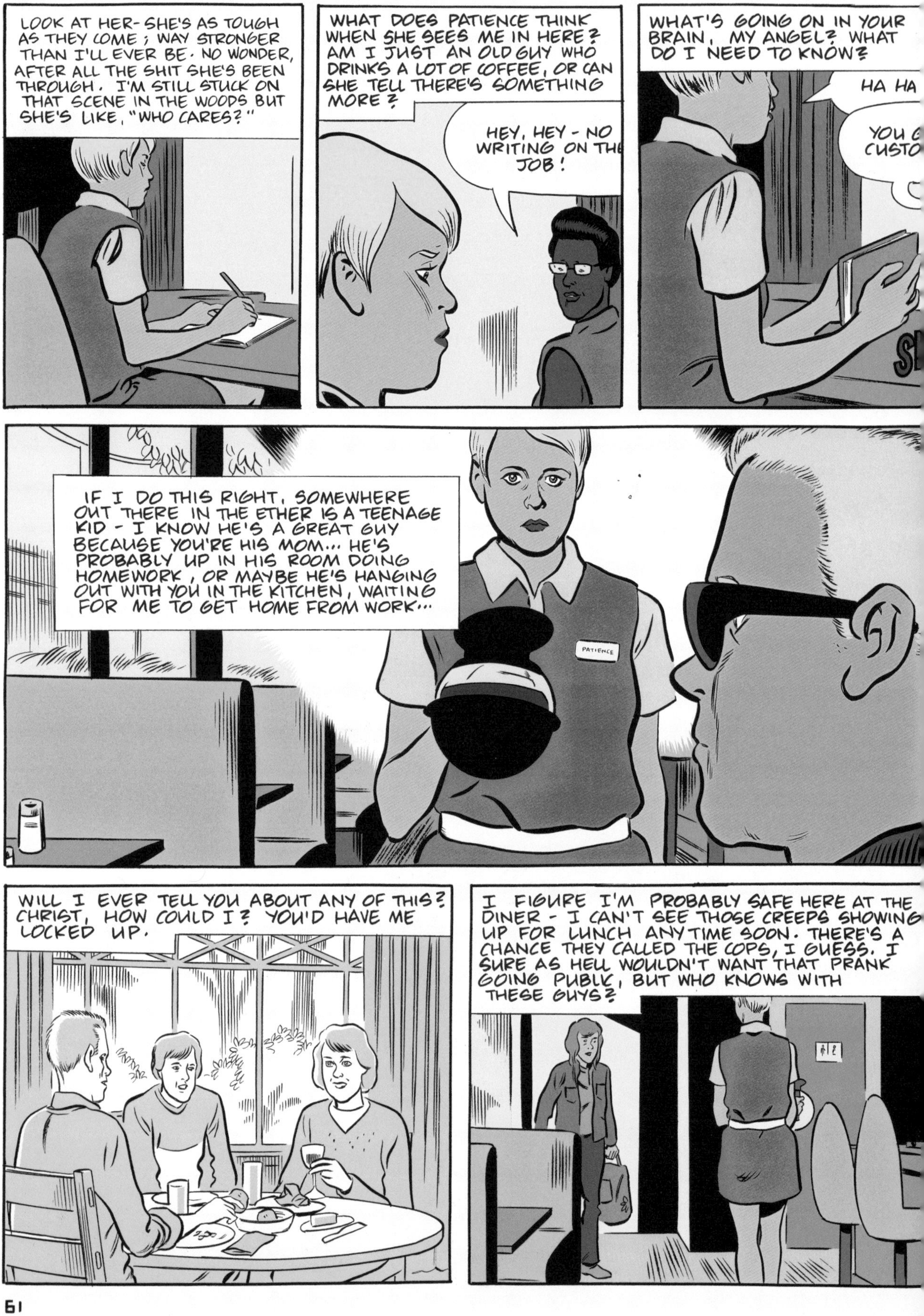

LOOK AT HER- SHE'S AS TOUGH AS THEY COME ; WAY STRONGER THAN I'LL EVER BE. NO WONDER, AFTER ALL THE SHIT SHE'S BEEN THROUGH. I'M STILL STUCK ON THAT SCENE IN THE WOODS BUT SHE'S LIKE, "WHO CARES?"
WHAT DOES PATIENCE THINK WHEN SHE SEES ME IN HERE? AM I JUST AN OLD GUY WHO DRINKS A LOT OF COFFEE, OR CAN SHE TELL THERE'S SOMETHING MORE?
HEY, HEY - NO WRITING ON THE JOB!
WHAT'S GOING ON IN YOUR BRAIN, MY ANGEL? WHAT DO I NEED TO KNOW?
HA HA
IF I DO THIS RIGHT, SOMEWHERE OUT THERE IN THE ETHER IS A TEENAGE KID - I KNOW HE'S A GREAT GUY BECAUSE YOU'RE HIS MOM... HE'S PROBABLY UP IN HIS ROOM DOING HOMEWORK, OR MAYBE HE'S HANGING OUT WITH YOU IN THE KITCHEN, WAITING FOR ME TO GET HOME FROM WORK...
PATIENCE
WILL I EVER TELL YOU ABOUT ANY OF THIS? CHRIST, HOW COULD I? YOU'D HAVE ME LOCKED UP.
I FIGURE I'M PROBABLY SAFE HERE AT THE DINER - I CAN'T SEE THOSE CREEPS SHOWING UP FOR LUNCH ANY TIME SOON. THERE'S A CHANCE THEY CALLED THE COPS, I GUESS. I SURE AS HELL WOULDN'T WANT THAT PRANK GOING PUBLIC, BUT WHO KNOWS WITH THESE GUYS?

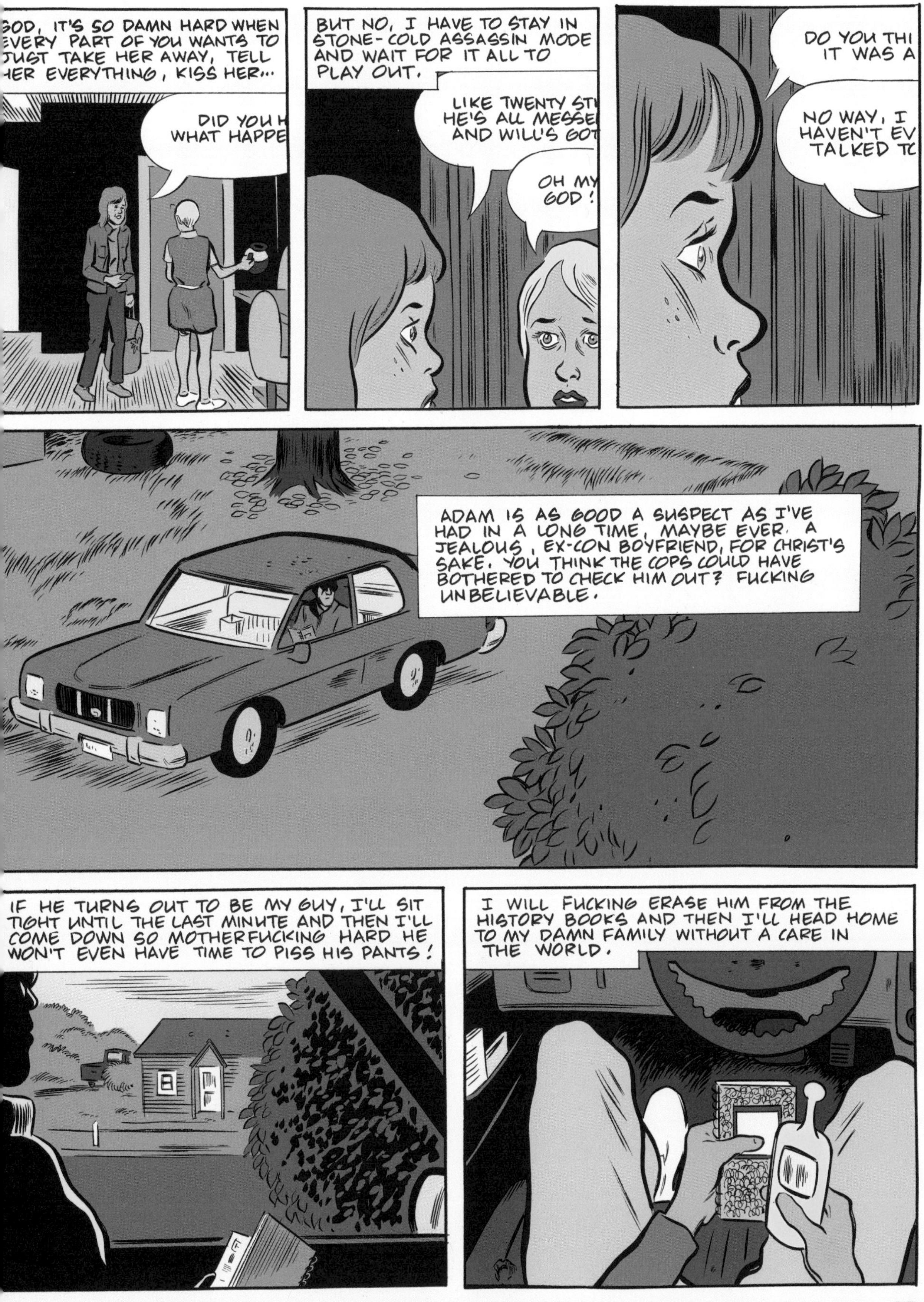
GOD, IT'S SO DAMN HARD WHEN EVERY PART OF YOU WANTS TO JUST TAKE HER AWAY, TELL HER EVERYTHING, KISS HER...
DID YOU H WHAT HAPPE
BUT NO, I HAVE TO STAY IN STONE-COLD ASSASSIN MODE AND WAIT FOR IT ALL TO PLAY OUT.
LIKE TWENTY ST HE'S ALL MESSE AND WILL'S GOT
OH MY GOD!
DO YOU THI IT WAS A
NO WAY, I HAVEN'T EV TALKED TC
ADAM IS AS GOOD A SUSPECT AS I'VE HAD IN A LONG TIME, MAYBE EVER. A JEALOUS, EX-CON BOYFRIEND, FOR CHRIST'S SAKE. YOU THINK THE COPS COULD HAVE BOTHERED TO CHECK HIM OUT? FUCKING UNBELIEVABLE.
IF HE TURNS OUT TO BE MY GUY, I'LL SIT TIGHT UNTIL THE LAST MINUTE AND THEN I'LL COME DOWN SO MOTHERFUCKING HARD HE WON'T EVEN HAVE TIME TO PISS HIS PANTS!
I WILL FUCKING ERASE HIM FROM THE HISTORY BOOKS AND THEN I'LL HEAD HOME TO MY DAMN FAMILY WITHOUT A CARE IN THE WORLD.

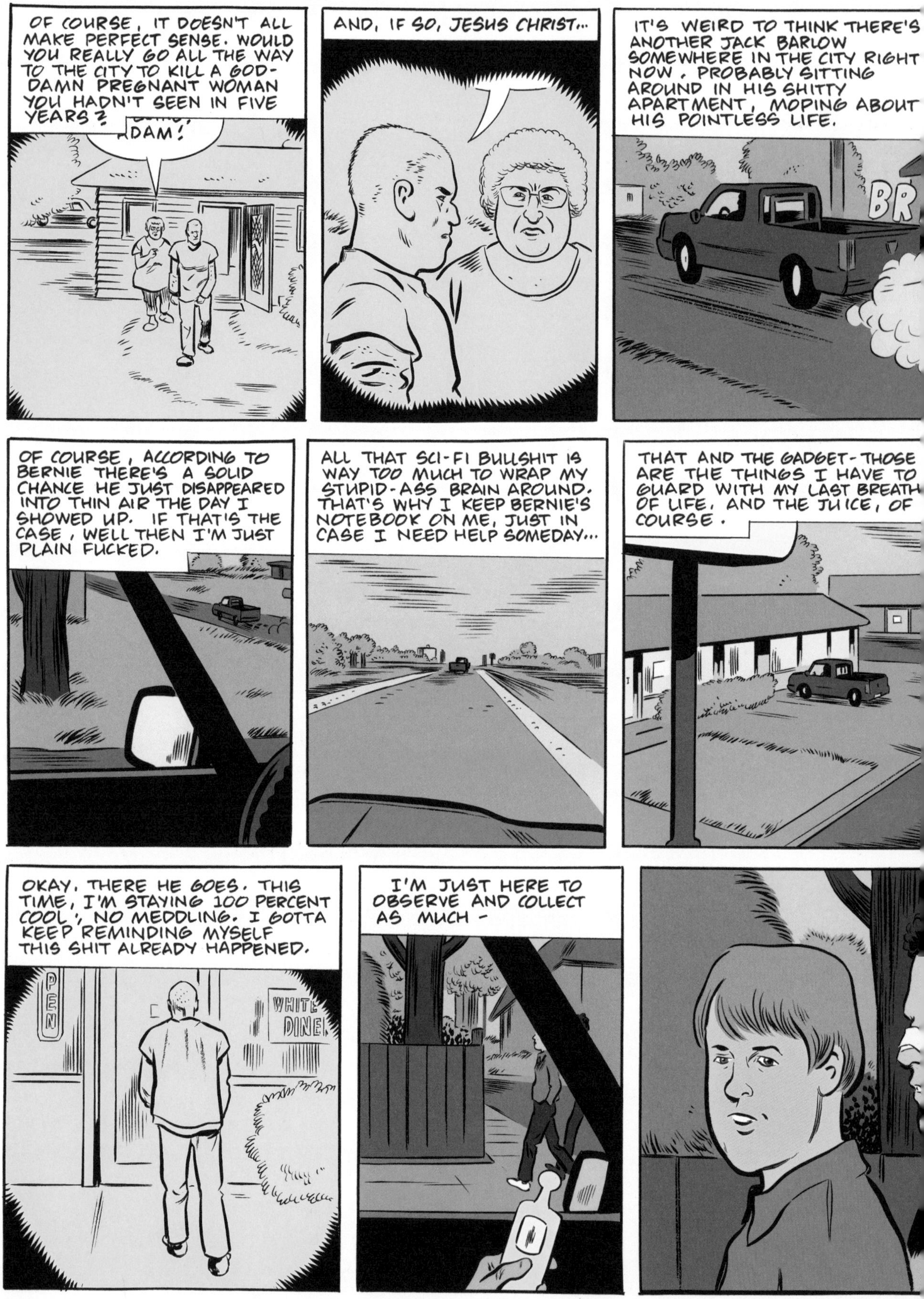
OF COURSE, IT DOESN'T ALL MAKE PERFECT SENSE. WOULD YOU REALLY GO ALL THE WAY TO THE CITY TO KILL A GOD-DAMN PREGNANT WOMAN YOU HADN'T SEEN IN FIVE YEARS?
DAM!
AND, IF SO, JESUS CHRIST...
IT'S WEIRD TO THINK THERE'S ANOTHER JACK BARLOW SOMEWHERE IN THE CITY RIGHT NOW. PROBABLY SITTING AROUND IN HIS SHITTY APARTMENT, MOPING ABOUT HIS POINTLESS LIFE.
BR
OF COURSE, ACCORDING TO BERNIE THERE'S A SOLID CHANCE HE JUST DISAPPEARED INTO THIN AIR THE DAY I SHOWED UP. IF THAT'S THE CASE, WELL THEN I'M JUST PLAIN FUCKED.
ALL THAT SCI-FI BULLSHIT IS WAY TOO MUCH TO WRAP MY STUPID-ASS BRAIN AROUND. THAT'S WHY I KEEP BERNIE'S NOTEBOOK ON ME, JUST IN CASE I NEED HELP SOMEDAY...
THAT AND THE GADGET- THOSE ARE THE THINGS I HAVE TO GUARD WITH MY LAST BREATH OF LIFE. AND THE JUICE, OF COURSE.
OKAY. THERE HE GOES. THIS TIME, I'M STAYING 100 PERCENT COOL, NO MEDDLING. I GOTTA KEEP REMINDING MYSELF THIS SHIT ALREADY HAPPENED.
PEN
WHITE
DINE
I'M JUST HERE TO OBSERVE AND COLLECT AS MUCH -

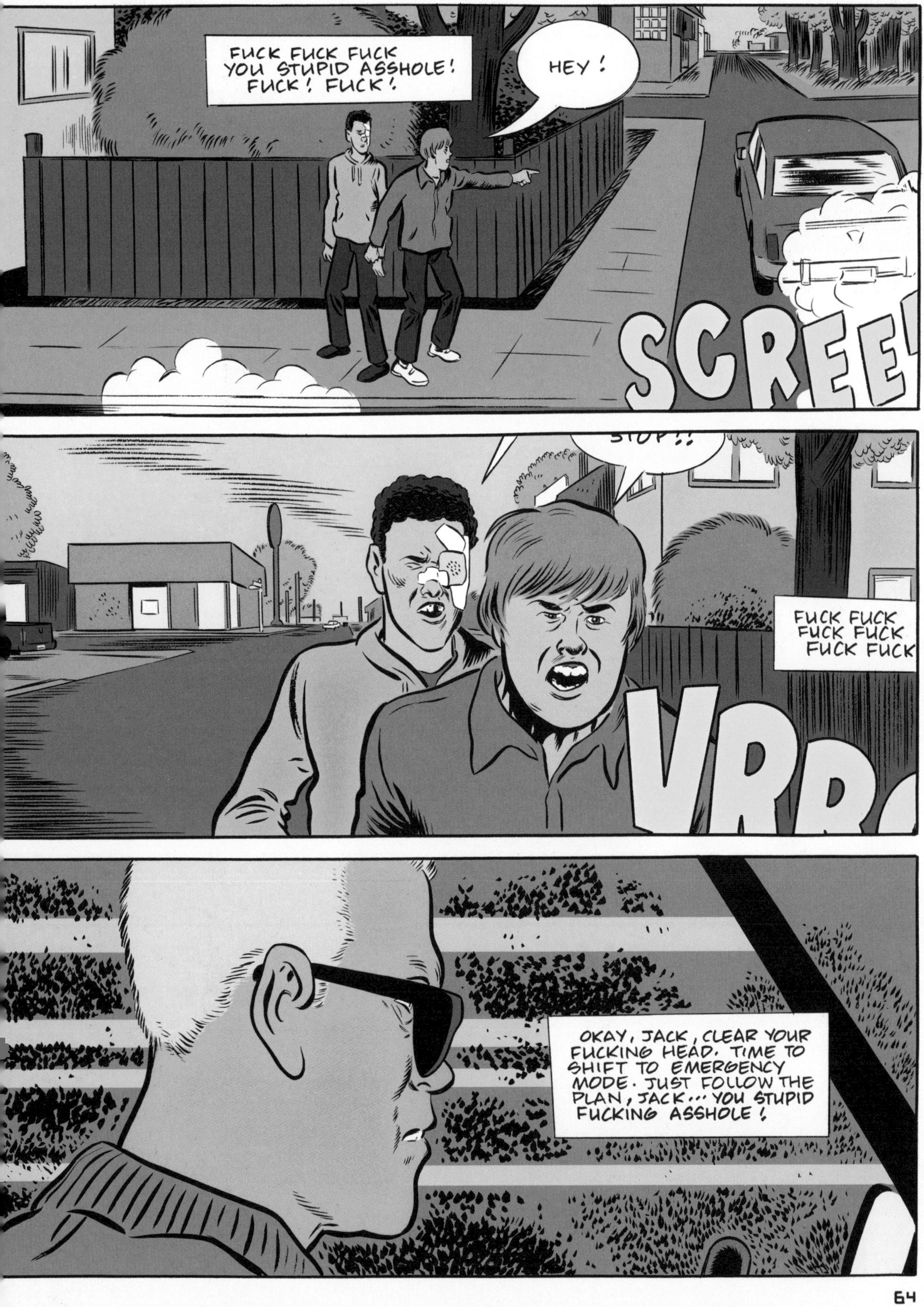
FUCK FUCK FUCK YOU STUPID ASSHOLE! FUCK! FUCK!
HEY!
SCREE
STOP!!
FUCK FUCK FUCK FUCK FUCK FUCK
VRR
OKAY, JACK, CLEAR YOUR FUCKING HEAD. TIME TO SHIFT TO EMERGENCY MODE. JUST FOLLOW THE PLAN, JACK... YOU STUPID FUCKING ASSHOLE!

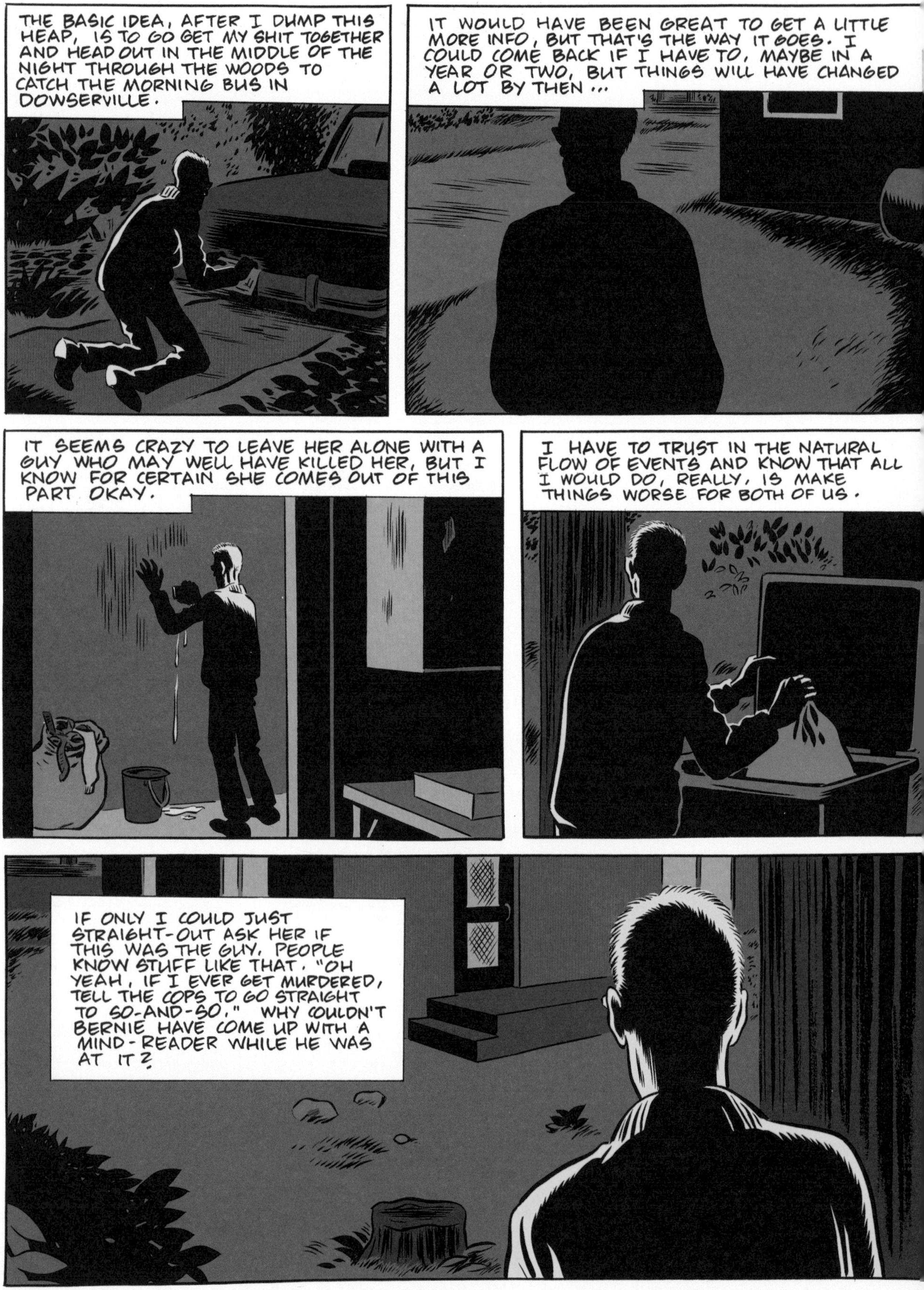
THE BASIC IDEA, AFTER I DUMP THIS HEAP, IS TO GO GET MY SHIT TOGETHER AND HEAD OUT IN THE MIDDLE OF THE NIGHT THROUGH THE WOODS TO CATCH THE MORNING BUS IN DOWSERVILLE.
IT WOULD HAVE BEEN GREAT TO GET A LITTLE MORE INFO, BUT THAT'S THE WAY IT GOES. I COULD COME BACK IF I HAVE TO, MAYBE IN A YEAR OR TWO, BUT THINGS WILL HAVE CHANGED A LOT BY THEN...
IT SEEMS CRAZY TO LEAVE HER ALONE WITH A GUY WHO MAY WELL HAVE KILLED HER, BUT I KNOW FOR CERTAIN SHE COMES OUT OF THIS PART OKAY.
I HAVE TO TRUST IN THE NATURAL FLOW OF EVENTS AND KNOW THAT ALL I WOULD DO, REALLY, IS MAKE THINGS WORSE FOR BOTH OF US.
IF ONLY I COULD JUST STRAIGHT-OUT ASK HER IF THIS WAS THE GUY. PEOPLE KNOW STUFF LIKE THAT. "OH YEAH, IF I EVER GET MURDERED, TELL THE COPS TO GO STRAIGHT TO SO-AND-SO." WHY COULDN'T BERNIE HAVE COME UP WITH A MIND-READER WHILE HE WAS AT IT?

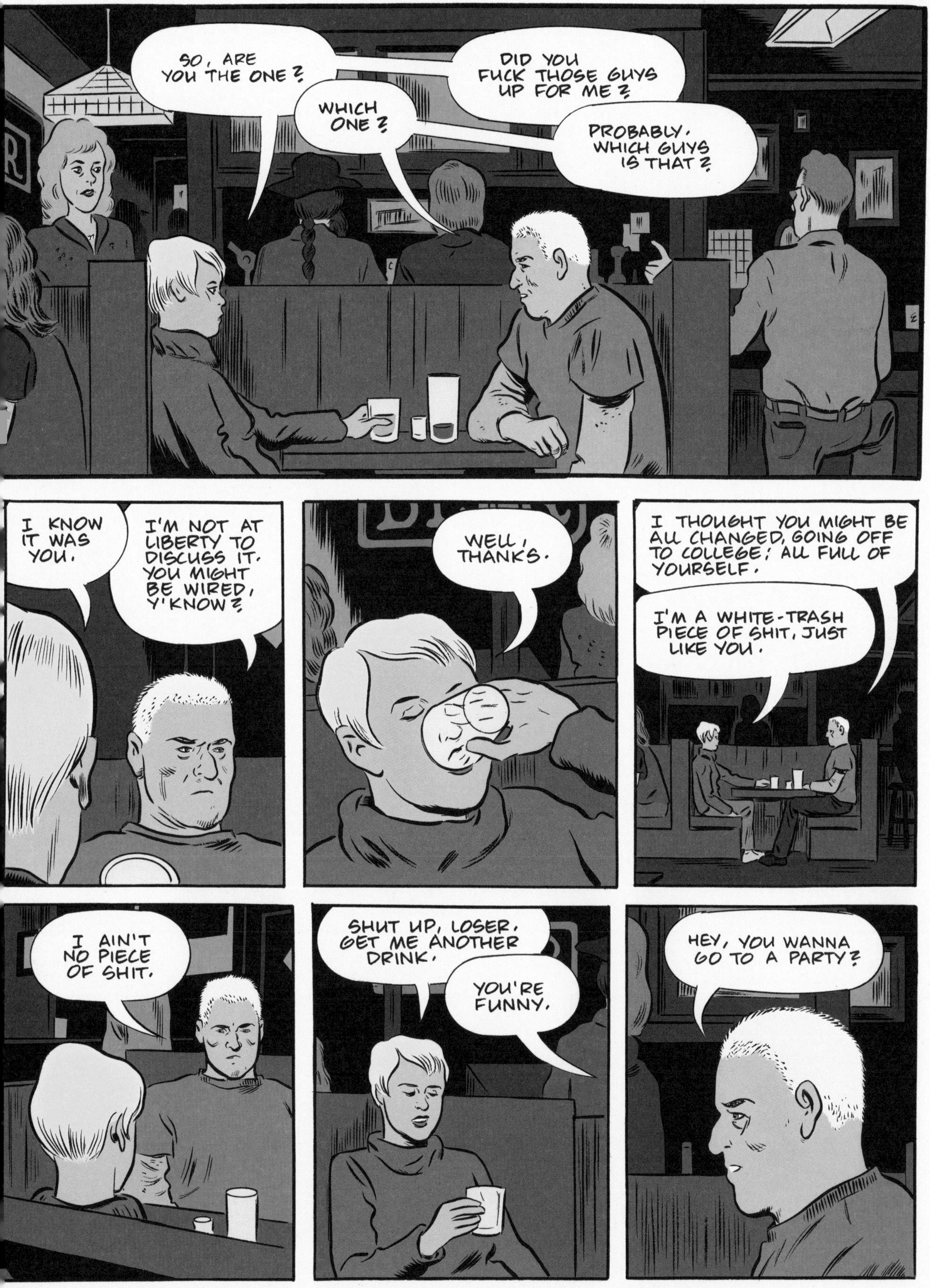

SO, ARE YOU THE ONE?
WHICH ONE?
DID YOU FUCK THOSE GUYS UP FOR ME?
PROBABLY. WHICH GUYS IS THAT?
I KNOW IT WAS YOU.
I'M NOT AT LIBERTY TO DISCUSS IT. YOU MIGHT BE WIRED, Y'KNOW?
WELL, THANKS.
I THOUGHT YOU MIGHT BE ALL CHANGED, GOING OFF TO COLLEGE; ALL FULL OF YOURSELF.
I'M A WHITE-TRASH PIECE OF SHIT, JUST LIKE YOU.
I AIN'T NO PIECE OF SHIT.
SHUT UP, LOSER. GET ME ANOTHER DRINK.
YOU'RE FUNNY.
HEY, YOU WANNA GO TO A PARTY?

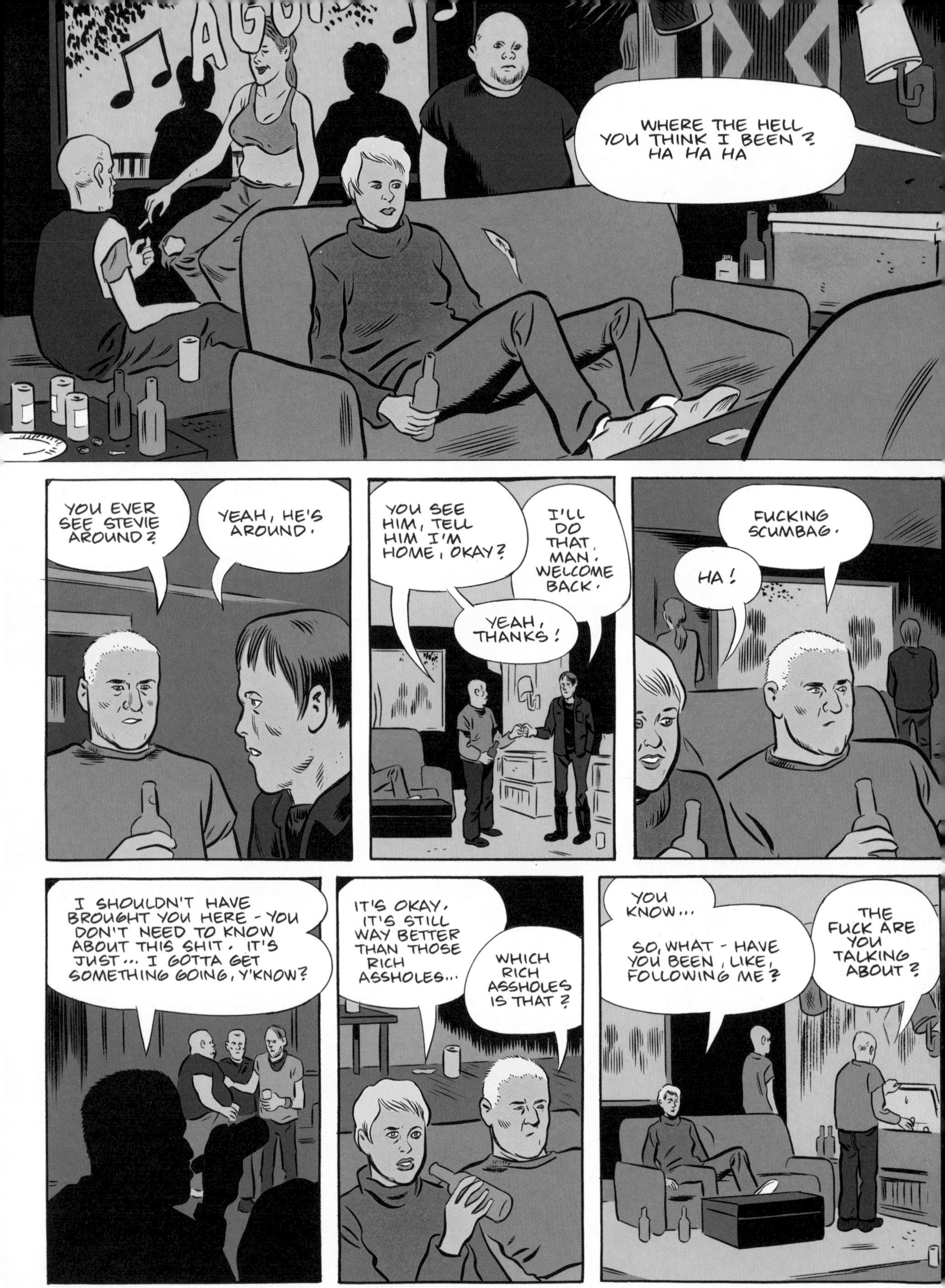

WHERE THE HELL YOU THINK I BEEN? HA HA HA
YOU EVER SEE STEVIE AROUND?
YEAH, HE'S AROUND.
YOU SEE HIM, TELL HIM I'M HOME, OKAY?
I'LL DO THAT MAN. WELCOME BACK.
YEAH, THANKS!
FUCKING SCUMBAG.
HA!
I SHOULDN'T HAVE BROUGHT YOU HERE - YOU DON'T NEED TO KNOW ABOUT THIS SHIT. IT'S JUST... I GOTTA GET SOMETHING GOING, Y'KNOW?
IT'S OKAY. IT'S STILL WAY BETTER THAN THOSE RICH ASSHOLES...
WHICH RICH ASSHOLES IS THAT?
YOU KNOW...
SO, WHAT - HAVE YOU BEEN, LIKE, FOLLOWING ME?
THE FUCK ARE YOU TALKING ABOUT?

SHIT, MAN, WHEN'D YOU GET OUT?

BEEN AT MY MOM'S A COUPLE WEEKS, BUT THAT'S WORSE'N JAIL, Y'KNOW?

HA HA

COME ON, MAN... JUST TELL ME.

YOU'RE FUCKING PARANOID. THIS IS MY FIRST DAY OUTTA HOUSE ARREST.

BUT, WHAT ABOUT... SO HOW'D YOU BEAT UP THOSE GUYS, THEN?

WHICH GUYS AGAIN?

I WENT ON A DATE WITH A FUCKING SCUMBAG AND THEN SOMEBODY KICKED HIS ASS - RING A BELL?

YOU BEEN GOIN' ON DATES? WHO WITH?

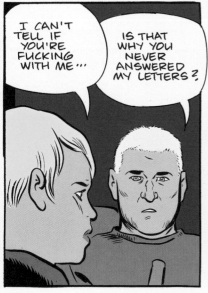

I CAN'T TELL IF YOU'RE FUCKING WITH ME...

IS THAT WHY YOU NEVER ANSWERED MY LETTERS?

I NEVER GOT ANY LETTERS, NOW, LOOK- ARE YOU SERIOUSLY TELLING ME YOU-

WHO THE FUCK IS THIS GUY? I THINK MAYBE I WILL KICK HIS ASS!

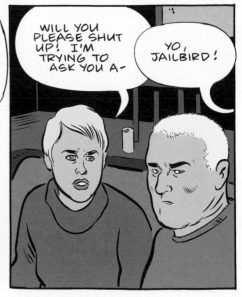

WILL YOU PLEASE SHUT UP! I'M TRYING TO ASK YOU A-

YO, JAILBIRD!

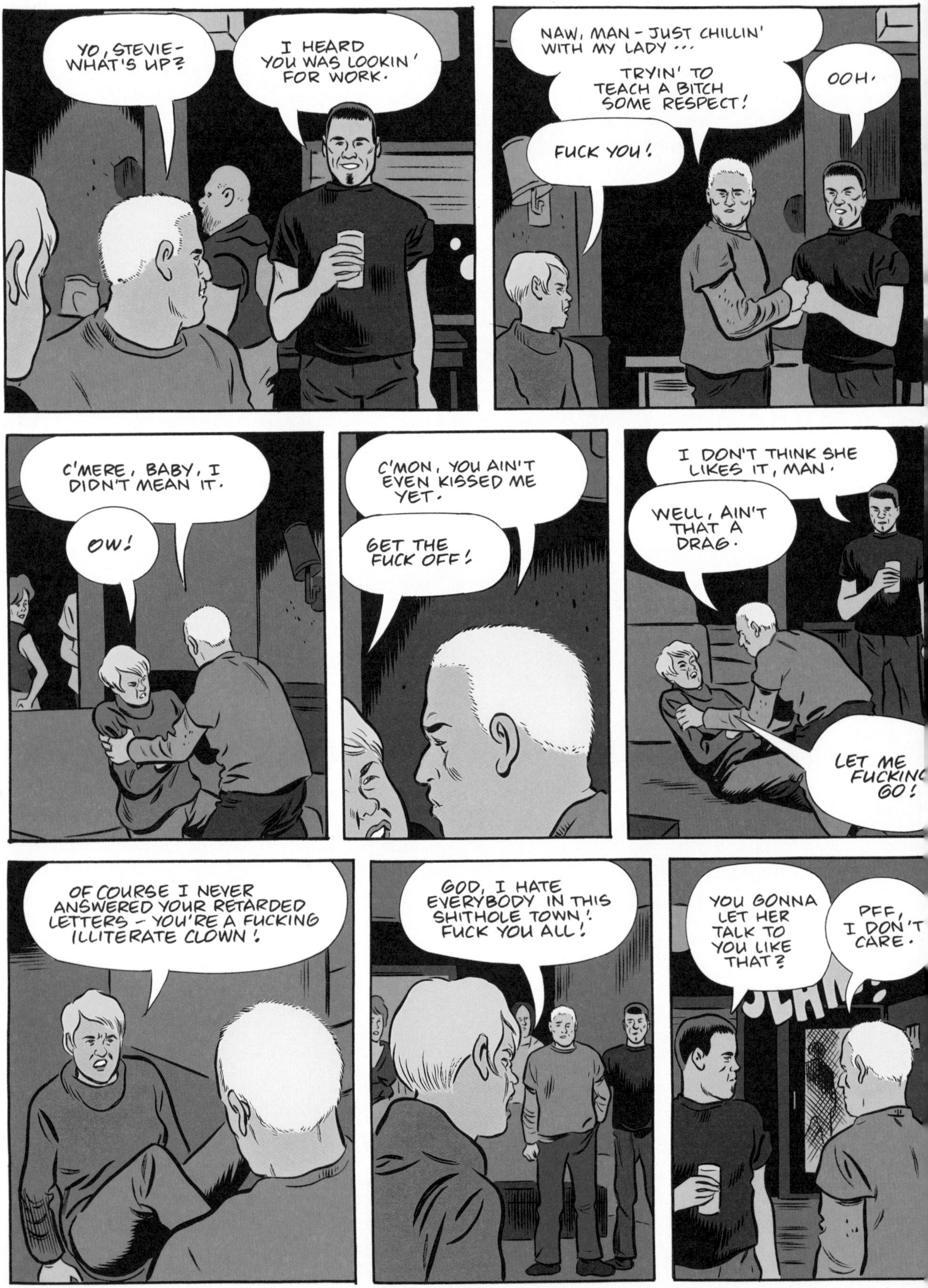
YO, STEVIE- WHAT'S UP?
I HEARD YOU WAS LOOKIN' FOR WORK.
NAW, MAN - JUST CHILLIN' WITH MY LADY ...
TRYIN' TO TEACH A BITCH SOME RESPECT!
OOH.
FUCK YOU!
C'MERE, BABY, I DIDN'T MEAN IT.
OW!
C'MON, YOU AIN'T EVEN KISSED ME YET.
GET THE FUCK OFF!
I DON'T THINK SHE LIKES IT, MAN.
WELL, AIN'T THAT A DRAG.
LET ME FUCKING GO!
OF COURSE I NEVER ANSWERED YOUR RETARDED LETTERS - YOU'RE A FUCKING ILLITERATE CLOWN!
GOD, I HATE EVERYBODY IN THIS SHITHOLE TOWN! FUCK YOU ALL!
YOU GONNA LET HER TALK TO YOU LIKE THAT?
PFF, I DON'T CARE.

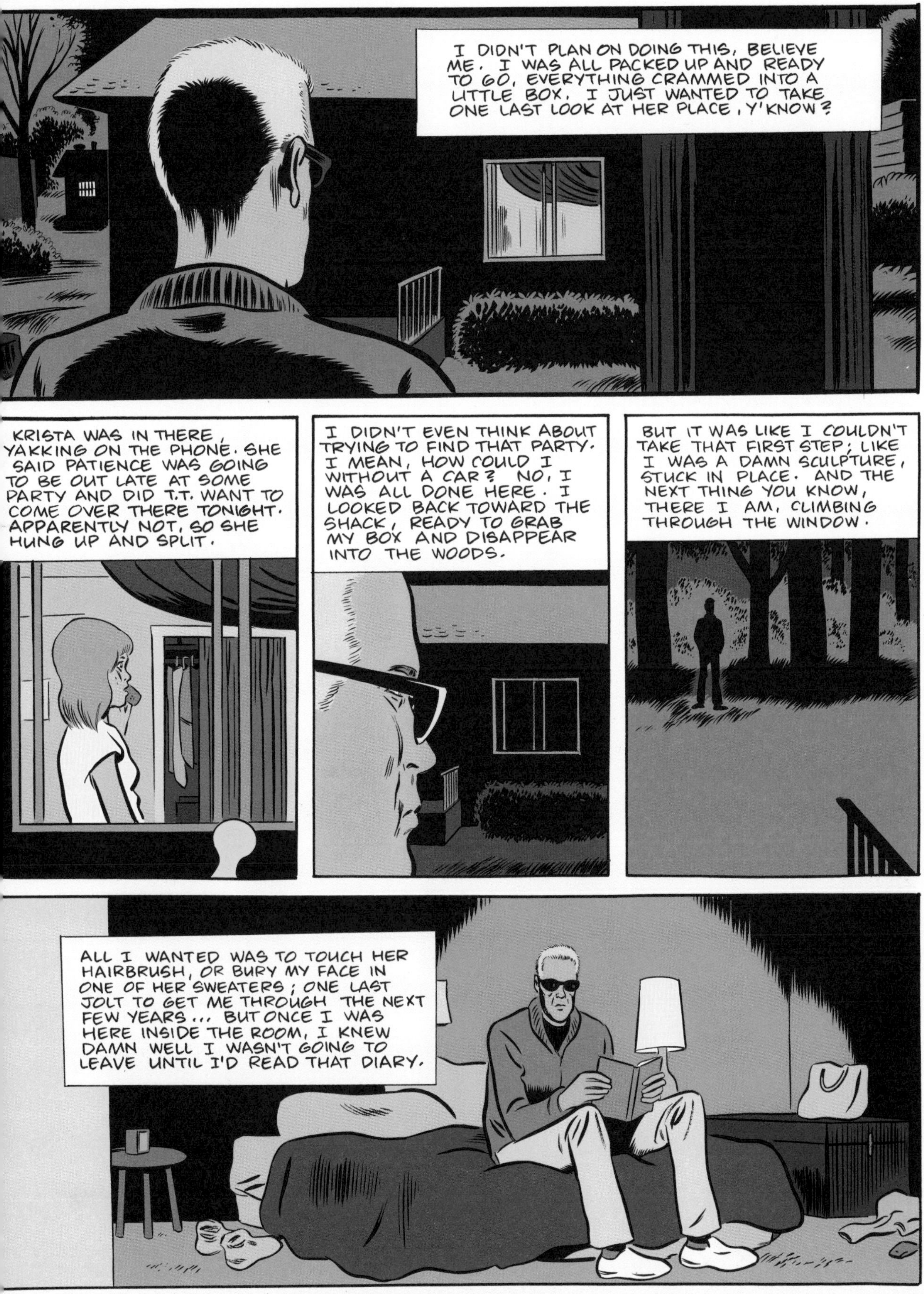
I DIDN'T PLAN ON DOING THIS, BELIEVE ME. I WAS ALL PACKED UP AND READY TO GO, EVERYTHING CRAMMED INTO A LITTLE BOX. I JUST WANTED TO TAKE ONE LAST LOOK AT HER PLACE, Y'KNOW?
KRISTA WAS IN THERE, YAKKING ON THE PHONE. SHE SAID PATIENCE WAS GOING TO BE OUT LATE AT SOME PARTY AND DID T.T. WANT TO COME OVER THERE TONIGHT. APPARENTLY NOT, SO SHE HUNG UP AND SPLIT.
I DIDN'T EVEN THINK ABOUT TRYING TO FIND THAT PARTY. I MEAN, HOW COULD I WITHOUT A CAR? NO, I WAS ALL DONE HERE. I LOOKED BACK TOWARD THE SHACK, READY TO GRAB MY BOX AND DISAPPEAR INTO THE WOODS.
BUT IT WAS LIKE I COULDN'T TAKE THAT FIRST STEP; LIKE I WAS A DAMN SCULPTURE, STUCK IN PLACE. AND THE NEXT THING YOU KNOW, THERE I AM, CLIMBING THROUGH THE WINDOW.
ALL I WANTED WAS TO TOUCH HER HAIRBRUSH, OR BURY MY FACE IN ONE OF HER SWEATERS; ONE LAST JOLT TO GET ME THROUGH THE NEXT FEW YEARS... BUT ONCE I WAS HERE INSIDE THE ROOM, I KNEW DAMN WELL I WASN'T GOING TO LEAVE UNTIL I'D READ THAT DIARY.

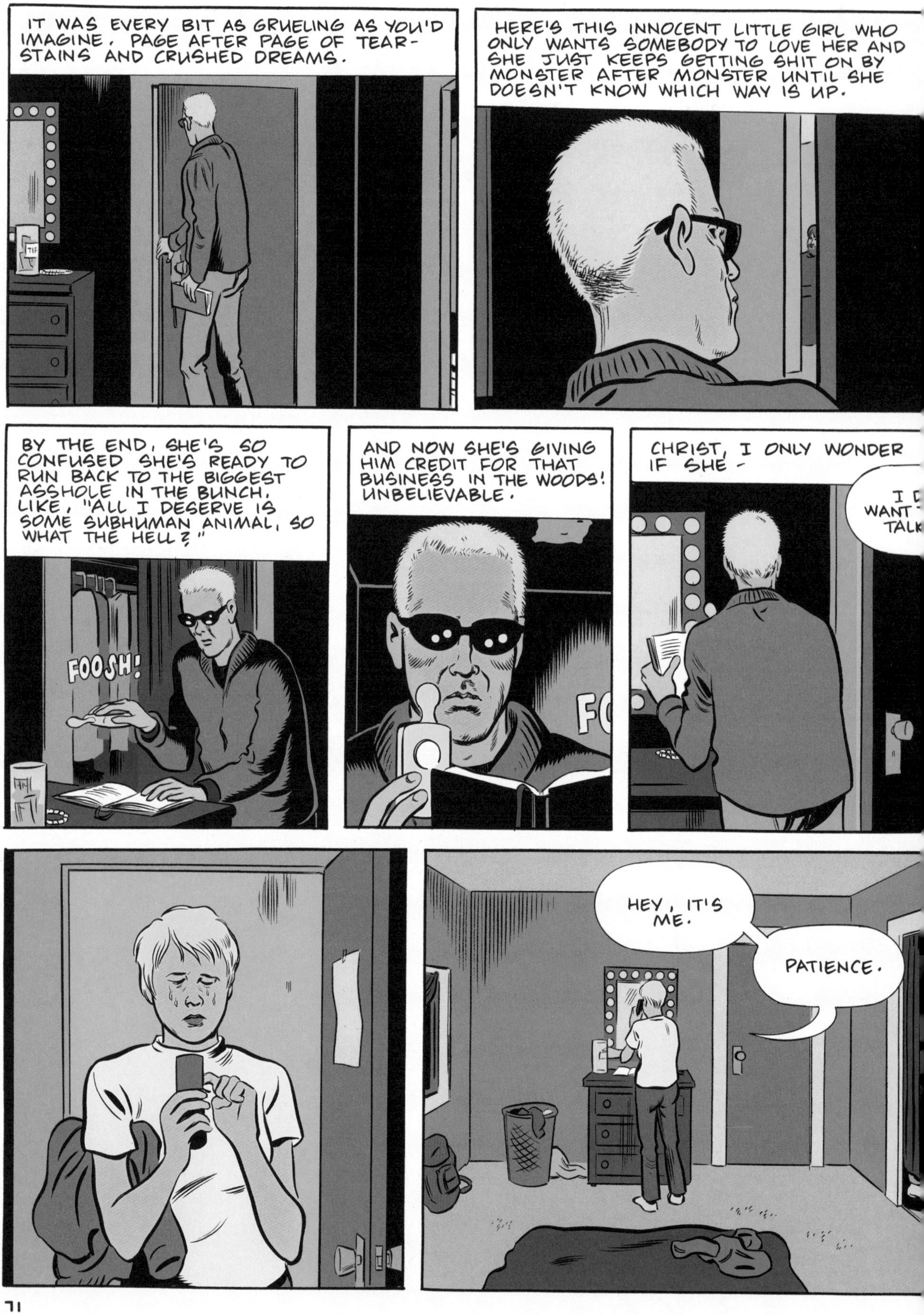
IT WAS EVERY BIT AS GRUELING AS YOU'D IMAGINE, PAGE AFTER PAGE OF TEAR-STAINS AND CRUSHED DREAMS.
HERE'S THIS INNOCENT LITTLE GIRL WHO ONLY WANTS SOMEBODY TO LOVE HER AND SHE JUST KEEPS GETTING SHIT ON BY MONSTER AFTER MONSTER UNTIL SHE DOESN'T KNOW WHICH WAY IS UP.
BY THE END, SHE'S SO CONFUSED SHE'S READY TO RUN BACK TO THE BIGGEST ASSHOLE IN THE BUNCH. LIKE, "ALL I DESERVE IS SOME SUBHUMAN ANIMAL, SO WHAT THE HELL?"
FOOSH!
AND NOW SHE'S GIVING HIM CREDIT FOR THAT BUSINESS IN THE WOODS! UNBELIEVABLE.
CHRIST, I ONLY WONDER IF SHE -
HEY, IT'S ME.
PATIENCE.

I JUST... I WANTED TO TELL YOU I CAN'T COME IN TOMORROW...

NO, I JUST...

I THINK I NEED TO GET OUT OF HERE. I...

NO, NO... I'M REALLY SORRY, NANCY, I JUST...

I HAVE TO GO. BYE.

≟ SOB ≟

WHAT THE HELL? WHERE'S THE REST OF MY MONEY?

KRISTA! YOU FUCKING LITTLE CRIMINAL!

THIS ISN'T EVEN ENOUGH FOR A BUS TICKET!

AND WHO THE FUCK SAID YOU COULD READ MY DIARY, YOU LITTLE—

DON'T WORRY A ME - SHE EXPECTI

72

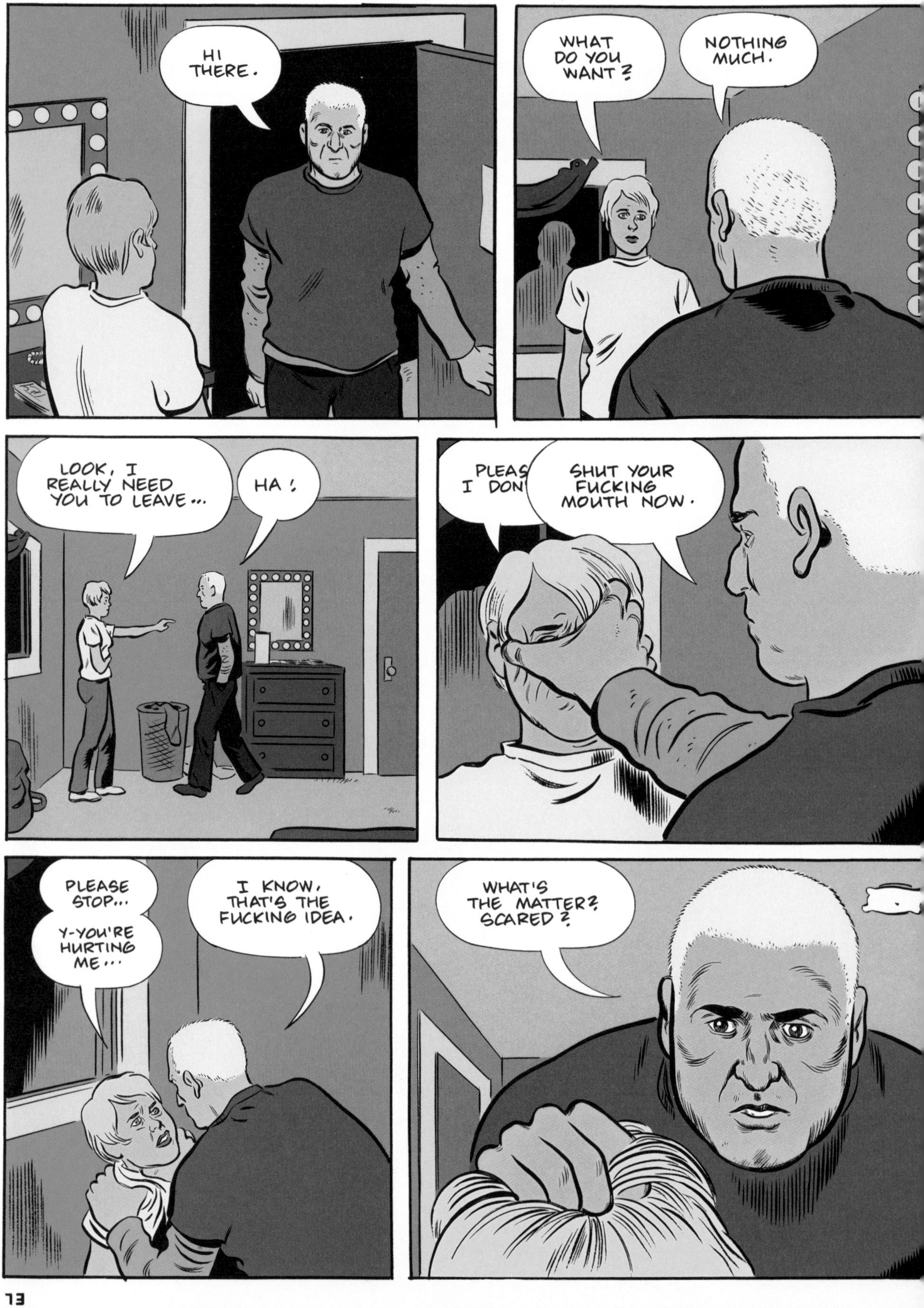
HI THERE.
WHAT DO YOU WANT?
NOTHING MUCH.
LOOK, I REALLY NEED YOU TO LEAVE...
HA!
PLEAS I DON
SHUT YOUR FUCKING MOUTH NOW.
PLEASE STOP...
Y-YOU'RE HURTING ME...
I KNOW, THAT'S THE FUCKING IDEA.
WHAT'S THE MATTER? SCARED?

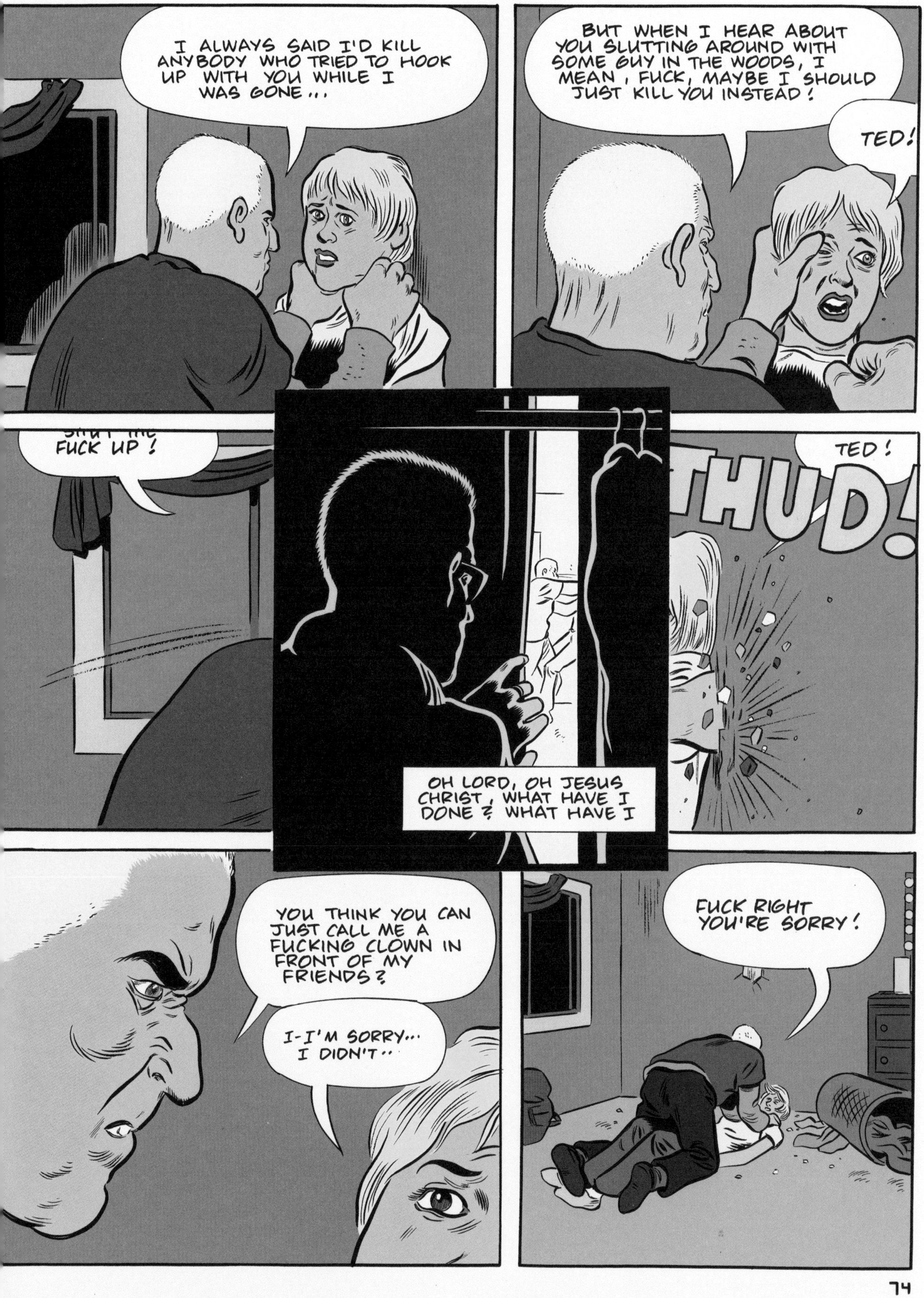
I ALWAYS SAID I'D KILL ANYBODY WHO TRIED TO HOOK UP WITH YOU WHILE I WAS GONE...
BUT WHEN I HEAR ABOUT YOU SLUTTING AROUND WITH SOME GUY IN THE WOODS, I MEAN, FUCK, MAYBE I SHOULD JUST KILL YOU INSTEAD!
TED!
FUCK UP!
OH LORD, OH JESUS CHRIST, WHAT HAVE I DONE? WHAT HAVE I
TED!
THUD!
YOU THINK YOU CAN JUST CALL ME A FUCKING CLOWN IN FRONT OF MY FRIENDS?
I-I'M SORRY... I DIDN'T..
FUCK RIGHT YOU'RE SORRY!

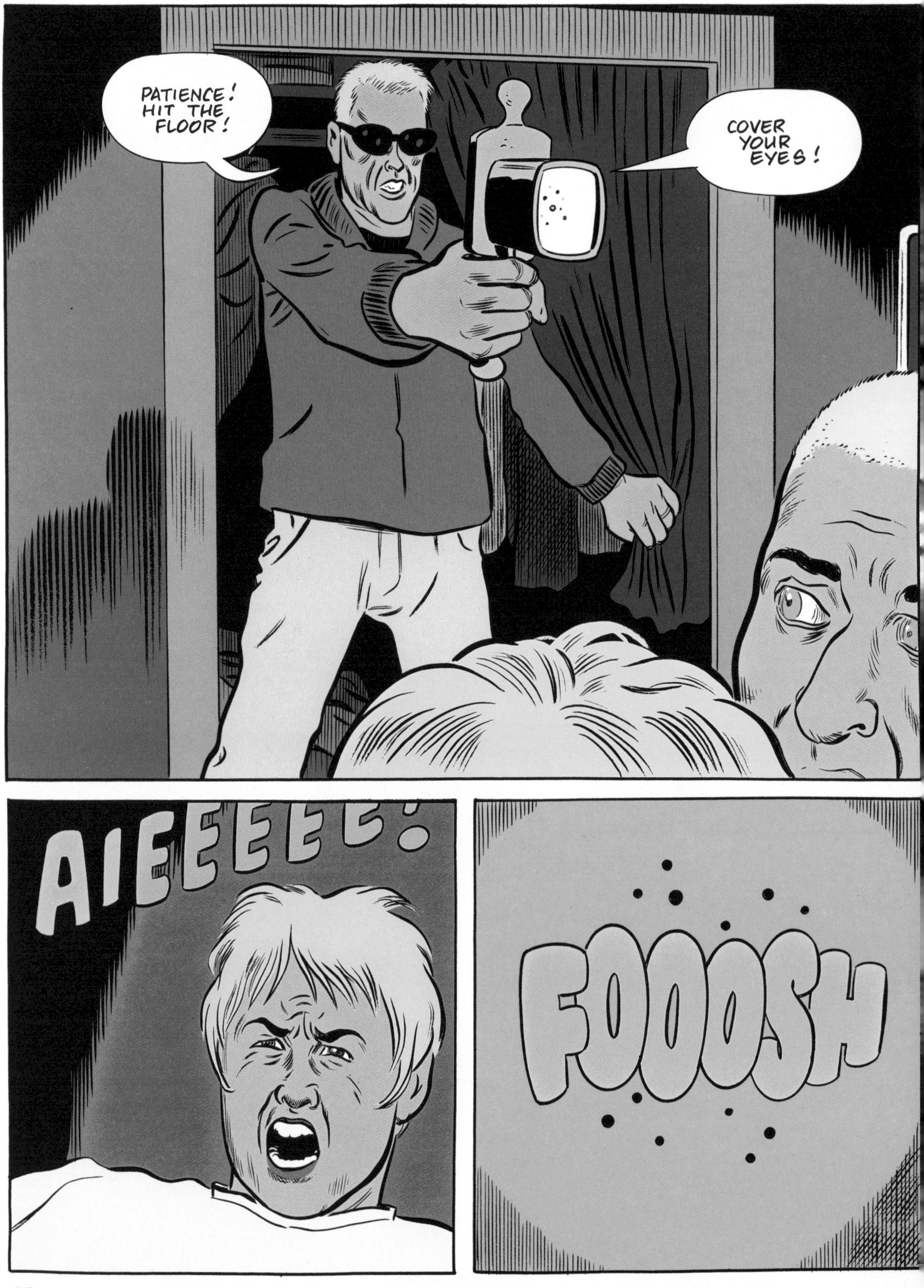
PATIENCE! HIT THE FLOOR!
COVER YOUR EYES!
AIEEEEE!
FOOOSH

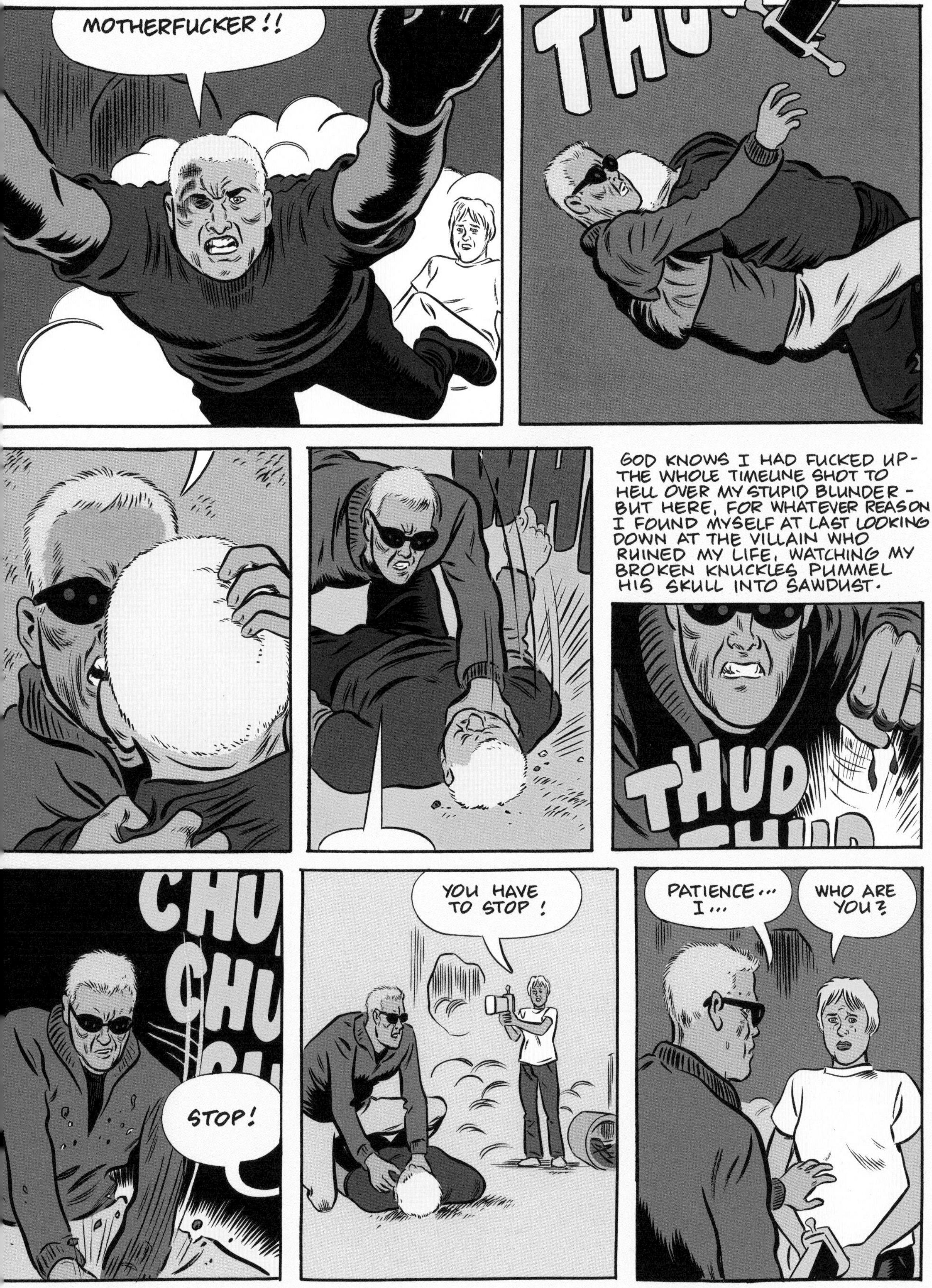
MOTHERFUCKER!!
THU
GOD KNOWS I HAD FUCKED UP - THE WHOLE TIMELINE SHOT TO HELL OVER MY STUPID BLUNDER - BUT HERE, FOR WHATEVER REASON, I FOUND MYSELF AT LAST LOOKING DOWN AT THE VILLAIN WHO RUINED MY LIFE, WATCHING MY BROKEN KNUCKLES PUMMEL HIS SKULL INTO SAWDUST.
THUD
CHU
CHU
STOP!
YOU HAVE TO STOP!
PATIENCE... I...
WHO ARE YOU?

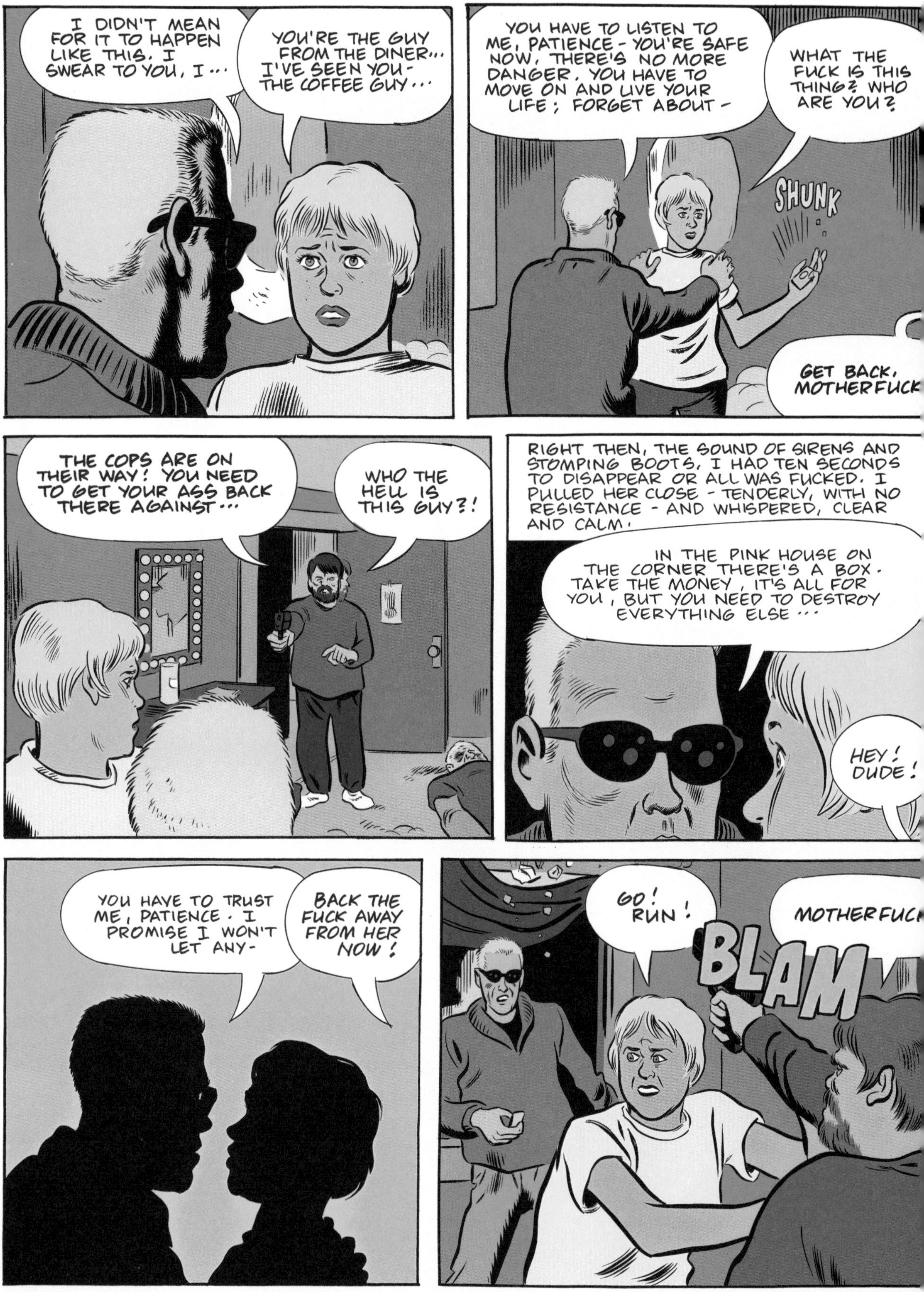
I DIDN'T MEAN FOR IT TO HAPPEN LIKE THIS. I SWEAR TO YOU, I...
YOU'RE THE GUY FROM THE DINER... I'VE SEEN YOU- THE COFFEE GUY...
YOU HAVE TO LISTEN TO ME, PATIENCE - YOU'RE SAFE NOW, THERE'S NO MORE DANGER. YOU HAVE TO MOVE ON AND LIVE YOUR LIFE; FORGET ABOUT -
WHAT THE FUCK IS THIS THING? WHO ARE YOU?
SHUNK
GET BACK, MOTHERFUCK
THE COPS ARE ON THEIR WAY! YOU NEED TO GET YOUR ASS BACK THERE AGAINST...
WHO THE HELL IS THIS GUY?!
RIGHT THEN, THE SOUND OF SIRENS AND STOMPING BOOTS, I HAD TEN SECONDS TO DISAPPEAR OR ALL WAS FUCKED. I PULLED HER CLOSE - TENDERLY, WITH NO RESISTANCE - AND WHISPERED, CLEAR AND CALM.
IN THE PINK HOUSE ON THE CORNER THERE'S A BOX. TAKE THE MONEY, IT'S ALL FOR YOU, BUT YOU NEED TO DESTROY EVERYTHING ELSE...
HEY! DUDE!
YOU HAVE TO TRUST ME, PATIENCE. I PROMISE I WON'T LET ANY-
BACK THE FUCK AWAY FROM HER NOW!
GO! RUN!
MOTHERFUCK
BLAM

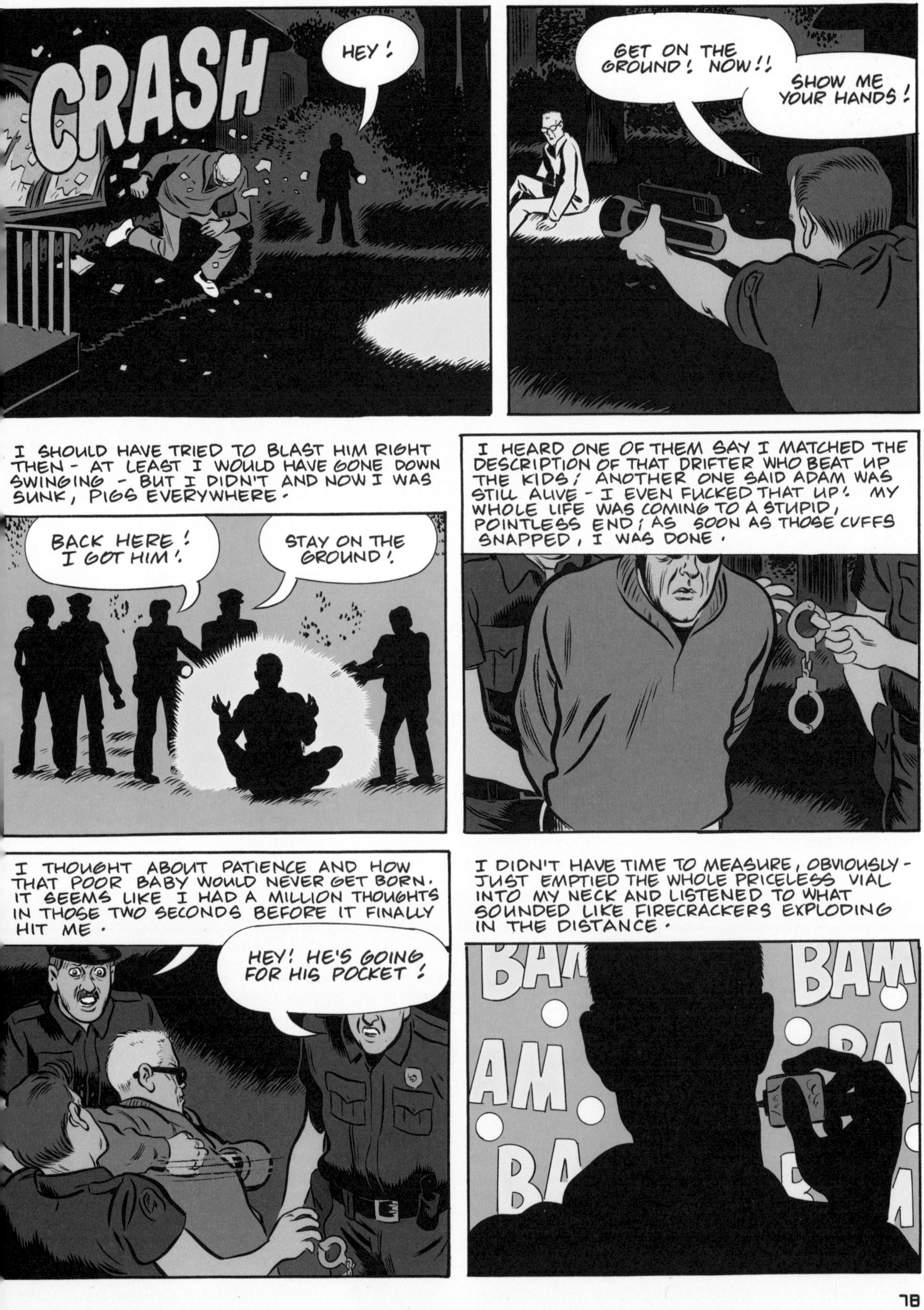
CRASH
HEY!
GET ON THE GROUND! NOW!!
SHOW ME YOUR HANDS!
I SHOULD HAVE TRIED TO BLAST HIM RIGHT THEN - AT LEAST I WOULD HAVE GONE DOWN SWINGING - BUT I DIDN'T AND NOW I WAS SUNK, PIGS EVERYWHERE.
BACK HERE! I GOT HIM!
STAY ON THE GROUND!
I HEARD ONE OF THEM SAY I MATCHED THE DESCRIPTION OF THAT DRIFTER WHO BEAT UP THE KIDS; ANOTHER ONE SAID ADAM WAS STILL ALIVE - I EVEN FUCKED THAT UP! MY WHOLE LIFE WAS COMING TO A STUPID, POINTLESS END; AS SOON AS THOSE CUFFS SNAPPED, I WAS DONE.
I THOUGHT ABOUT PATIENCE AND HOW THAT POOR BABY WOULD NEVER GET BORN. IT SEEMS LIKE I HAD A MILLION THOUGHTS IN THOSE TWO SECONDS BEFORE IT FINALLY HIT ME.
HEY! HE'S GOING FOR HIS POCKET!
I DIDN'T HAVE TIME TO MEASURE, OBVIOUSLY - JUST EMPTIED THE WHOLE PRICELESS VIAL INTO MY NECK AND LISTENED TO WHAT SOUNDED LIKE FIRECRACKERS EXPLODING IN THE DISTANCE.
BAM

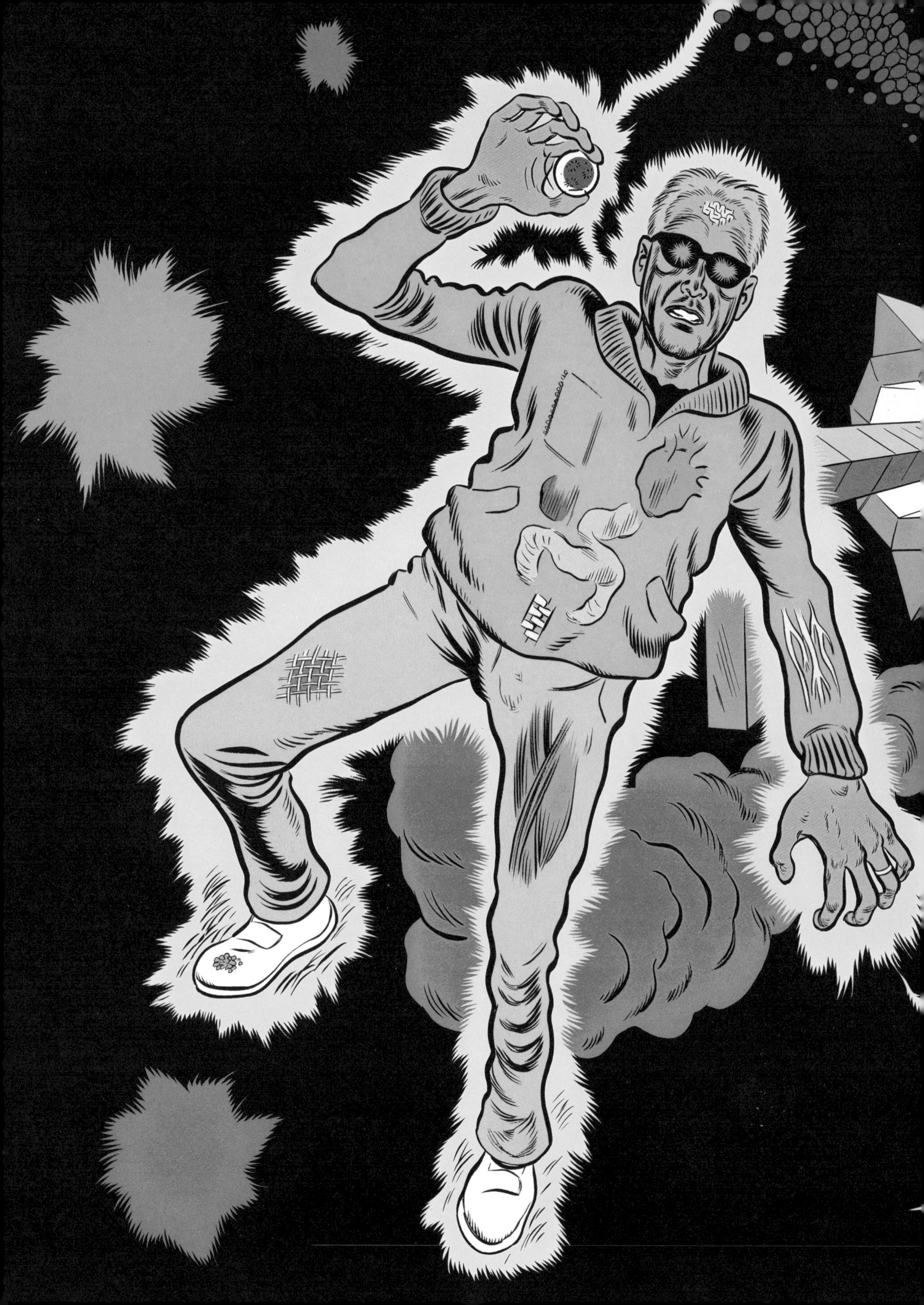

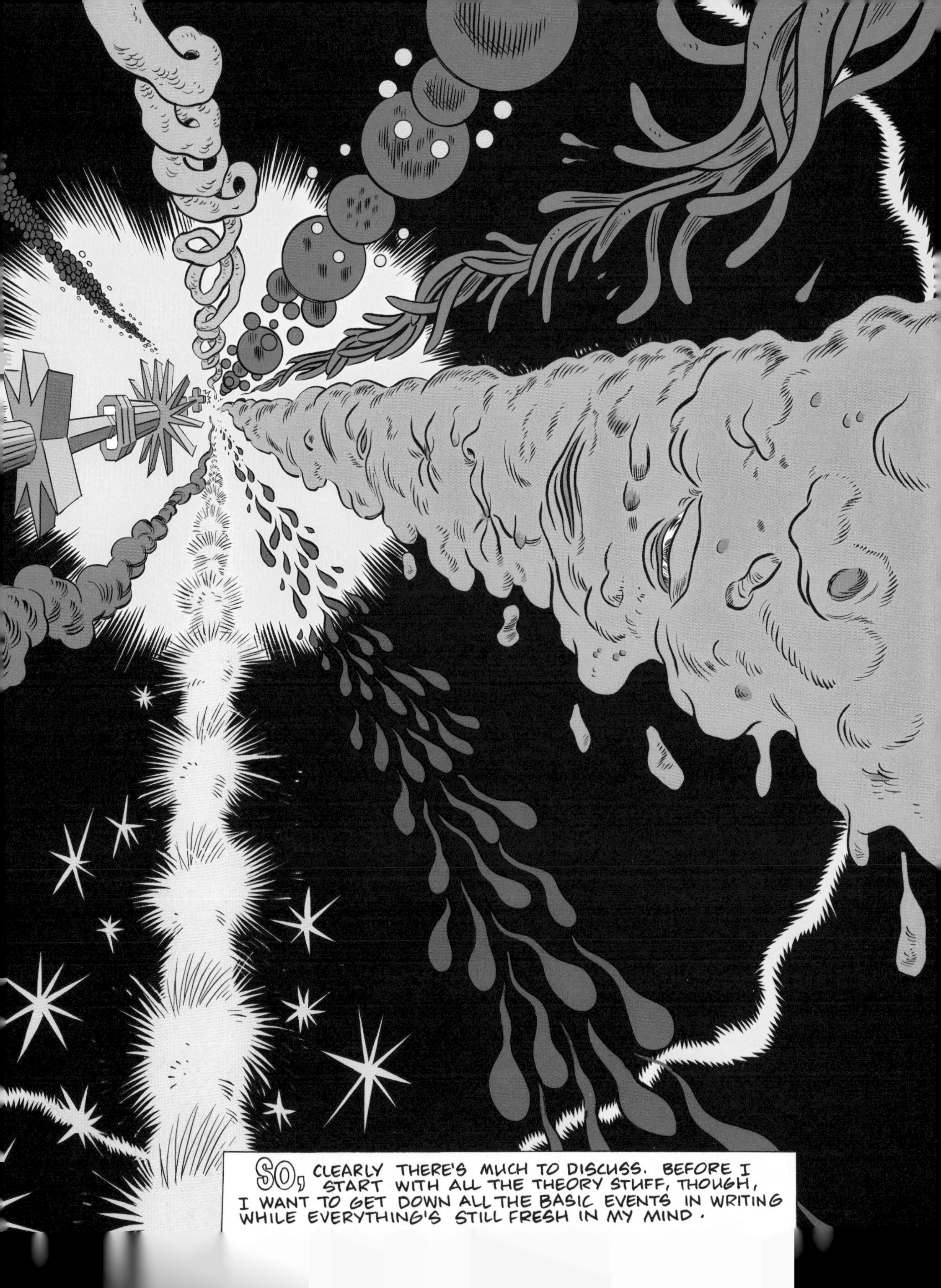
SO, CLEARLY THERE'S MUCH TO DISCUSS. BEFORE I START WITH ALL THE THEORY STUFF, THOUGH, I WANT TO GET DOWN ALL THE BASIC EVENTS IN WRITING WHILE EVERYTHING'S STILL FRESH IN MY MIND.

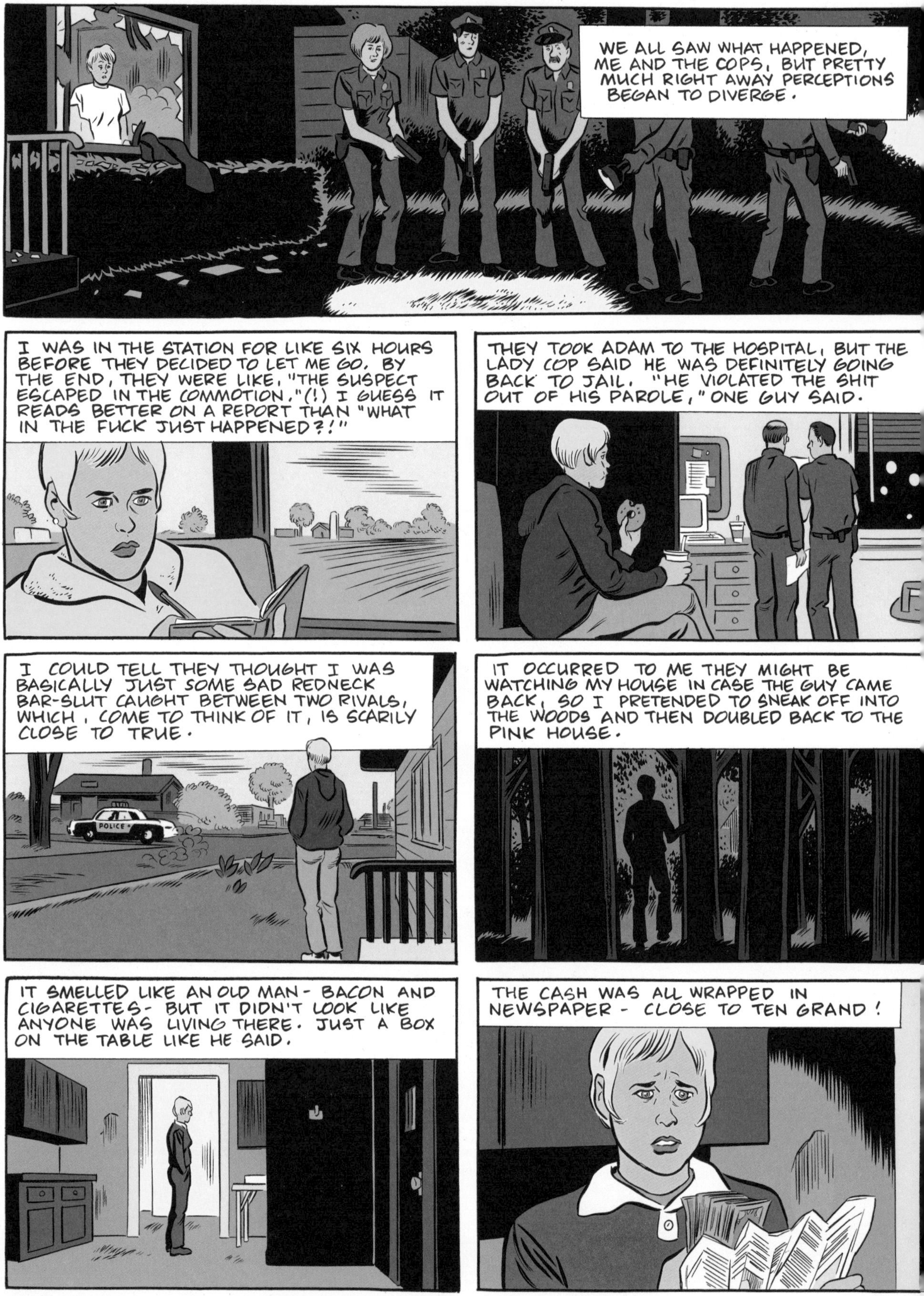
WE ALL SAW WHAT HAPPENED, ME AND THE COPS, BUT PRETTY MUCH RIGHT AWAY PERCEPTIONS BEGAN TO DIVERGE.
I WAS IN THE STATION FOR LIKE SIX HOURS BEFORE THEY DECIDED TO LET ME GO. BY THE END, THEY WERE LIKE, "THE SUSPECT ESCAPED IN THE COMMOTION." (!) I GUESS IT READS BETTER ON A REPORT THAN "WHAT IN THE FUCK JUST HAPPENED?!"
THEY TOOK ADAM TO THE HOSPITAL, BUT THE LADY COP SAID HE WAS DEFINITELY GOING BACK TO JAIL. "HE VIOLATED THE SHIT OUT OF HIS PAROLE," ONE GUY SAID.
I COULD TELL THEY THOUGHT I WAS BASICALLY JUST SOME SAD REDNECK BAR-SLUT CAUGHT BETWEEN TWO RIVALS, WHICH, COME TO THINK OF IT, IS SCARILY CLOSE TO TRUE.
POLICE
IT OCCURRED TO ME THEY MIGHT BE WATCHING MY HOUSE IN CASE THE GUY CAME BACK, SO I PRETENDED TO SNEAK OFF INTO THE WOODS AND THEN DOUBLED BACK TO THE PINK HOUSE.
IT SMELLED LIKE AN OLD MAN - BACON AND CIGARETTES - BUT IT DIDN'T LOOK LIKE ANYONE WAS LIVING THERE. JUST A BOX ON THE TABLE LIKE HE SAID.
THE CASH WAS ALL WRAPPED IN NEWSPAPER - CLOSE TO TEN GRAND!

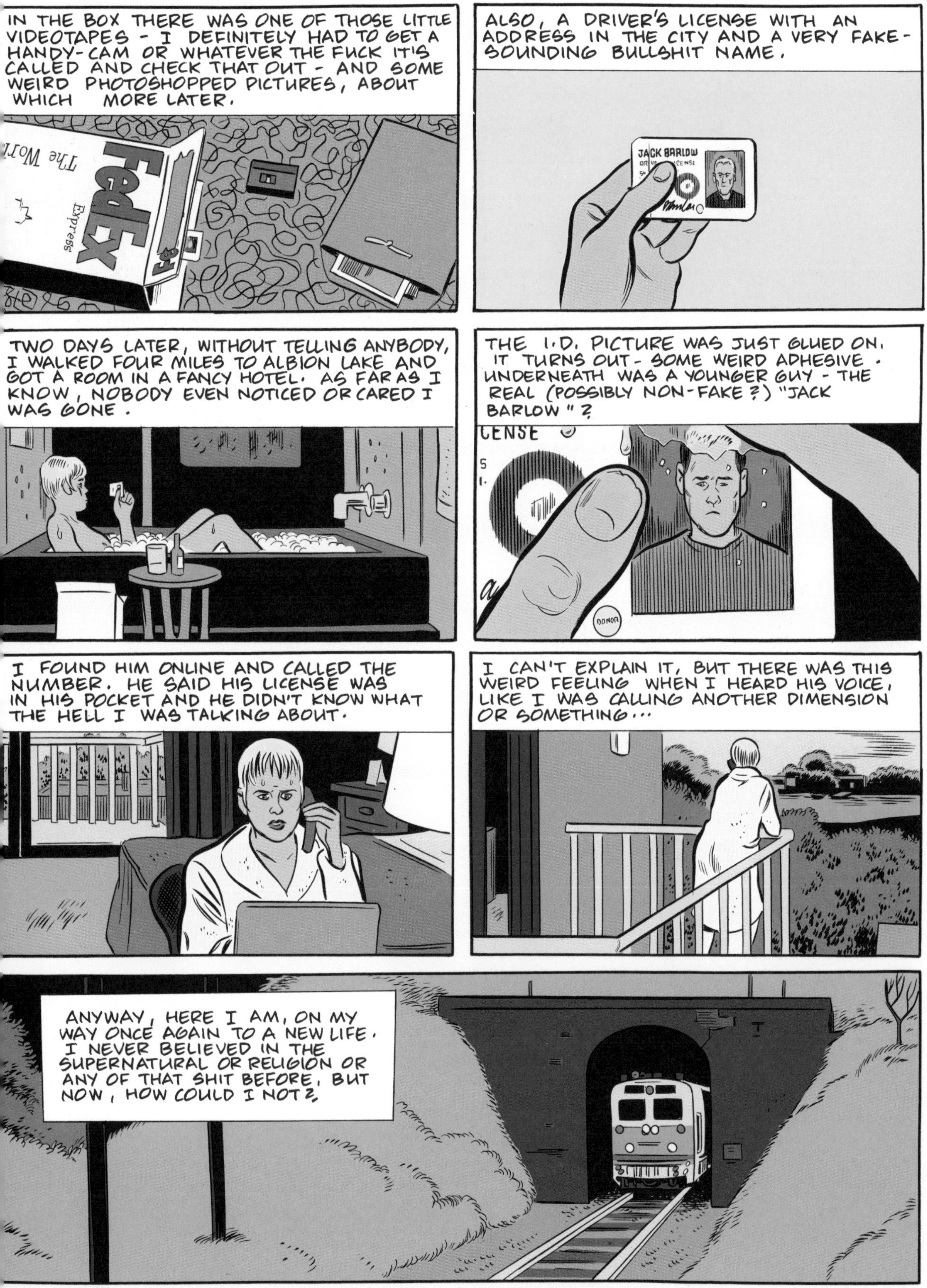
IN THE BOX THERE WAS ONE OF THOSE LITTLE VIDEOTAPES - I DEFINITELY HAD TO GET A HANDY-CAM OR WHATEVER THE FUCK IT'S CALLED AND CHECK THAT OUT - AND SOME WEIRD PHOTOSHOPPED PICTURES, ABOUT WHICH MORE LATER.
FedEx Express
ALSO, A DRIVER'S LICENSE WITH AN ADDRESS IN THE CITY AND A VERY FAKE-SOUNDING BULLSHIT NAME.
JACK BARLOW
TWO DAYS LATER, WITHOUT TELLING ANYBODY, I WALKED FOUR MILES TO ALBION LAKE AND GOT A ROOM IN A FANCY HOTEL. AS FAR AS I KNOW, NOBODY EVEN NOTICED OR CARED I WAS GONE.
THE I.D. PICTURE WAS JUST GLUED ON, IT TURNS OUT - SOME WEIRD ADHESIVE. UNDERNEATH WAS A YOUNGER GUY - THE REAL (POSSIBLY NON-FAKE?) "JACK BARLOW"?
DONOR
I FOUND HIM ONLINE AND CALLED THE NUMBER. HE SAID HIS LICENSE WAS IN HIS POCKET AND HE DIDN'T KNOW WHAT THE HELL I WAS TALKING ABOUT.
I CAN'T EXPLAIN IT, BUT THERE WAS THIS WEIRD FEELING WHEN I HEARD HIS VOICE, LIKE I WAS CALLING ANOTHER DIMENSION OR SOMETHING...
ANYWAY, HERE I AM, ON MY WAY ONCE AGAIN TO A NEW LIFE. I NEVER BELIEVED IN THE SUPERNATURAL OR RELIGION OR ANY OF THAT SHIT BEFORE, BUT NOW, HOW COULD I NOT?

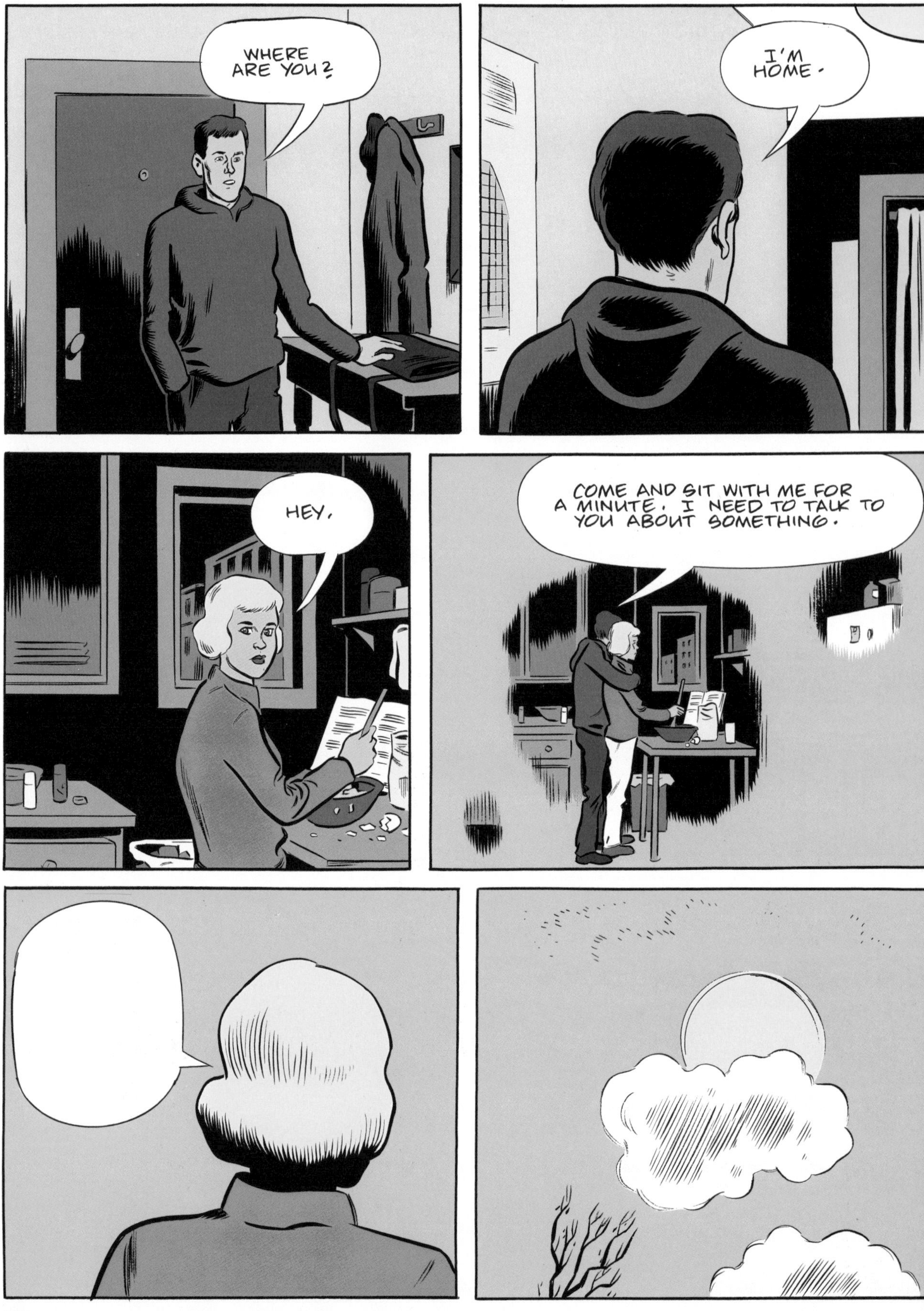
WHERE ARE YOU?
I'M HOME.
HEY.
COME AND SIT WITH ME FOR A MINUTE. I NEED TO TALK TO YOU ABOUT SOMETHING.

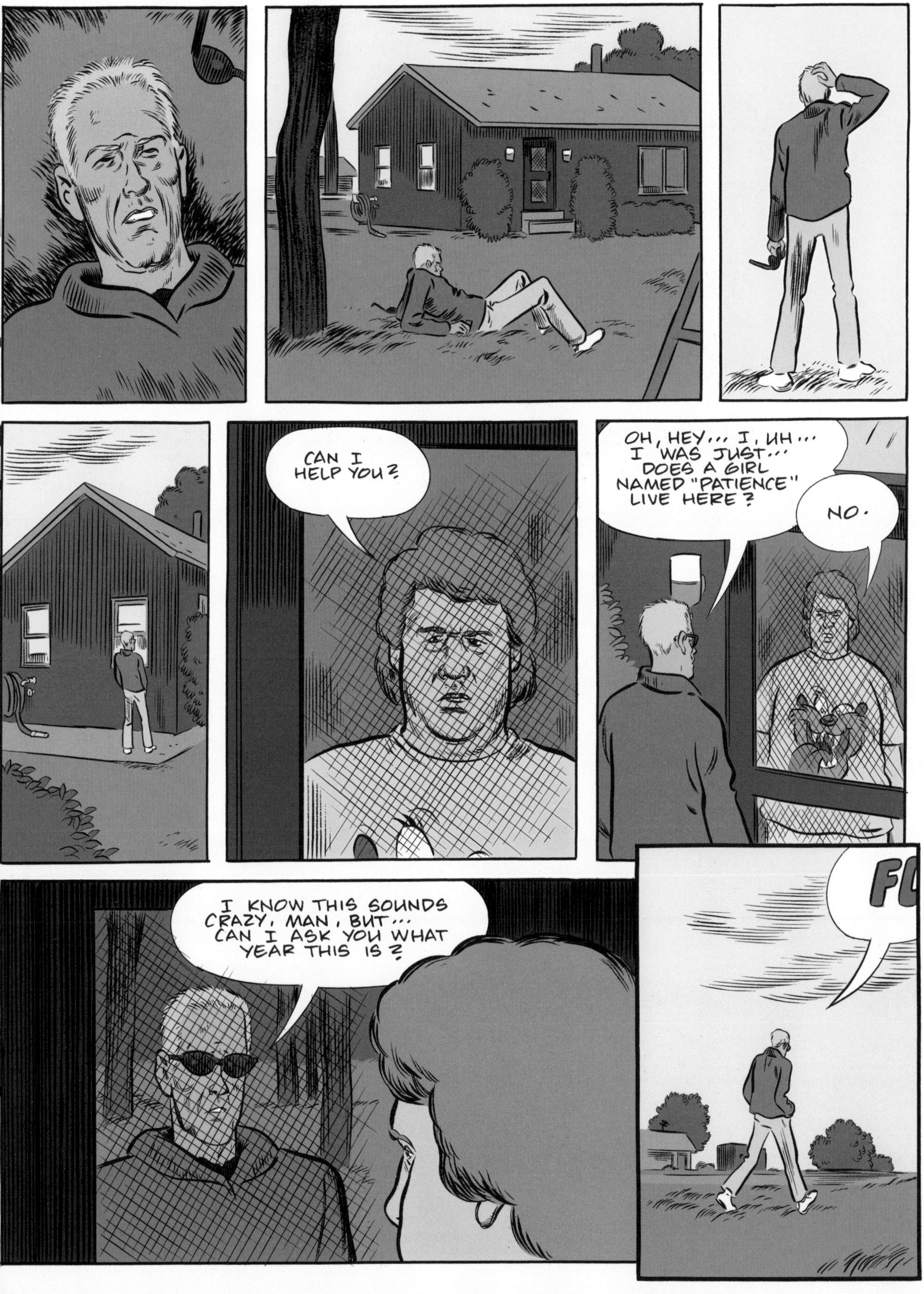

CAN I HELP YOU?
OH, HEY... I, UH... I WAS JUST... DOES A GIRL NAMED "PATIENCE" LIVE HERE?
NO.
I KNOW THIS SOUNDS CRAZY, MAN, BUT... CAN I ASK YOU WHAT YEAR THIS IS?

19

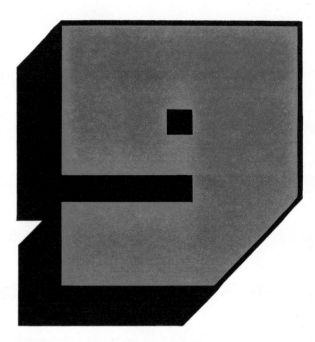

SO HERE I AM, SEPARATED BY A LIFETIME FROM MY BELOVED ANGEL AND THE VILLAIN WHO MURDERED HER.

ALL THE YEARS OF PLANNING, EVERYTHING, ALL IN THE TOILET. NOTHING LEFT BUT A USELESS GIZMO, A NOTEBOOK FULL OF GIBBERISH, AND A CRUMMY TWELVE-DOLLAR PHONE.

I'VE GOT NO JUICE, NO I.D., MAYBE FIFTEEN BUCKS IN MY POCKET... YEAH, THINGS ARE REALLY GOING GREAT.

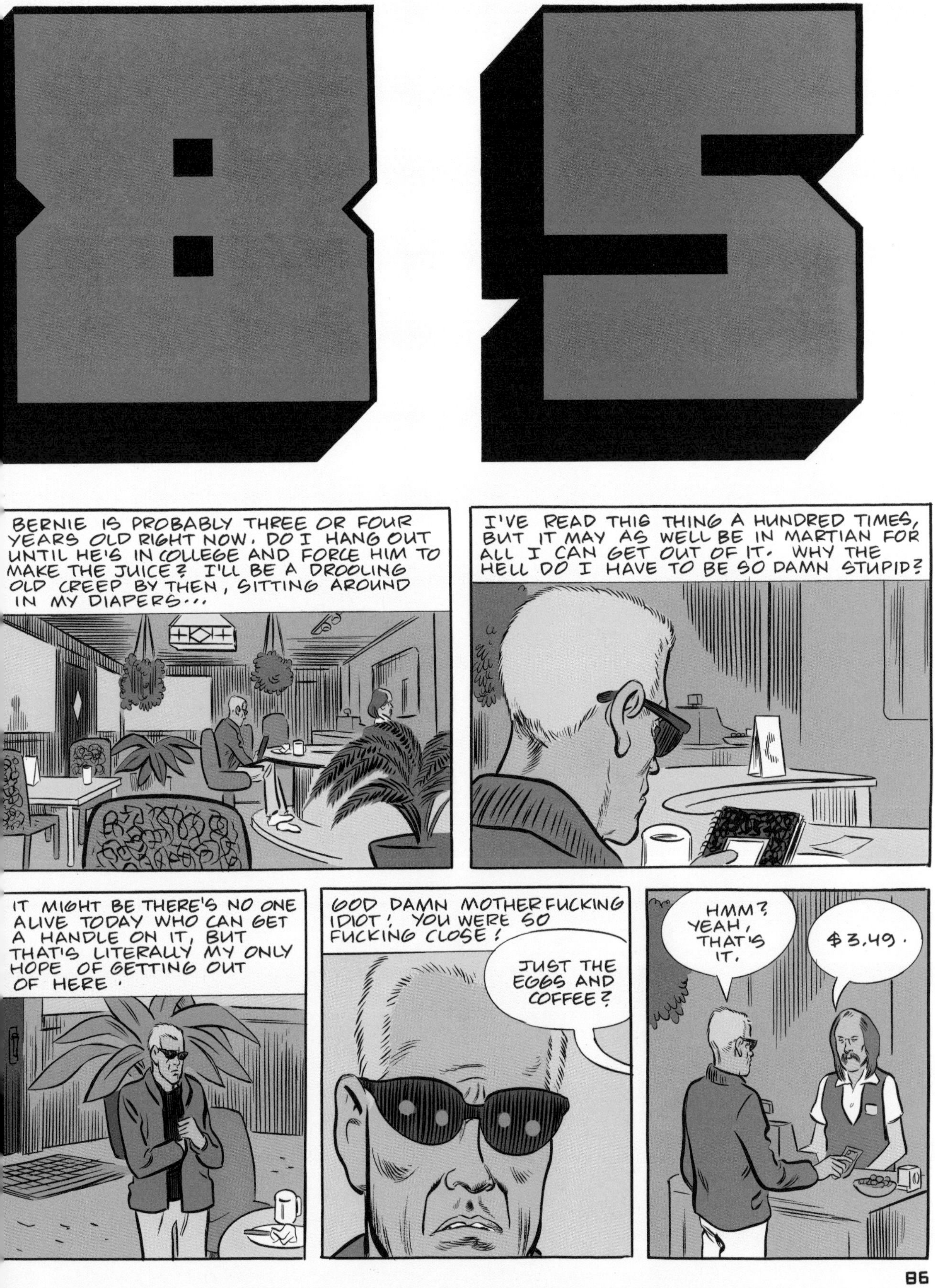
8:5
BERNIE IS PROBABLY THREE OR FOUR YEARS OLD RIGHT NOW. DO I HANG OUT UNTIL HE'S IN COLLEGE AND FORCE HIM TO MAKE THE JUICE? I'LL BE A DROOLING OLD CREEP BY THEN, SITTING AROUND IN MY DIAPERS...
I'VE READ THIS THING A HUNDRED TIMES, BUT IT MAY AS WELL BE IN MARTIAN FOR ALL I CAN GET OUT OF IT. WHY THE HELL DO I HAVE TO BE SO DAMN STUPID?
IT MIGHT BE THERE'S NO ONE ALIVE TODAY WHO CAN GET A HANDLE ON IT, BUT THAT'S LITERALLY MY ONLY HOPE OF GETTING OUT OF HERE.
GOD DAMN MOTHERFUCKING IDIOT! YOU WERE SO FUCKING CLOSE!
JUST THE EGGS AND COFFEE?
HMM? YEAH, THAT'S IT.
$3.49.

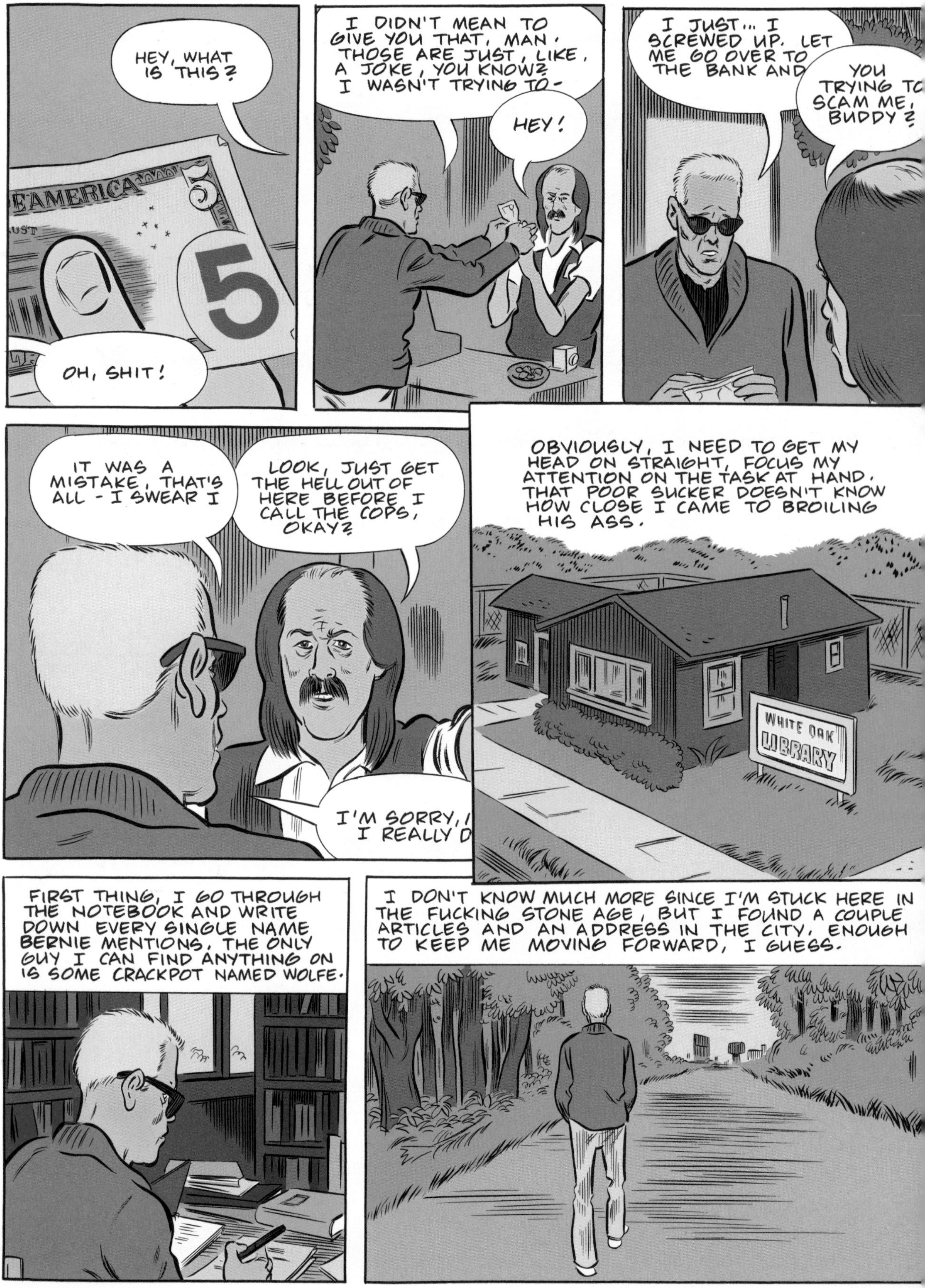

HEY, WHAT IS THIS?
AMERICA
5
OH, SHIT!
I DIDN'T MEAN TO GIVE YOU THAT, MAN. THOSE ARE JUST, LIKE, A JOKE, YOU KNOW? I WASN'T TRYING TO-
HEY!
I JUST... I SCREWED UP. LET ME GO OVER TO THE BANK AND
YOU TRYING TO SCAM ME, BUDDY?
IT WAS A MISTAKE, THAT'S ALL - I SWEAR I
LOOK, JUST GET THE HELL OUT OF HERE BEFORE I CALL THE COPS, OKAY?
I'M SORRY, I I REALLY D
OBVIOUSLY, I NEED TO GET MY HEAD ON STRAIGHT, FOCUS MY ATTENTION ON THE TASK AT HAND. THAT POOR SUCKER DOESN'T KNOW HOW CLOSE I CAME TO BROILING HIS ASS.
WHITE OAK LIBRARY
FIRST THING, I GO THROUGH THE NOTEBOOK AND WRITE DOWN EVERY SINGLE NAME BERNIE MENTIONS. THE ONLY GUY I CAN FIND ANYTHING ON IS SOME CRACKPOT NAMED WOLFE.
I DON'T KNOW MUCH MORE SINCE I'M STUCK HERE IN THE FUCKING STONE AGE, BUT I FOUND A COUPLE ARTICLES AND AN ADDRESS IN THE CITY. ENOUGH TO KEEP ME MOVING FORWARD, I GUESS.

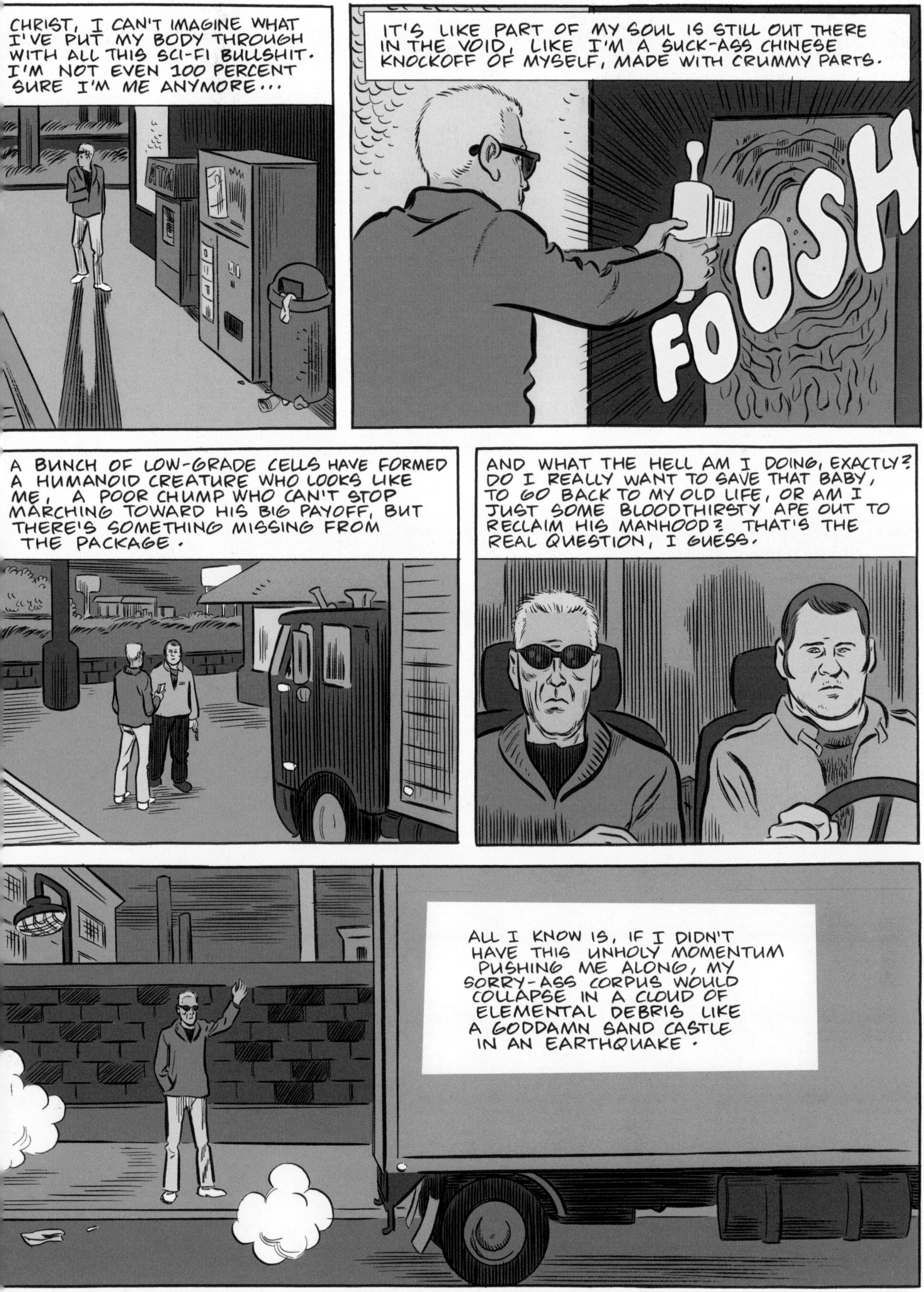
CHRIST, I CAN'T IMAGINE WHAT I'VE PUT MY BODY THROUGH WITH ALL THIS SCI-FI BULLSHIT. I'M NOT EVEN 100 PERCENT SURE I'M ME ANYMORE...
ATM
IT'S LIKE PART OF MY SOUL IS STILL OUT THERE IN THE VOID, LIKE I'M A SUCK-ASS CHINESE KNOCKOFF OF MYSELF, MADE WITH CRUMMY PARTS.
FOOSH
A BUNCH OF LOW-GRADE CELLS HAVE FORMED A HUMANOID CREATURE WHO LOOKS LIKE ME, A POOR CHUMP WHO CAN'T STOP MARCHING TOWARD HIS BIG PAYOFF, BUT THERE'S SOMETHING MISSING FROM THE PACKAGE.
AND WHAT THE HELL AM I DOING, EXACTLY? DO I REALLY WANT TO SAVE THAT BABY, TO GO BACK TO MY OLD LIFE, OR AM I JUST SOME BLOODTHIRSTY APE OUT TO RECLAIM HIS MANHOOD? THAT'S THE REAL QUESTION, I GUESS.
ALL I KNOW IS, IF I DIDN'T HAVE THIS UNHOLY MOMENTUM PUSHING ME ALONG, MY SORRY-ASS CORPUS WOULD COLLAPSE IN A CLOUD OF ELEMENTAL DEBRIS LIKE A GODDAMN SAND CASTLE IN AN EARTHQUAKE.

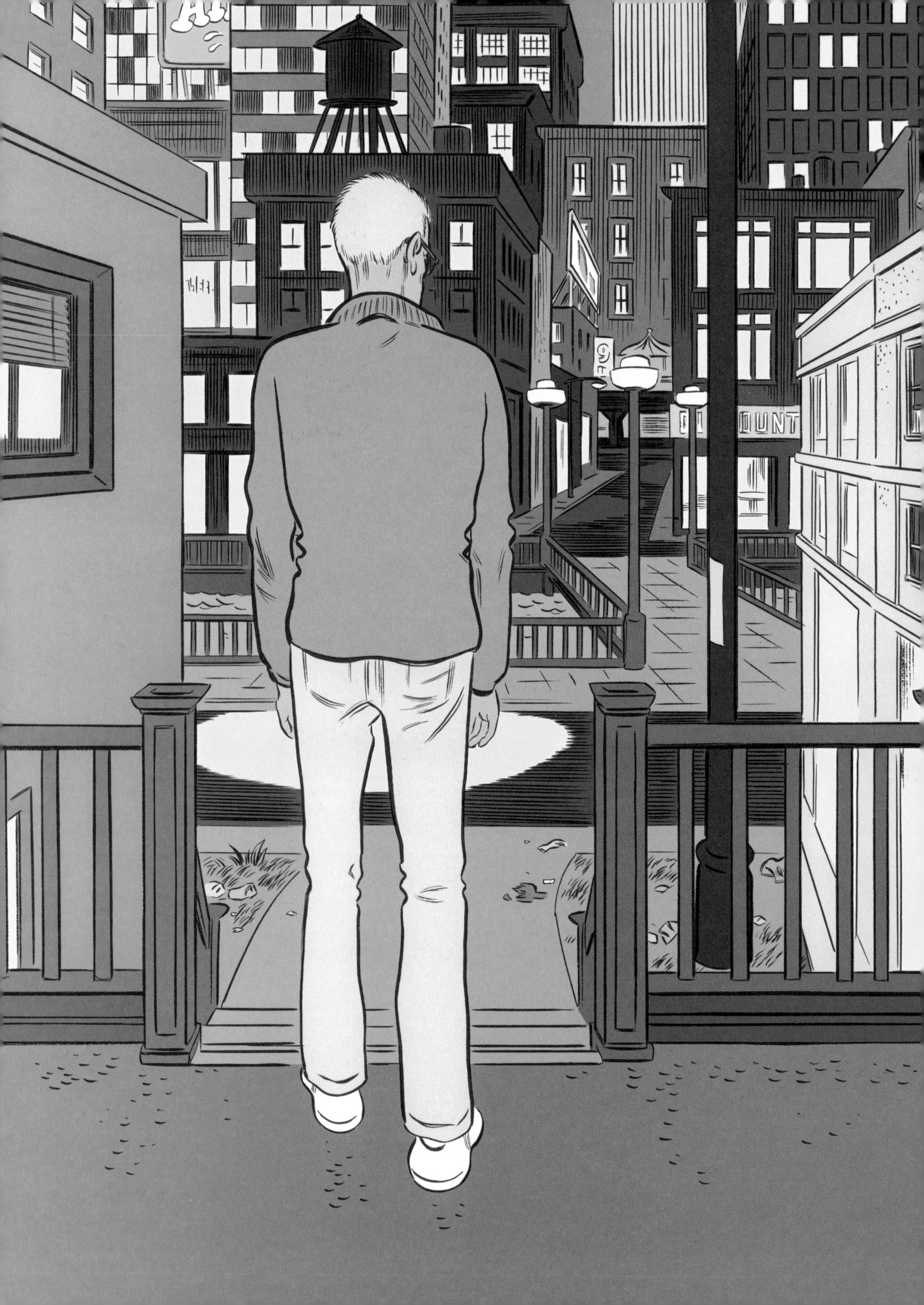

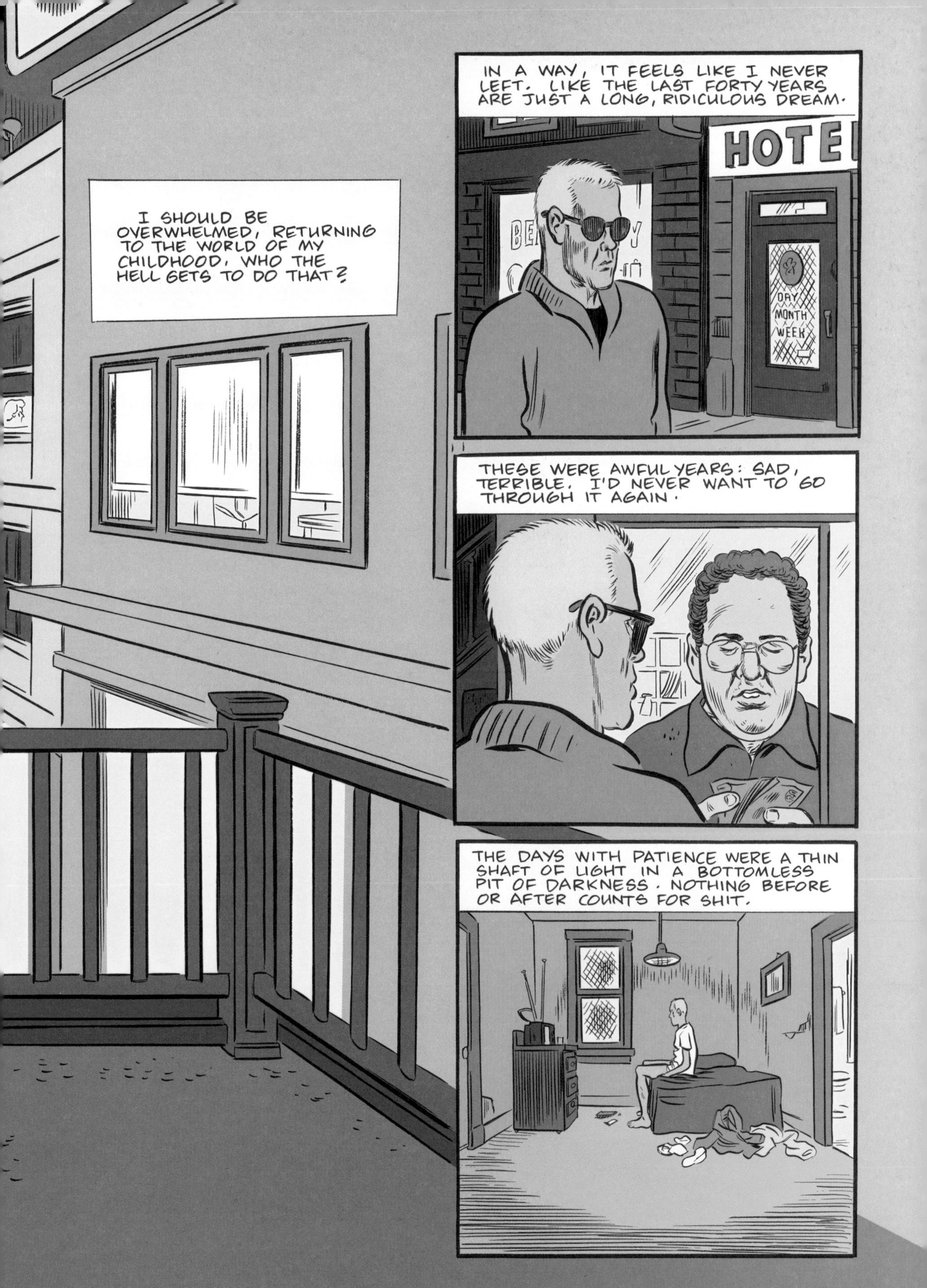
I SHOULD BE OVERWHELMED, RETURNING TO THE WORLD OF MY CHILDHOOD. WHO THE HELL GETS TO DO THAT?
IN A WAY, IT FEELS LIKE I NEVER LEFT. LIKE THE LAST FORTY YEARS ARE JUST A LONG, RIDICULOUS DREAM.
HOTE
DAY
MONTH
WEEK
THESE WERE AWFUL YEARS: SAD, TERRIBLE. I'D NEVER WANT TO GO THROUGH IT AGAIN.
THE DAYS WITH PATIENCE WERE A THIN SHAFT OF LIGHT IN A BOTTOMLESS PIT OF DARKNESS. NOTHING BEFORE OR AFTER COUNTS FOR SHIT.

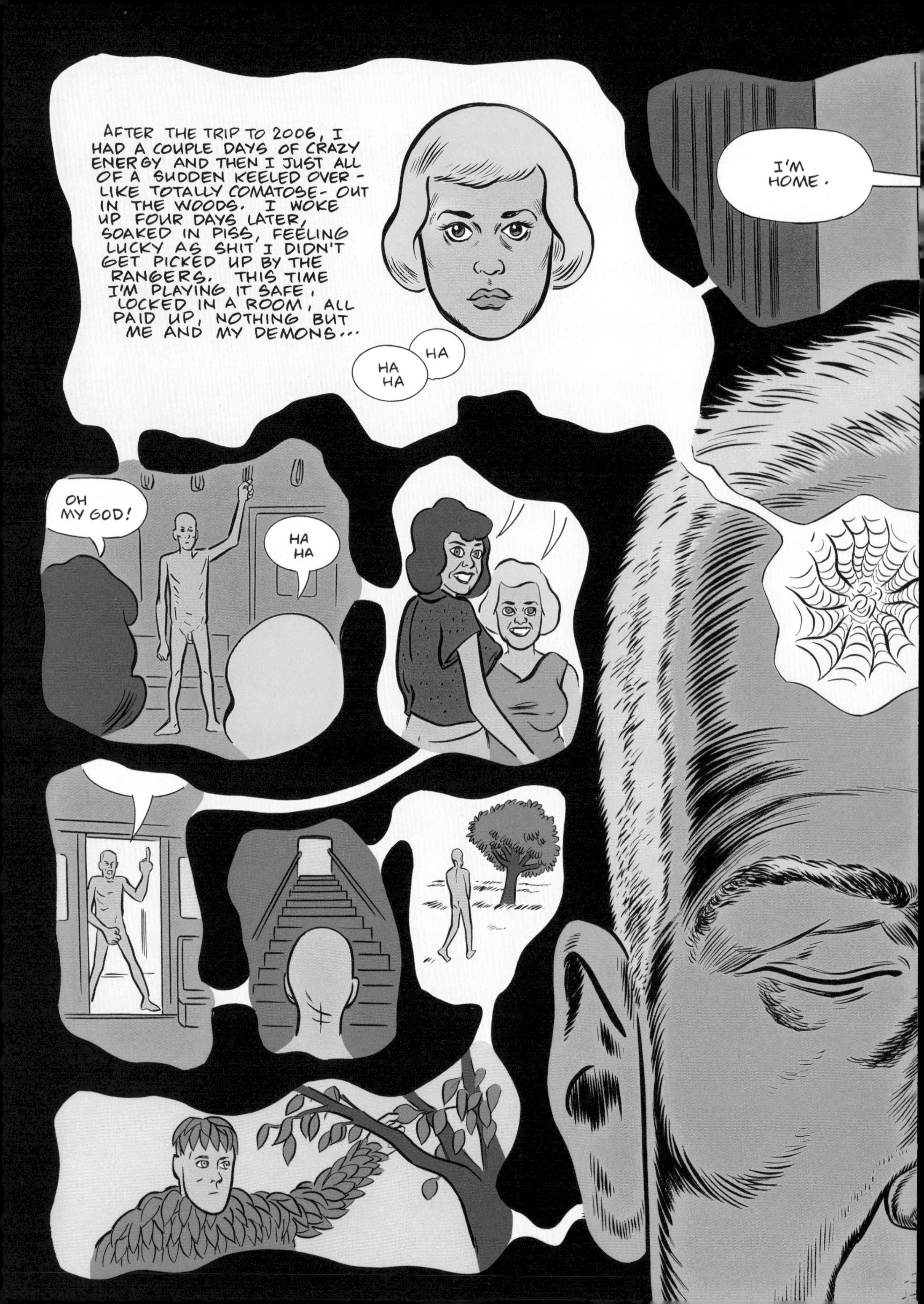
AFTER THE TRIP TO 2006, I HAD A COUPLE DAYS OF CRAZY ENERGY AND THEN I JUST ALL OF A SUDDEN KEELED OVER - LIKE TOTALLY COMATOSE- OUT IN THE WOODS. I WOKE UP FOUR DAYS LATER, SOAKED IN PISS, FEELING LUCKY AS SHIT I DIDN'T GET PICKED UP BY THE RANGERS. THIS TIME I'M PLAYING IT SAFE, LOCKED IN A ROOM, ALL PAID UP, NOTHING BUT ME AND MY DEMONS...
I'M HOME.
HA HA
HA
OH MY GOD!
HA HA

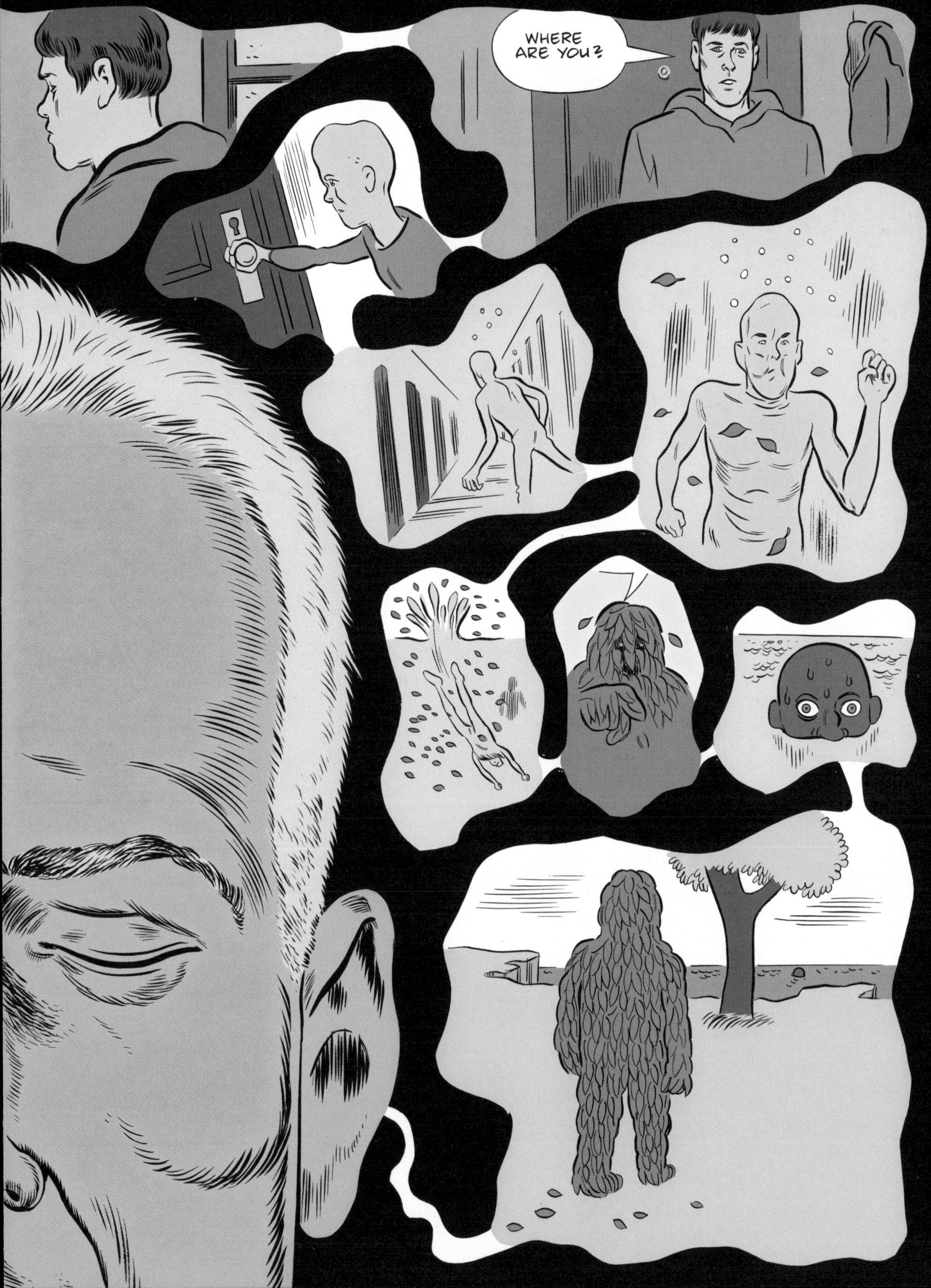
WHERE ARE YOU?

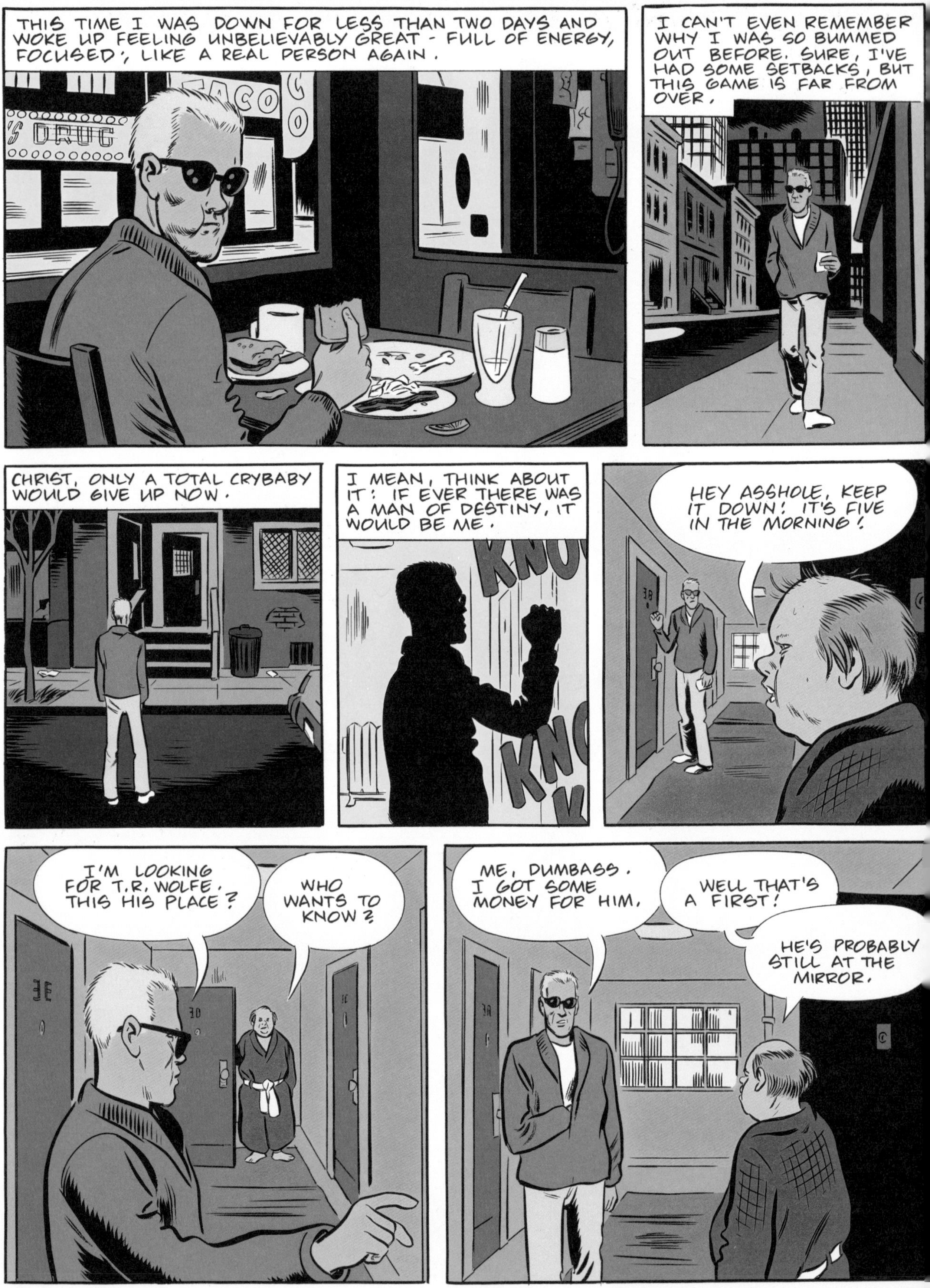
THIS TIME I WAS DOWN FOR LESS THAN TWO DAYS AND WOKE UP FEELING UNBELIEVABLY GREAT - FULL OF ENERGY, FOCUSED; LIKE A REAL PERSON AGAIN.
DRUG
TACO
I CAN'T EVEN REMEMBER WHY I WAS SO BUMMED OUT BEFORE. SURE, I'VE HAD SOME SETBACKS, BUT THIS GAME IS FAR FROM OVER.
CHRIST, ONLY A TOTAL CRYBABY WOULD GIVE UP NOW.
I MEAN, THINK ABOUT IT: IF EVER THERE WAS A MAN OF DESTINY, IT WOULD BE ME.
KNO
KNO
KNO
HEY ASSHOLE, KEEP IT DOWN! IT'S FIVE IN THE MORNING!
I'M LOOKING FOR T.R. WOLFE. THIS HIS PLACE?
WHO WANTS TO KNOW?
ME, DUMBASS. I GOT SOME MONEY FOR HIM.
WELL THAT'S A FIRST!
HE'S PROBABLY STILL AT THE MIRROR.

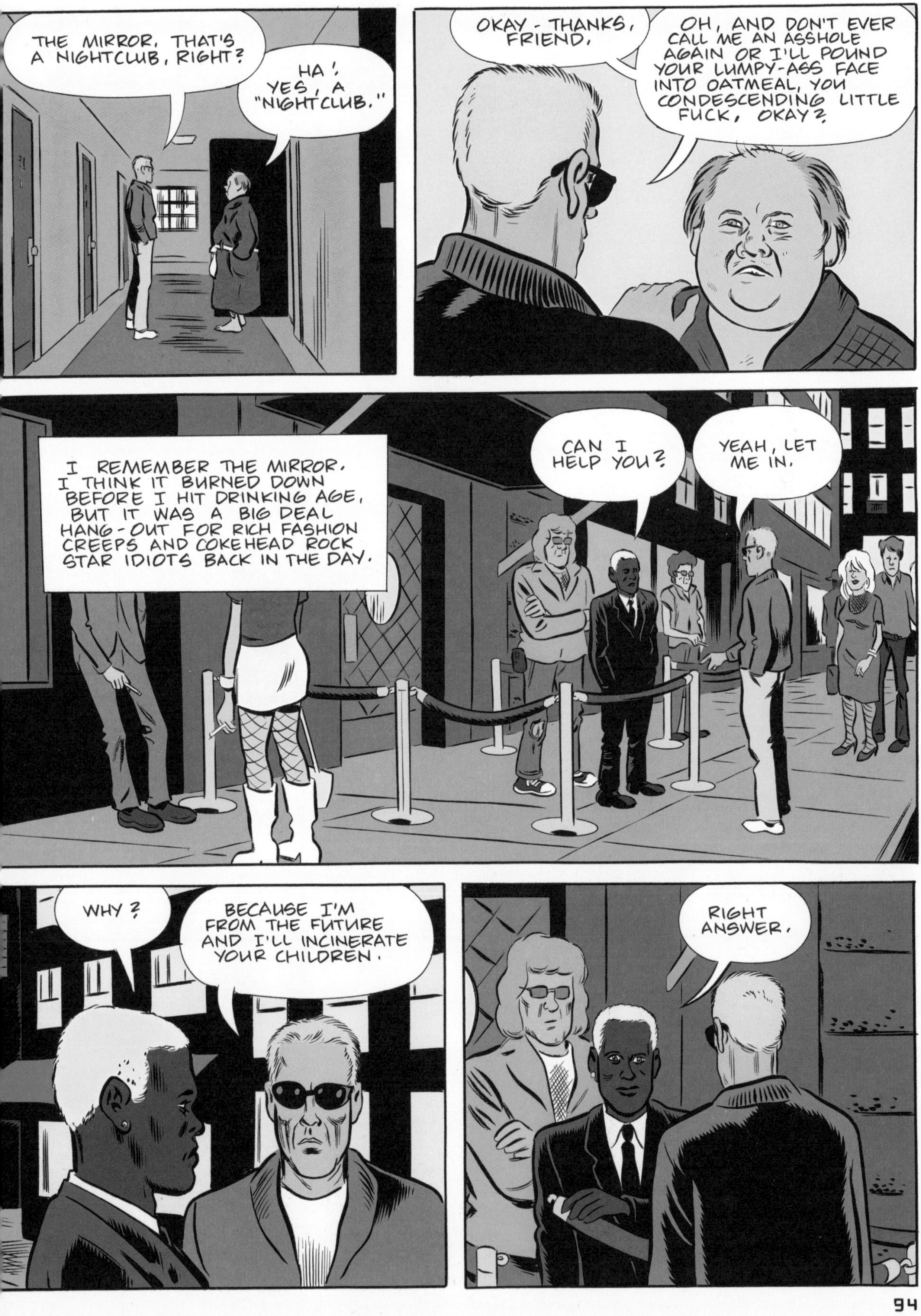
THE MIRROR, THAT'S A NIGHTCLUB, RIGHT?
HA! YES, A "NIGHTCLUB."
OKAY - THANKS, FRIEND.
OH, AND DON'T EVER CALL ME AN ASSHOLE AGAIN OR I'LL POUND YOUR LUMPY-ASS FACE INTO OATMEAL, YOU CONDESCENDING LITTLE FUCK, OKAY?
I REMEMBER THE MIRROR. I THINK IT BURNED DOWN BEFORE I HIT DRINKING AGE, BUT IT WAS A BIG DEAL HANG-OUT FOR RICH FASHION CREEPS AND COKEHEAD ROCK STAR IDIOTS BACK IN THE DAY.
CAN I HELP YOU?
YEAH, LET ME IN.
WHY?
BECAUSE I'M FROM THE FUTURE AND I'LL INCINERATE YOUR CHILDREN.
RIGHT ANSWER.

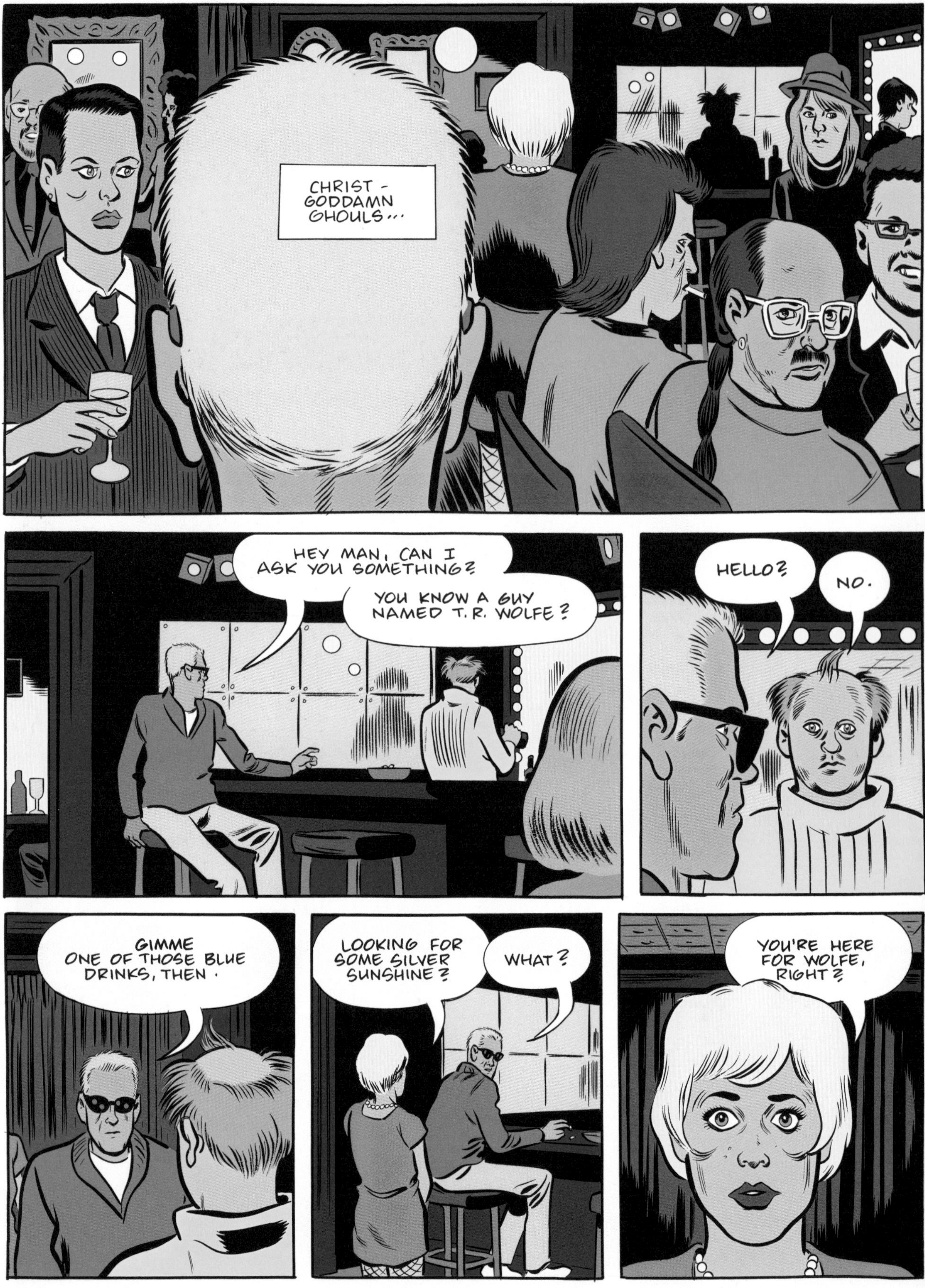

CHRIST - GODDAMN GHOULS...
HEY MAN, CAN I ASK YOU SOMETHING?
YOU KNOW A GUY NAMED T.R. WOLFE?
HELLO?
NO.
GIMME ONE OF THOSE BLUE DRINKS, THEN.
LOOKING FOR SOME SILVER SUNSHINE?
WHAT?
YOU'RE HERE FOR WOLFE, RIGHT?

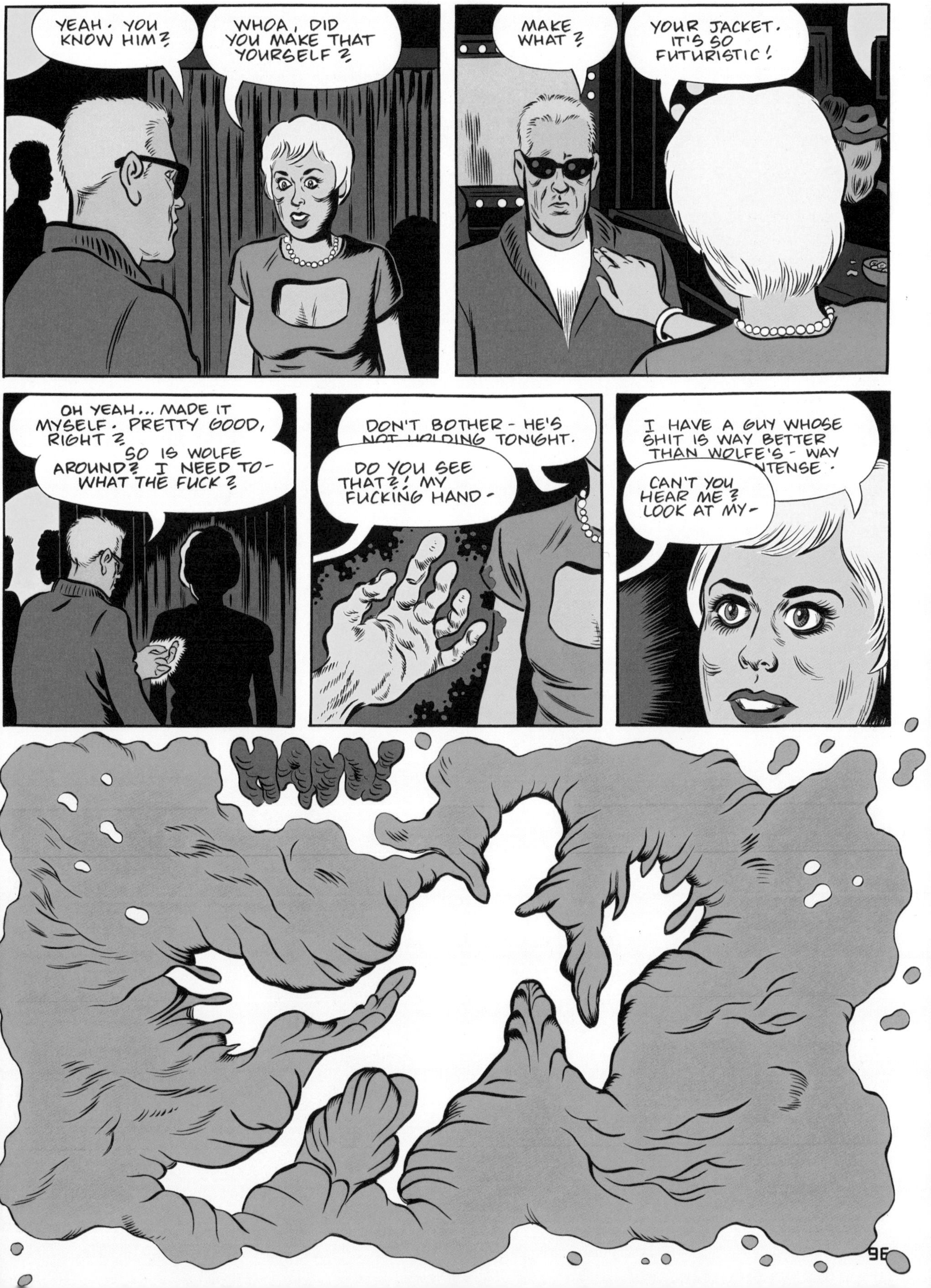
YEAH. YOU KNOW HIM?
WHOA, DID YOU MAKE THAT YOURSELF?
MAKE WHAT?
YOUR JACKET. IT'S SO FUTURISTIC!
OH YEAH... MADE IT MYSELF. PRETTY GOOD, RIGHT?
SO IS WOLFE AROUND? I NEED TO- WHAT THE FUCK?
DON'T BOTHER- HE'S NOT HOLDING TONIGHT.
DO YOU SEE THAT?! MY FUCKING HAND-
I HAVE A GUY WHOSE SHIT IS WAY BETTER THAN WOLFE'S- WAY
NTENSE.
CAN'T YOU HEAR ME? LOOK AT MY-

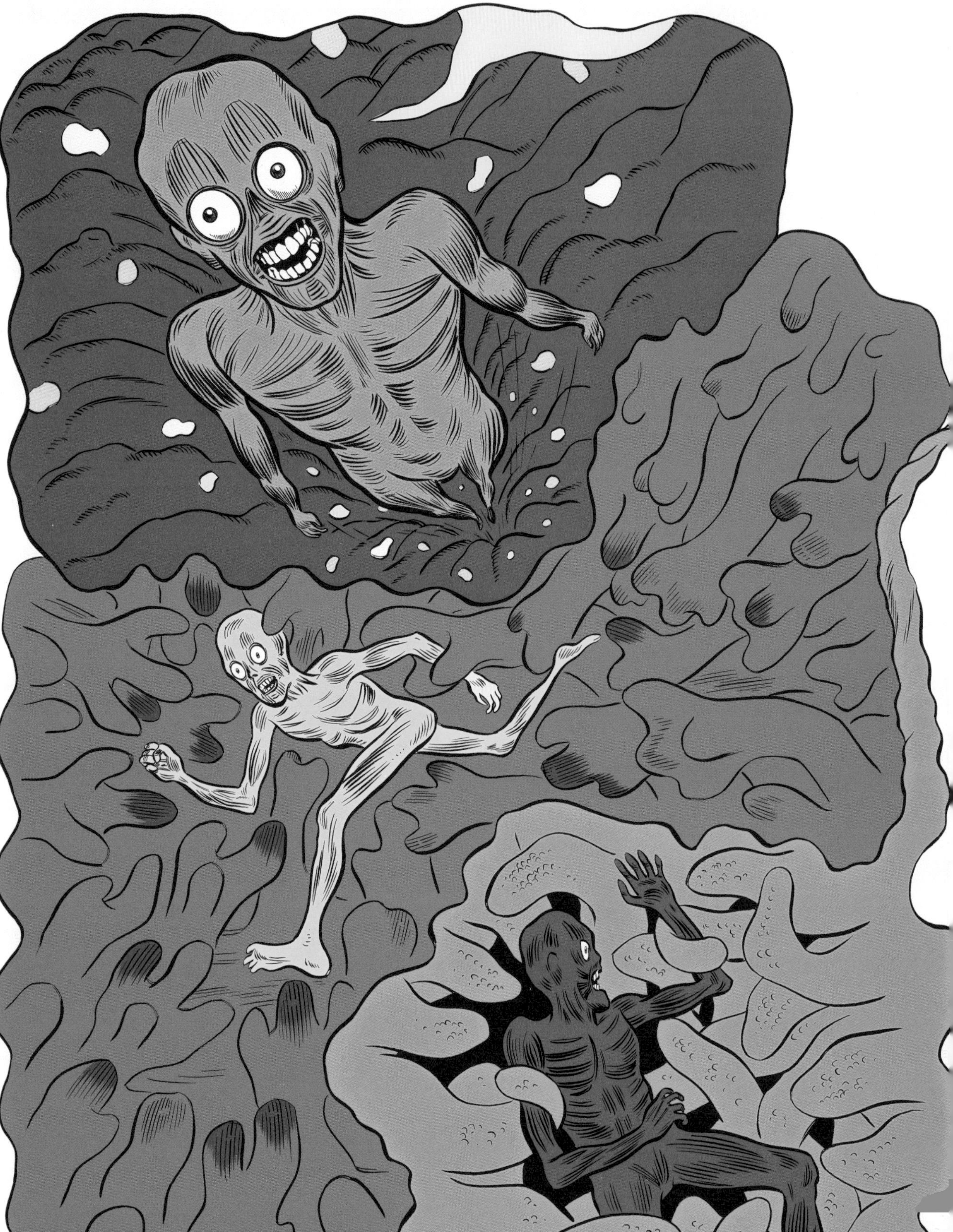

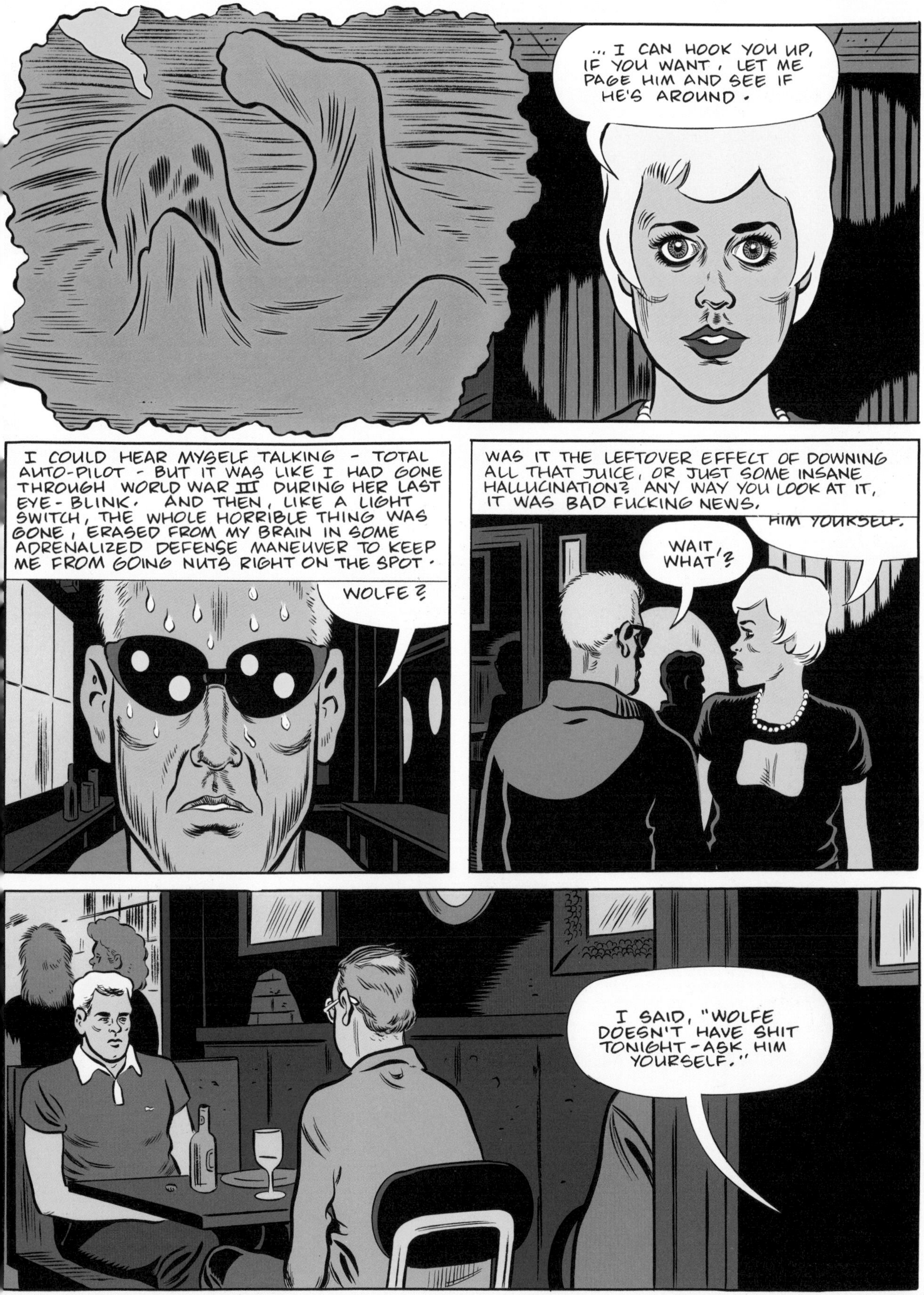
...I CAN HOOK YOU UP, IF YOU WANT, LET ME PAGE HIM AND SEE IF HE'S AROUND.
I COULD HEAR MYSELF TALKING - TOTAL AUTO-PILOT - BUT IT WAS LIKE I HAD GONE THROUGH WORLD WAR III DURING HER LAST EYE-BLINK. AND THEN, LIKE A LIGHT SWITCH, THE WHOLE HORRIBLE THING WAS GONE, ERASED FROM MY BRAIN IN SOME ADRENALIZED DEFENSE MANEUVER TO KEEP ME FROM GOING NUTS RIGHT ON THE SPOT.
WOLFE?
WAS IT THE LEFTOVER EFFECT OF DOWNING ALL THAT JUICE, OR JUST SOME INSANE HALLUCINATION? ANY WAY YOU LOOK AT IT, IT WAS BAD FUCKING NEWS.
HIM YOURSELF.
WAIT, WHAT?
I SAID, "WOLFE DOESN'T HAVE SHIT TONIGHT-ASK HIM YOURSELF."

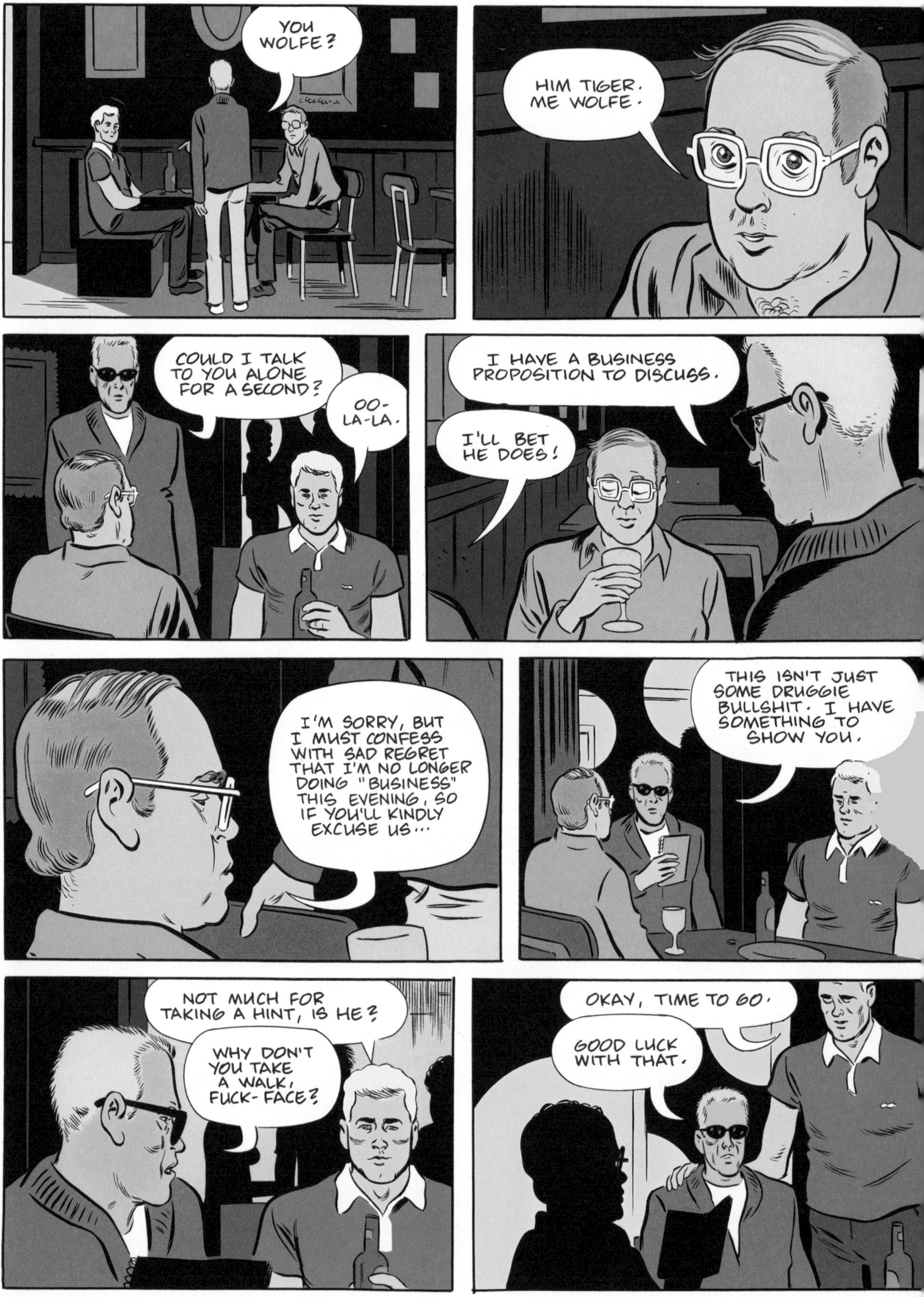
YOU WOLFE?
HIM TIGER. ME WOLFE.
COULD I TALK TO YOU ALONE FOR A SECOND?
OO-LA-LA.
I HAVE A BUSINESS PROPOSITION TO DISCUSS.
I'LL BET HE DOES!
I'M SORRY, BUT I MUST CONFESS WITH SAD REGRET THAT I'M NO LONGER DOING "BUSINESS" THIS EVENING, SO IF YOU'LL KINDLY EXCUSE US...
THIS ISN'T JUST SOME DRUGGIE BULLSHIT. I HAVE SOMETHING TO SHOW YOU.
NOT MUCH FOR TAKING A HINT, IS HE?
WHY DON'T YOU TAKE A WALK, FUCK-FACE?
OKAY, TIME TO GO.
GOOD LUCK WITH THAT.

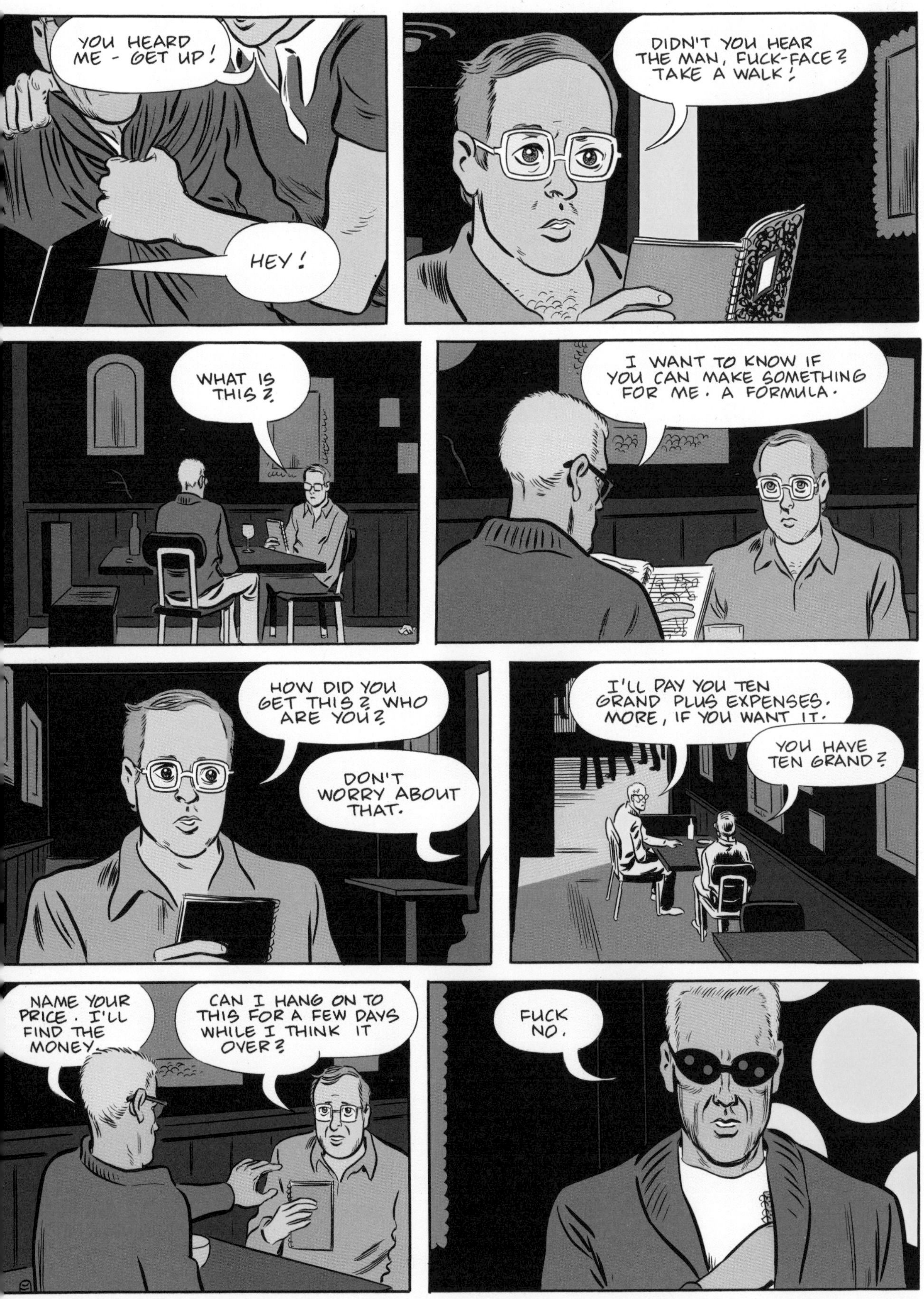
YOU HEARD ME - GET UP!
HEY!
DIDN'T YOU HEAR THE MAN, FUCK-FACE? TAKE A WALK!
WHAT IS THIS?
I WANT TO KNOW IF YOU CAN MAKE SOMETHING FOR ME. A FORMULA.
HOW DID YOU GET THIS? WHO ARE YOU?
DON'T WORRY ABOUT THAT.
I'LL PAY YOU TEN GRAND PLUS EXPENSES. MORE, IF YOU WANT IT.
YOU HAVE TEN GRAND?
NAME YOUR PRICE. I'LL FIND THE MONEY.
CAN I HANG ON TO THIS FOR A FEW DAYS WHILE I THINK IT OVER?
FUCK NO.

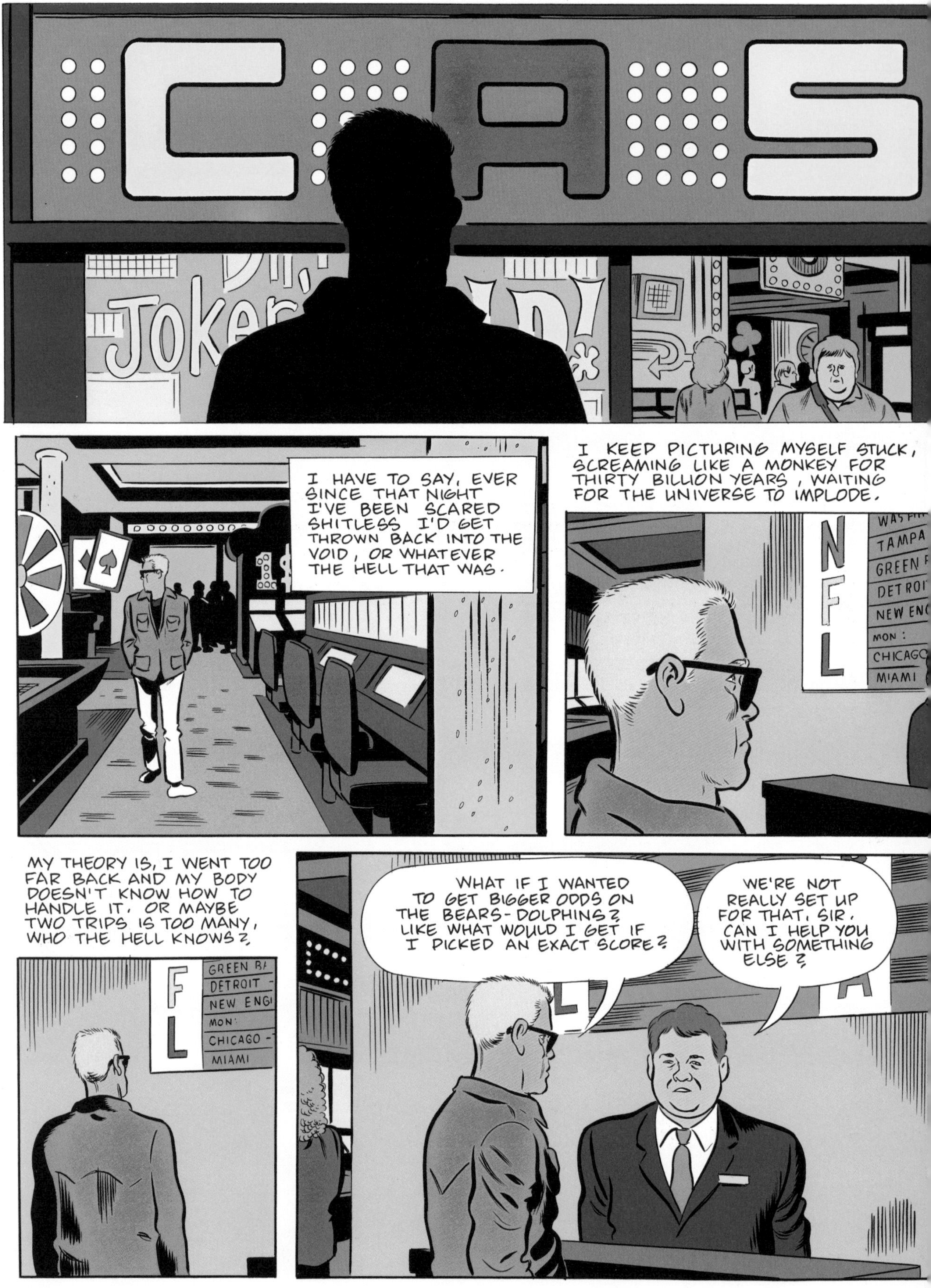
CAS
Joker'
I HAVE TO SAY, EVER SINCE THAT NIGHT I'VE BEEN SCARED SHITLESS I'D GET THROWN BACK INTO THE VOID, OR WHATEVER THE HELL THAT WAS.
I KEEP PICTURING MYSELF STUCK, SCREAMING LIKE A MONKEY FOR THIRTY BILLION YEARS, WAITING FOR THE UNIVERSE TO IMPLODE.
NFL
TAMPA
DETROI
MON :
MIAMI
MY THEORY IS, I WENT TOO FAR BACK AND MY BODY DOESN'T KNOW HOW TO HANDLE IT. OR MAYBE TWO TRIPS IS TOO MANY, WHO THE HELL KNOWS?
FL
DETROIT
MON:
CHICAGO
MIAMI
WHAT IF I WANTED TO GET BIGGER ODDS ON THE BEARS-DOLPHINS? LIKE WHAT WOULD I GET IF I PICKED AN EXACT SCORE?
WE'RE NOT REALLY SET UP FOR THAT, SIR. CAN I HELP YOU WITH SOMETHING ELSE?

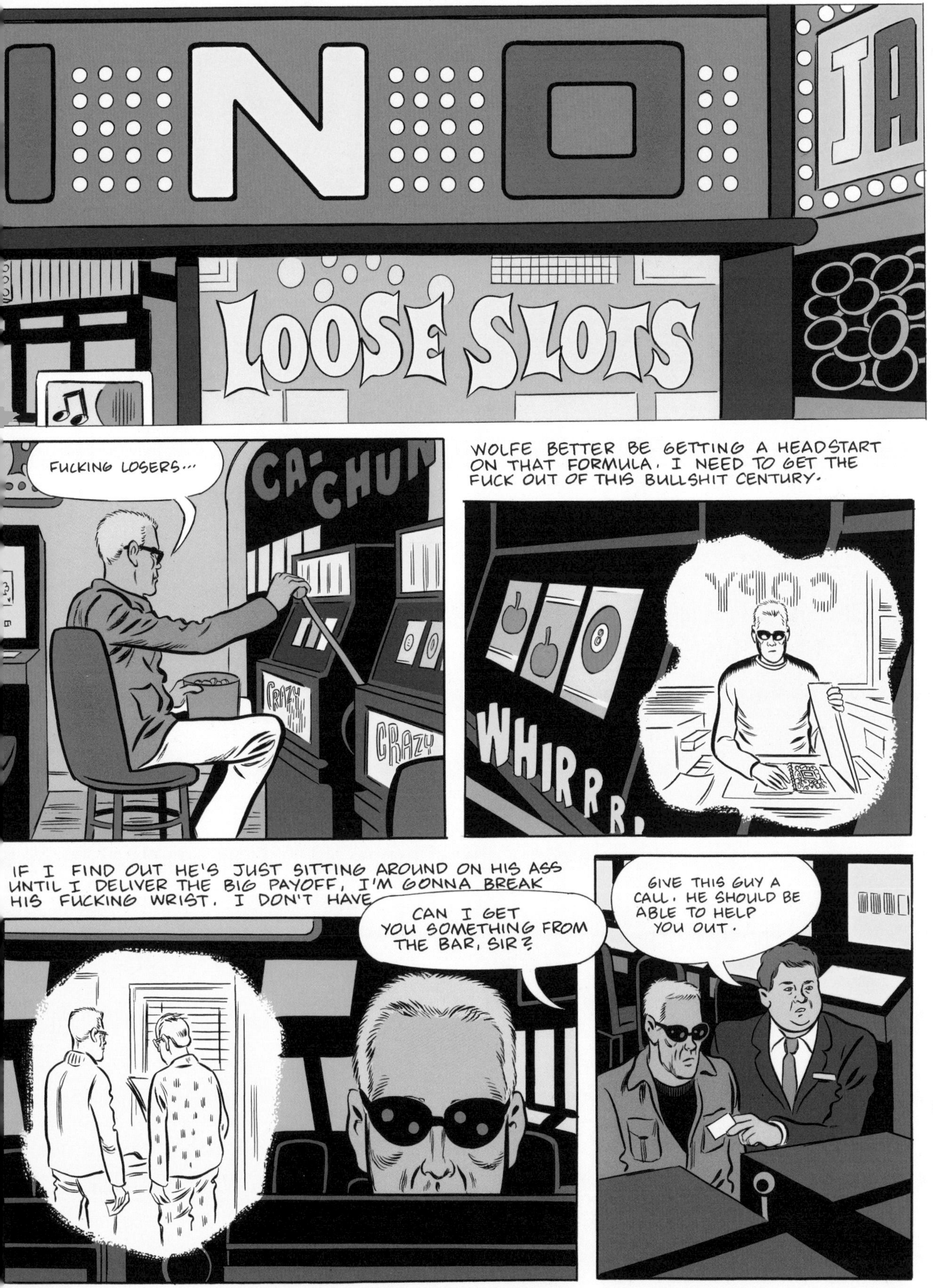
LOOSE SLOTS
FUCKING LOSERS...
CA-CHUN
CRAZY
CRAZY
WOLFE BETTER BE GETTING A HEADSTART ON THAT FORMULA. I NEED TO GET THE FUCK OUT OF THIS BULLSHIT CENTURY.
WHIRRR.
IF I FIND OUT HE'S JUST SITTING AROUND ON HIS ASS UNTIL I DELIVER THE BIG PAYOFF, I'M GONNA BREAK HIS FUCKING WRIST. I DON'T HAVE
CAN I GET YOU SOMETHING FROM THE BAR, SIR?
GIVE THIS GUY A CALL. HE SHOULD BE ABLE TO HELP YOU OUT.

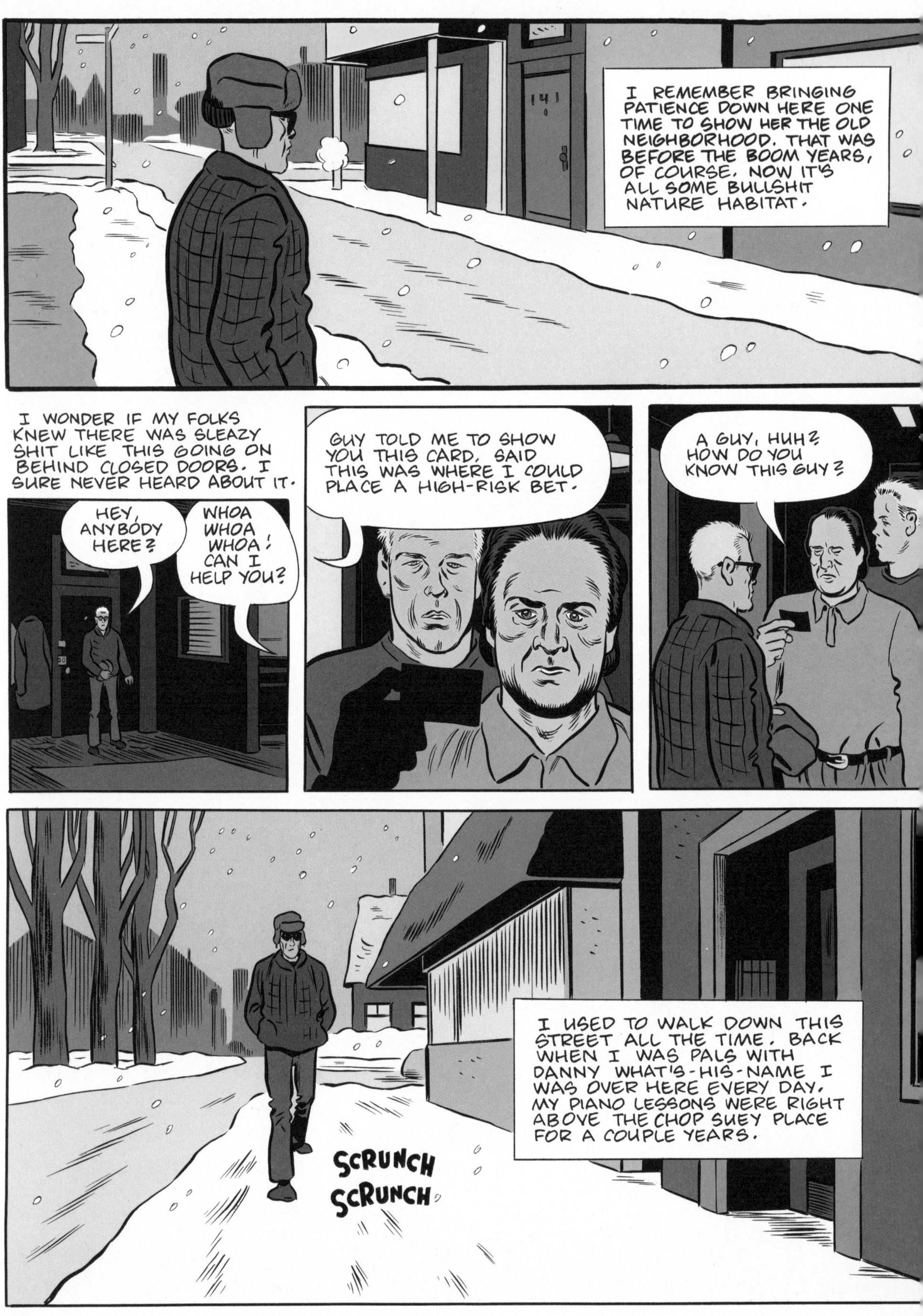
I REMEMBER BRINGING PATIENCE DOWN HERE ONE TIME TO SHOW HER THE OLD NEIGHBORHOOD. THAT WAS BEFORE THE BOOM YEARS, OF COURSE. NOW IT'S ALL SOME BULLSHIT NATURE HABITAT.
I WONDER IF MY FOLKS KNEW THERE WAS SLEAZY SHIT LIKE THIS GOING ON BEHIND CLOSED DOORS. I SURE NEVER HEARD ABOUT IT.
HEY, ANYBODY HERE?
WHOA WHOA WHOA! CAN I HELP YOU?
GUY TOLD ME TO SHOW YOU THIS CARD. SAID THIS WAS WHERE I COULD PLACE A HIGH-RISK BET.
A GUY, HUH? HOW DO YOU KNOW THIS GUY?
I USED TO WALK DOWN THIS STREET ALL THE TIME. BACK WHEN I WAS PALS WITH DANNY WHAT'S-HIS-NAME I WAS OVER HERE EVERY DAY. MY PIANO LESSONS WERE RIGHT ABOVE THE CHOP SUEY PLACE FOR A COUPLE YEARS.
SCRUNCH
SCRUNCH

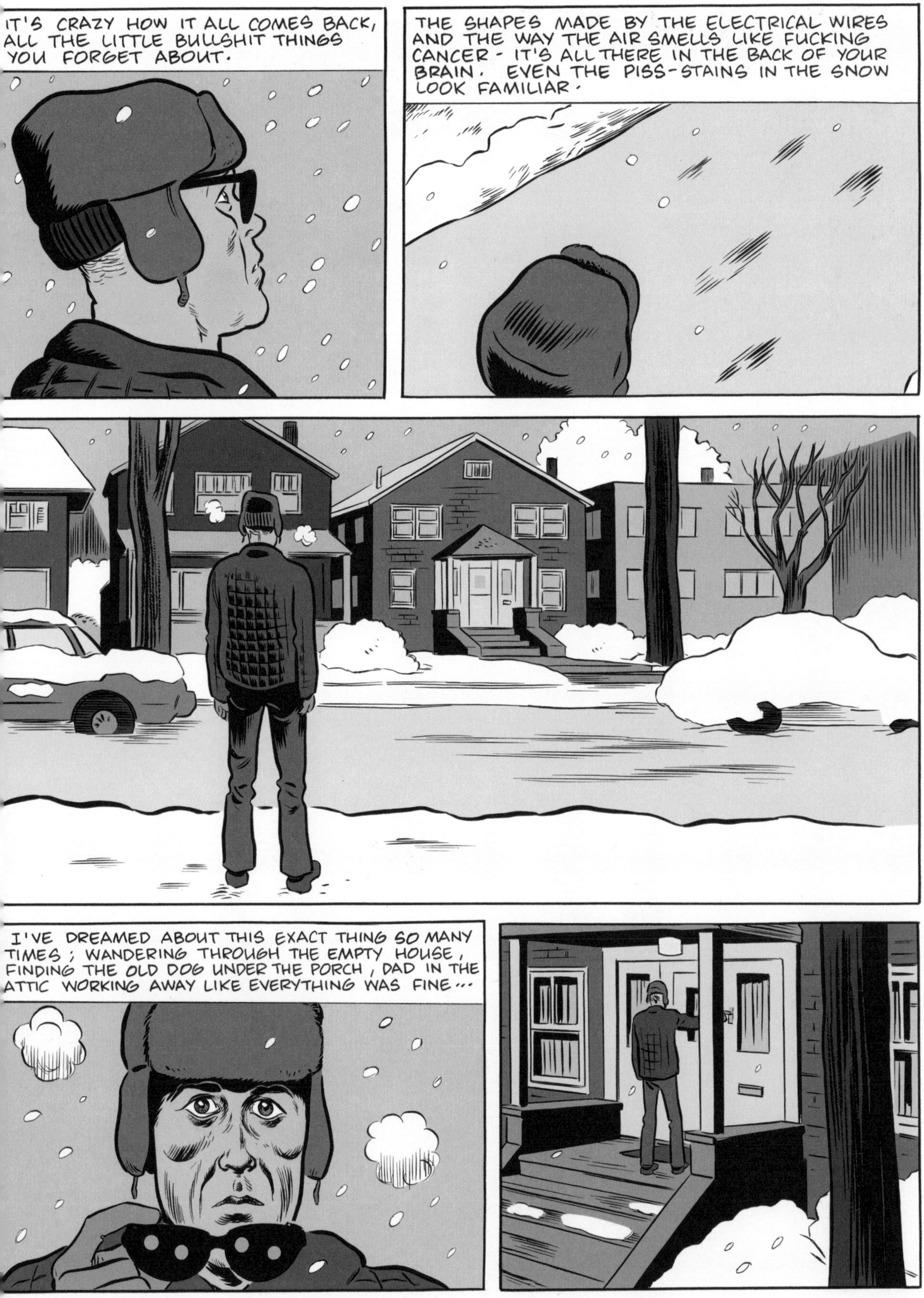
IT'S CRAZY HOW IT ALL COMES BACK, ALL THE LITTLE BULLSHIT THINGS YOU FORGET ABOUT.
THE SHAPES MADE BY THE ELECTRICAL WIRES AND THE WAY THE AIR SMELLS LIKE FUCKING CANCER - IT'S ALL THERE IN THE BACK OF YOUR BRAIN. EVEN THE PISS-STAINS IN THE SNOW LOOK FAMILIAR.
I'VE DREAMED ABOUT THIS EXACT THING SO MANY TIMES; WANDERING THROUGH THE EMPTY HOUSE, FINDING THE OLD DOG UNDER THE PORCH, DAD IN THE ATTIC WORKING AWAY LIKE EVERYTHING WAS FINE...

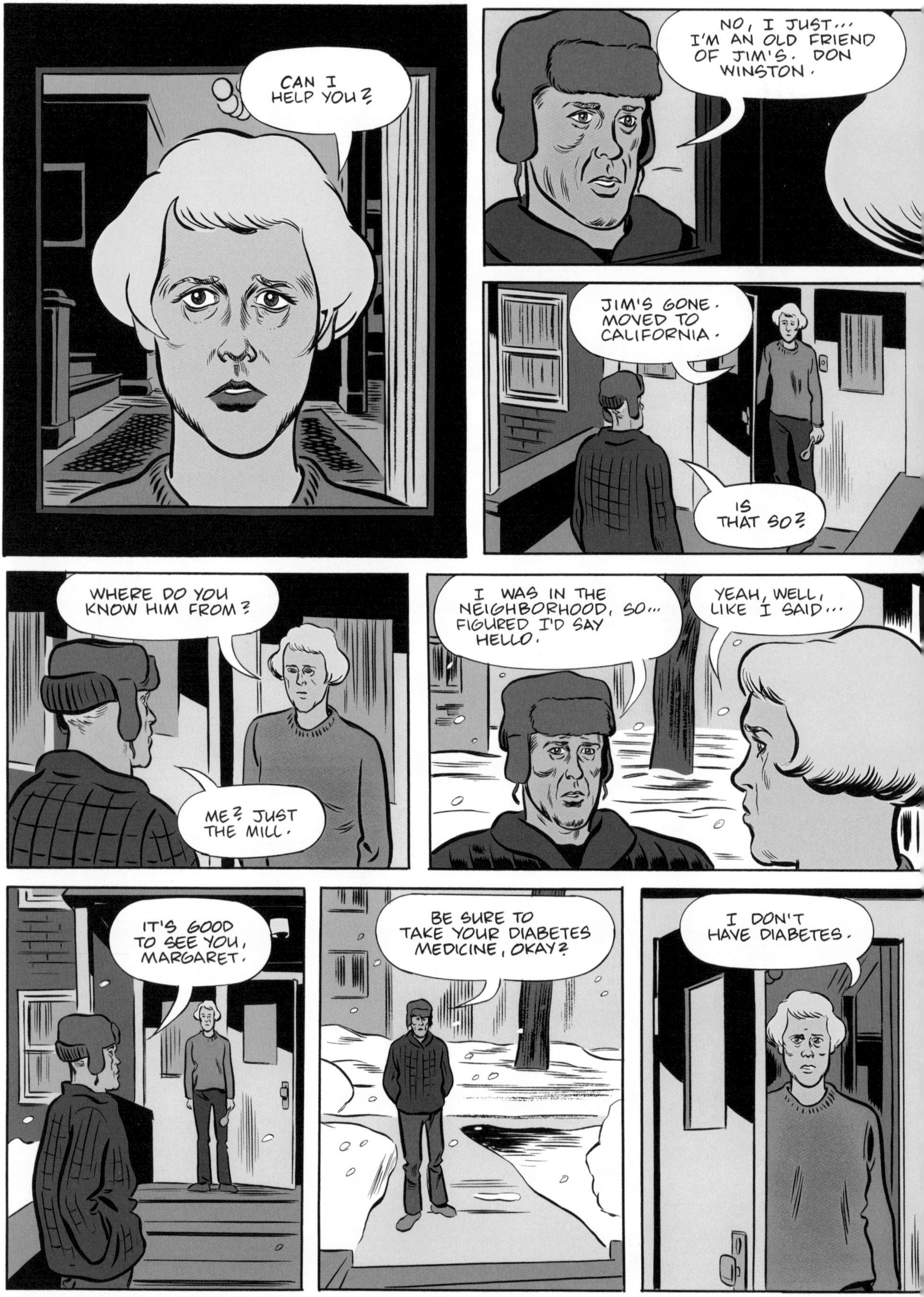
CAN I HELP YOU?
NO, I JUST... I'M AN OLD FRIEND OF JIM'S. DON WINSTON.
JIM'S GONE. MOVED TO CALIFORNIA.
IS THAT SO?
WHERE DO YOU KNOW HIM FROM?
ME? JUST THE MILL.
I WAS IN THE NEIGHBORHOOD, SO... FIGURED I'D SAY HELLO.
YEAH, WELL, LIKE I SAID...
IT'S GOOD TO SEE YOU, MARGARET.
BE SURE TO TAKE YOUR DIABETES MEDICINE, OKAY?
I DON'T HAVE DIABETES.

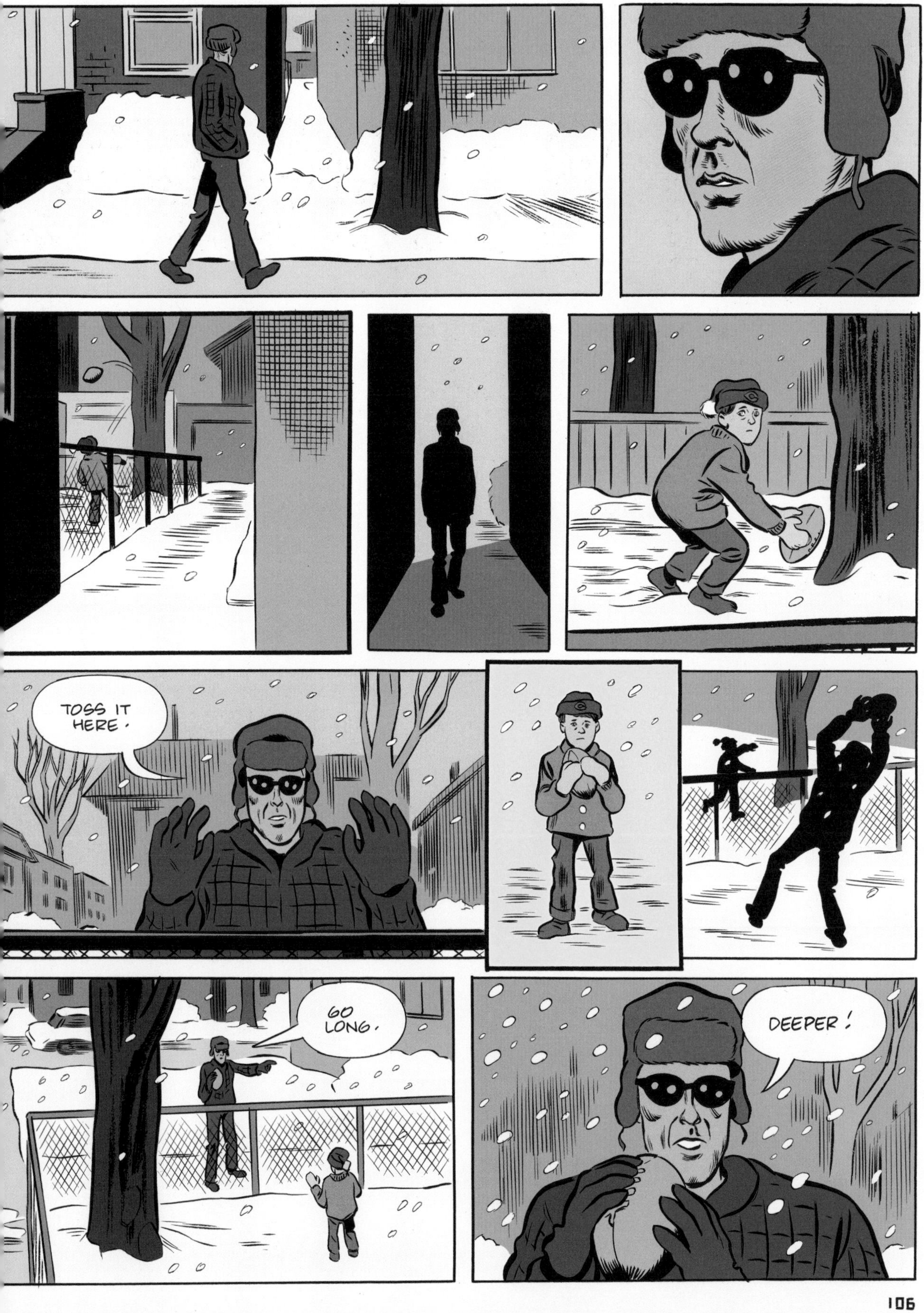
TOSS IT HERE.
GO LONG.
DEEPER!

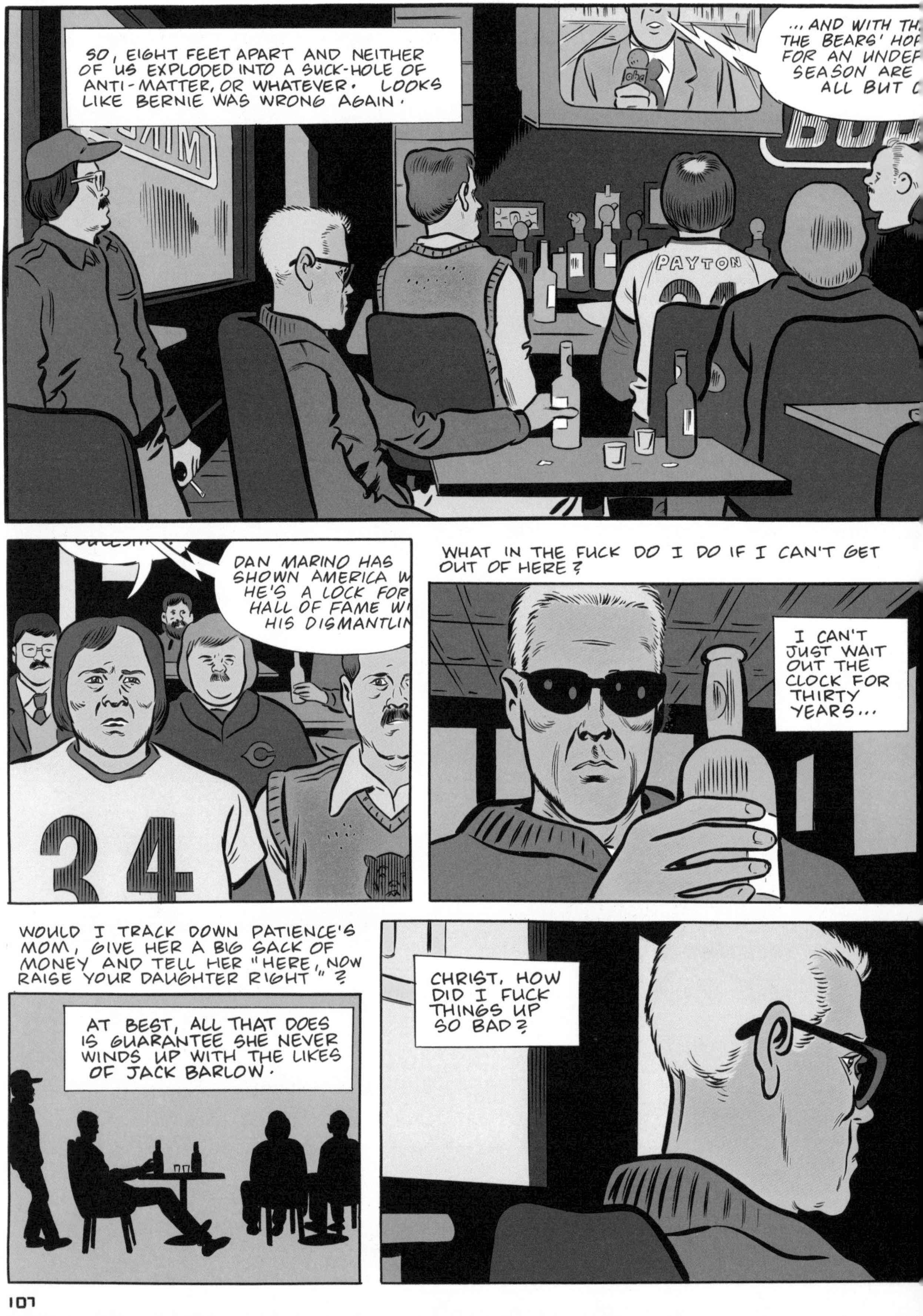
SO, EIGHT FEET APART AND NEITHER OF US EXPLODED INTO A SUCK-HOLE OF ANTI-MATTER, OR WHATEVER. LOOKS LIKE BERNIE WAS WRONG AGAIN.
...AND WITH TH THE BEARS' HOP FOR AN UNDER SEASON ARE ALL BUT
PAYTON
DAN MARINO HAS SHOWN AMERICA W HE'S A LOCK FOR HALL OF FAME WI HIS DISMANTLIN
WHAT IN THE FUCK DO I DO IF I CAN'T GET OUT OF HERE?
I CAN'T JUST WAIT OUT THE CLOCK FOR THIRTY YEARS...
WOULD I TRACK DOWN PATIENCE'S MOM, GIVE HER A BIG SACK OF MONEY AND TELL HER "HERE, NOW RAISE YOUR DAUGHTER RIGHT"?
AT BEST, ALL THAT DOES IS GUARANTEE SHE NEVER WINDS UP WITH THE LIKES OF JACK BARLOW.
CHRIST, HOW DID I FUCK THINGS UP SO BAD?

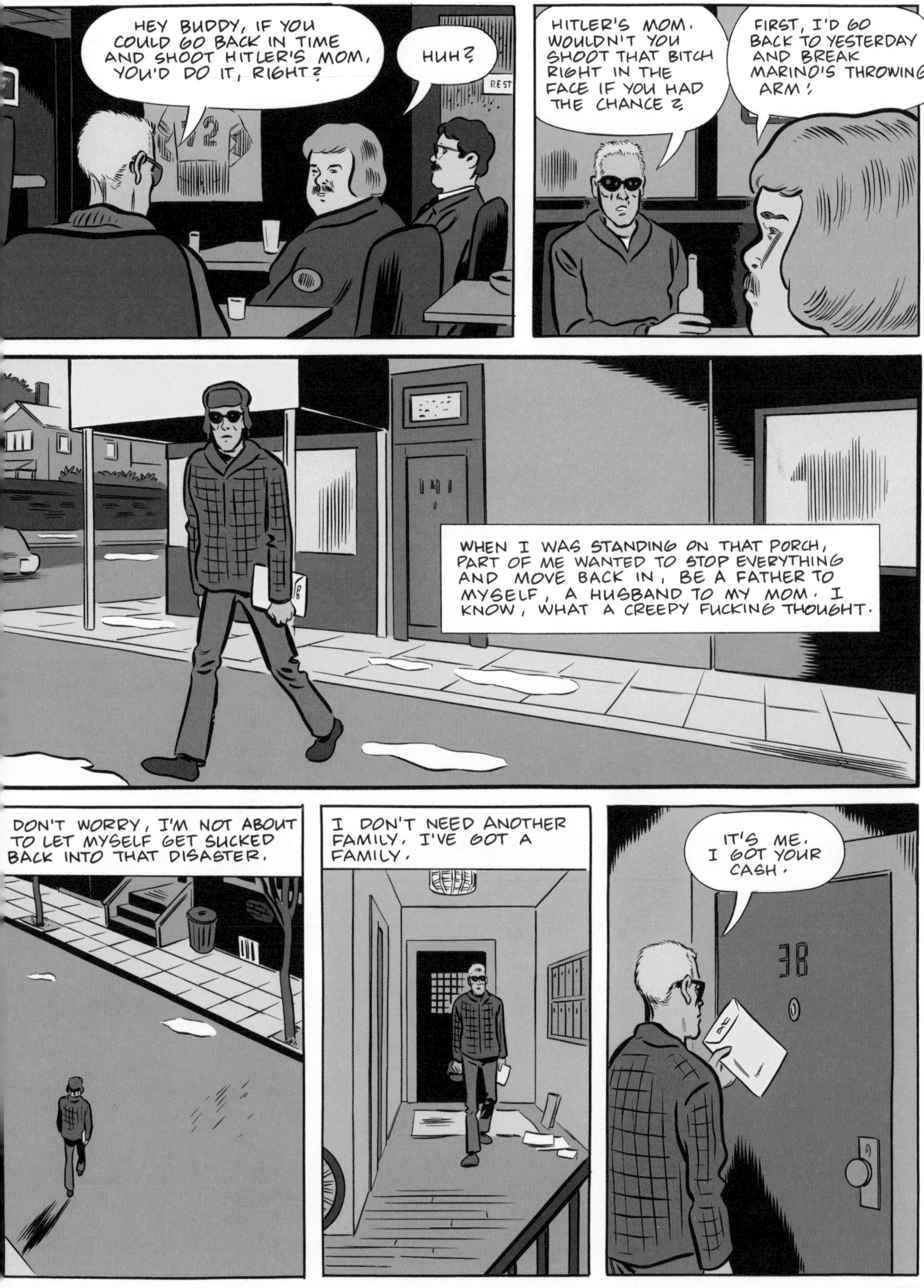
HEY BUDDY, IF YOU COULD GO BACK IN TIME AND SHOOT HITLER'S MOM, YOU'D DO IT, RIGHT?
HUH?
REST
HITLER'S MOM. WOULDN'T YOU SHOOT THAT BITCH RIGHT IN THE FACE IF YOU HAD THE CHANCE?
FIRST, I'D GO BACK TO YESTERDAY AND BREAK MARINO'S THROWING ARM!
141
WHEN I WAS STANDING ON THAT PORCH, PART OF ME WANTED TO STOP EVERYTHING AND MOVE BACK IN, BE A FATHER TO MYSELF, A HUSBAND TO MY MOM. I KNOW, WHAT A CREEPY FUCKING THOUGHT.
DON'T WORRY, I'M NOT ABOUT TO LET MYSELF GET SUCKED BACK INTO THAT DISASTER.
I DON'T NEED ANOTHER FAMILY. I'VE GOT A FAMILY.
IT'S ME. I GOT YOUR CASH.
38

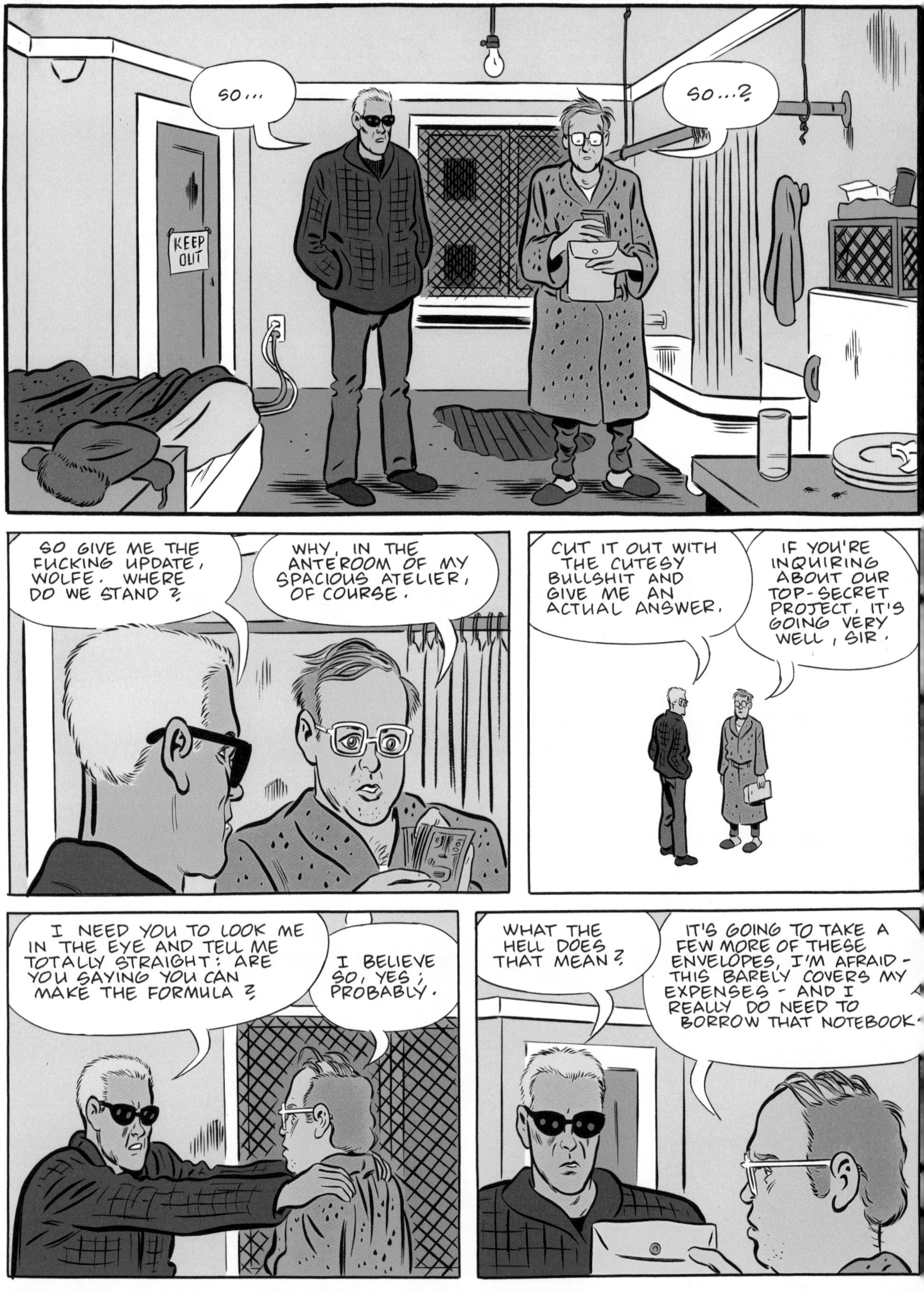
SO...
SO...?
SO GIVE ME THE FUCKING UPDATE, WOLFE. WHERE DO WE STAND?
WHY, IN THE ANTEROOM OF MY SPACIOUS ATELIER, OF COURSE.
CUT IT OUT WITH THE CUTESY BULLSHIT AND GIVE ME AN ACTUAL ANSWER.
IF YOU'RE INQUIRING ABOUT OUR TOP-SECRET PROJECT, IT'S GOING VERY WELL, SIR.
I NEED YOU TO LOOK ME IN THE EYE AND TELL ME TOTALLY STRAIGHT: ARE YOU SAYING YOU CAN MAKE THE FORMULA?
I BELIEVE SO, YES; PROBABLY.
WHAT THE HELL DOES THAT MEAN?
IT'S GOING TO TAKE A FEW MORE OF THESE ENVELOPES, I'M AFRAID - THIS BARELY COVERS MY EXPENSES - AND I REALLY DO NEED TO BORROW THAT NOTEBOOK.

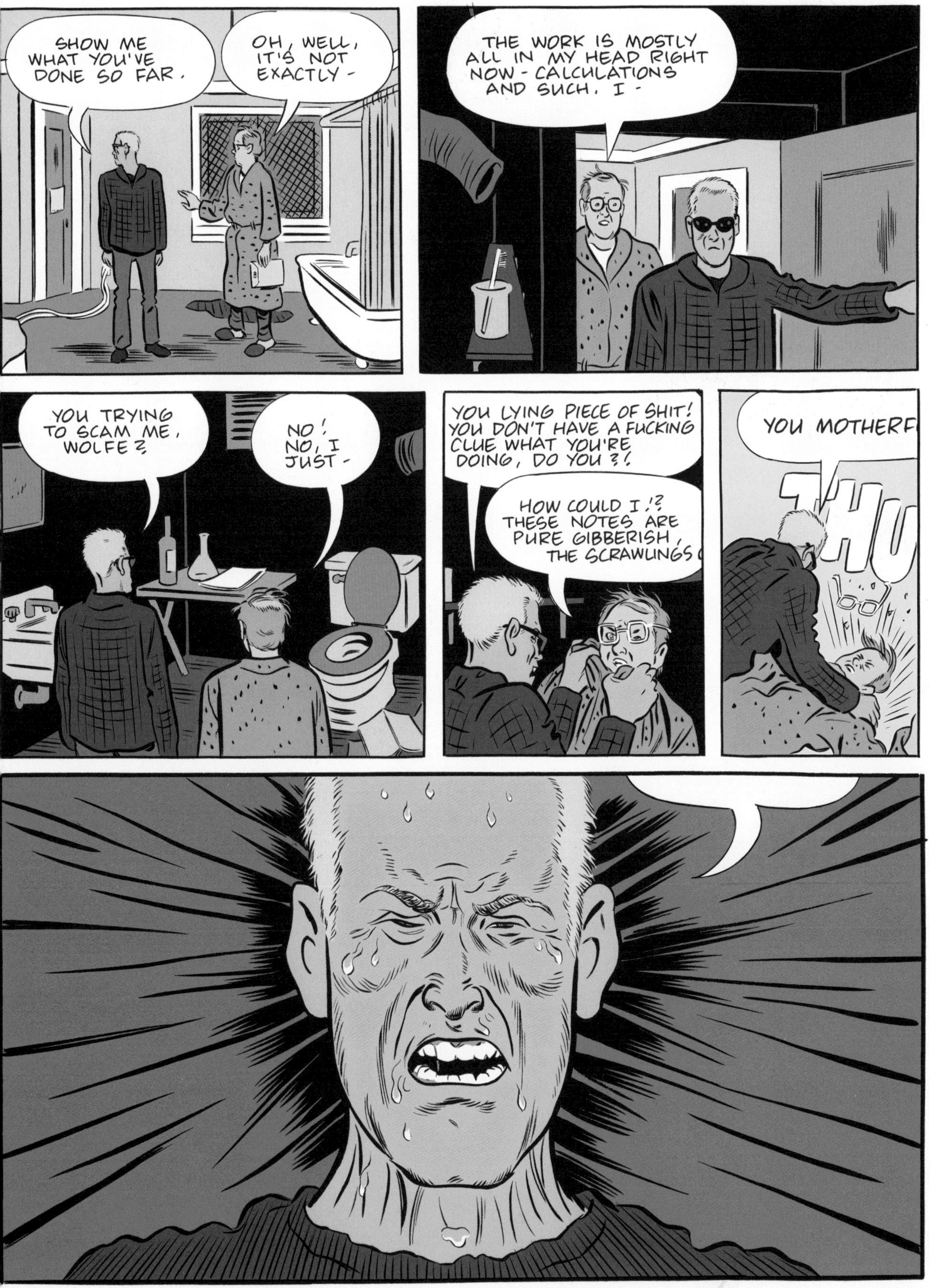
SHOW ME WHAT YOU'VE DONE SO FAR.
OH, WELL, IT'S NOT EXACTLY -
THE WORK IS MOSTLY ALL IN MY HEAD RIGHT NOW - CALCULATIONS AND SUCH. I -
YOU TRYING TO SCAM ME, WOLFE?
NO! NO, I JUST -
YOU LYING PIECE OF SHIT! YOU DON'T HAVE A FUCKING CLUE WHAT YOU'RE DOING, DO YOU?!
HOW COULD I!? THESE NOTES ARE PURE GIBBERISH, THE SCRAWLINGS
YOU MOTHERF

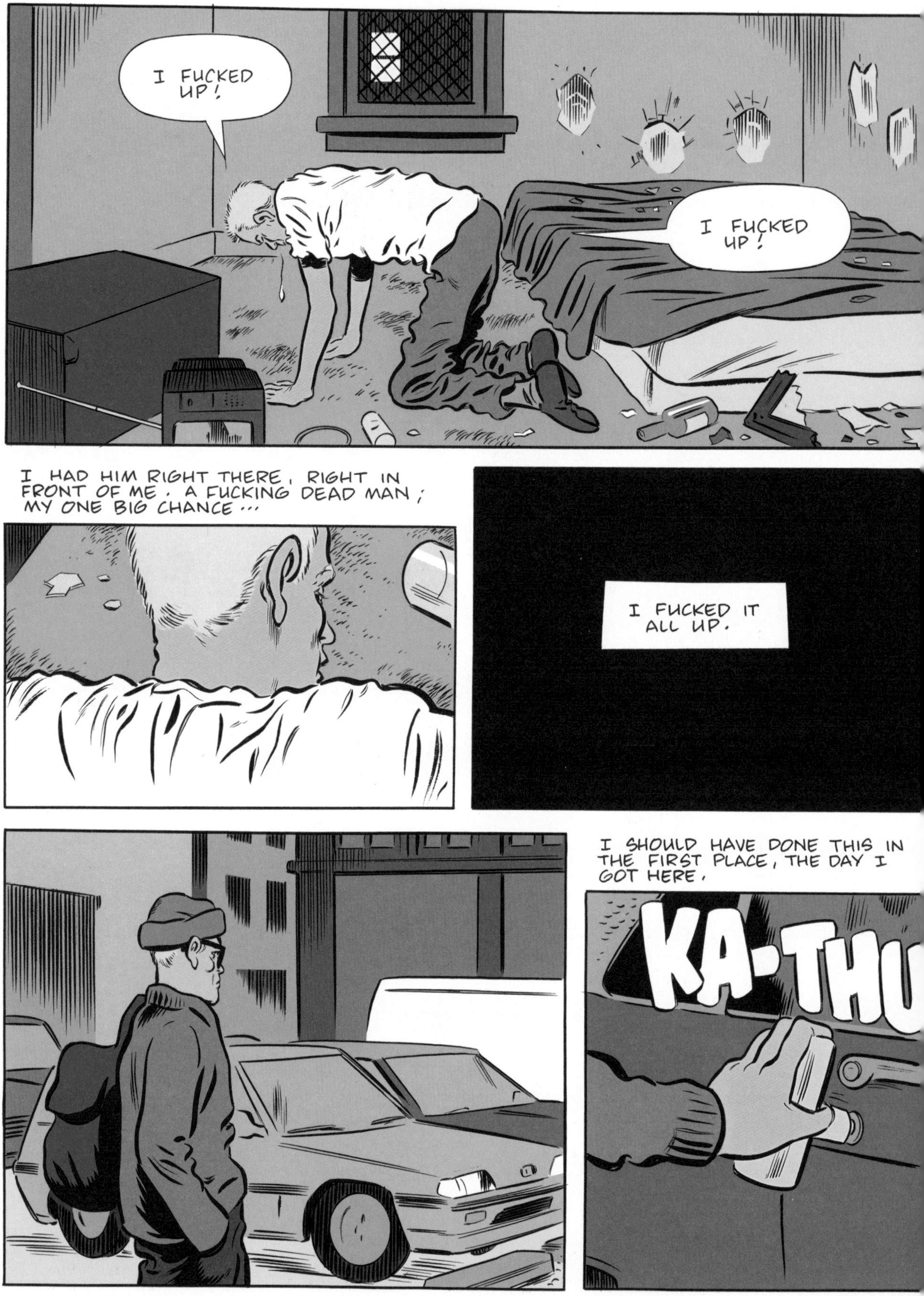
I FUCKED UP!
I FUCKED UP!
I HAD HIM RIGHT THERE, RIGHT IN FRONT OF ME. A FUCKING DEAD MAN; MY ONE BIG CHANCE...
I FUCKED IT ALL UP.
I SHOULD HAVE DONE THIS IN THE FIRST PLACE, THE DAY I GOT HERE.
KA-THU

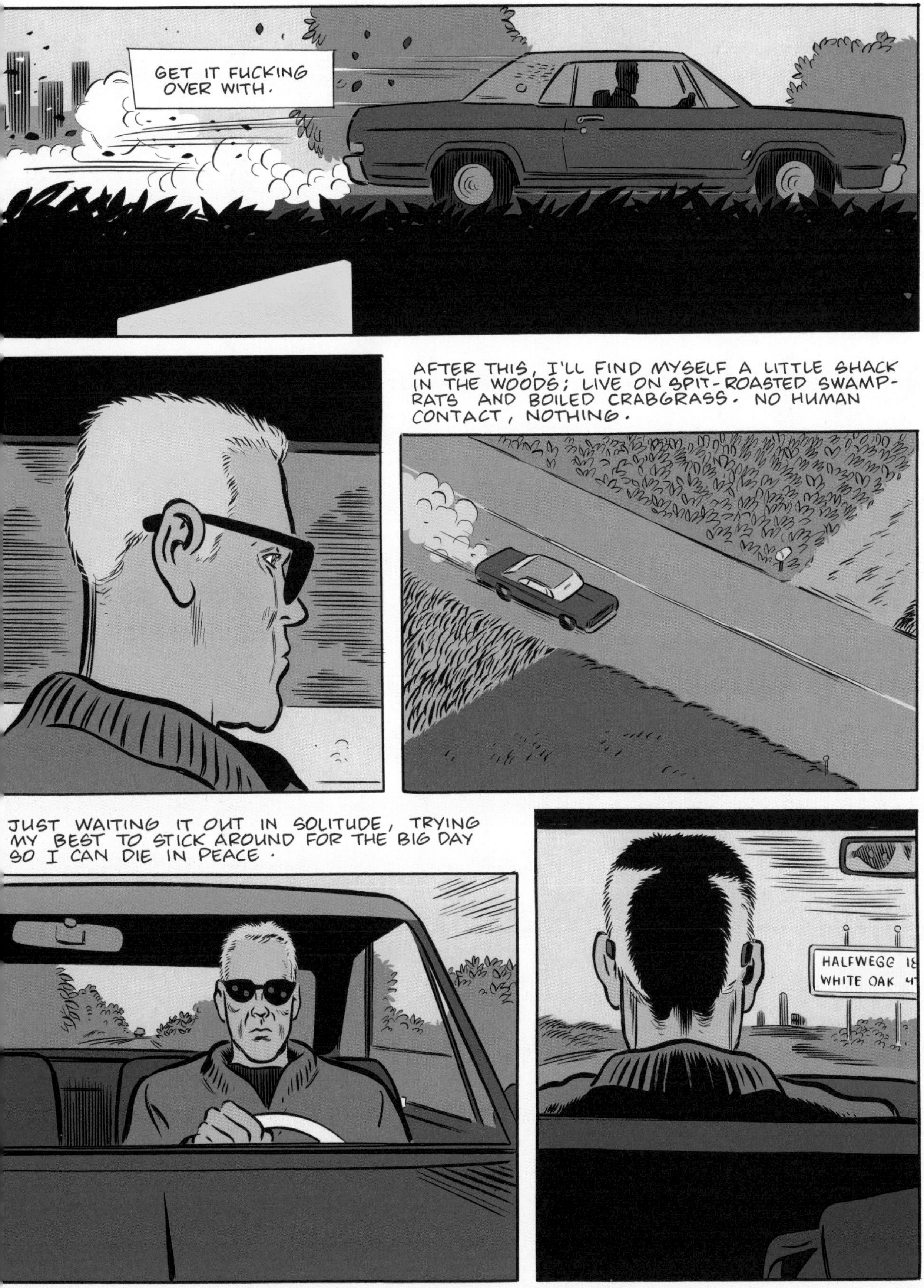
GET IT FUCKING OVER WITH.
AFTER THIS, I'LL FIND MYSELF A LITTLE SHACK IN THE WOODS; LIVE ON SPIT-ROASTED SWAMP-RATS AND BOILED CRABGRASS. NO HUMAN CONTACT, NOTHING.
JUST WAITING IT OUT IN SOLITUDE, TRYING MY BEST TO STICK AROUND FOR THE BIG DAY SO I CAN DIE IN PEACE.
HALFWEGE 18
WHITE OAK 4

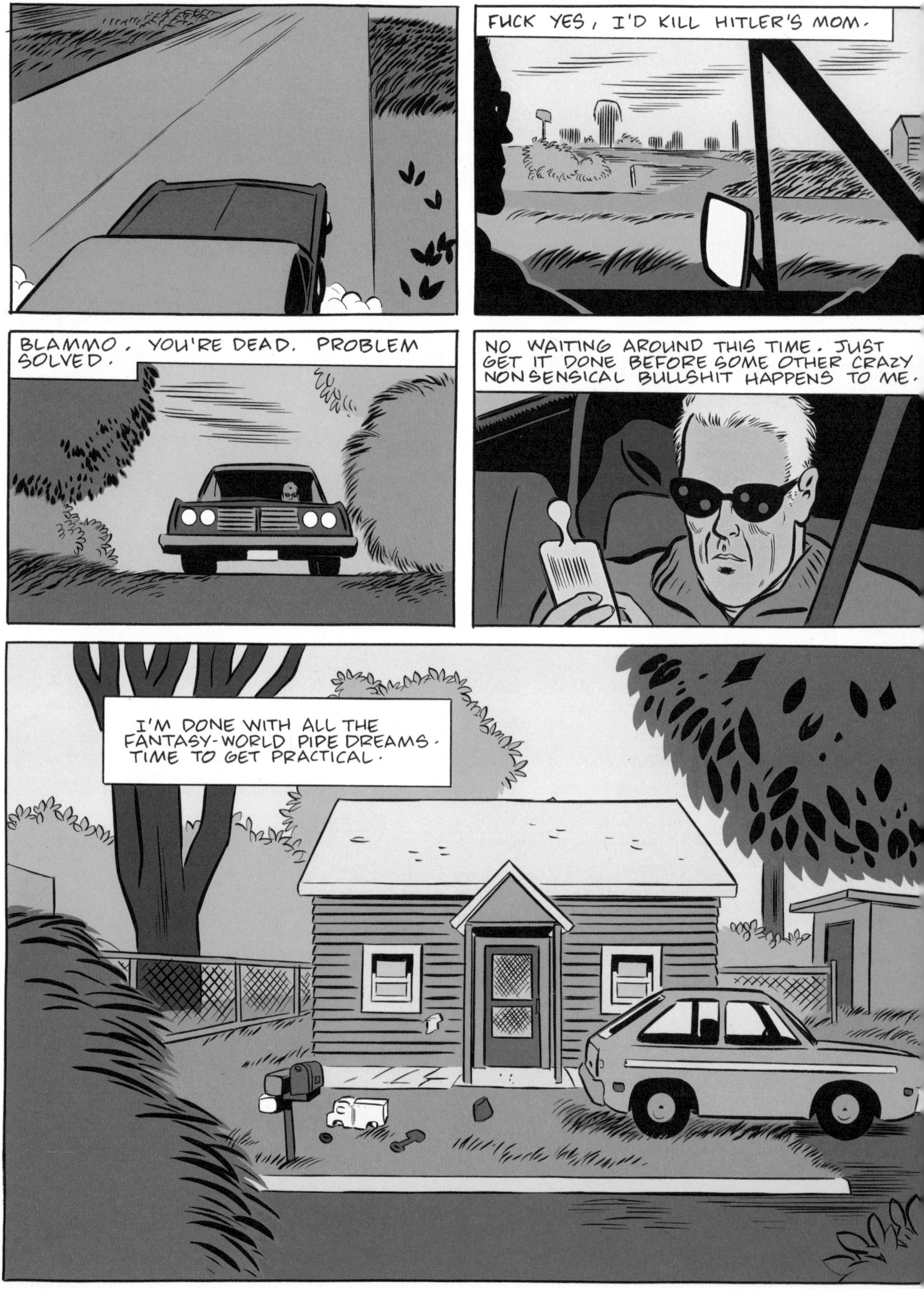
FUCK YES, I'D KILL HITLER'S MOM.
BLAMMO. YOU'RE DEAD. PROBLEM SOLVED.
NO WAITING AROUND THIS TIME. JUST GET IT DONE BEFORE SOME OTHER CRAZY NONSENSICAL BULLSHIT HAPPENS TO ME.
I'M DONE WITH ALL THE FANTASY-WORLD PIPE DREAMS. TIME TO GET PRACTICAL.

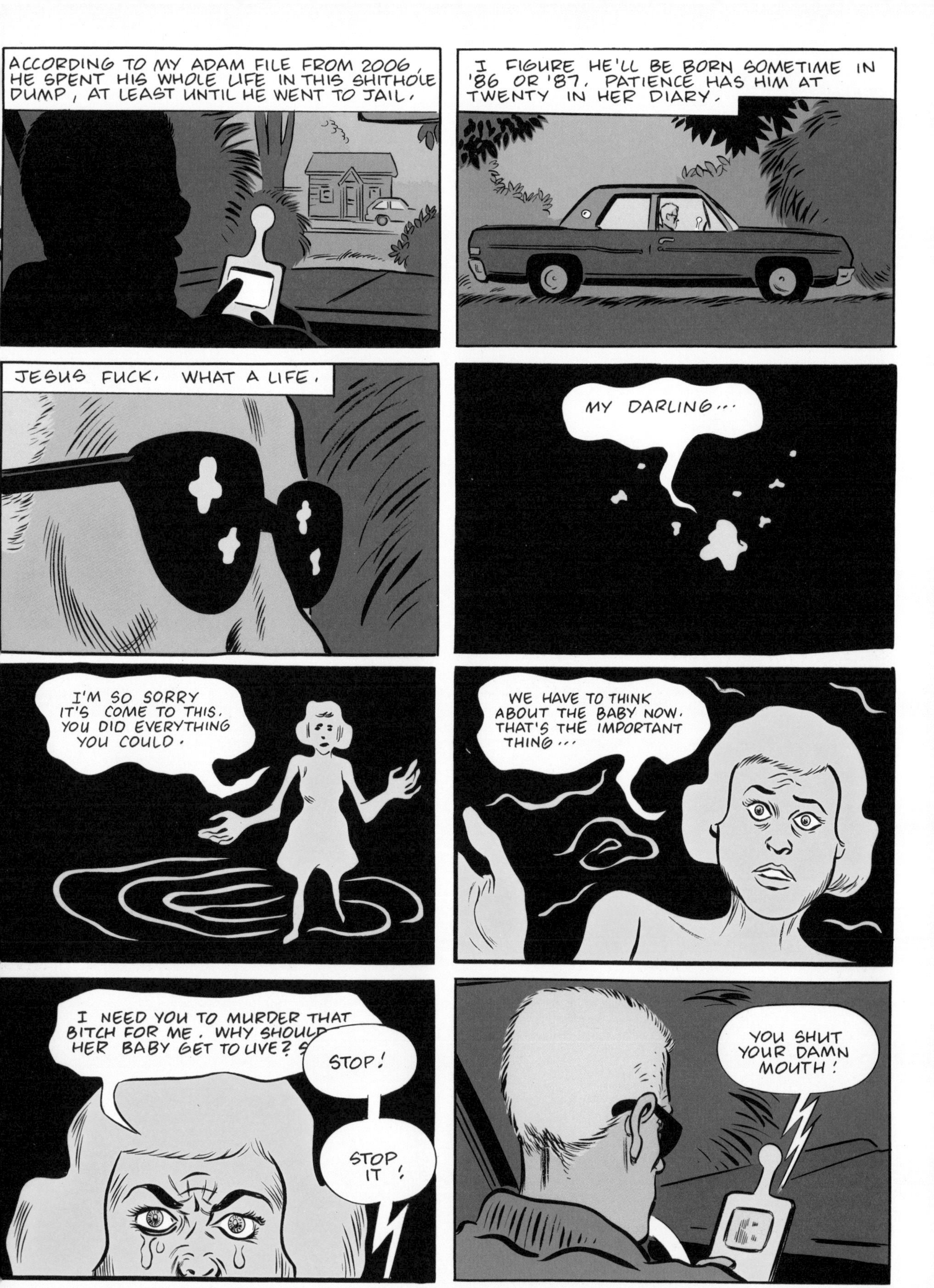
ACCORDING TO MY ADAM FILE FROM 2006, HE SPENT HIS WHOLE LIFE IN THIS SHITHOLE DUMP, AT LEAST UNTIL HE WENT TO JAIL.
I FIGURE HE'LL BE BORN SOMETIME IN '86 OR '87. PATIENCE HAS HIM AT TWENTY IN HER DIARY.
JESUS FUCK. WHAT A LIFE.
MY DARLING...
I'M SO SORRY IT'S COME TO THIS. YOU DID EVERYTHING YOU COULD.
WE HAVE TO THINK ABOUT THE BABY NOW. THAT'S THE IMPORTANT THING...
I NEED YOU TO MURDER THAT BITCH FOR ME. WHY SHOULD HER BABY GET TO LIVE?
STOP!
STOP IT!
YOU SHUT YOUR DAMN MOUTH!

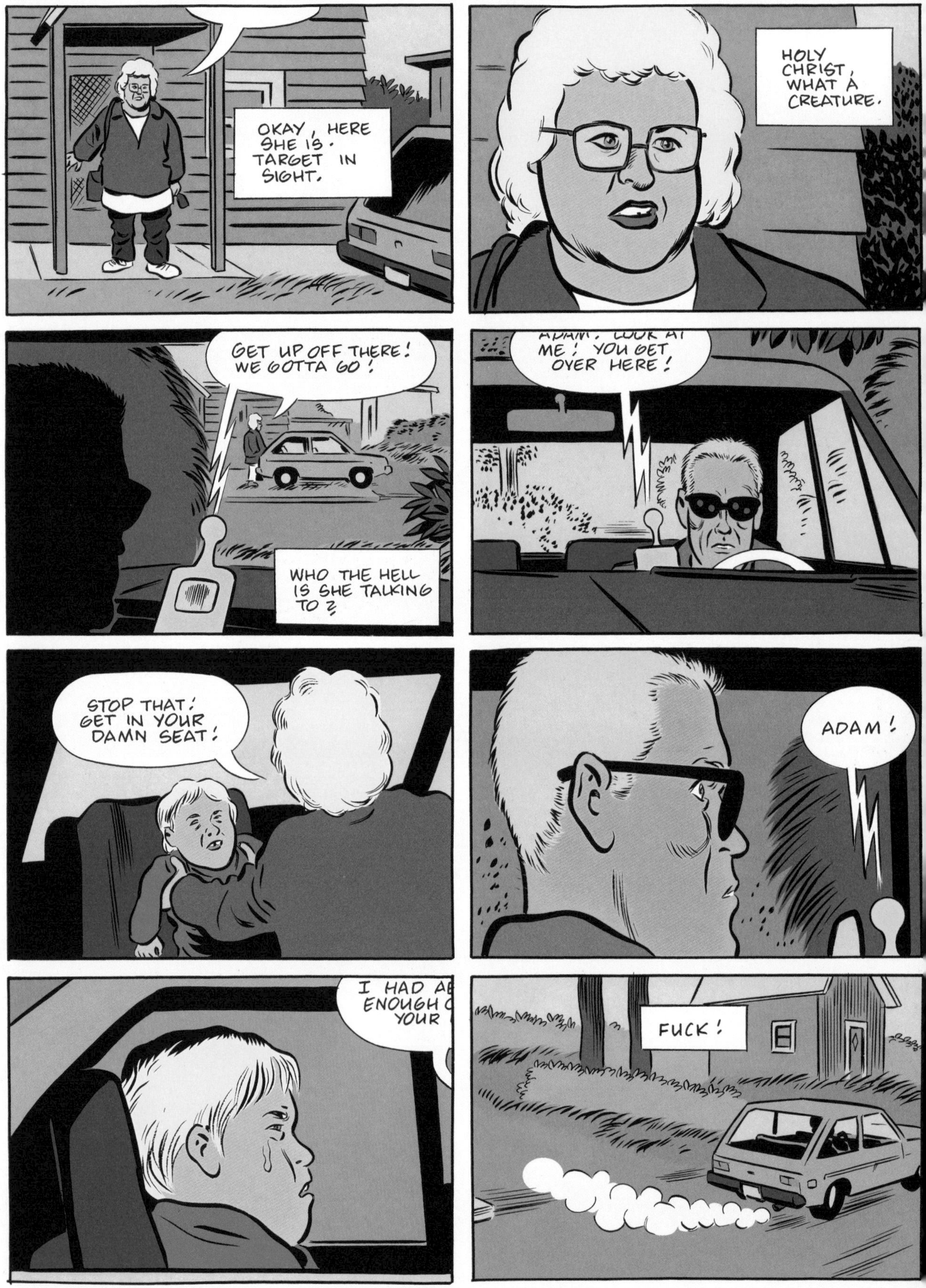
OKAY, HERE SHE IS. TARGET IN SIGHT.
HOLY CHRIST, WHAT A CREATURE.
GET UP OFF THERE! WE GOTTA GO!
WHO THE HELL IS SHE TALKING TO?
ADAM! LOOK AT ME! YOU GET OVER HERE!
STOP THAT! GET IN YOUR DAMN SEAT!
ADAM!
I HAD A
ENOUGH
YOUR
FUCK!

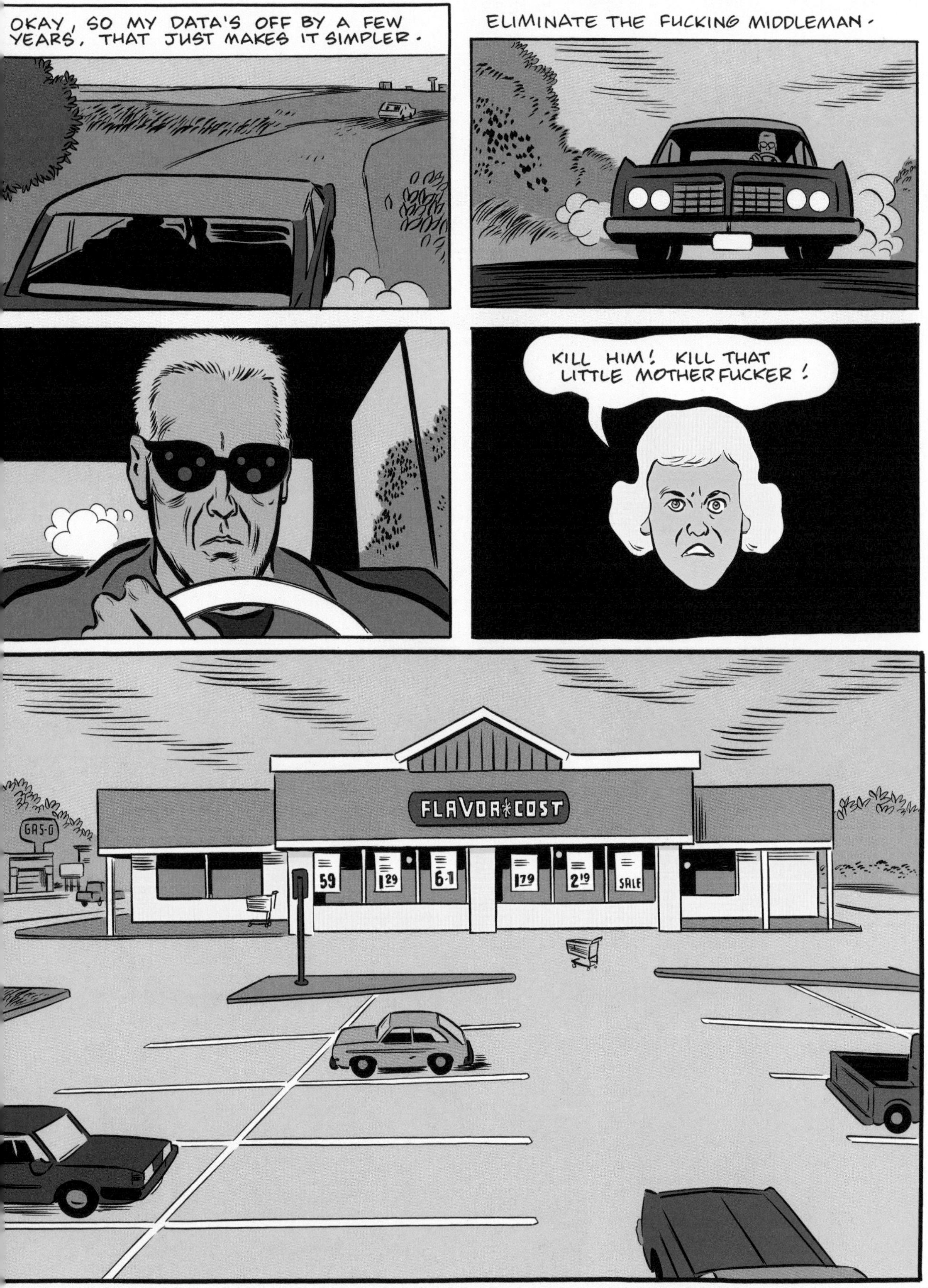
OKAY, SO MY DATA'S OFF BY A FEW YEARS, THAT JUST MAKES IT SIMPLER.
ELIMINATE THE FUCKING MIDDLEMAN.
KILL HIM! KILL THAT LITTLE MOTHERFUCKER!
GAS-O
FLAVOR*COST
59
1.29
6.1
1.79
2.19
SALE

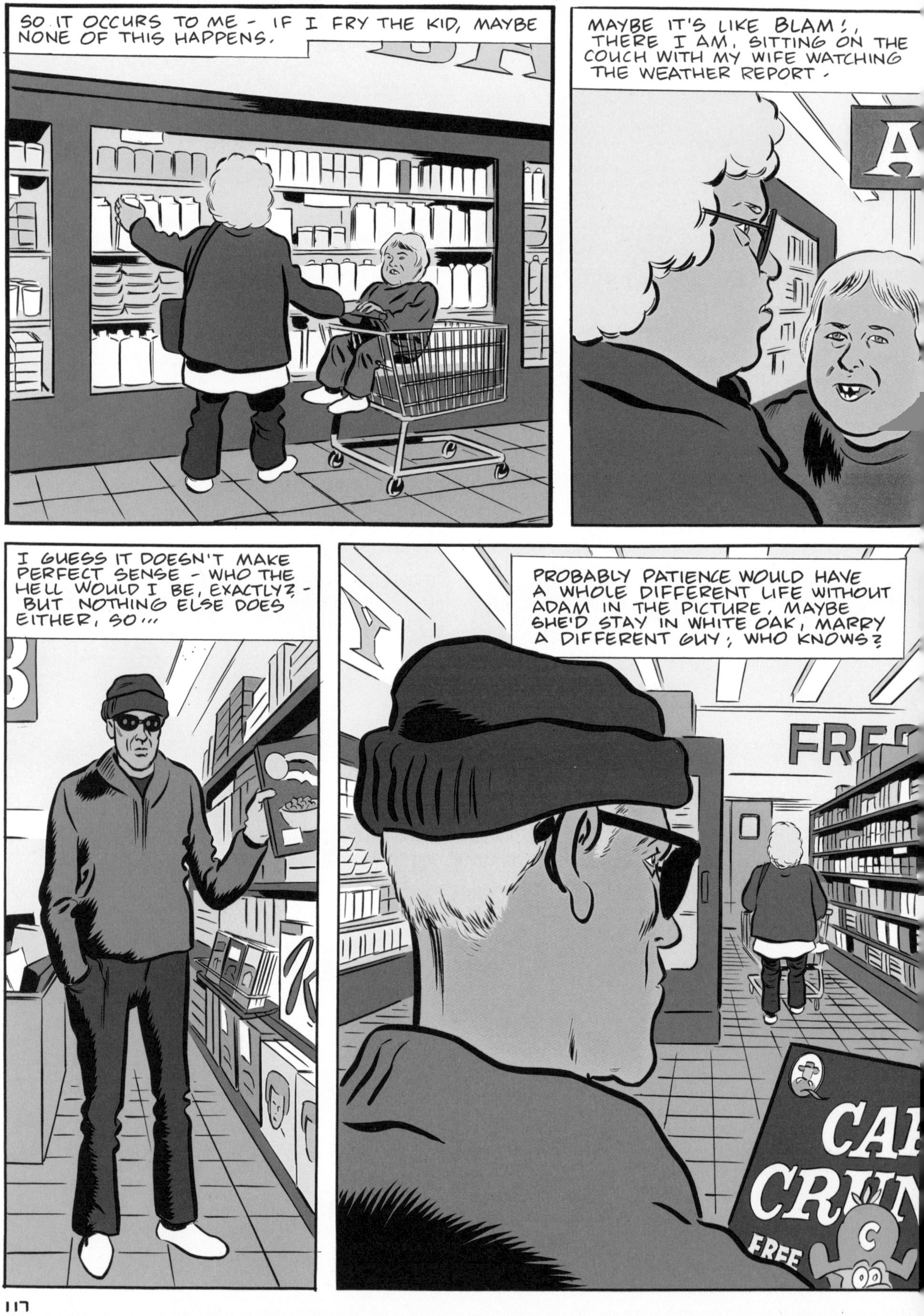
SO IT OCCURS TO ME - IF I FRY THE KID, MAYBE NONE OF THIS HAPPENS.
MAYBE IT'S LIKE BLAM!, THERE I AM, SITTING ON THE COUCH WITH MY WIFE WATCHING THE WEATHER REPORT.
I GUESS IT DOESN'T MAKE PERFECT SENSE - WHO THE HELL WOULD I BE, EXACTLY? - BUT NOTHING ELSE DOES EITHER, SO...
PROBABLY PATIENCE WOULD HAVE A WHOLE DIFFERENT LIFE WITHOUT ADAM IN THE PICTURE, MAYBE SHE'D STAY IN WHITE OAK, MARRY A DIFFERENT GUY; WHO KNOWS?
FRE
FREE

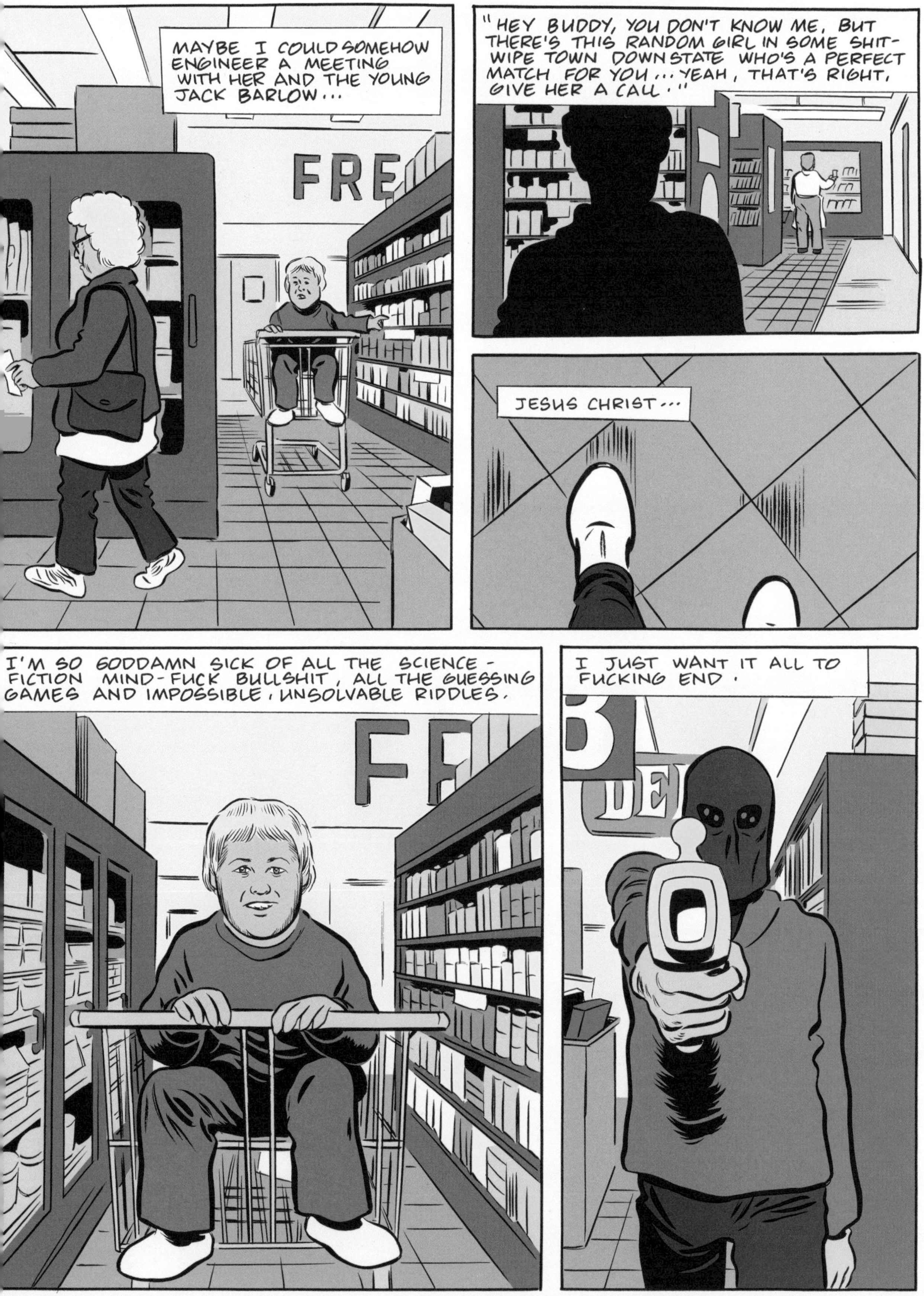
MAYBE I COULD SOMEHOW ENGINEER A MEETING WITH HER AND THE YOUNG JACK BARLOW...
FRE
"HEY BUDDY, YOU DON'T KNOW ME, BUT THERE'S THIS RANDOM GIRL IN SOME SHIT-WIPE TOWN DOWNSTATE WHO'S A PERFECT MATCH FOR YOU... YEAH, THAT'S RIGHT, GIVE HER A CALL."
JESUS CHRIST...
I'M SO GODDAMN SICK OF ALL THE SCIENCE-FICTION MIND-FUCK BULLSHIT, ALL THE GUESSING GAMES AND IMPOSSIBLE, UNSOLVABLE RIDDLES.
I JUST WANT IT ALL TO FUCKING END.

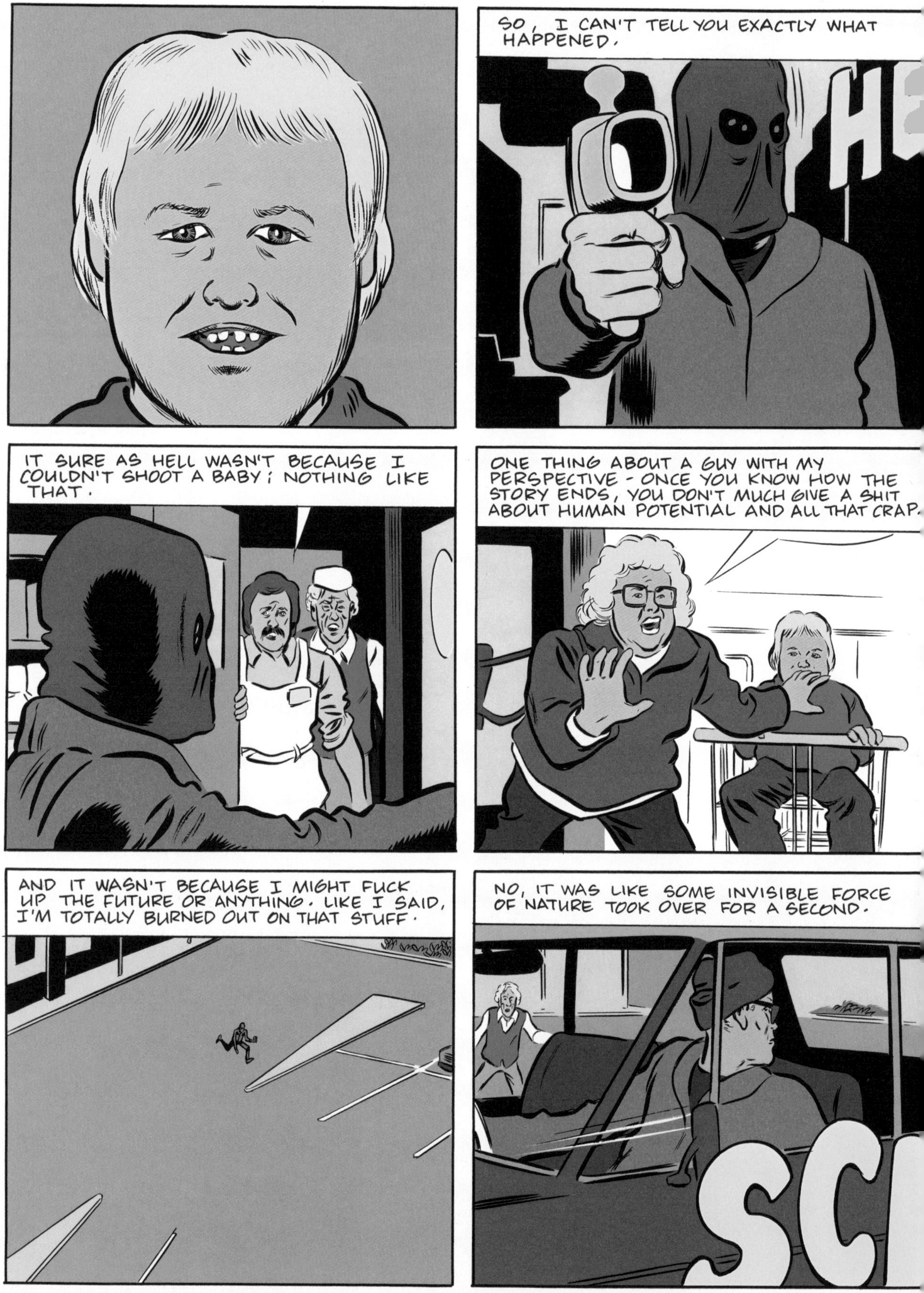
SO, I CAN'T TELL YOU EXACTLY WHAT HAPPENED.
IT SURE AS HELL WASN'T BECAUSE I COULDN'T SHOOT A BABY; NOTHING LIKE THAT.
ONE THING ABOUT A GUY WITH MY PERSPECTIVE - ONCE YOU KNOW HOW THE STORY ENDS, YOU DON'T MUCH GIVE A SHIT ABOUT HUMAN POTENTIAL AND ALL THAT CRAP.
AND IT WASN'T BECAUSE I MIGHT FUCK UP THE FUTURE OR ANYTHING. LIKE I SAID, I'M TOTALLY BURNED OUT ON THAT STUFF.
NO, IT WAS LIKE SOME INVISIBLE FORCE OF NATURE TOOK OVER FOR A SECOND.

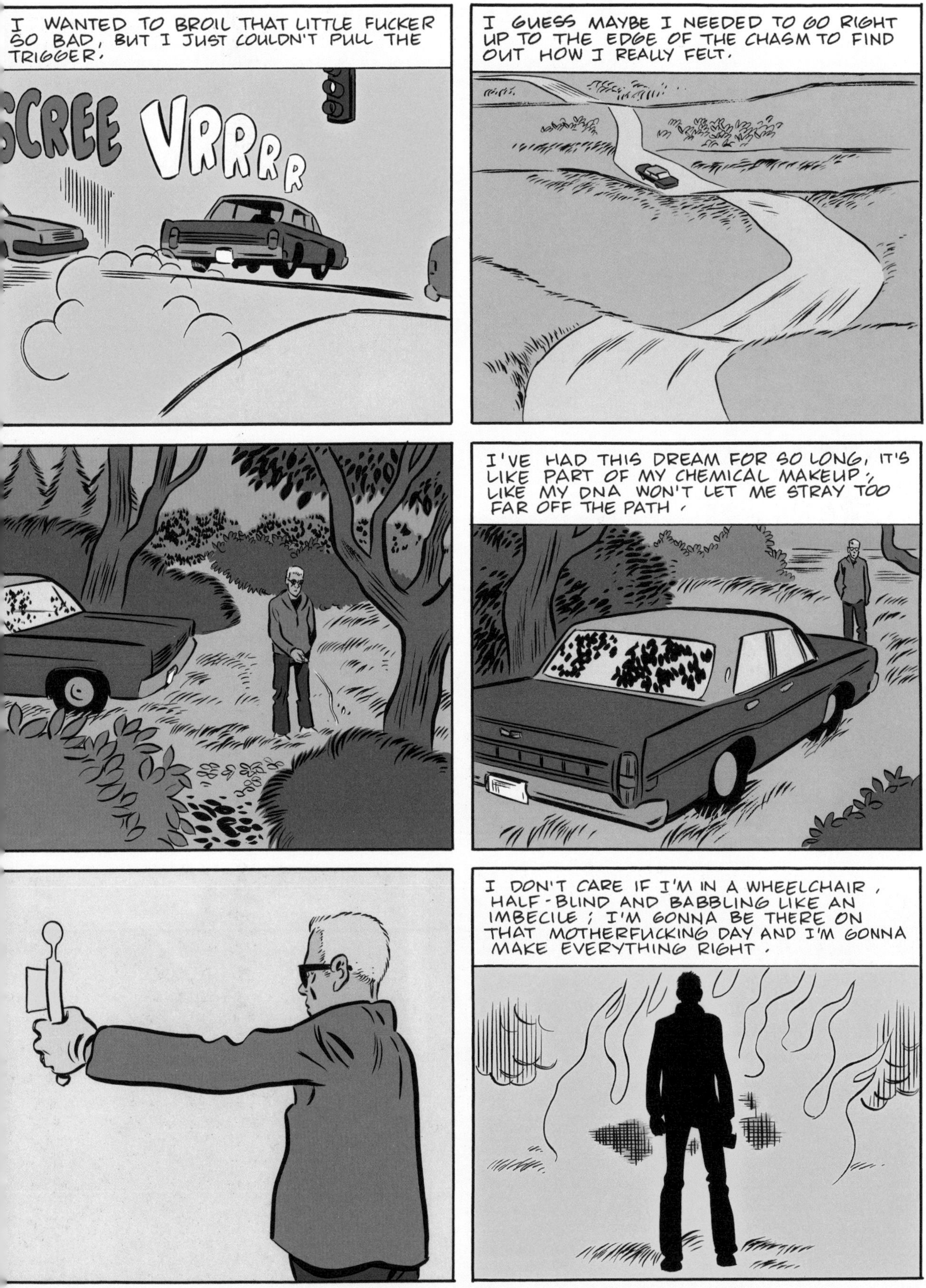
I WANTED TO BROIL THAT LITTLE FUCKER SO BAD, BUT I JUST COULDN'T PULL THE TRIGGER.
SCREE
VRRRRR
I GUESS MAYBE I NEEDED TO GO RIGHT UP TO THE EDGE OF THE CHASM TO FIND OUT HOW I REALLY FELT.
I'VE HAD THIS DREAM FOR SO LONG, IT'S LIKE PART OF MY CHEMICAL MAKEUP; LIKE MY DNA WON'T LET ME STRAY TOO FAR OFF THE PATH.
I DON'T CARE IF I'M IN A WHEELCHAIR, HALF-BLIND AND BABBLING LIKE AN IMBECILE; I'M GONNA BE THERE ON THAT MOTHERFUCKING DAY AND I'M GONNA MAKE EVERYTHING RIGHT.

I DECIDED I WASN'T GOING TO SHIT ON MYSELF FOR THIS ONE. AT LEAST IT HELPED CLEAR MY HEAD, RIGHT? "I JUST HAVE TO MAKE IT BACK TO THE CITY, LAY LOW AND LET IT BLOW OVER" - THAT'S WHAT I WAS THINKING. "DON'T WORRY, NOBODY SAW YOUR FACE."

BUT IT'S NEVER THAT EASY, IS IT?

COCKSUCKER!

THE SUSPECT IS BEING DESCRIBED AS A WHITE-MIDDLE-AGED CAUCASIAN MALE, TALL AND SLEND

TV

SHOOTI ATTEM

FUCK FUCK FUCK!

WHO THE HELL THOUGHT THERE WERE SECURITY CAMERAS IN 1985?

I NEED TO SKIP OUT ASAP-HEAD UP NORTH, FIND MY LITTLE SHACK. IT'S ONLY A MATTER OF TIME BEFORE SOME ASSHO

BA B

BAM BAM BAM

WHO IS IT?

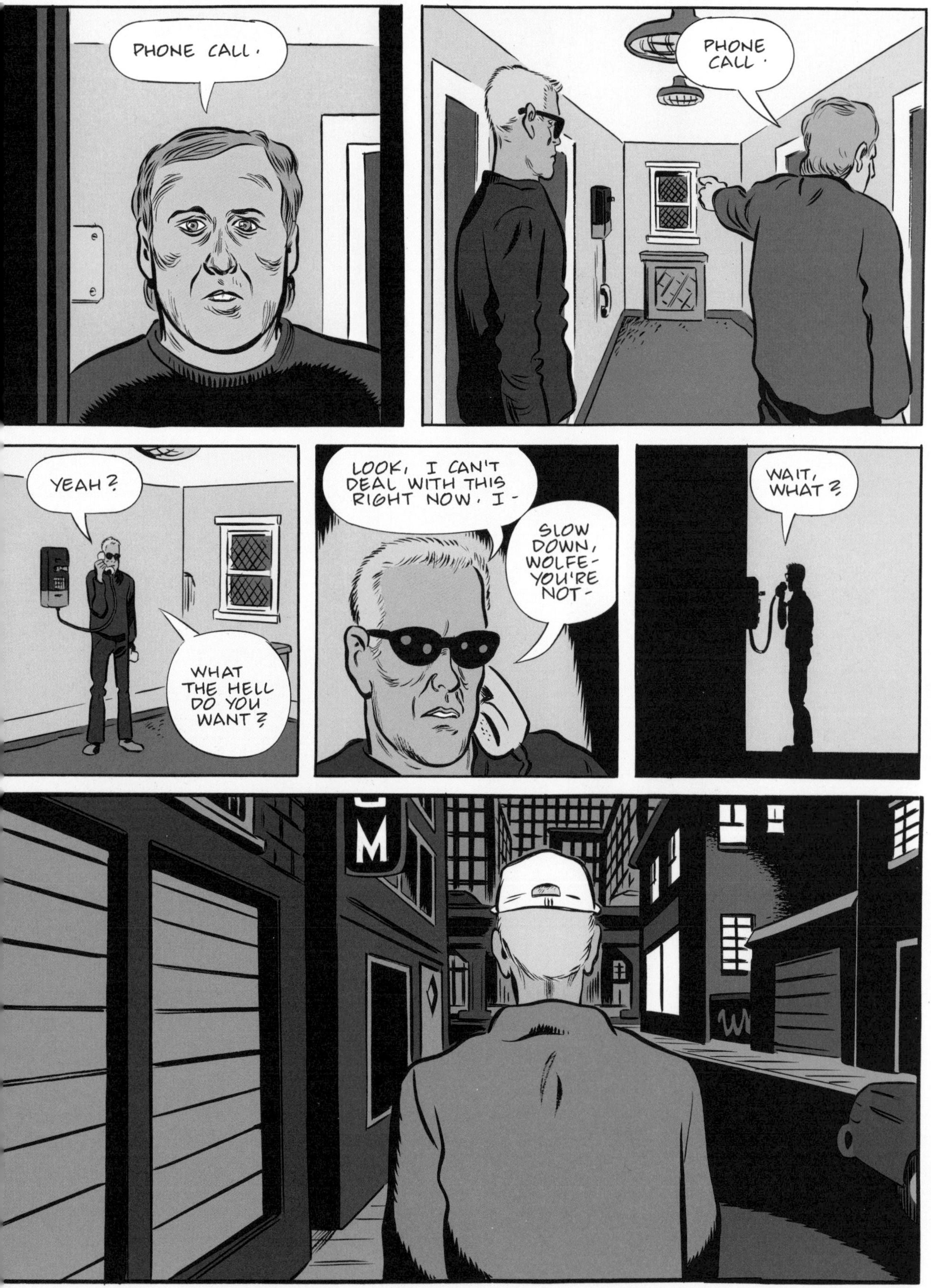
PHONE CALL.
PHONE CALL.
YEAH?
WHAT THE HELL DO YOU WANT?
LOOK, I CAN'T DEAL WITH THIS RIGHT NOW. I-
SLOW DOWN, WOLFE- YOU'RE NOT-
WAIT, WHAT?

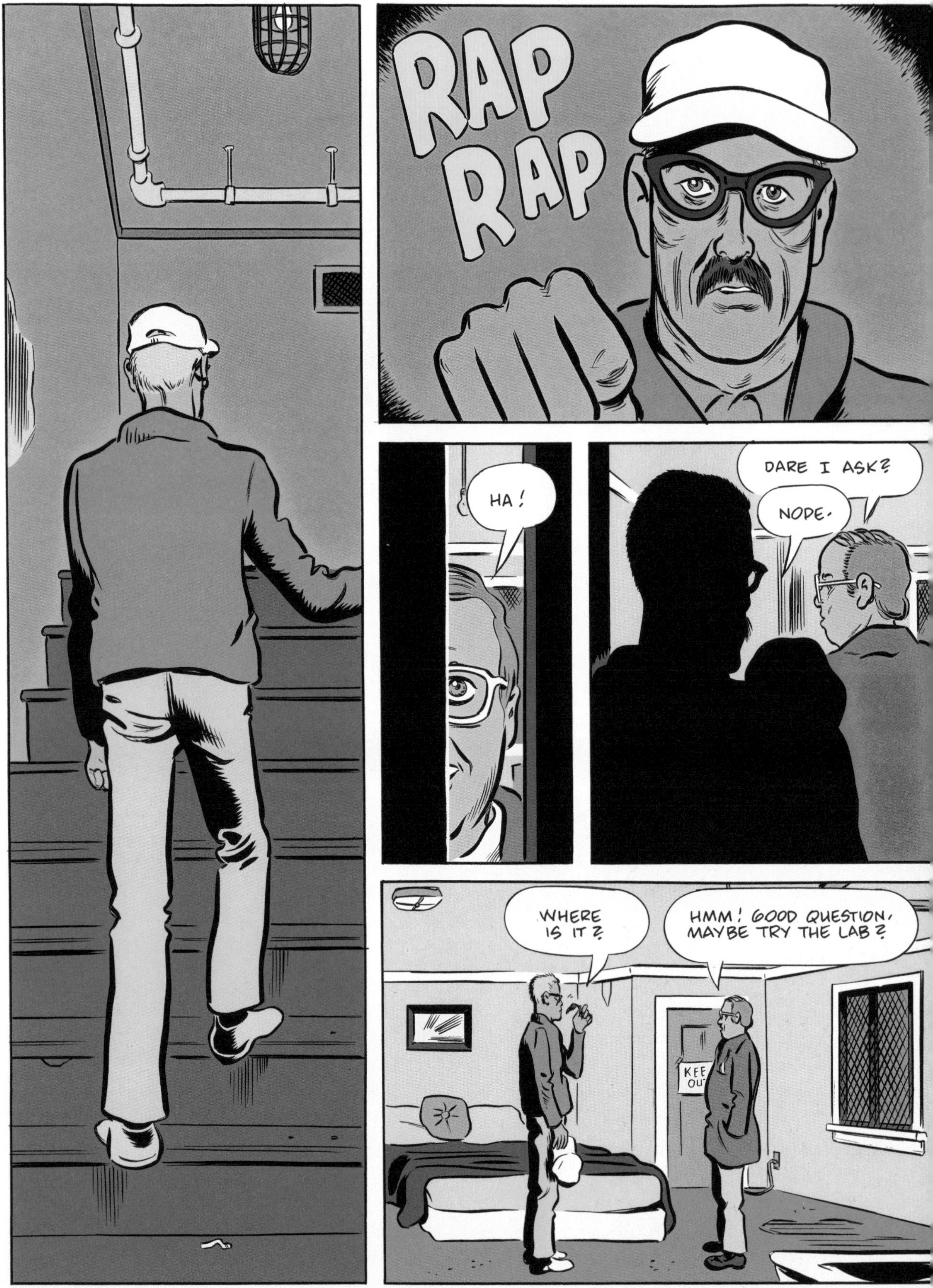
RAP
RAP
HA!
DARE I ASK?
NOPE.
WHERE IS IT?
HMM! GOOD QUESTION. MAYBE TRY THE LAB?
KEEP OUT

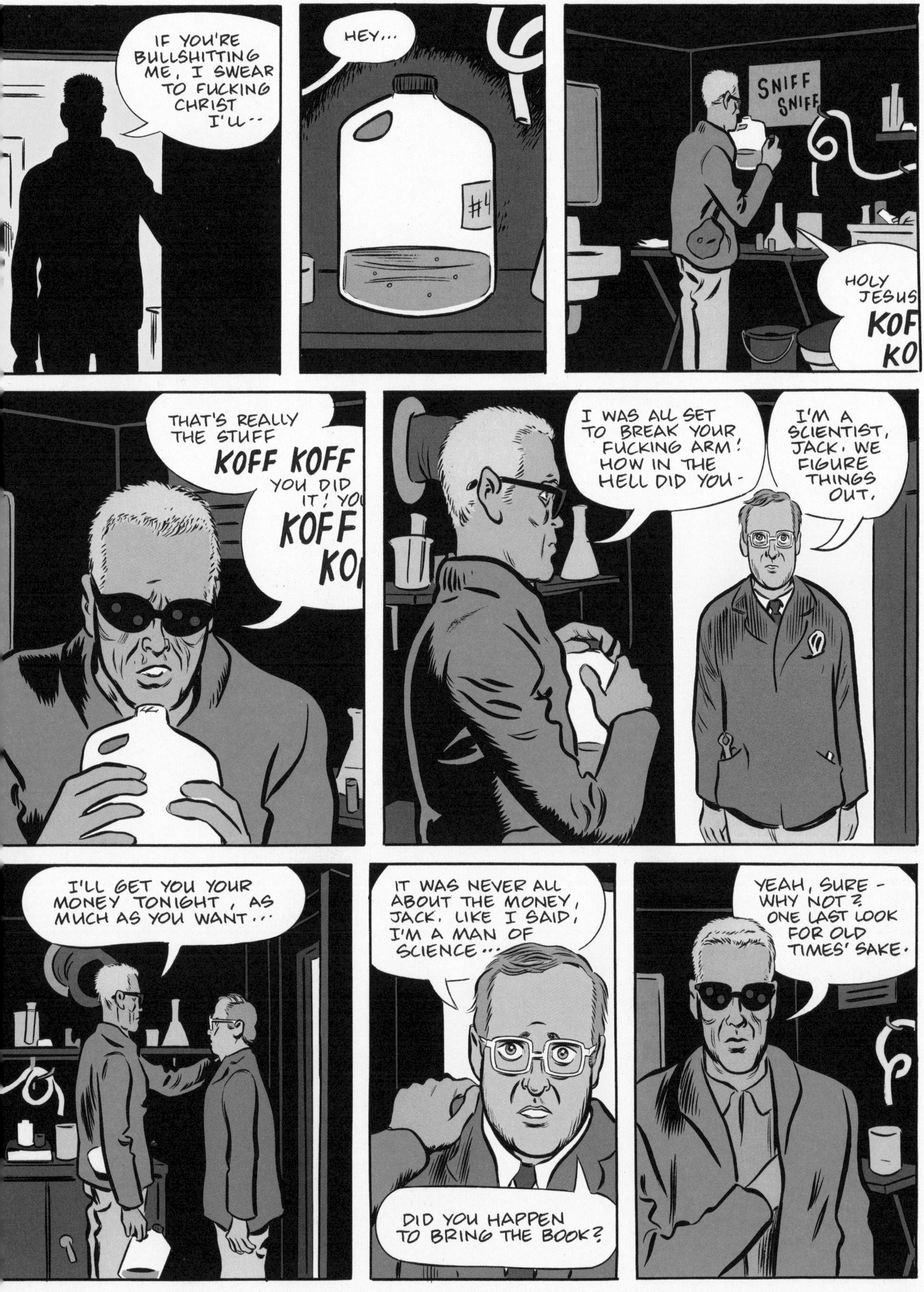
IF YOU'RE BULLSHITTING ME, I SWEAR TO FUCKING CHRIST I'LL--
HEY...
#4
SNIFF SNIFF
HOLY JESUS
KOF KO
THAT'S REALLY THE STUFF
KOFF KOFF
YOU DID IT! YOU
KOFF KO
I WAS ALL SET TO BREAK YOUR FUCKING ARM! HOW IN THE HELL DID YOU-
I'M A SCIENTIST, JACK. WE FIGURE THINGS OUT.
I'LL GET YOU YOUR MONEY TONIGHT, AS MUCH AS YOU WANT...
IT WAS NEVER ALL ABOUT THE MONEY, JACK. LIKE I SAID, I'M A MAN OF SCIENCE...
DID YOU HAPPEN TO BRING THE BOOK?
YEAH, SURE - WHY NOT? ONE LAST LOOK FOR OLD TIMES' SAKE.

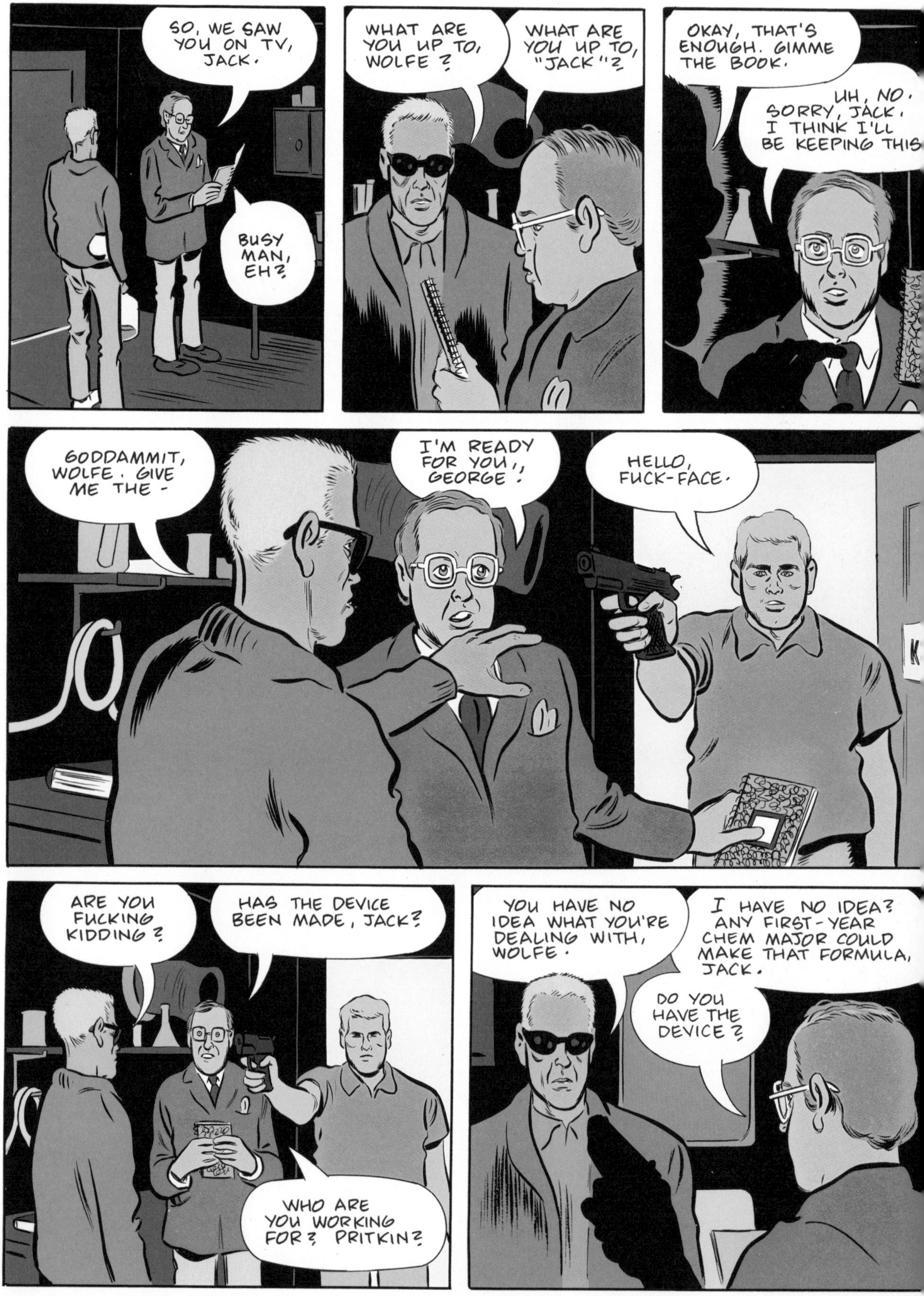
SO, WE SAW YOU ON TV, JACK.
BUSY MAN, EH?
WHAT ARE YOU UP TO, WOLFE?
WHAT ARE YOU UP TO, "JACK"?
OKAY, THAT'S ENOUGH. GIMME THE BOOK.
UH, NO. SORRY, JACK. I THINK I'LL BE KEEPING THIS
GODDAMMIT, WOLFE. GIVE ME THE-
I'M READY FOR YOU, GEORGE!
HELLO, FUCK-FACE.
ARE YOU FUCKING KIDDING?
HAS THE DEVICE BEEN MADE, JACK?
WHO ARE YOU WORKING FOR? PRITKIN?
YOU HAVE NO IDEA WHAT YOU'RE DEALING WITH, WOLFE.
I HAVE NO IDEA? ANY FIRST-YEAR CHEM MAJOR COULD MAKE THAT FORMULA, JACK.
DO YOU HAVE THE DEVICE?

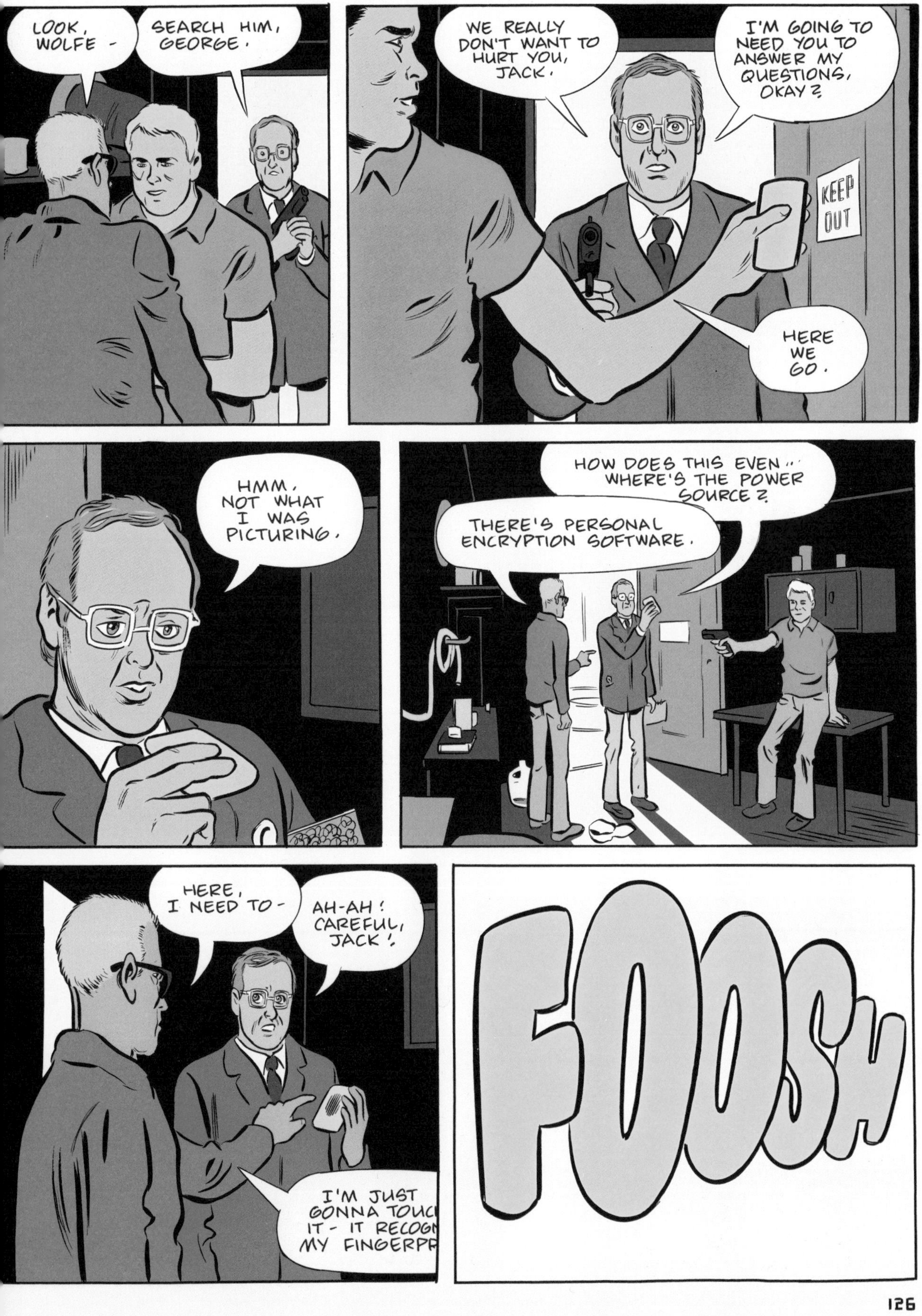
LOOK, WOLFE -
SEARCH HIM, GEORGE.
WE REALLY DON'T WANT TO HURT YOU, JACK.
I'M GOING TO NEED YOU TO ANSWER MY QUESTIONS, OKAY?
HERE WE GO.
HMM, NOT WHAT I WAS PICTURING.
HOW DOES THIS EVEN... WHERE'S THE POWER SOURCE?
THERE'S PERSONAL ENCRYPTION SOFTWARE.
KEEP OUT
HERE, I NEED TO -
AH-AH! CAREFUL, JACK!
I'M JUST GONNA TOUC
IT - IT RECOGN
MY FINGERPR
FOOSH

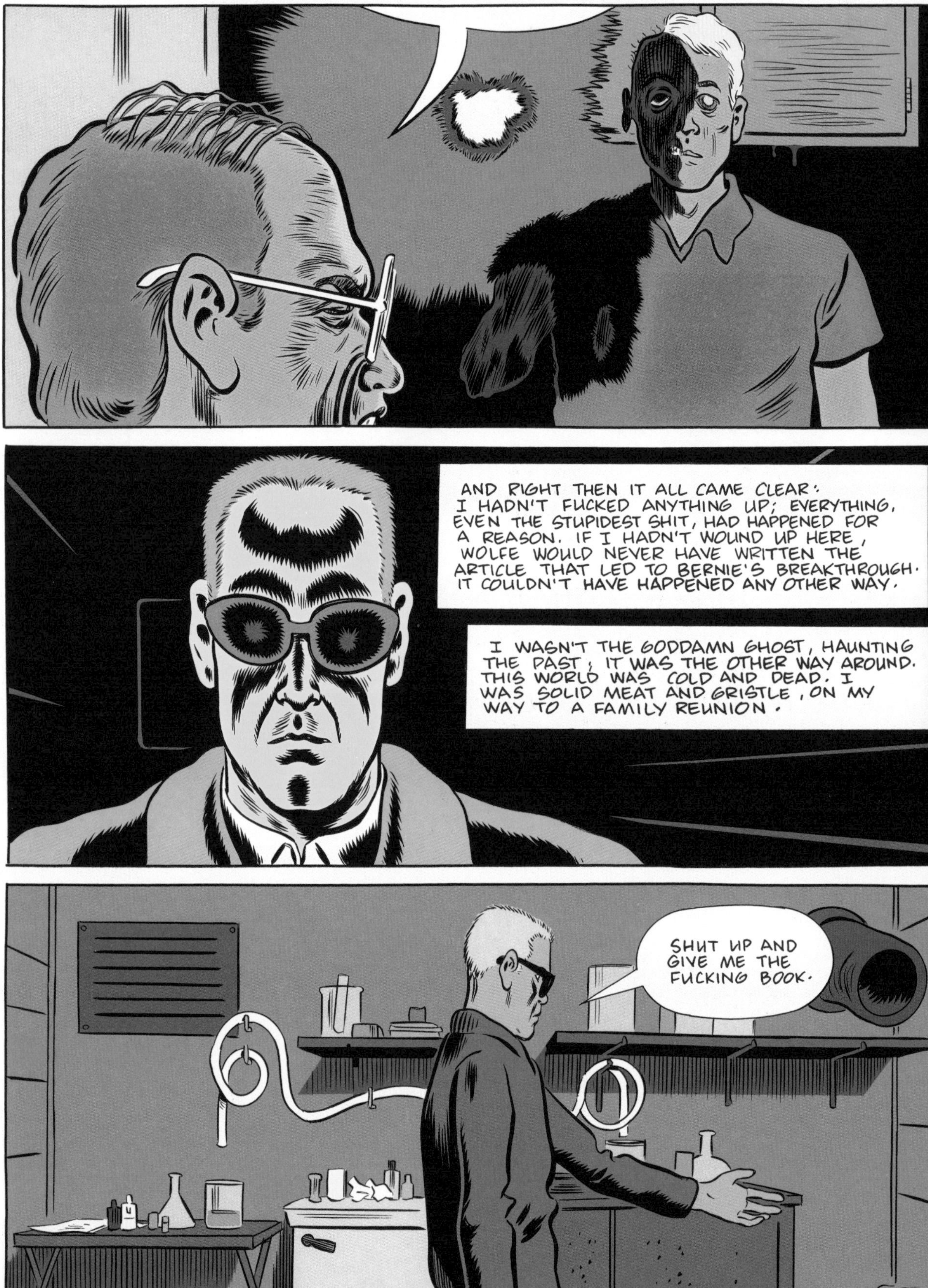
AND RIGHT THEN IT ALL CAME CLEAR: I HADN'T FUCKED ANYTHING UP; EVERYTHING, EVEN THE STUPIDEST SHIT, HAD HAPPENED FOR A REASON. IF I HADN'T WOUND UP HERE, WOLFE WOULD NEVER HAVE WRITTEN THE ARTICLE THAT LED TO BERNIE'S BREAKTHROUGH. IT COULDN'T HAVE HAPPENED ANY OTHER WAY.
I WASN'T THE GODDAMN GHOST, HAUNTING THE PAST; IT WAS THE OTHER WAY AROUND. THIS WORLD WAS COLD AND DEAD. I WAS SOLID MEAT AND GRISTLE, ON MY WAY TO A FAMILY REUNION.
SHUT UP AND GIVE ME THE FUCKING BOOK.

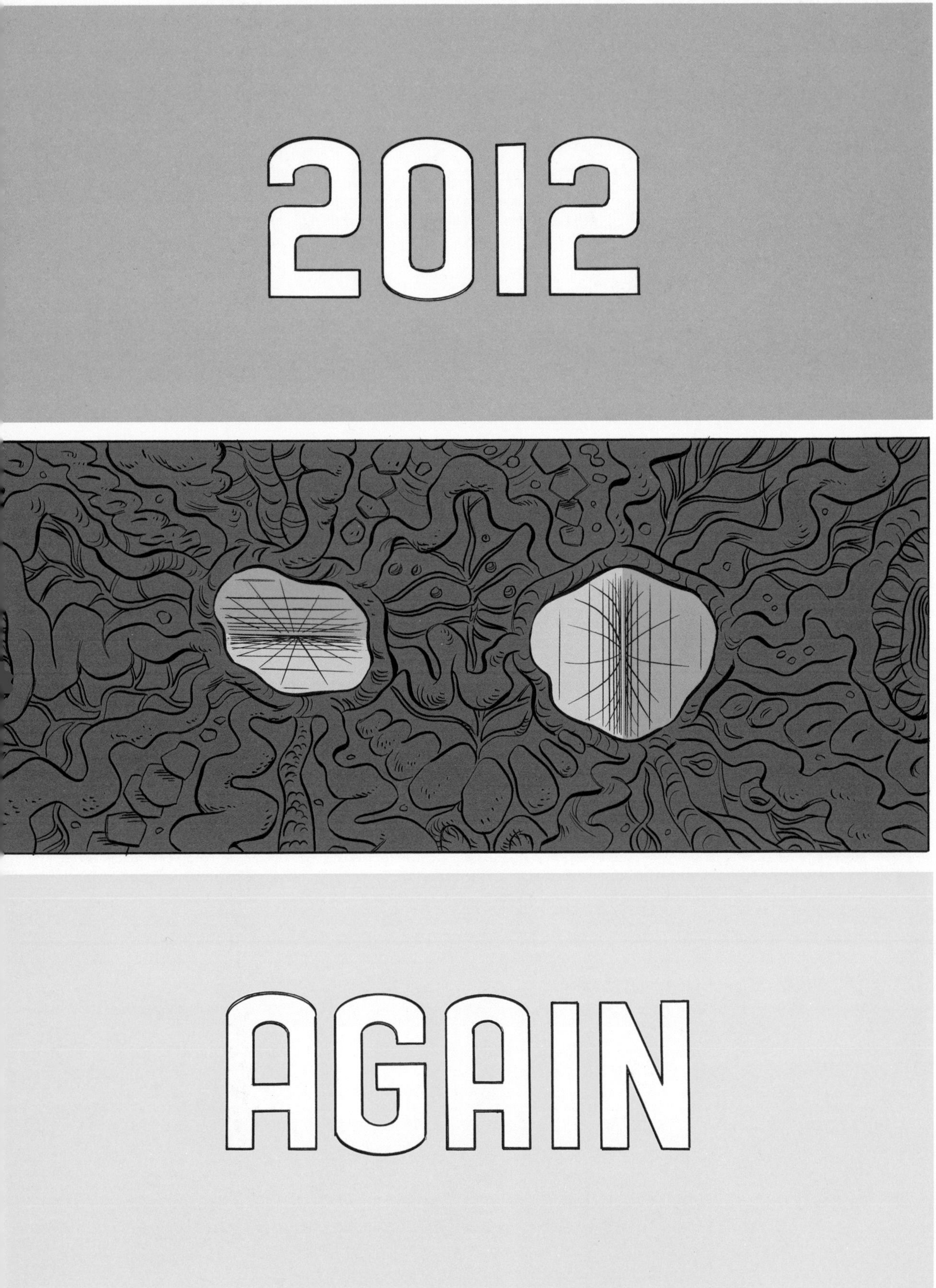
2012
AGAIN

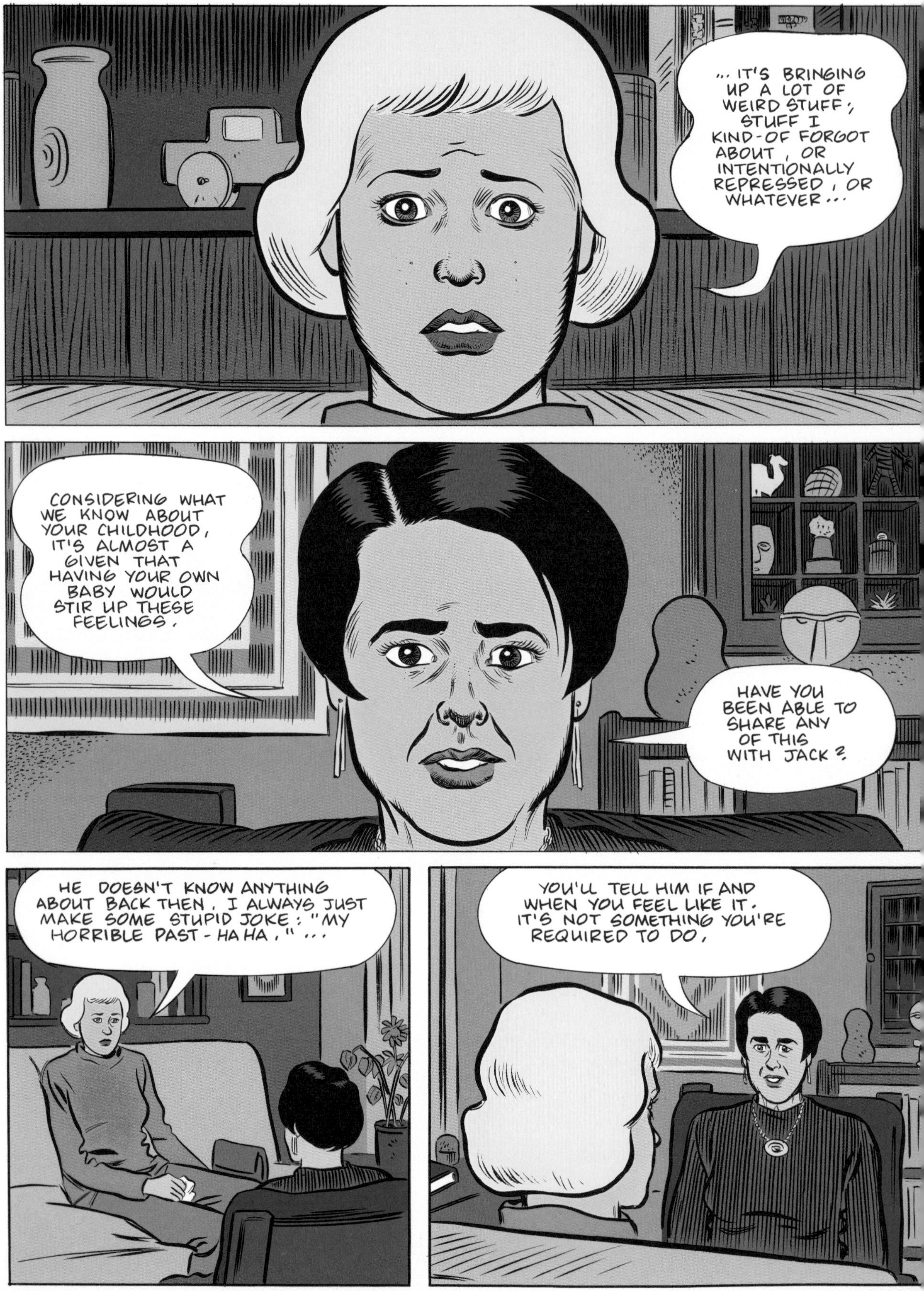
... IT'S BRINGING UP A LOT OF WEIRD STUFF; STUFF I KIND-OF FORGOT ABOUT, OR INTENTIONALLY REPRESSED, OR WHATEVER...
CONSIDERING WHAT WE KNOW ABOUT YOUR CHILDHOOD, IT'S ALMOST A GIVEN THAT HAVING YOUR OWN BABY WOULD STIR UP THESE FEELINGS.
HAVE YOU BEEN ABLE TO SHARE ANY OF THIS WITH JACK?
HE DOESN'T KNOW ANYTHING ABOUT BACK THEN. I ALWAYS JUST MAKE SOME STUPID JOKE: "MY HORRIBLE PAST - HA HA." ...
YOU'LL TELL HIM IF AND WHEN YOU FEEL LIKE IT. IT'S NOT SOMETHING YOU'RE REQUIRED TO DO.

IT'S NOT JUST THE PSYCHOLOGICAL TORMENT, OR WHATEVER, THERE WERE GENUINELY WEIRD THINGS THAT HAPPENED BACK THEN ; THINGS I CAN'T EVEN BEGIN TO EXPLAIN...

LIKE WHAT ?

LIKE THAT WHOLE CRAZY NIGHT WITH MY EX ! I DON'T EVEN KNOW WHO THAT GUY WAS... HE WAS JUST THERE IN THE ROOM, AND THEN HE WAS GONE. THERE WAS ALL THIS... I DON'T KNOW, I JUST...

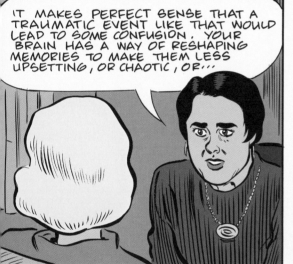

IT MAKES PERFECT SENSE THAT A TRAUMATIC EVENT LIKE THAT WOULD LEAD TO SOME CONFUSION. YOUR BRAIN HAS A WAY OF RESHAPING MEMORIES TO MAKE THEM LESS UPSETTING, OR CHAOTIC, OR...

YOU THINK I HAD, LIKE, A PSYCHOTIC HALLUCINATION ? I DON'T KNOW - IT ALL SEEMED REALLY REAL... AND WHAT ABOUT THE BOX ? THAT WAS DEFINITELY REAL...

NO, NO, NO, OF COURSE IT'S ALL REAL. EVERYTHING IS COMPLETELY VALID EMOTIONALLY. I JUST WOULDN'T GET TOO HUNG UP ON ALL THE DETAILS...

IS THERE MAYBE SOME MEDICATION I COULD TRY IF THINGS GET WORSE ?

LET'S START WITH THAT NEXT TIME, OKAY ? THERE'S SOMETHING I NEED TO ASK YOU ABOUT YOUR INSURANCE.

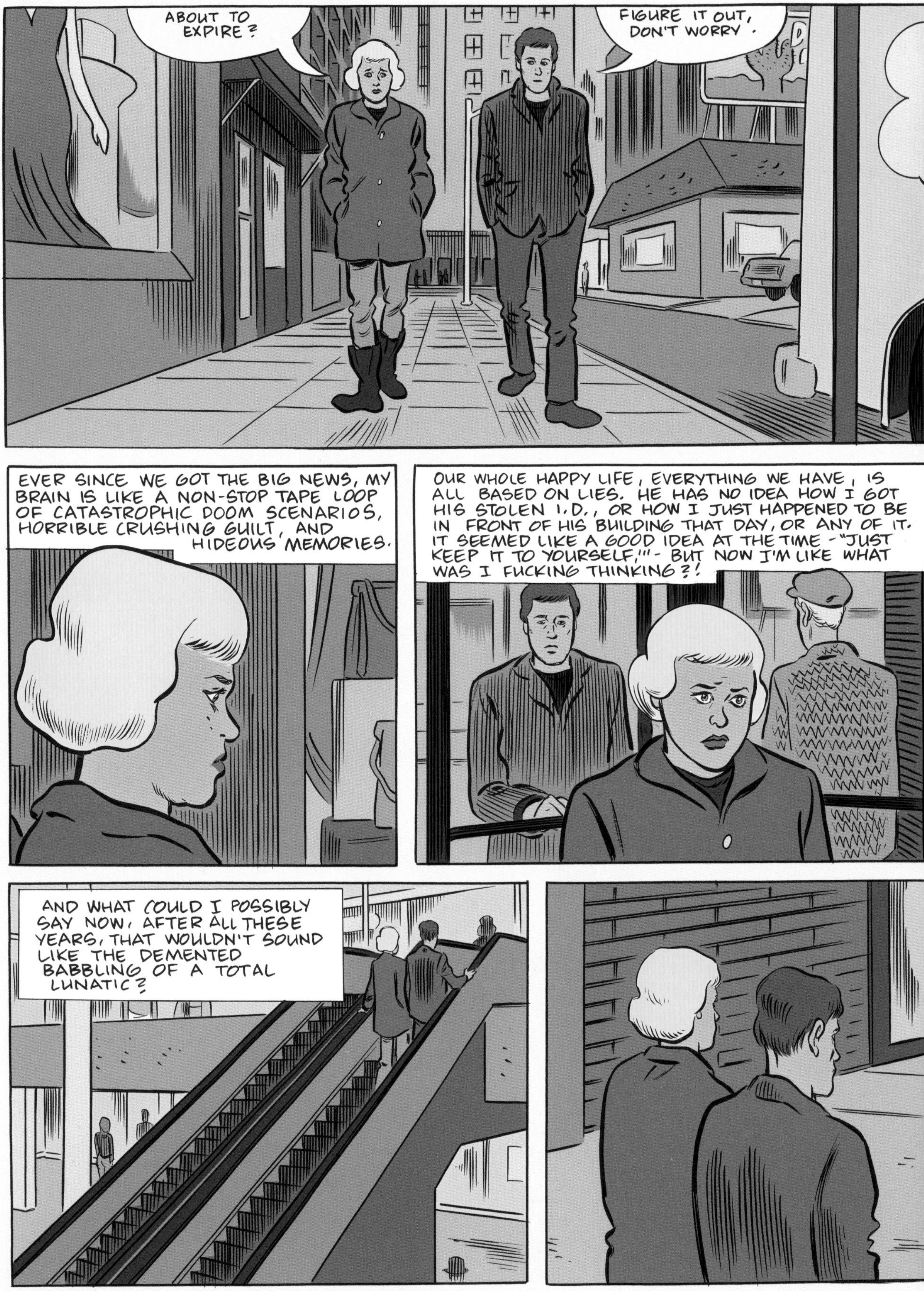
ABOUT TO EXPIRE?
FIGURE IT OUT, DON'T WORRY.
EVER SINCE WE GOT THE BIG NEWS, MY BRAIN IS LIKE A NON-STOP TAPE LOOP OF CATASTROPHIC DOOM SCENARIOS, HORRIBLE CRUSHING GUILT, AND HIDEOUS MEMORIES.
OUR WHOLE HAPPY LIFE, EVERYTHING WE HAVE, IS ALL BASED ON LIES. HE HAS NO IDEA HOW I GOT HIS STOLEN I.D., OR HOW I JUST HAPPENED TO BE IN FRONT OF HIS BUILDING THAT DAY, OR ANY OF IT. IT SEEMED LIKE A GOOD IDEA AT THE TIME - "JUST KEEP IT TO YOURSELF," - BUT NOW I'M LIKE WHAT WAS I FUCKING THINKING?!
AND WHAT COULD I POSSIBLY SAY NOW, AFTER ALL THESE YEARS, THAT WOULDN'T SOUND LIKE THE DEMENTED BABBLING OF A TOTAL LUNATIC?

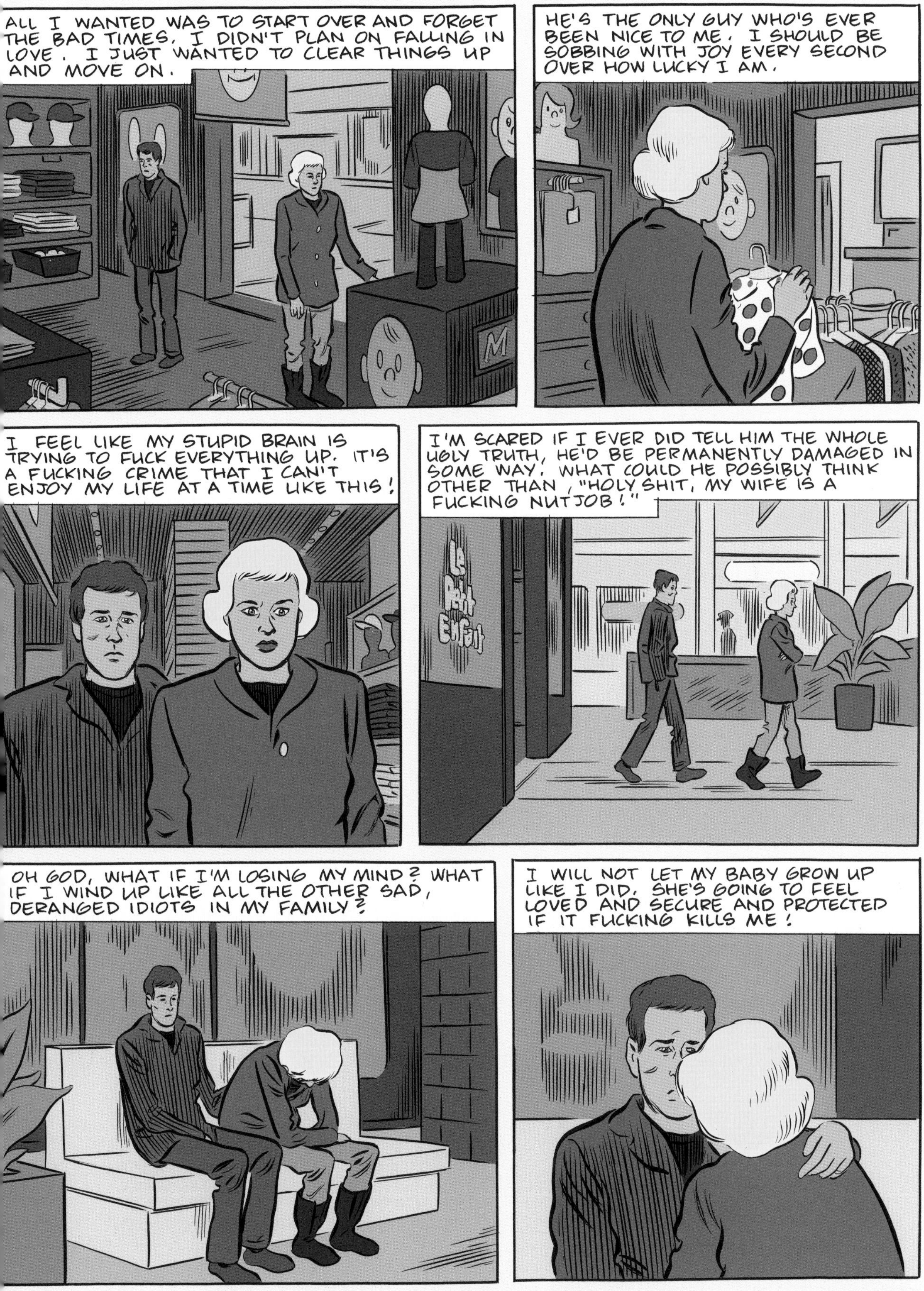
ALL I WANTED WAS TO START OVER AND FORGET THE BAD TIMES. I DIDN'T PLAN ON FALLING IN LOVE. I JUST WANTED TO CLEAR THINGS UP AND MOVE ON.
M
HE'S THE ONLY GUY WHO'S EVER BEEN NICE TO ME. I SHOULD BE SOBBING WITH JOY EVERY SECOND OVER HOW LUCKY I AM.
I FEEL LIKE MY STUPID BRAIN IS TRYING TO FUCK EVERYTHING UP. IT'S A FUCKING CRIME THAT I CAN'T ENJOY MY LIFE AT A TIME LIKE THIS!
I'M SCARED IF I EVER DID TELL HIM THE WHOLE UGLY TRUTH, HE'D BE PERMANENTLY DAMAGED IN SOME WAY. WHAT COULD HE POSSIBLY THINK OTHER THAN, "HOLY SHIT, MY WIFE IS A FUCKING NUTJOB!"
Le Petit Enfant
OH GOD, WHAT IF I'M LOSING MY MIND? WHAT IF I WIND UP LIKE ALL THE OTHER SAD, DERANGED IDIOTS IN MY FAMILY?
I WILL NOT LET MY BABY GROW UP LIKE I DID. SHE'S GOING TO FEEL LOVED AND SECURE AND PROTECTED IF IT FUCKING KILLS ME!

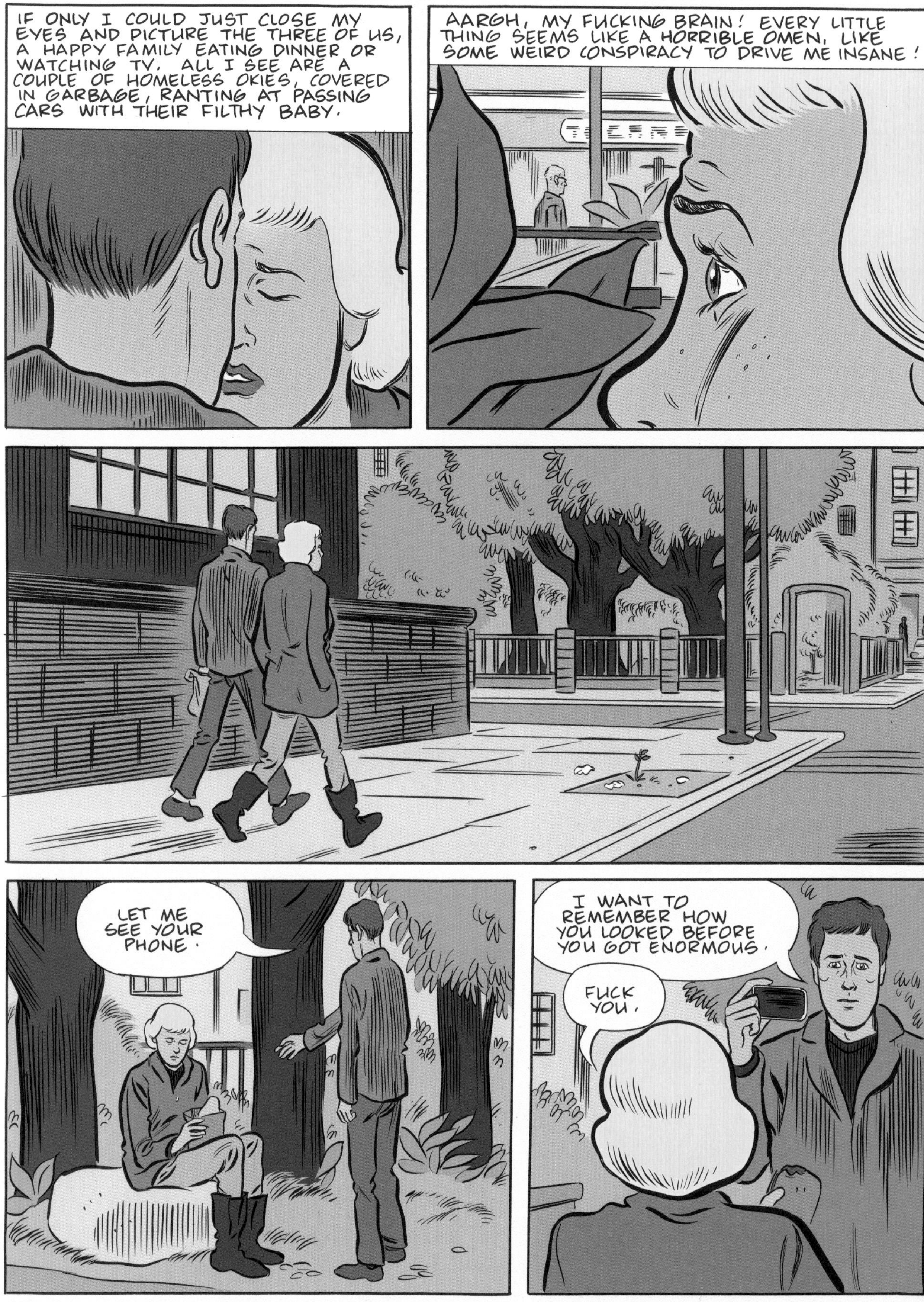
IF ONLY I COULD JUST CLOSE MY EYES AND PICTURE THE THREE OF US, A HAPPY FAMILY EATING DINNER OR WATCHING TV. ALL I SEE ARE A COUPLE OF HOMELESS OKIES, COVERED IN GARBAGE, RANTING AT PASSING CARS WITH THEIR FILTHY BABY.
AARGH, MY FUCKING BRAIN! EVERY LITTLE THING SEEMS LIKE A HORRIBLE OMEN, LIKE SOME WEIRD CONSPIRACY TO DRIVE ME INSANE!
LET ME SEE YOUR PHONE.
I WANT TO REMEMBER HOW YOU LOOKED BEFORE YOU GOT ENORMOUS.
FUCK YOU.

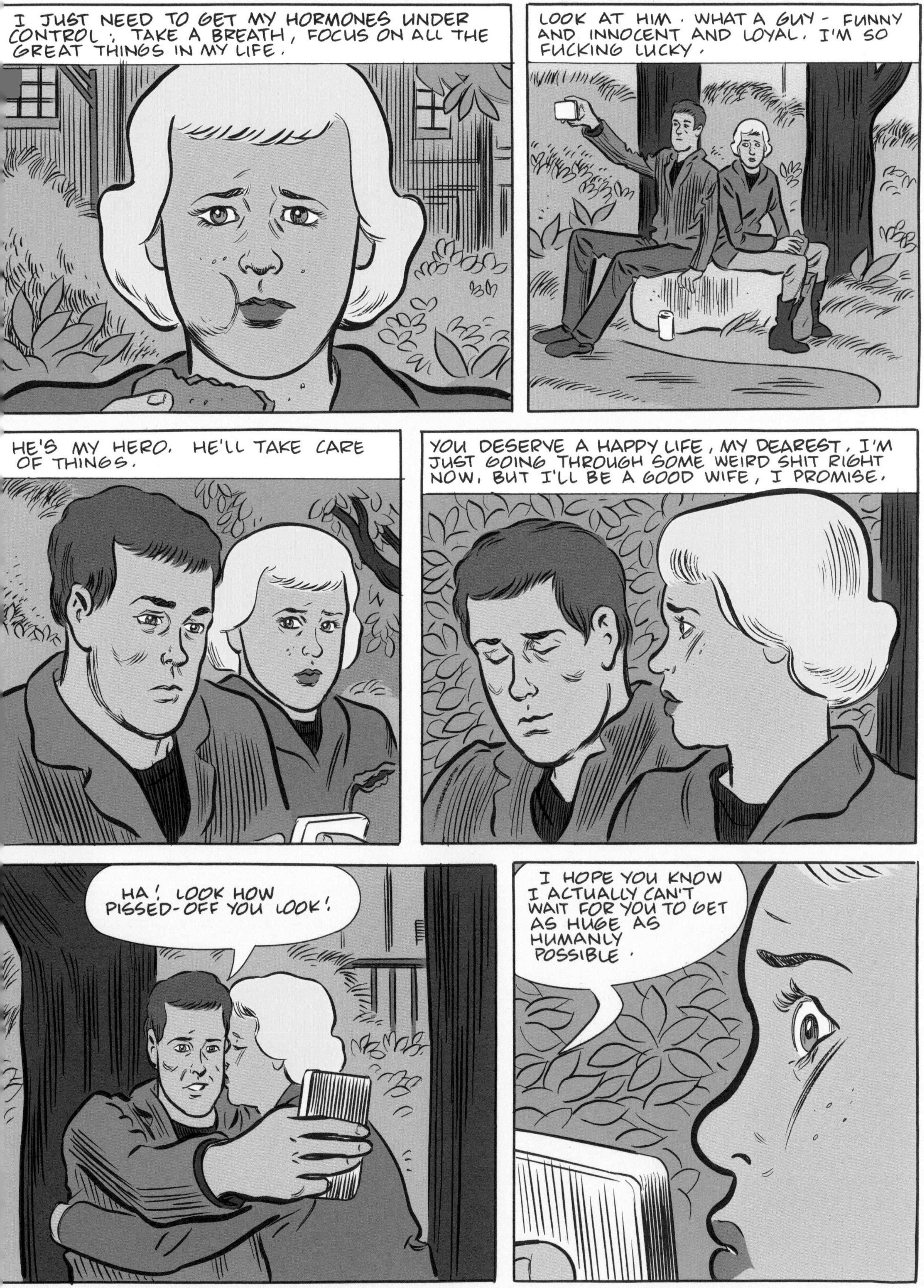
I JUST NEED TO GET MY HORMONES UNDER CONTROL; TAKE A BREATH, FOCUS ON ALL THE GREAT THINGS IN MY LIFE.
LOOK AT HIM. WHAT A GUY - FUNNY AND INNOCENT AND LOYAL. I'M SO FUCKING LUCKY.
HE'S MY HERO. HE'LL TAKE CARE OF THINGS.
YOU DESERVE A HAPPY LIFE, MY DEAREST. I'M JUST GOING THROUGH SOME WEIRD SHIT RIGHT NOW, BUT I'LL BE A GOOD WIFE, I PROMISE.
HA! LOOK HOW PISSED-OFF YOU LOOK!
I HOPE YOU KNOW I ACTUALLY CAN'T WAIT FOR YOU TO GET AS HUGE AS HUMANLY POSSIBLE.

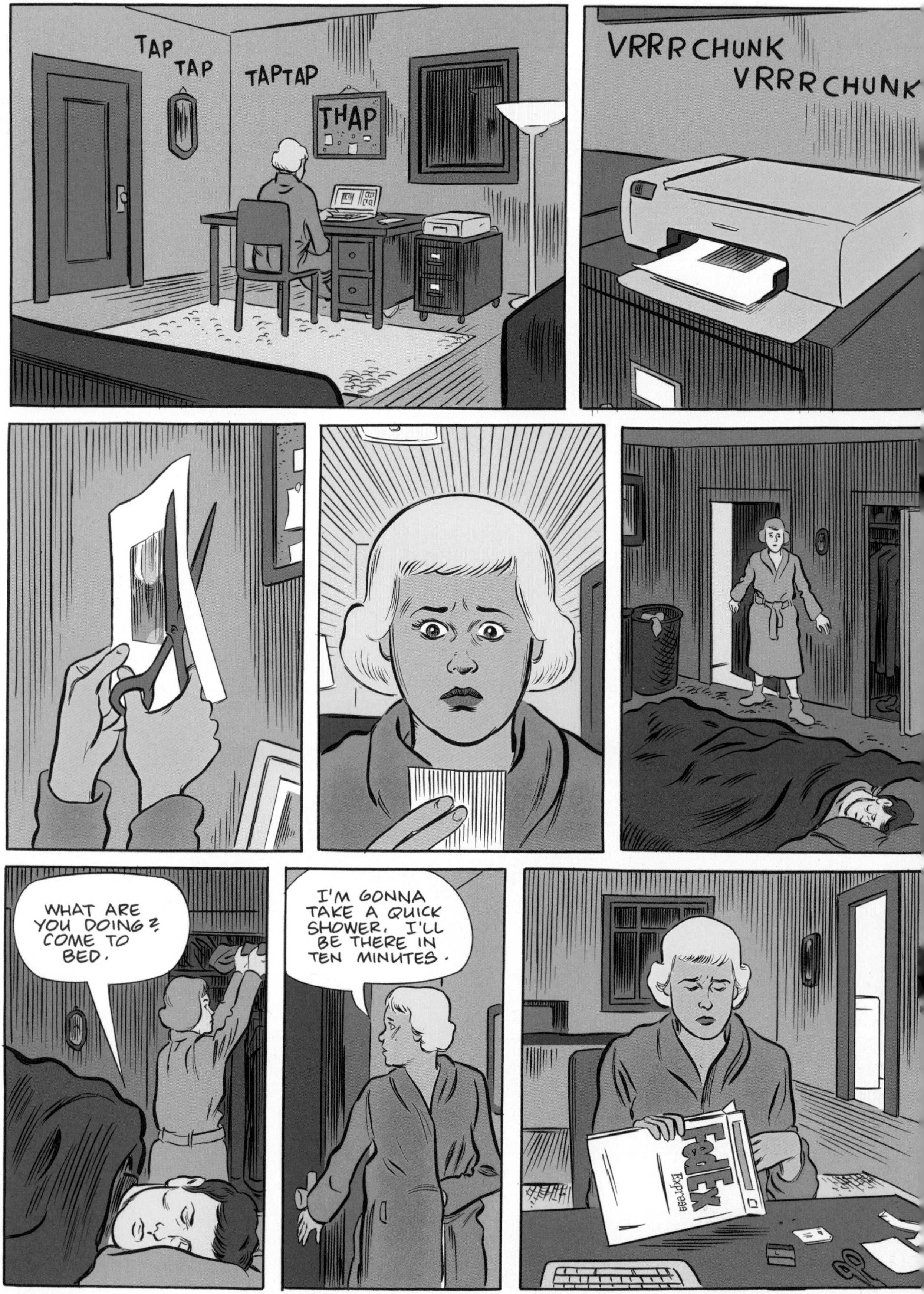
TAP
TAP
TAPTAP
THAP
VRRRCHUNK
VRRRCHUNK
WHAT ARE YOU DOING? COME TO BED.
I'M GONNA TAKE A QUICK SHOWER. I'LL BE THERE IN TEN MINUTES.
FedEx
Express

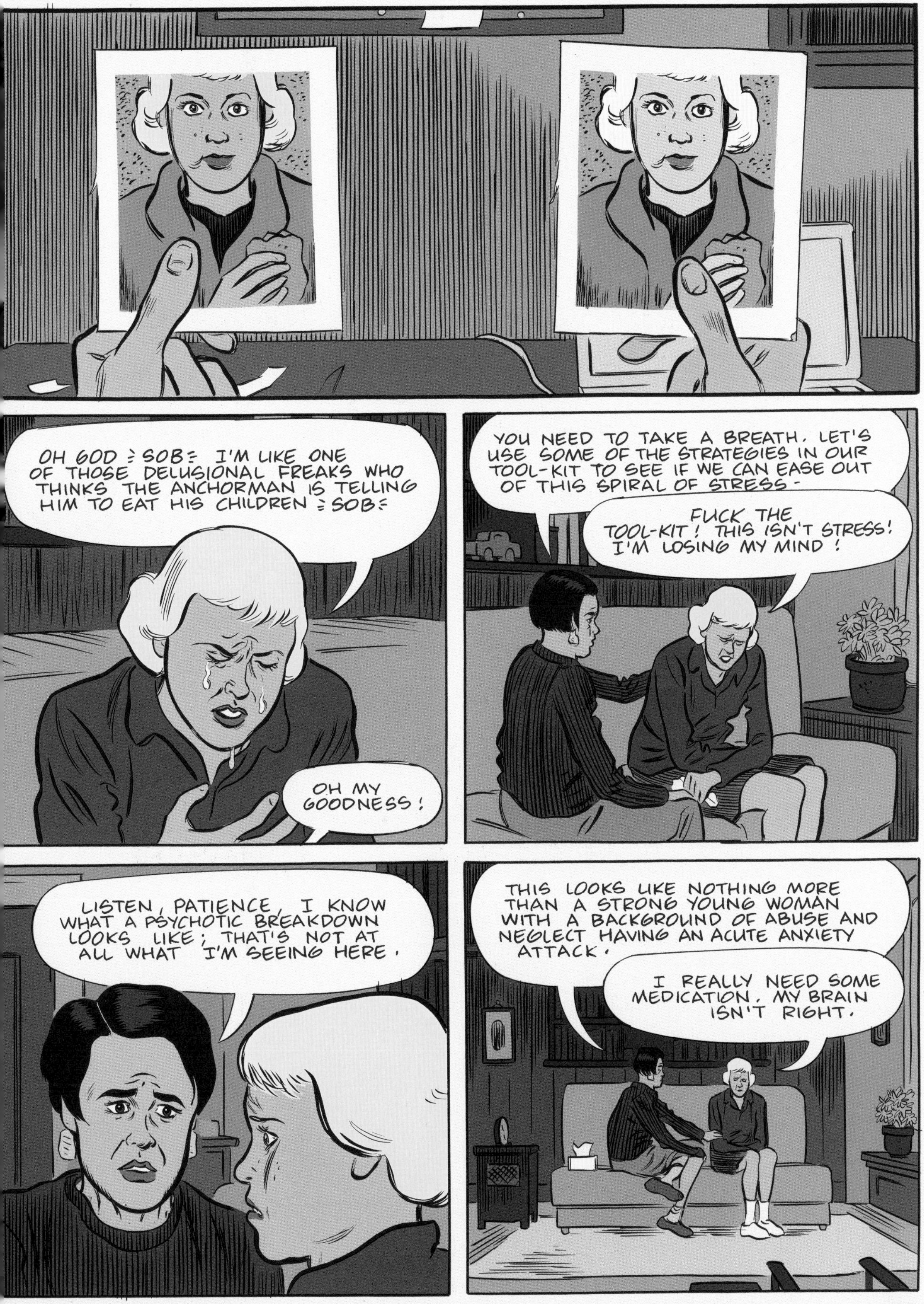
OH GOD =SOB= I'M LIKE ONE OF THOSE DELUSIONAL FREAKS WHO THINKS THE ANCHORMAN IS TELLING HIM TO EAT HIS CHILDREN =SOB=
OH MY GOODNESS!
YOU NEED TO TAKE A BREATH. LET'S USE SOME OF THE STRATEGIES IN OUR TOOL-KIT TO SEE IF WE CAN EASE OUT OF THIS SPIRAL OF STRESS-
FUCK THE TOOL-KIT! THIS ISN'T STRESS! I'M LOSING MY MIND!
LISTEN, PATIENCE, I KNOW WHAT A PSYCHOTIC BREAKDOWN LOOKS LIKE; THAT'S NOT AT ALL WHAT I'M SEEING HERE.
THIS LOOKS LIKE NOTHING MORE THAN A STRONG YOUNG WOMAN WITH A BACKGROUND OF ABUSE AND NEGLECT HAVING AN ACUTE ANXIETY ATTACK.
I REALLY NEED SOME MEDICATION. MY BRAIN ISN'T RIGHT.

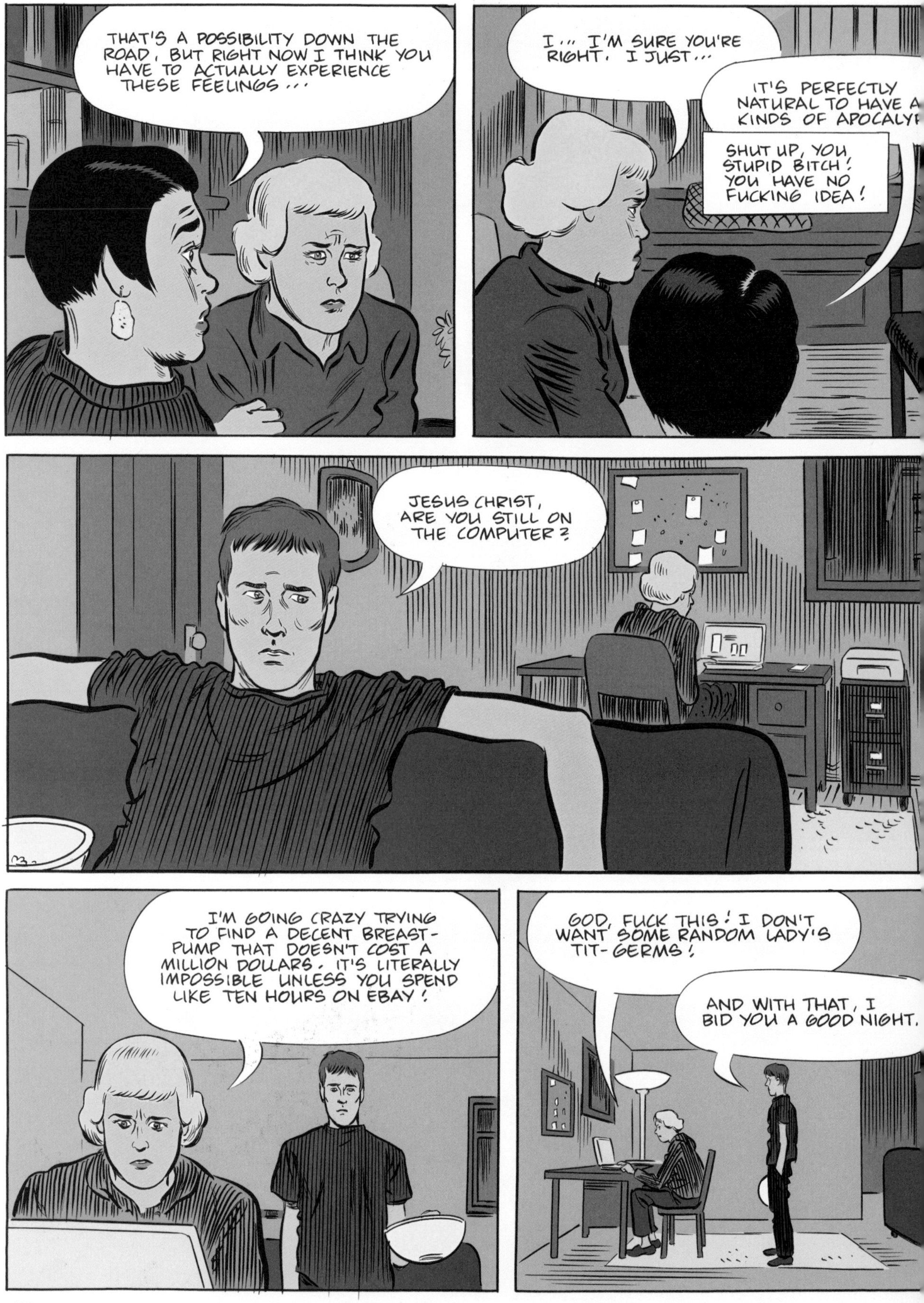
THAT'S A POSSIBILITY DOWN THE ROAD, BUT RIGHT NOW I THINK YOU HAVE TO ACTUALLY EXPERIENCE THESE FEELINGS...
I... I'M SURE YOU'RE RIGHT. I JUST...
IT'S PERFECTLY NATURAL TO HAVE A KINDS OF APOCALYP
SHUT UP, YOU STUPID BITCH! YOU HAVE NO FUCKING IDEA!
JESUS CHRIST, ARE YOU STILL ON THE COMPUTER?
I'M GOING CRAZY TRYING TO FIND A DECENT BREAST-PUMP THAT DOESN'T COST A MILLION DOLLARS. IT'S LITERALLY IMPOSSIBLE UNLESS YOU SPEND LIKE TEN HOURS ON EBAY!
GOD, FUCK THIS! I DON'T WANT SOME RANDOM LADY'S TIT-GERMS!
AND WITH THAT, I BID YOU A GOOD NIGHT.

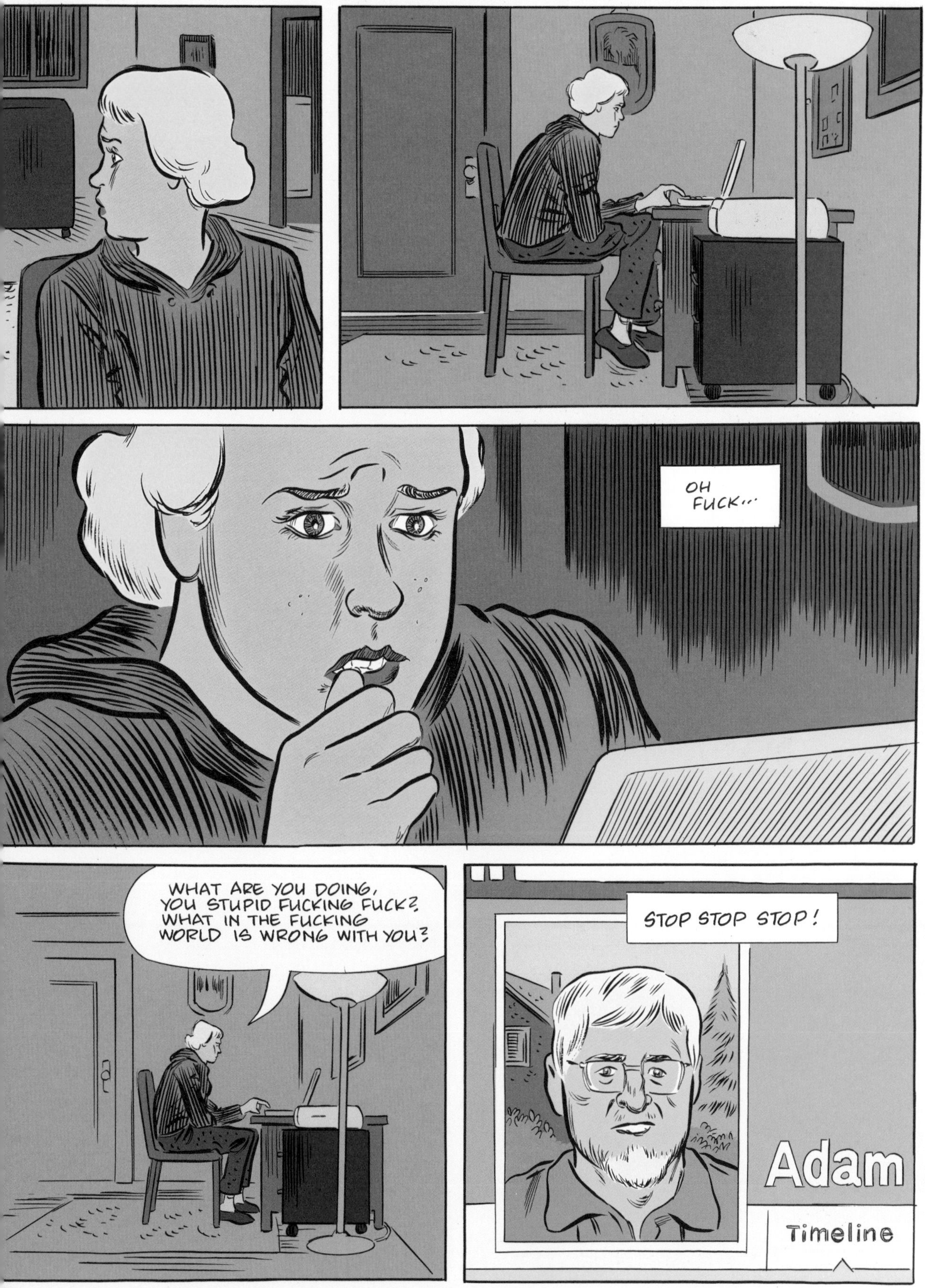
OH FUCK...
WHAT ARE YOU DOING, YOU STUPID FUCKING FUCK? WHAT IN THE FUCKING WORLD IS WRONG WITH YOU?
STOP STOP STOP!
Adam
Timeline

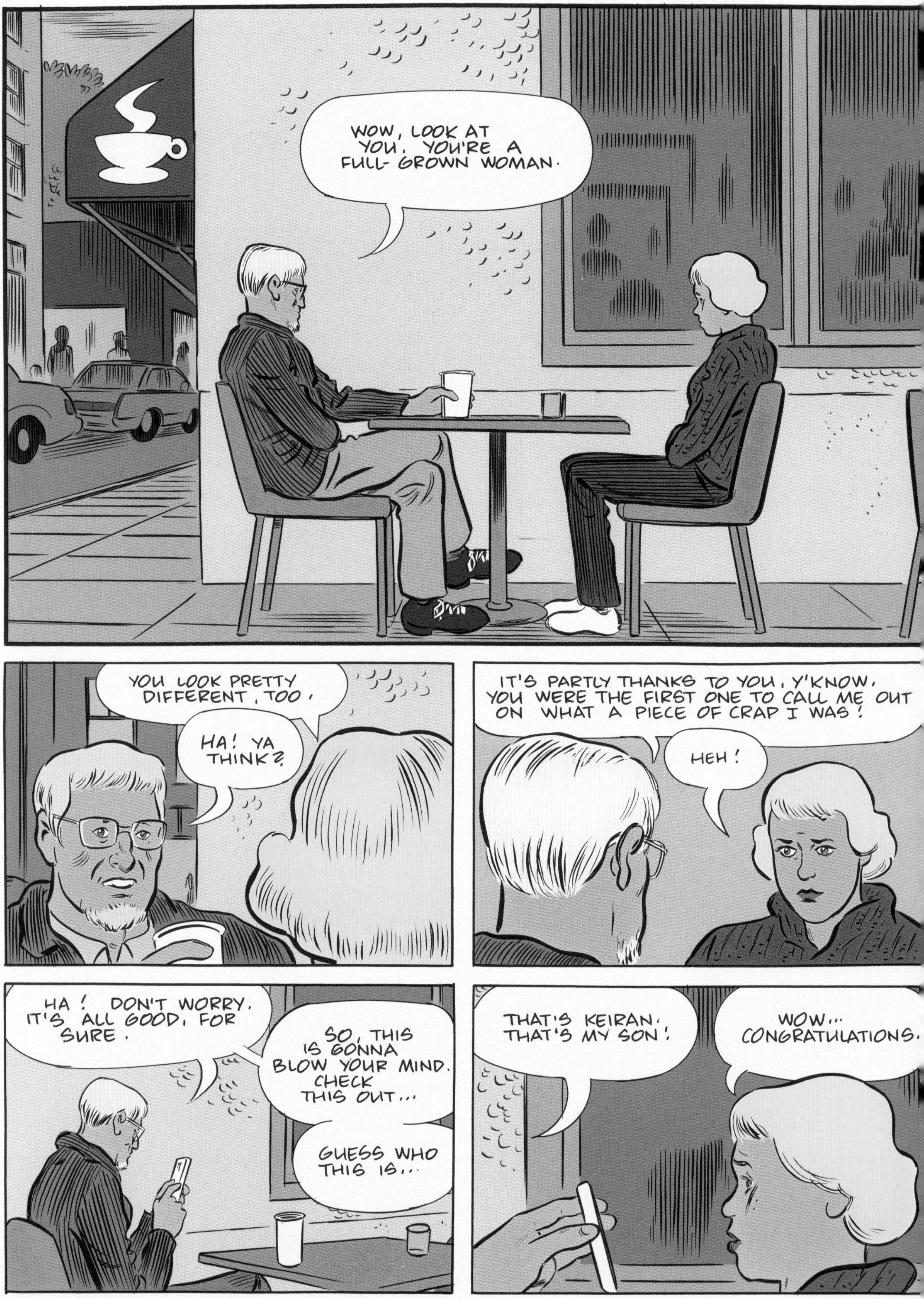
WOW, LOOK AT YOU. YOU'RE A FULL-GROWN WOMAN.
YOU LOOK PRETTY DIFFERENT, TOO.
HA! YA THINK?
IT'S PARTLY THANKS TO YOU, Y'KNOW. YOU WERE THE FIRST ONE TO CALL ME OUT ON WHAT A PIECE OF CRAP I WAS!
HEH!
HA! DON'T WORRY. IT'S ALL GOOD, FOR SURE.
SO, THIS IS GONNA BLOW YOUR MIND. CHECK THIS OUT...
GUESS WHO THIS IS...
THAT'S KEIRAN. THAT'S MY SON!
WOW... CONGRATULATIONS.

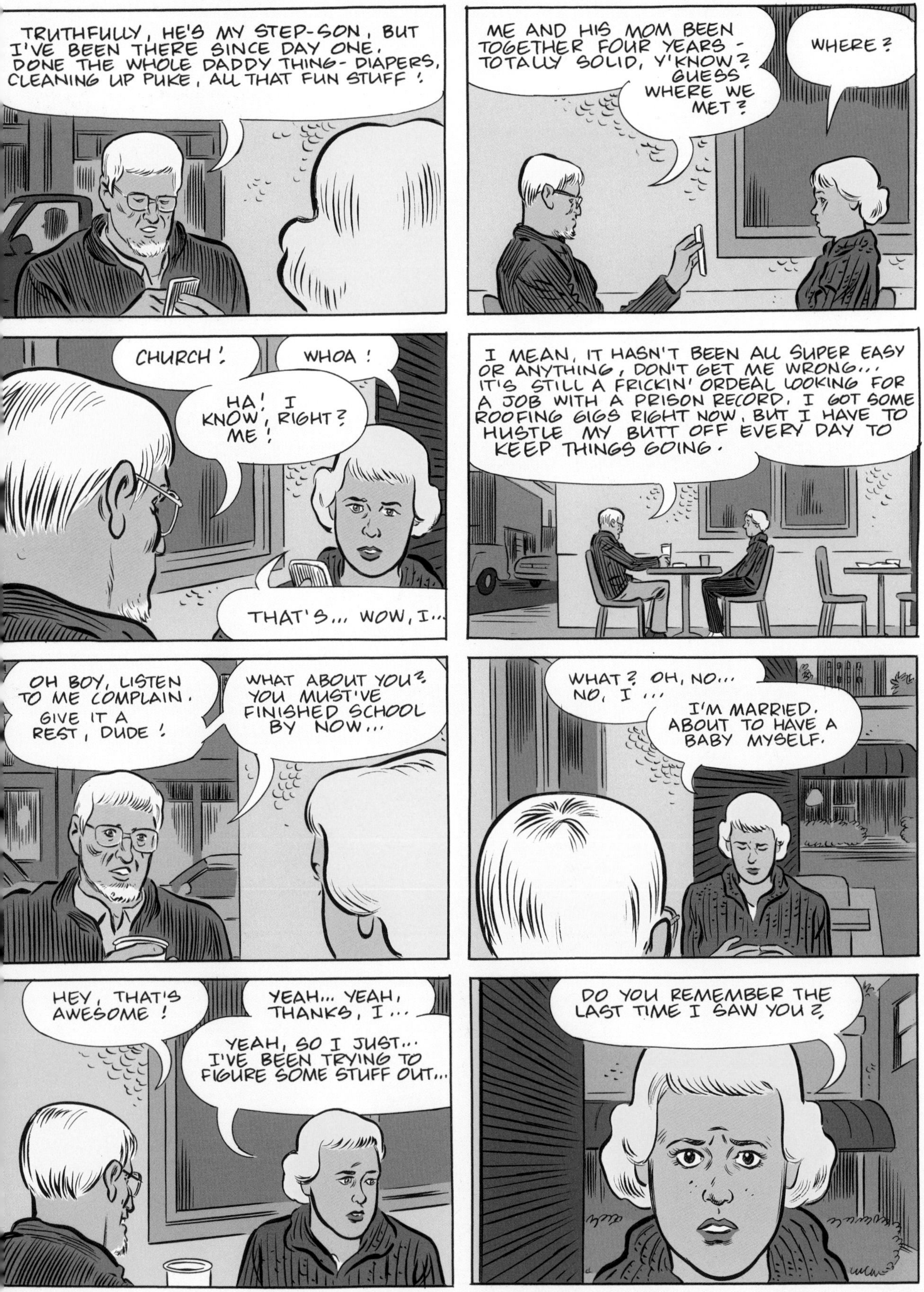
TRUTHFULLY, HE'S MY STEP-SON, BUT I'VE BEEN THERE SINCE DAY ONE. DONE THE WHOLE DADDY THING- DIAPERS, CLEANING UP PUKE, ALL THAT FUN STUFF!
ME AND HIS MOM BEEN TOGETHER FOUR YEARS - TOTALLY SOLID, Y'KNOW?
GUESS WHERE WE MET?
WHERE?
CHURCH!
WHOA!
HA! I KNOW, RIGHT? ME!
THAT'S... WOW, I...
I MEAN, IT HASN'T BEEN ALL SUPER EASY OR ANYTHING, DON'T GET ME WRONG... IT'S STILL A FRICKIN' ORDEAL LOOKING FOR A JOB WITH A PRISON RECORD. I GOT SOME ROOFING GIGS RIGHT NOW, BUT I HAVE TO HUSTLE MY BUTT OFF EVERY DAY TO KEEP THINGS GOING.
OH BOY, LISTEN TO ME COMPLAIN. GIVE IT A REST, DUDE!
WHAT ABOUT YOU? YOU MUST'VE FINISHED SCHOOL BY NOW...
WHAT? OH, NO... NO, I ...
I'M MARRIED. ABOUT TO HAVE A BABY MYSELF.
HEY, THAT'S AWESOME!
YEAH... YEAH, THANKS, I...
YEAH, SO I JUST... I'VE BEEN TRYING TO FIGURE SOME STUFF OUT...
DO YOU REMEMBER THE LAST TIME I SAW YOU?

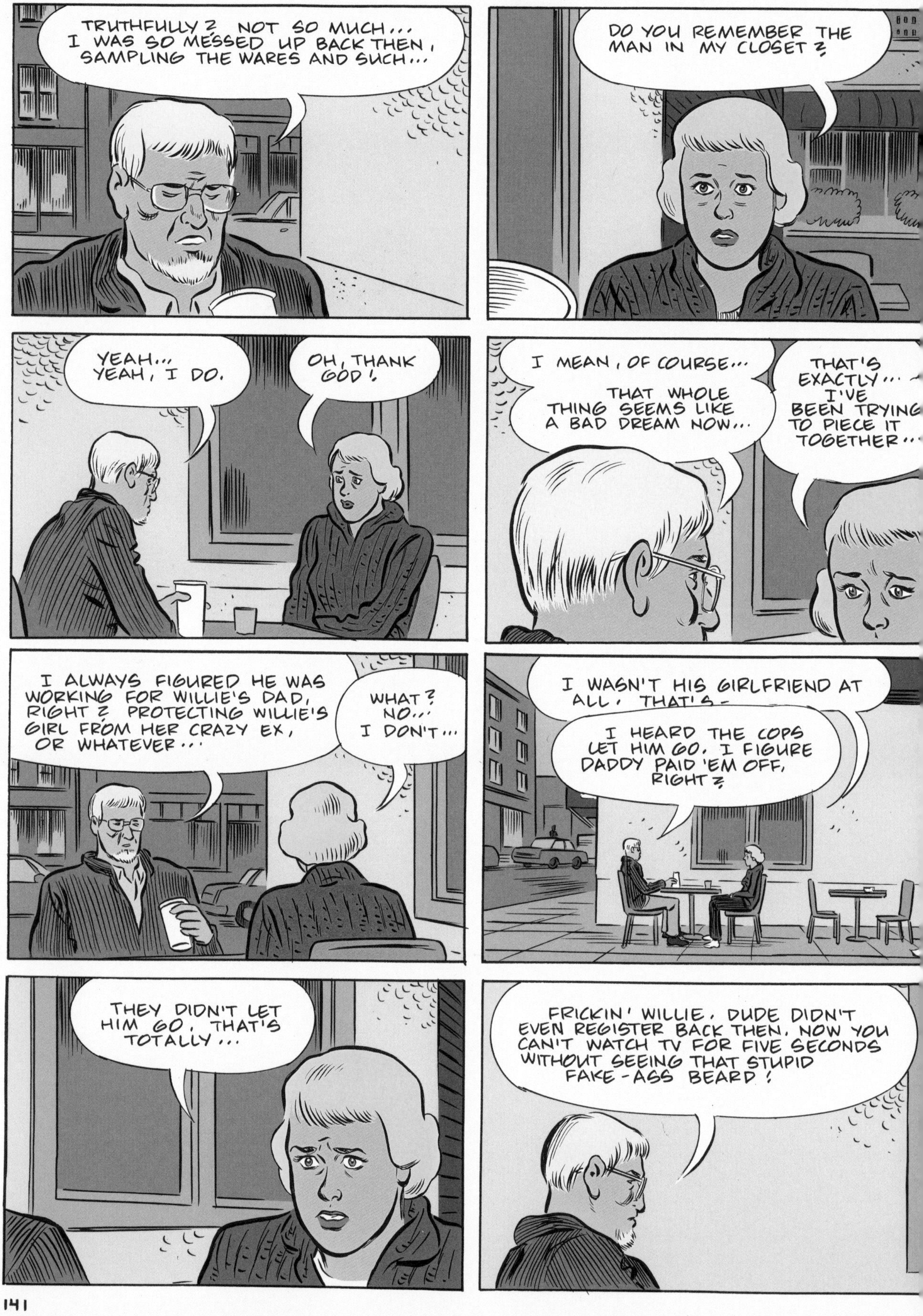
TRUTHFULLY? NOT SO MUCH... I WAS SO MESSED UP BACK THEN, SAMPLING THE WARES AND SUCH...
DO YOU REMEMBER THE MAN IN MY CLOSET?
YEAH... YEAH, I DO.
OH, THANK GOD!
I MEAN, OF COURSE...
THAT WHOLE THING SEEMS LIKE A BAD DREAM NOW...
THAT'S EXACTLY... I'VE BEEN TRYING TO PIECE IT TOGETHER...
I ALWAYS FIGURED HE WAS WORKING FOR WILLIE'S DAD, RIGHT? PROTECTING WILLIE'S GIRL FROM HER CRAZY EX, OR WHATEVER...
WHAT? NO... I DON'T...
I WASN'T HIS GIRLFRIEND AT ALL, THAT'S-
I HEARD THE COPS LET HIM GO. I FIGURE DADDY PAID 'EM OFF, RIGHT?
THEY DIDN'T LET HIM GO, THAT'S TOTALLY...
FRICKIN' WILLIE, DUDE DIDN'T EVEN REGISTER BACK THEN. NOW YOU CAN'T WATCH TV FOR FIVE SECONDS WITHOUT SEEING THAT STUPID FAKE-ASS BEARD!

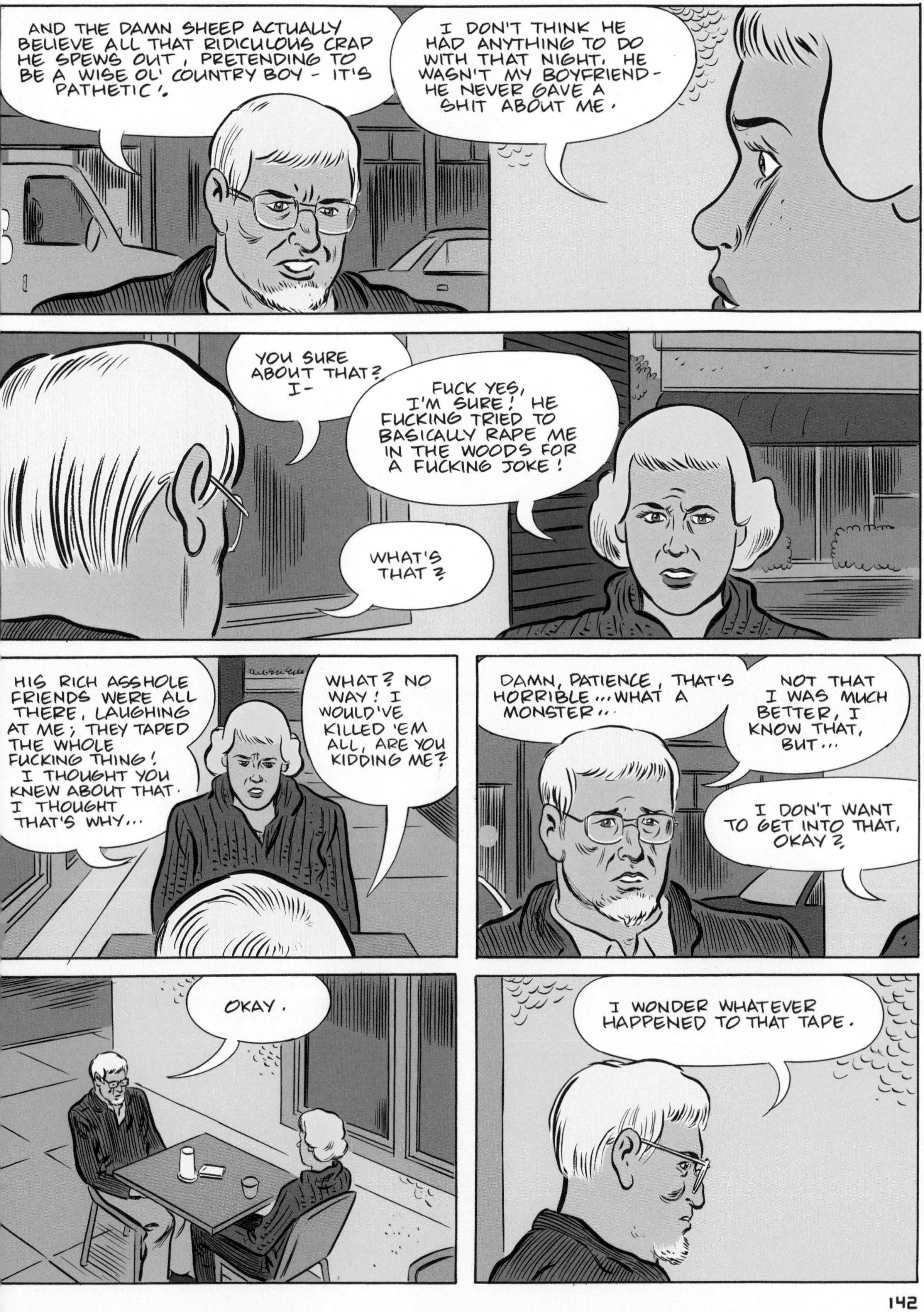
AND THE DAMN SHEEP ACTUALLY BELIEVE ALL THAT RIDICULOUS CRAP HE SPEWS OUT, PRETENDING TO BE A WISE OL' COUNTRY BOY - IT'S PATHETIC!
I DON'T THINK HE HAD ANYTHING TO DO WITH THAT NIGHT. HE WASN'T MY BOYFRIEND - HE NEVER GAVE A SHIT ABOUT ME.
YOU SURE ABOUT THAT? I-
FUCK YES, I'M SURE! HE FUCKING TRIED TO BASICALLY RAPE ME IN THE WOODS FOR A FUCKING JOKE!
WHAT'S THAT?
HIS RICH ASSHOLE FRIENDS WERE ALL THERE, LAUGHING AT ME; THEY TAPED THE WHOLE FUCKING THING! I THOUGHT YOU KNEW ABOUT THAT. I THOUGHT THAT'S WHY...
WHAT? NO WAY! I WOULD'VE KILLED 'EM ALL, ARE YOU KIDDING ME?
DAMN, PATIENCE, THAT'S HORRIBLE... WHAT A MONSTER...
NOT THAT I WAS MUCH BETTER, I KNOW THAT, BUT...
I DON'T WANT TO GET INTO THAT, OKAY?
OKAY.
I WONDER WHATEVER HAPPENED TO THAT TAPE.

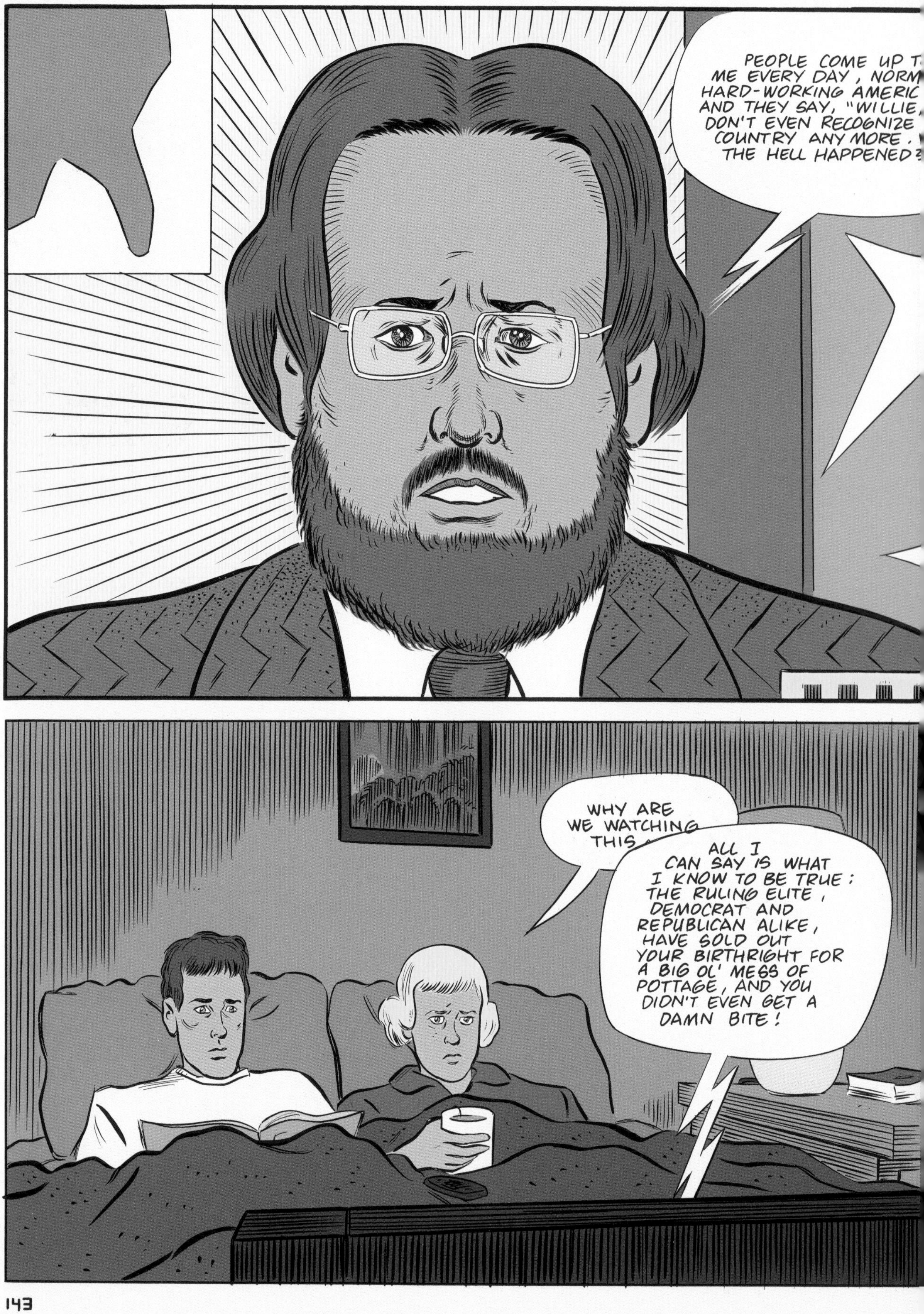

PEOPLE COME UP T
ME EVERY DAY, NORM
HARD-WORKING AMERIC
AND THEY SAY, "WILLIE,
DON'T EVEN RECOGNIZE
COUNTRY ANY MORE.
THE HELL HAPPENED?
WHY ARE WE WATCHING THIS
ALL I CAN SAY IS WHAT I KNOW TO BE TRUE: THE RULING ELITE, DEMOCRAT AND REPUBLICAN ALIKE, HAVE SOLD OUT YOUR BIRTHRIGHT FOR A BIG OL' MESS OF POTTAGE, AND YOU DIDN'T EVEN GET A DAMN BITE!

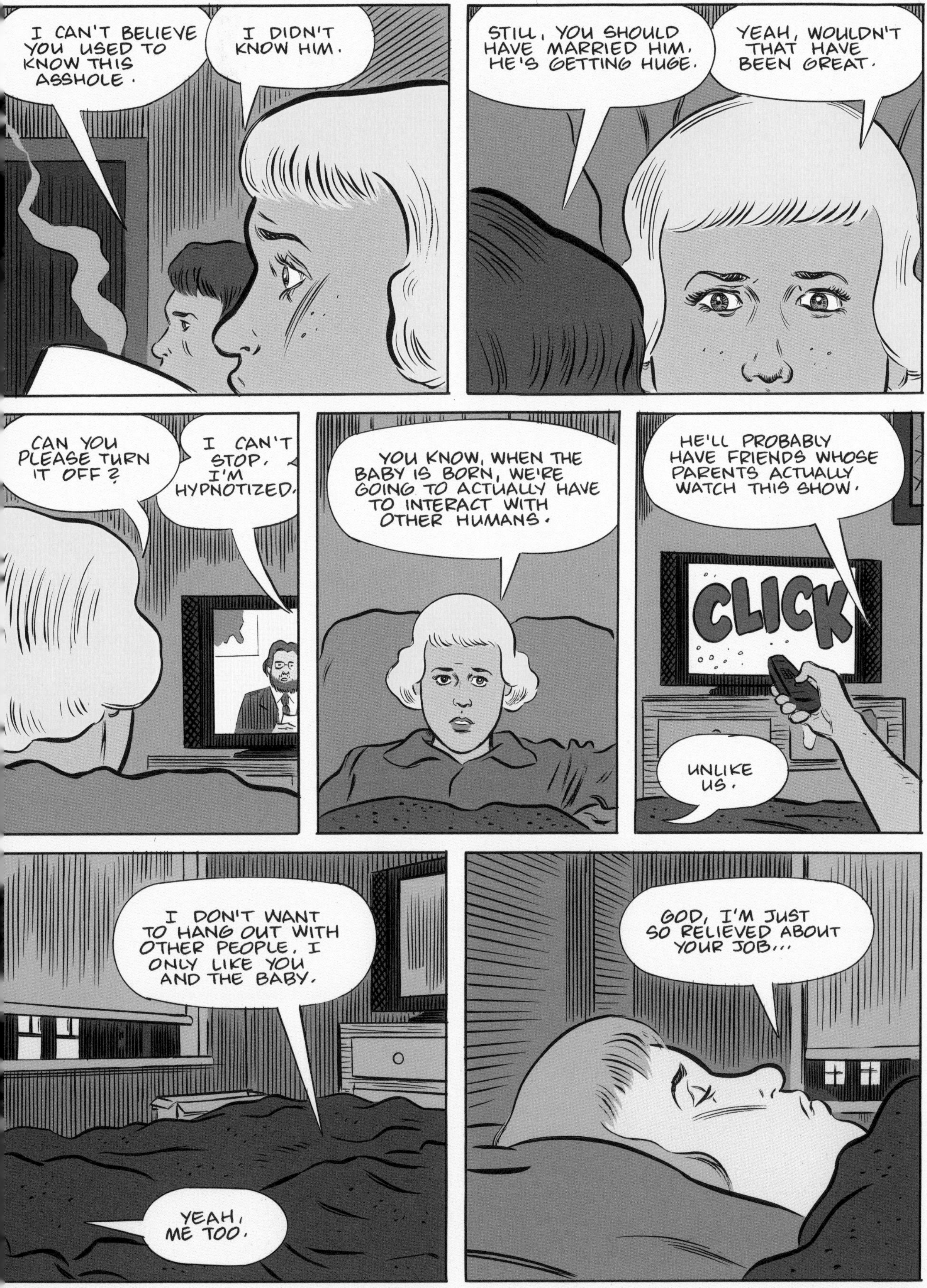
I CAN'T BELIEVE YOU USED TO KNOW THIS ASSHOLE.
I DIDN'T KNOW HIM.
STILL, YOU SHOULD HAVE MARRIED HIM. HE'S GETTING HUGE.
YEAH, WOULDN'T THAT HAVE BEEN GREAT.
CAN YOU PLEASE TURN IT OFF?
I CAN'T STOP. I'M HYPNOTIZED.
YOU KNOW, WHEN THE BABY IS BORN, WE'RE GOING TO ACTUALLY HAVE TO INTERACT WITH OTHER HUMANS.
HE'LL PROBABLY HAVE FRIENDS WHOSE PARENTS ACTUALLY WATCH THIS SHOW.
CLICK
UNLIKE US.
I DON'T WANT TO HANG OUT WITH OTHER PEOPLE. I ONLY LIKE YOU AND THE BABY.
YEAH, ME TOO.
GOD, I'M JUST SO RELIEVED ABOUT YOUR JOB...

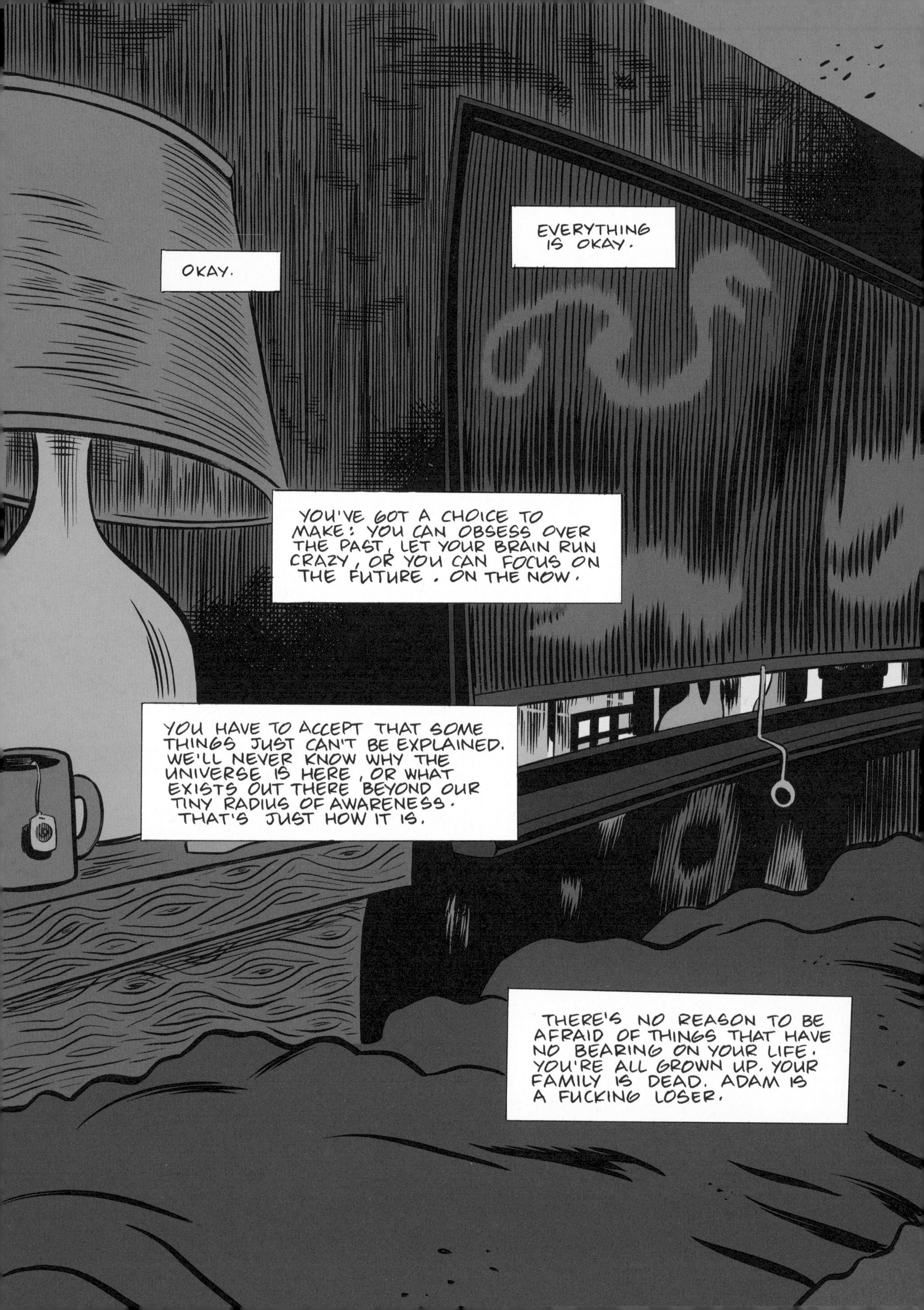
OKAY.
EVERYTHING IS OKAY.
YOU'VE GOT A CHOICE TO MAKE: YOU CAN OBSESS OVER THE PAST, LET YOUR BRAIN RUN CRAZY, OR YOU CAN FOCUS ON THE FUTURE. ON THE NOW.
YOU HAVE TO ACCEPT THAT SOME THINGS JUST CAN'T BE EXPLAINED. WE'LL NEVER KNOW WHY THE UNIVERSE IS HERE, OR WHAT EXISTS OUT THERE BEYOND OUR TINY RADIUS OF AWARENESS. THAT'S JUST HOW IT IS.
THERE'S NO REASON TO BE AFRAID OF THINGS THAT HAVE NO BEARING ON YOUR LIFE. YOU'RE ALL GROWN UP. YOUR FAMILY IS DEAD. ADAM IS A FUCKING LOSER.

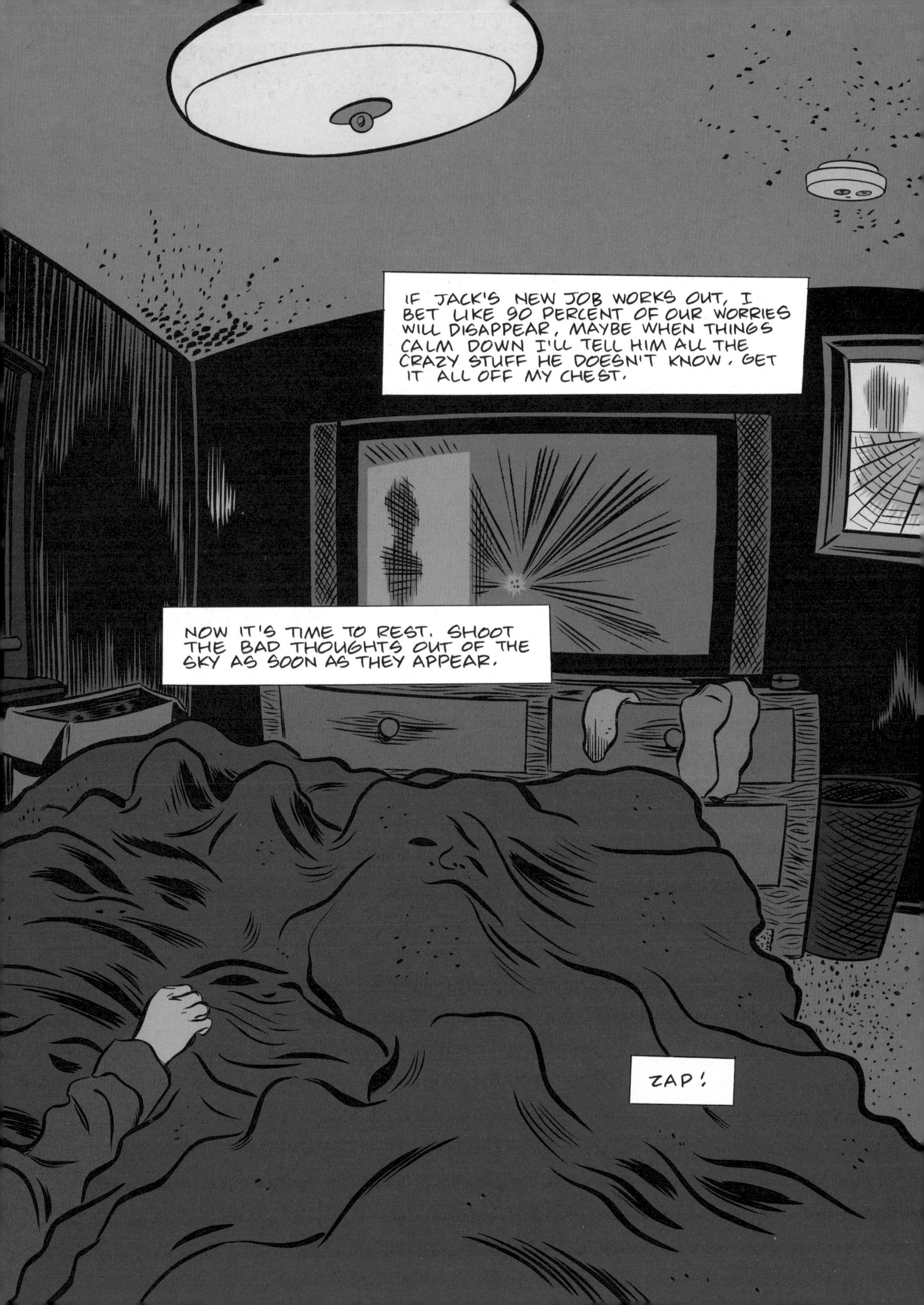
IF JACK'S NEW JOB WORKS OUT, I BET LIKE 90 PERCENT OF OUR WORRIES WILL DISAPPEAR. MAYBE WHEN THINGS CALM DOWN I'LL TELL HIM ALL THE CRAZY STUFF HE DOESN'T KNOW. GET IT ALL OFF MY CHEST.
NOW IT'S TIME TO REST. SHOOT THE BAD THOUGHTS OUT OF THE SKY AS SOON AS THEY APPEAR.
ZAP!

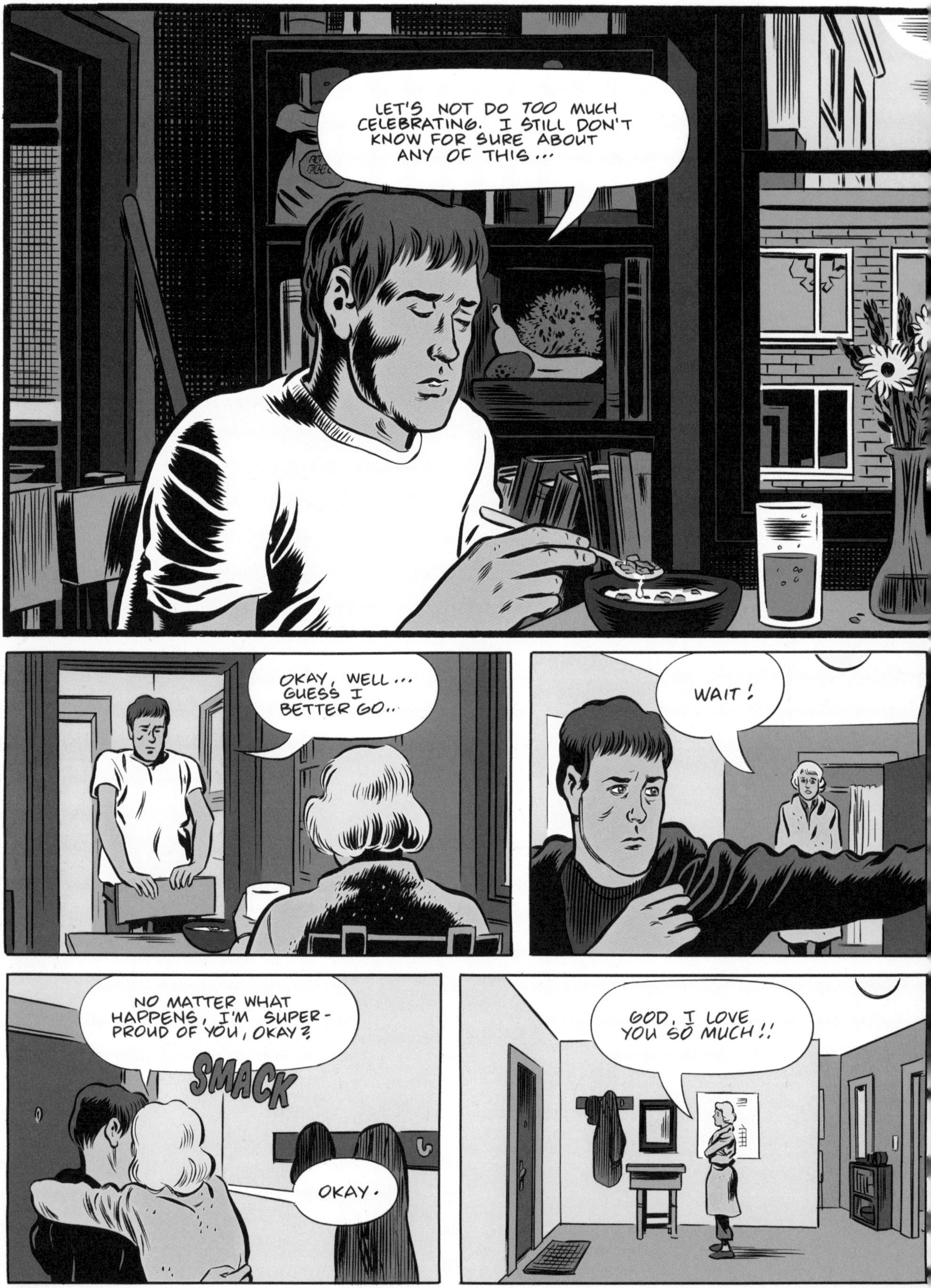
LET'S NOT DO TOO MUCH CELEBRATING. I STILL DON'T KNOW FOR SURE ABOUT ANY OF THIS...
OKAY, WELL... GUESS I BETTER GO...
WAIT!
NO MATTER WHAT HAPPENS, I'M SUPER-PROUD OF YOU, OKAY?
SMACK
OKAY.
GOD, I LOVE YOU SO MUCH!!

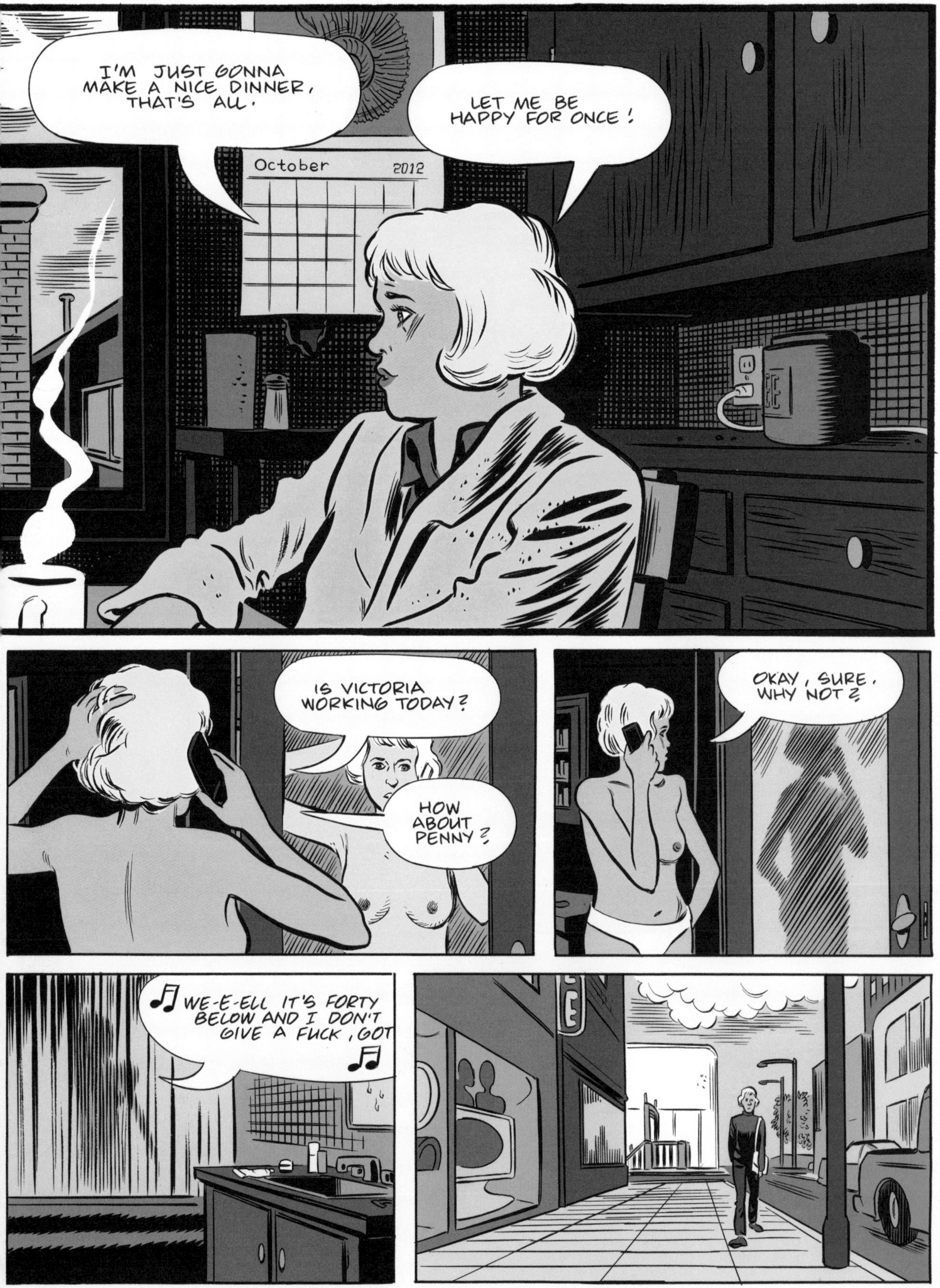
I'M JUST GONNA MAKE A NICE DINNER, THAT'S ALL.
LET ME BE HAPPY FOR ONCE!
October 2012
IS VICTORIA WORKING TODAY?
HOW ABOUT PENNY?
OKAY, SURE. WHY NOT?
♫ WE-E-ELL IT'S FORTY BELOW AND I DON'T GIVE A FUCK, GOT ♫

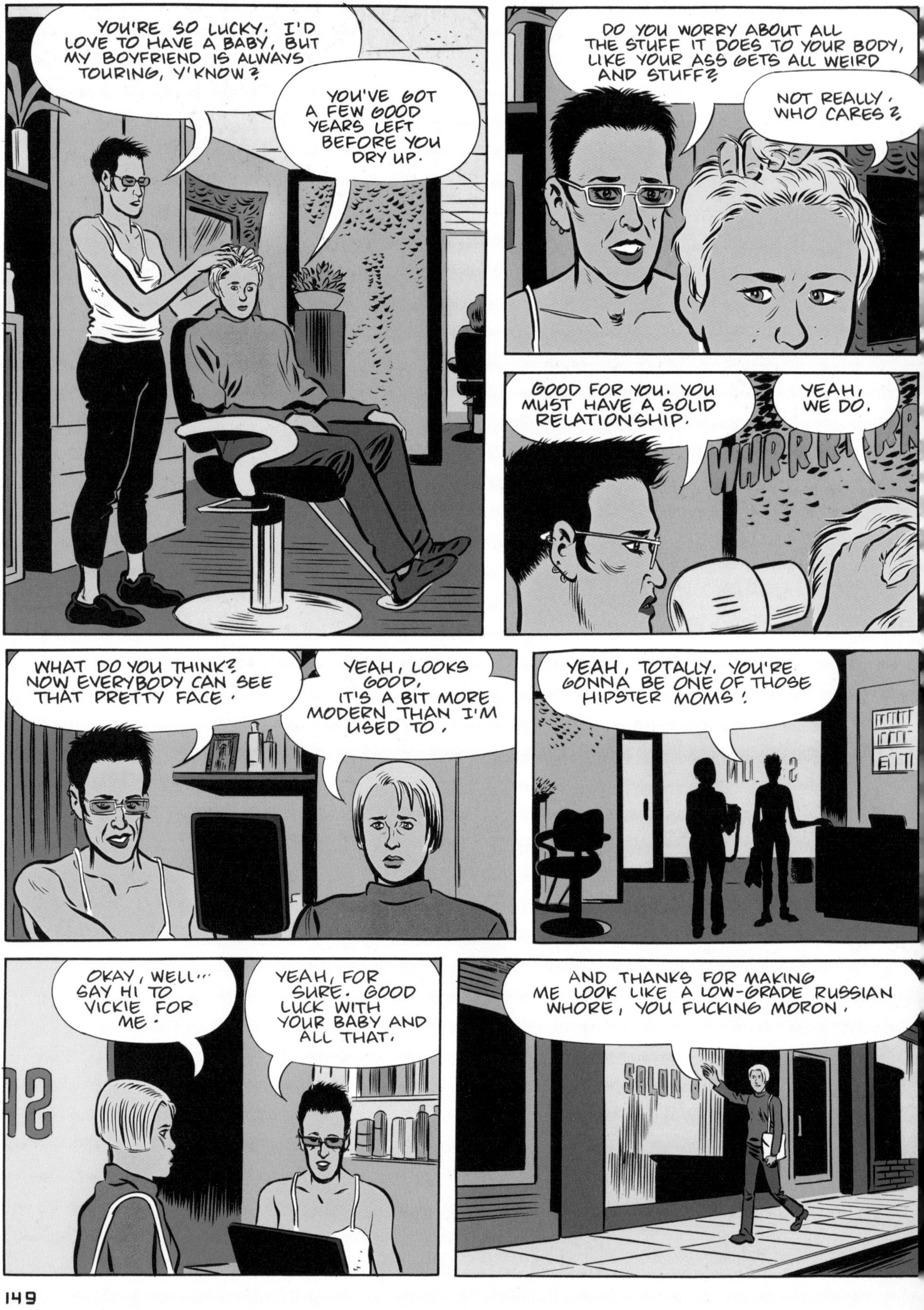
YOU'RE SO LUCKY. I'D LOVE TO HAVE A BABY, BUT MY BOYFRIEND IS ALWAYS TOURING, Y'KNOW?
YOU'VE GOT A FEW GOOD YEARS LEFT BEFORE YOU DRY UP.
DO YOU WORRY ABOUT ALL THE STUFF IT DOES TO YOUR BODY, LIKE YOUR ASS GETS ALL WEIRD AND STUFF?
NOT REALLY. WHO CARES?
GOOD FOR YOU. YOU MUST HAVE A SOLID RELATIONSHIP.
YEAH, WE DO.
WHRRR
WHAT DO YOU THINK? NOW EVERYBODY CAN SEE THAT PRETTY FACE.
YEAH, LOOKS GOOD. IT'S A BIT MORE MODERN THAN I'M USED TO.
YEAH, TOTALLY. YOU'RE GONNA BE ONE OF THOSE HIPSTER MOMS!
OKAY, WELL... SAY HI TO VICKIE FOR ME.
YEAH, FOR SURE. GOOD LUCK WITH YOUR BABY AND ALL THAT.
AND THANKS FOR MAKING ME LOOK LIKE A LOW-GRADE RUSSIAN WHORE, YOU FUCKING MORON.
SALON

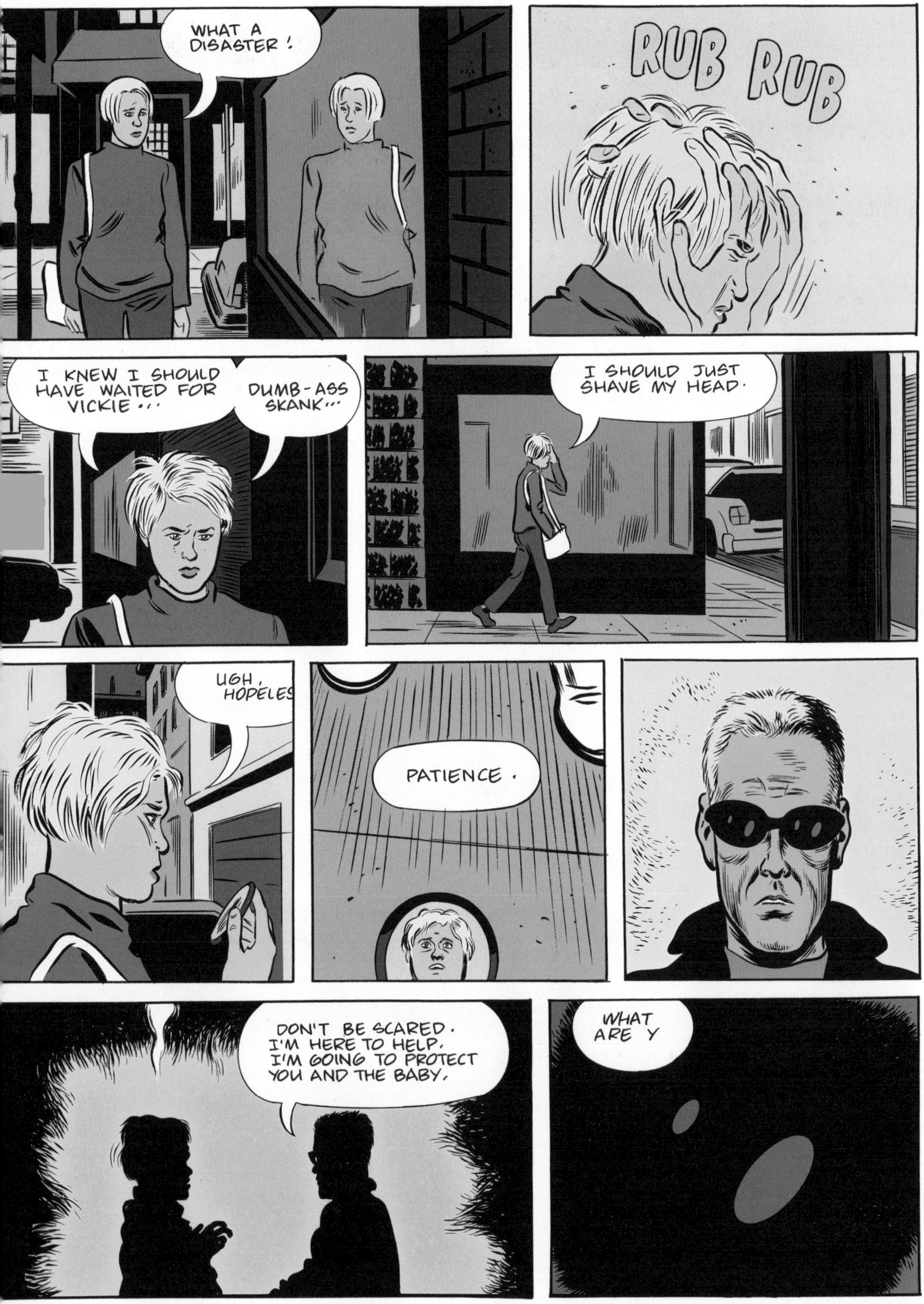
WHAT A DISASTER!
RUB RUB
I KNEW I SHOULD HAVE WAITED FOR VICKIE...
DUMB-ASS SKANK...
I SHOULD JUST SHAVE MY HEAD.
UGH, HOPELES
PATIENCE.
DON'T BE SCARED. I'M HERE TO HELP. I'M GOING TO PROTECT YOU AND THE BABY.
WHAT ARE Y

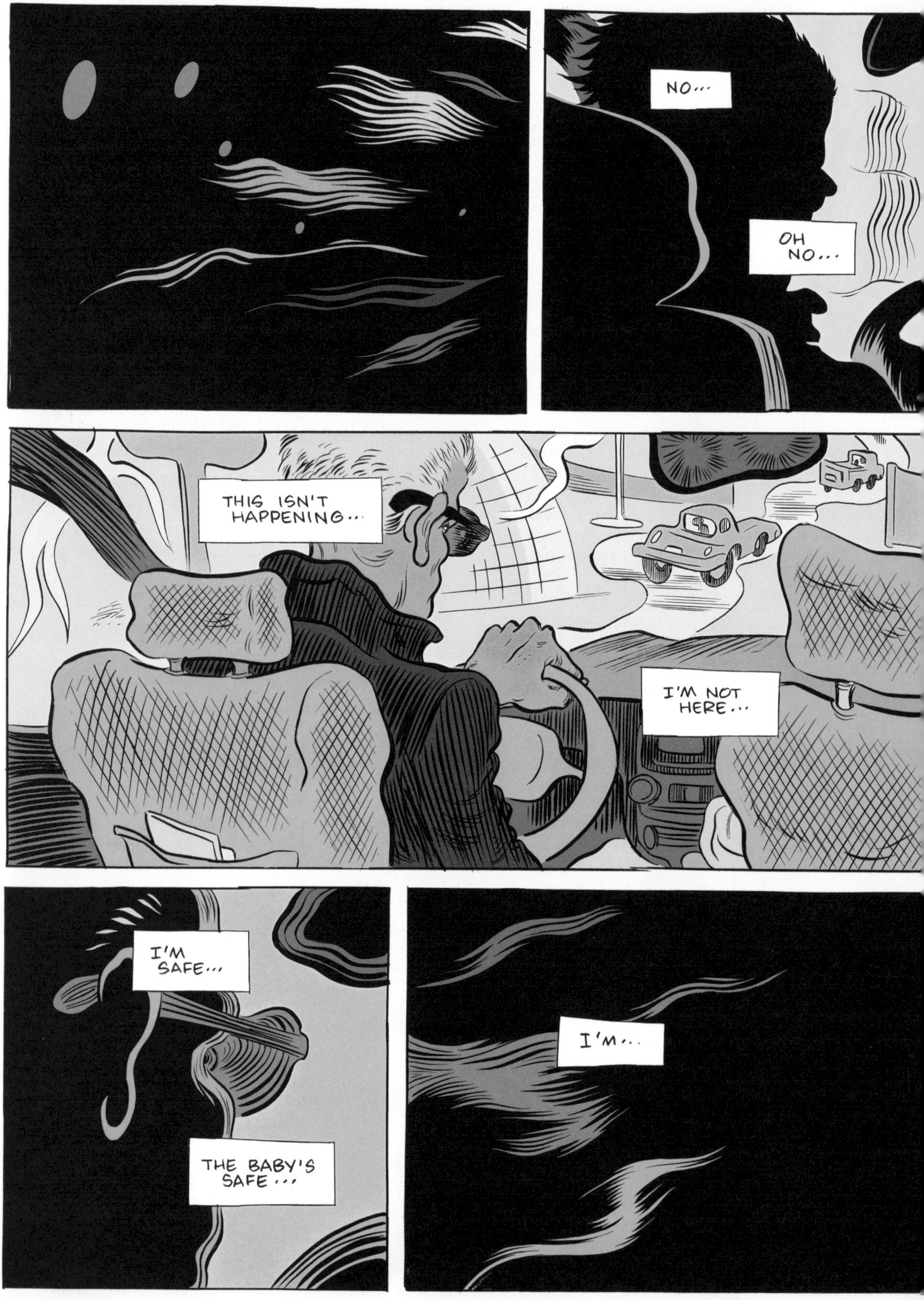
NO...
OH NO...
THIS ISN'T HAPPENING...
I'M NOT HERE...
I'M SAFE...
THE BABY'S SAFE...
I'M...

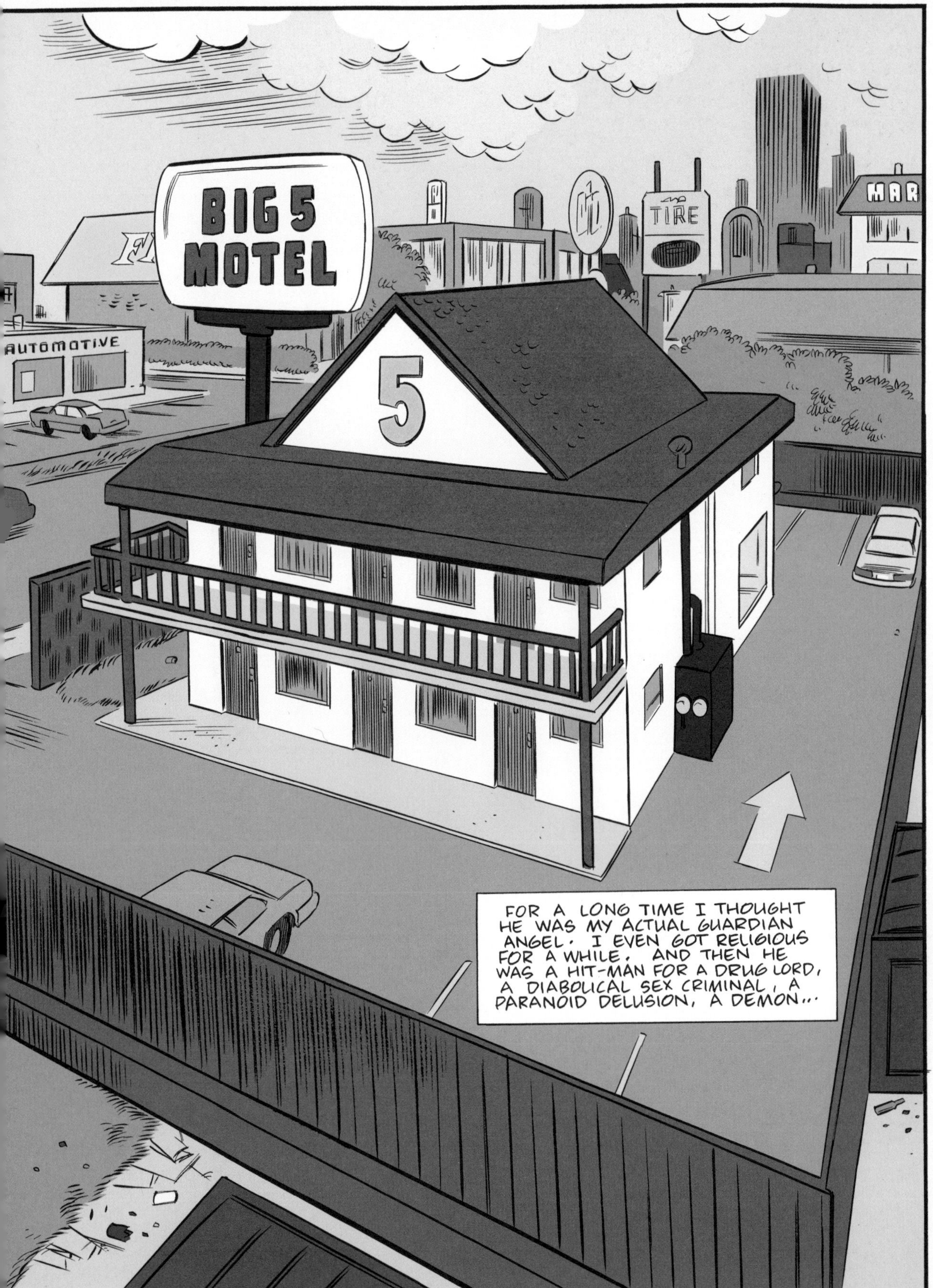
BIG 5 MOTEL
AUTOMOTIVE
TIRE
MAR
5
FOR A LONG TIME I THOUGHT HE WAS MY ACTUAL GUARDIAN ANGEL. I EVEN GOT RELIGIOUS FOR A WHILE. AND THEN HE WAS A HIT-MAN FOR A DRUG LORD, A DIABOLICAL SEX CRIMINAL, A PARANOID DELUSION, A DEMON...

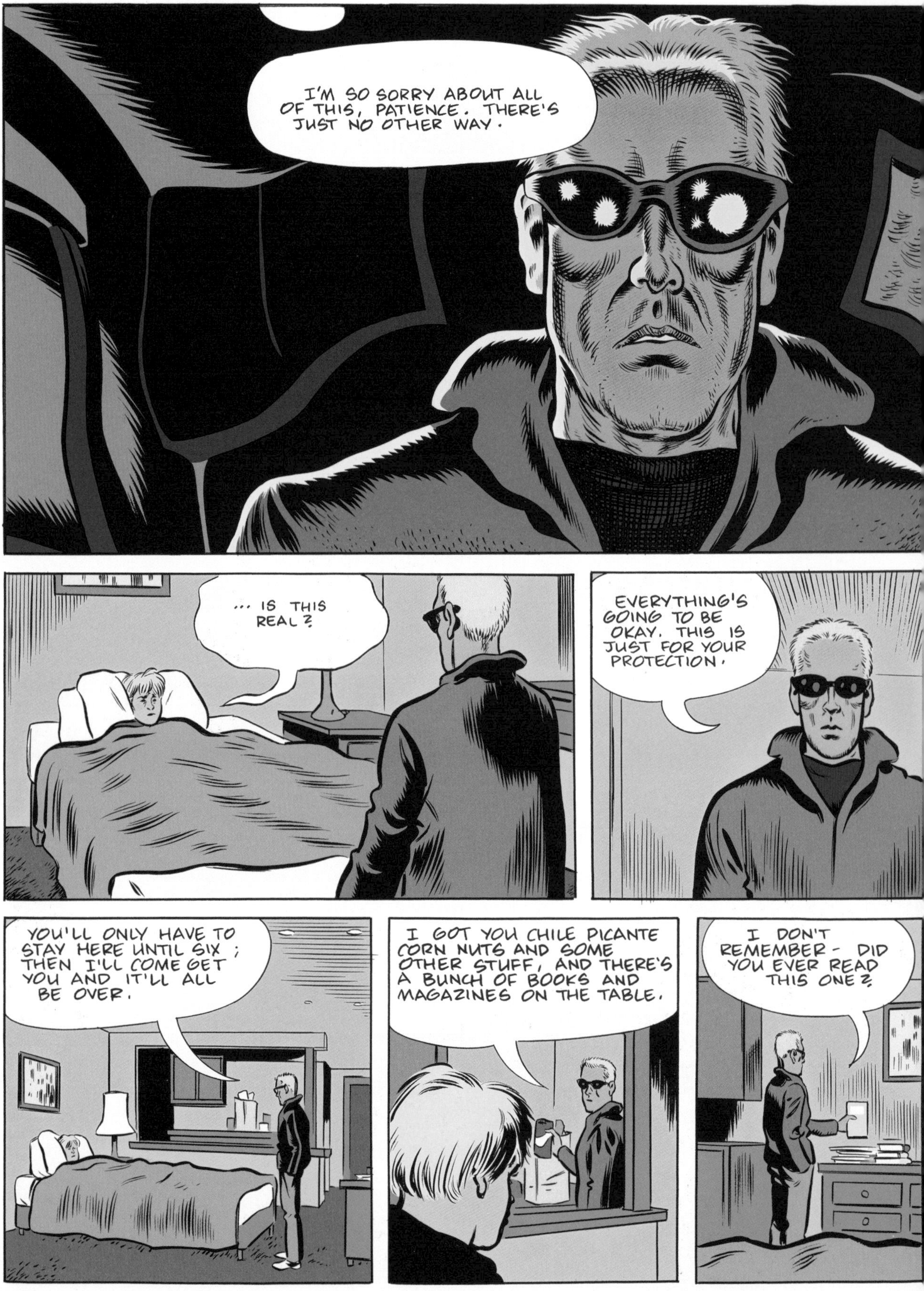
I'M SO SORRY ABOUT ALL OF THIS, PATIENCE. THERE'S JUST NO OTHER WAY.
... IS THIS REAL?
EVERYTHING'S GOING TO BE OKAY. THIS IS JUST FOR YOUR PROTECTION.
YOU'LL ONLY HAVE TO STAY HERE UNTIL SIX; THEN I'LL COME GET YOU AND IT'LL ALL BE OVER.
I GOT YOU CHILE PICANTE CORN NUTS AND SOME OTHER STUFF, AND THERE'S A BUNCH OF BOOKS AND MAGAZINES ON THE TABLE.
I DON'T REMEMBER - DID YOU EVER READ THIS ONE?

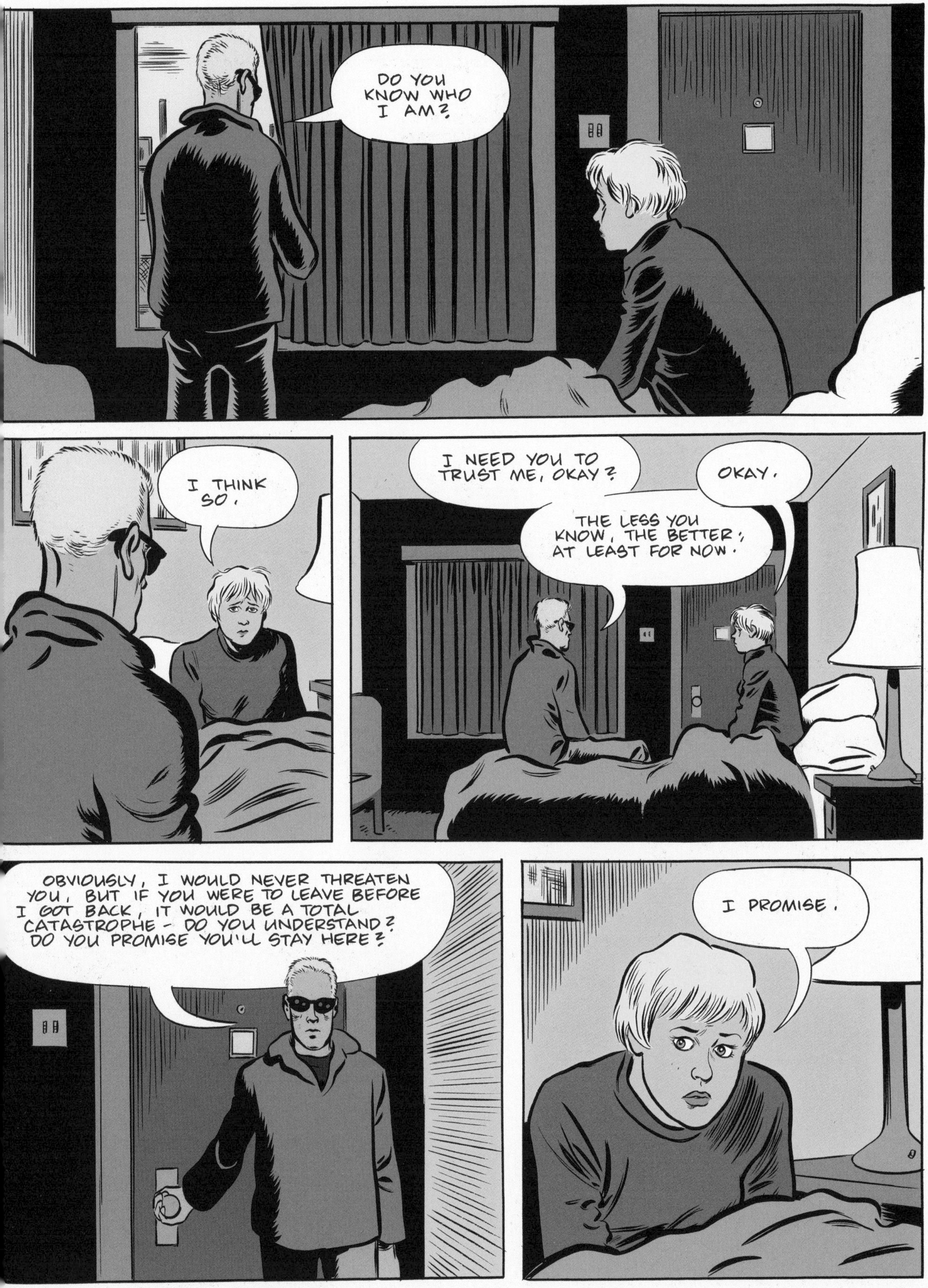

DO YOU KNOW WHO I AM?
I THINK SO.
I NEED YOU TO TRUST ME, OKAY?
OKAY.
THE LESS YOU KNOW, THE BETTER; AT LEAST FOR NOW.
OBVIOUSLY, I WOULD NEVER THREATEN YOU, BUT IF YOU WERE TO LEAVE BEFORE I GOT BACK, IT WOULD BE A TOTAL CATASTROPHE - DO YOU UNDERSTAND? DO YOU PROMISE YOU'LL STAY HERE?
I PROMISE.

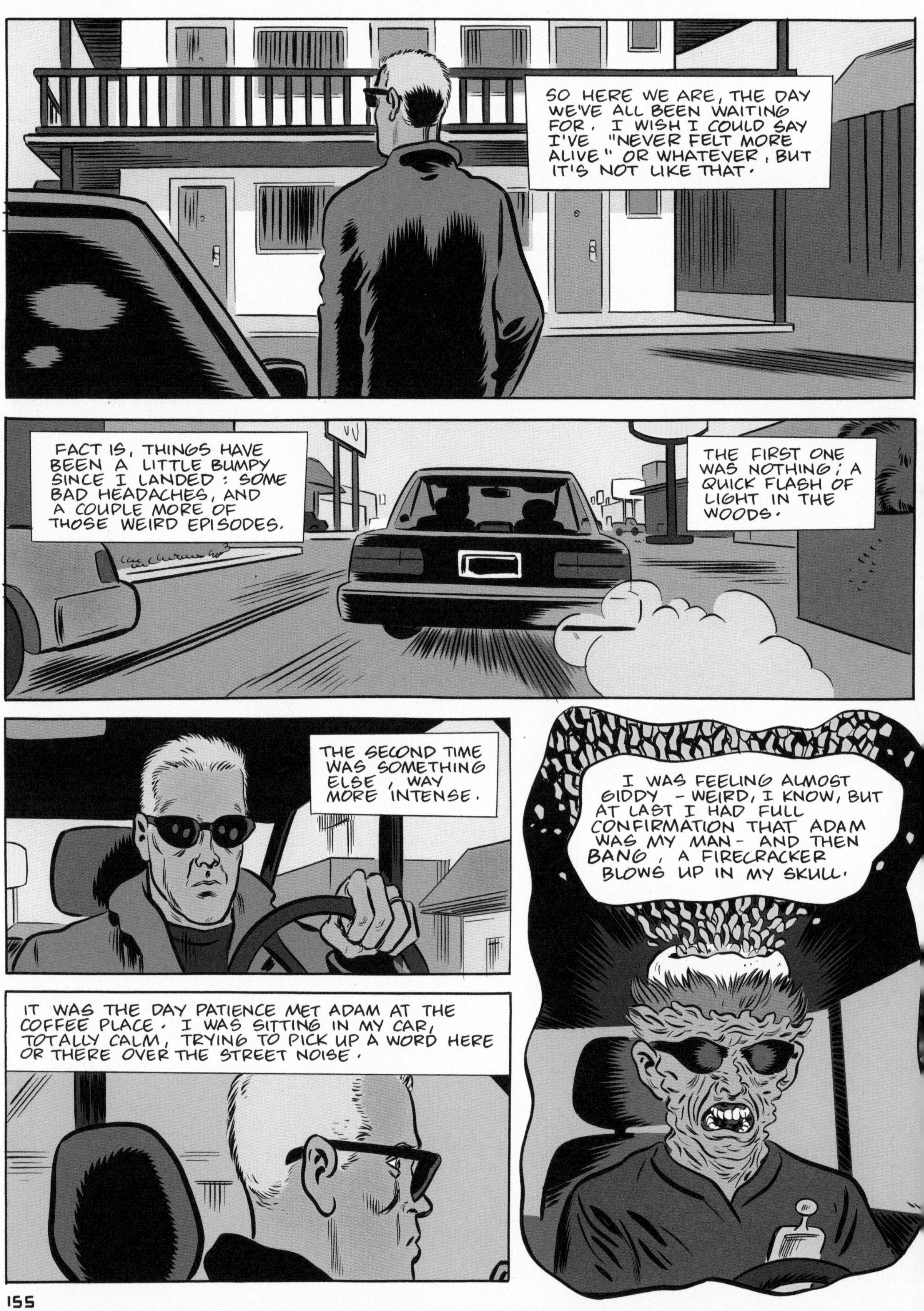
SO HERE WE ARE, THE DAY WE'VE ALL BEEN WAITING FOR. I WISH I COULD SAY I'VE "NEVER FELT MORE ALIVE" OR WHATEVER, BUT IT'S NOT LIKE THAT.
FACT IS, THINGS HAVE BEEN A LITTLE BUMPY SINCE I LANDED: SOME BAD HEADACHES, AND A COUPLE MORE OF THOSE WEIRD EPISODES.
THE FIRST ONE WAS NOTHING; A QUICK FLASH OF LIGHT IN THE WOODS.
THE SECOND TIME WAS SOMETHING ELSE, WAY MORE INTENSE.
IT WAS THE DAY PATIENCE MET ADAM AT THE COFFEE PLACE. I WAS SITTING IN MY CAR, TOTALLY CALM, TRYING TO PICK UP A WORD HERE OR THERE OVER THE STREET NOISE.
I WAS FEELING ALMOST GIDDY - WEIRD, I KNOW, BUT AT LAST I HAD FULL CONFIRMATION THAT ADAM WAS MY MAN- AND THEN BANG, A FIRECRACKER BLOWS UP IN MY SKULL.

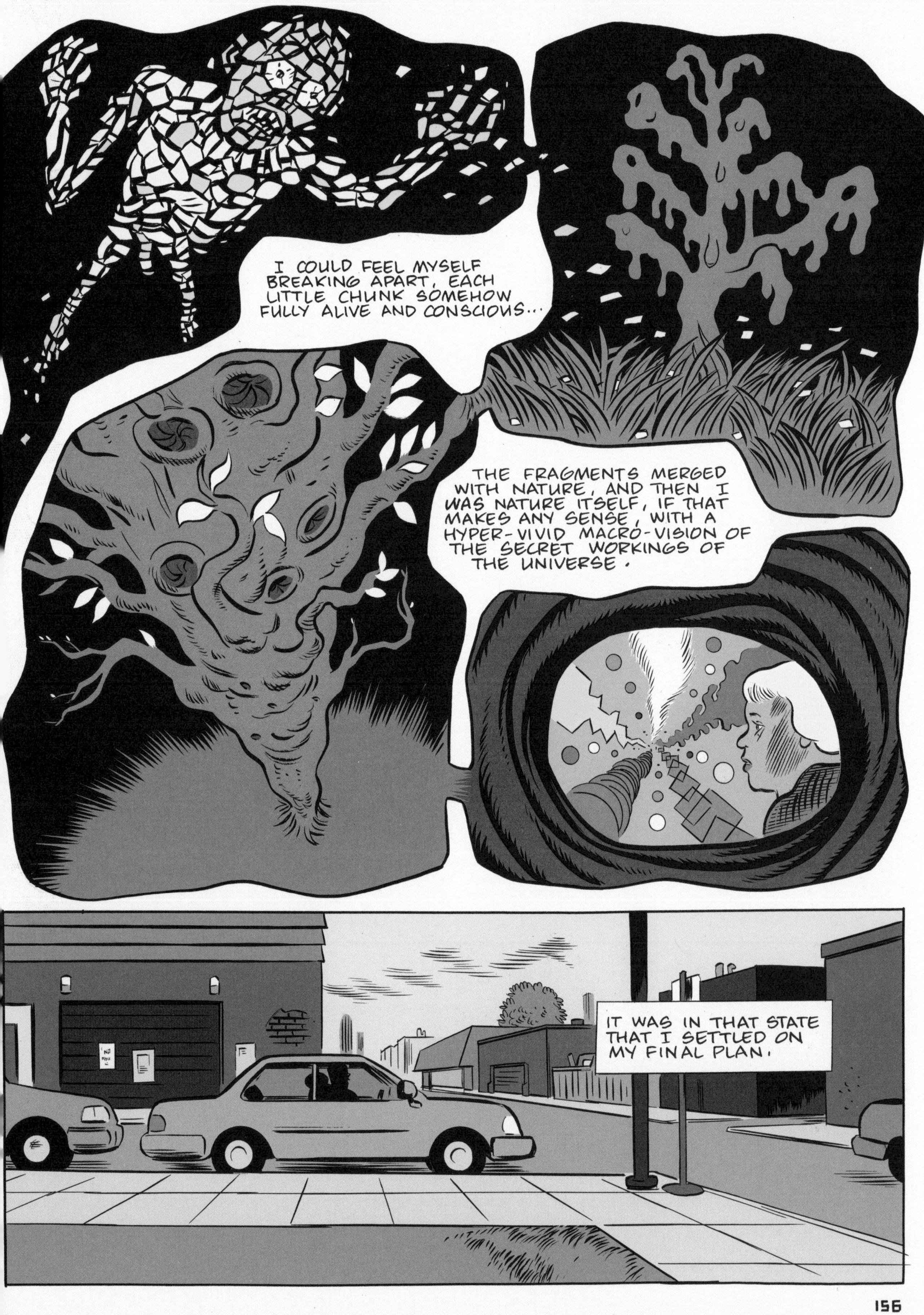
I COULD FEEL MYSELF BREAKING APART, EACH LITTLE CHUNK SOMEHOW FULLY ALIVE AND CONSCIOUS...
THE FRAGMENTS MERGED WITH NATURE, AND THEN I WAS NATURE ITSELF, IF THAT MAKES ANY SENSE, WITH A HYPER-VIVID MACRO-VISION OF THE SECRET WORKINGS OF THE UNIVERSE.
IT WAS IN THAT STATE THAT I SETTLED ON MY FINAL PLAN.

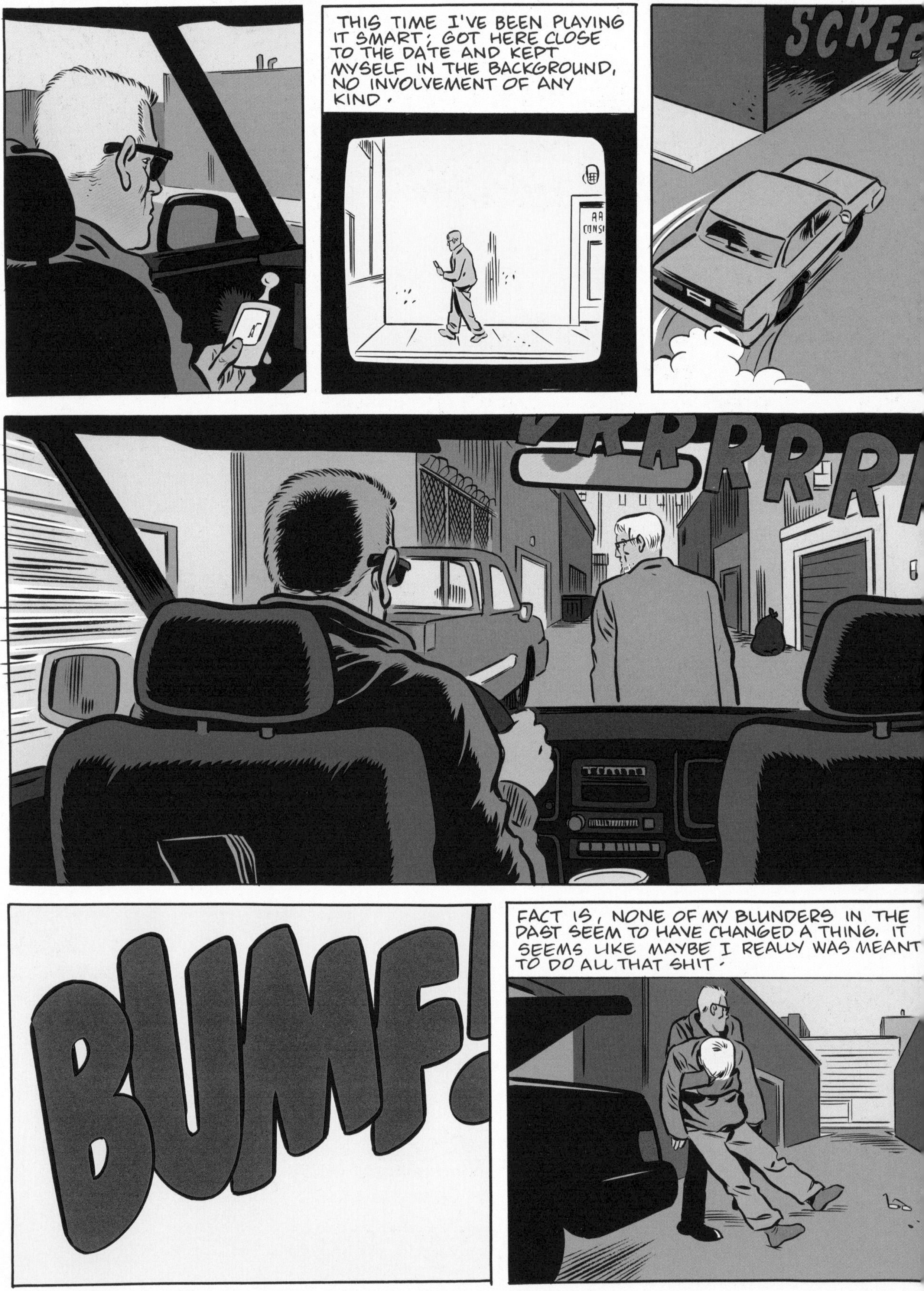
THIS TIME I'VE BEEN PLAYING IT SMART; GOT HERE CLOSE TO THE DATE AND KEPT MYSELF IN THE BACKGROUND, NO INVOLVEMENT OF ANY KIND.
SCREE
VRRRRR
BUMF!
FACT IS, NONE OF MY BLUNDERS IN THE PAST SEEM TO HAVE CHANGED A THING. IT SEEMS LIKE MAYBE I REALLY WAS MEANT TO DO ALL THAT SHIT.

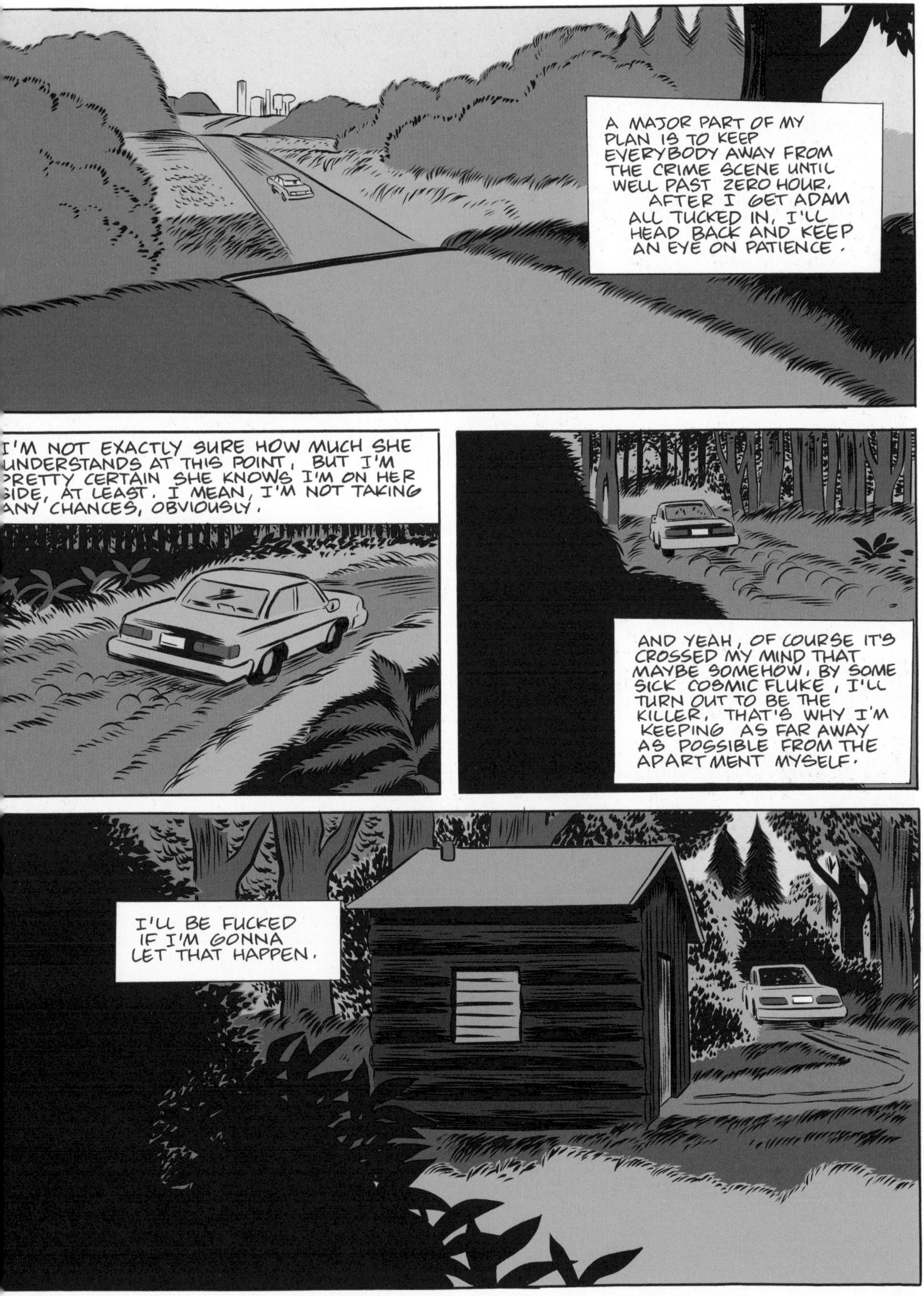
A MAJOR PART OF MY PLAN IS TO KEEP EVERYBODY AWAY FROM THE CRIME SCENE UNTIL WELL PAST ZERO HOUR. AFTER I GET ADAM ALL TUCKED IN, I'LL HEAD BACK AND KEEP AN EYE ON PATIENCE.
I'M NOT EXACTLY SURE HOW MUCH SHE UNDERSTANDS AT THIS POINT, BUT I'M PRETTY CERTAIN SHE KNOWS I'M ON HER SIDE, AT LEAST. I MEAN, I'M NOT TAKING ANY CHANCES, OBVIOUSLY.
AND YEAH, OF COURSE IT'S CROSSED MY MIND THAT MAYBE SOMEHOW, BY SOME SICK COSMIC FLUKE, I'LL TURN OUT TO BE THE KILLER. THAT'S WHY I'M KEEPING AS FAR AWAY AS POSSIBLE FROM THE APARTMENT MYSELF.
I'LL BE FUCKED IF I'M GONNA LET THAT HAPPEN.

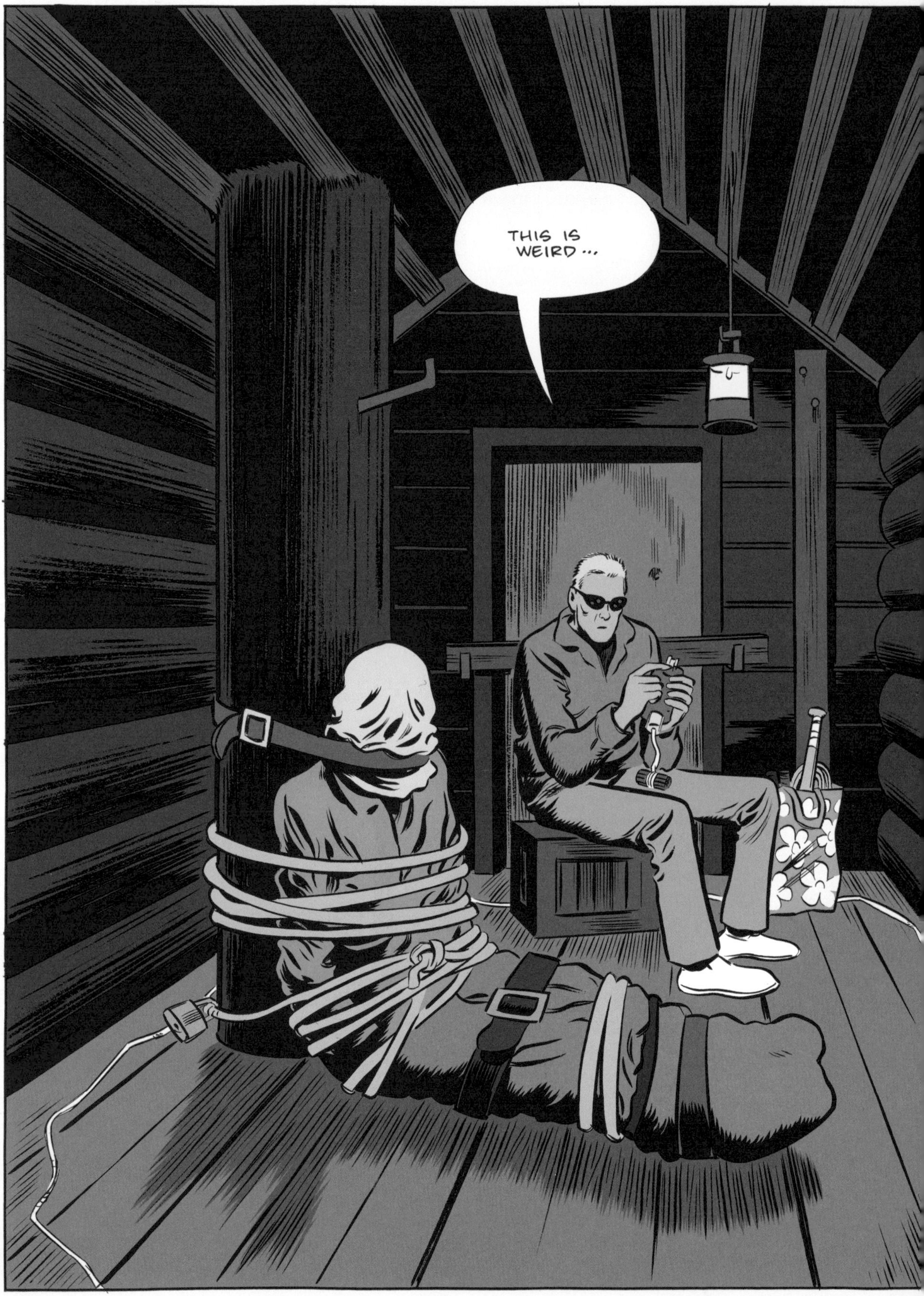
THIS IS WEIRD...

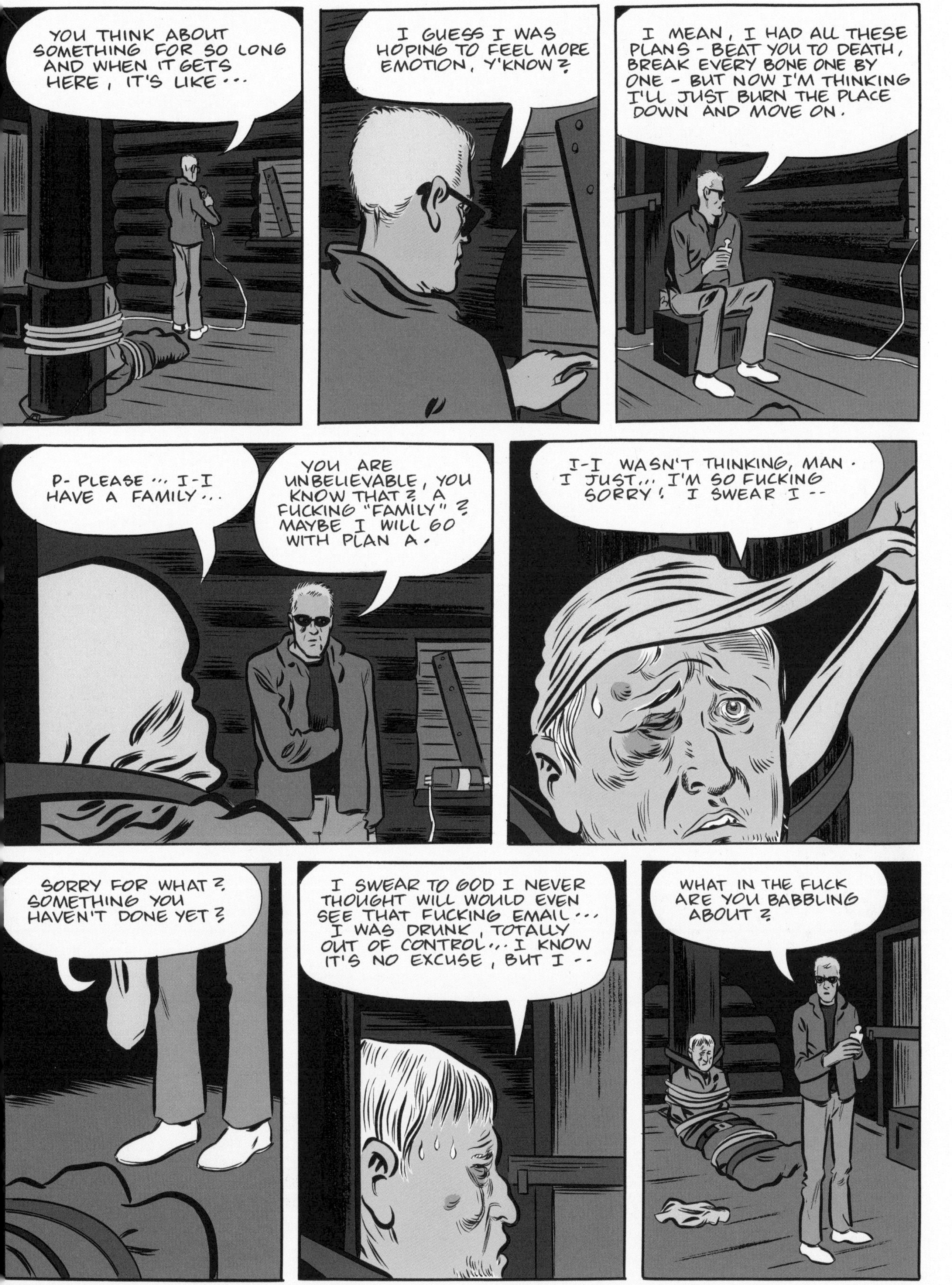
YOU THINK ABOUT SOMETHING FOR SO LONG AND WHEN IT GETS HERE, IT'S LIKE...
I GUESS I WAS HOPING TO FEEL MORE EMOTION, Y'KNOW?
I MEAN, I HAD ALL THESE PLANS - BEAT YOU TO DEATH, BREAK EVERY BONE ONE BY ONE - BUT NOW I'M THINKING I'LL JUST BURN THE PLACE DOWN AND MOVE ON.
P-PLEASE... I-I HAVE A FAMILY...
YOU ARE UNBELIEVABLE, YOU KNOW THAT? A FUCKING "FAMILY"? MAYBE I WILL GO WITH PLAN A.
I-I WASN'T THINKING, MAN. I JUST... I'M SO FUCKING SORRY! I SWEAR I--
SORRY FOR WHAT? SOMETHING YOU HAVEN'T DONE YET?
I SWEAR TO GOD I NEVER THOUGHT WILL WOULD EVEN SEE THAT FUCKING EMAIL... I WAS DRUNK, TOTALLY OUT OF CONTROL... I KNOW IT'S NO EXCUSE, BUT I--
WHAT IN THE FUCK ARE YOU BABBLING ABOUT?

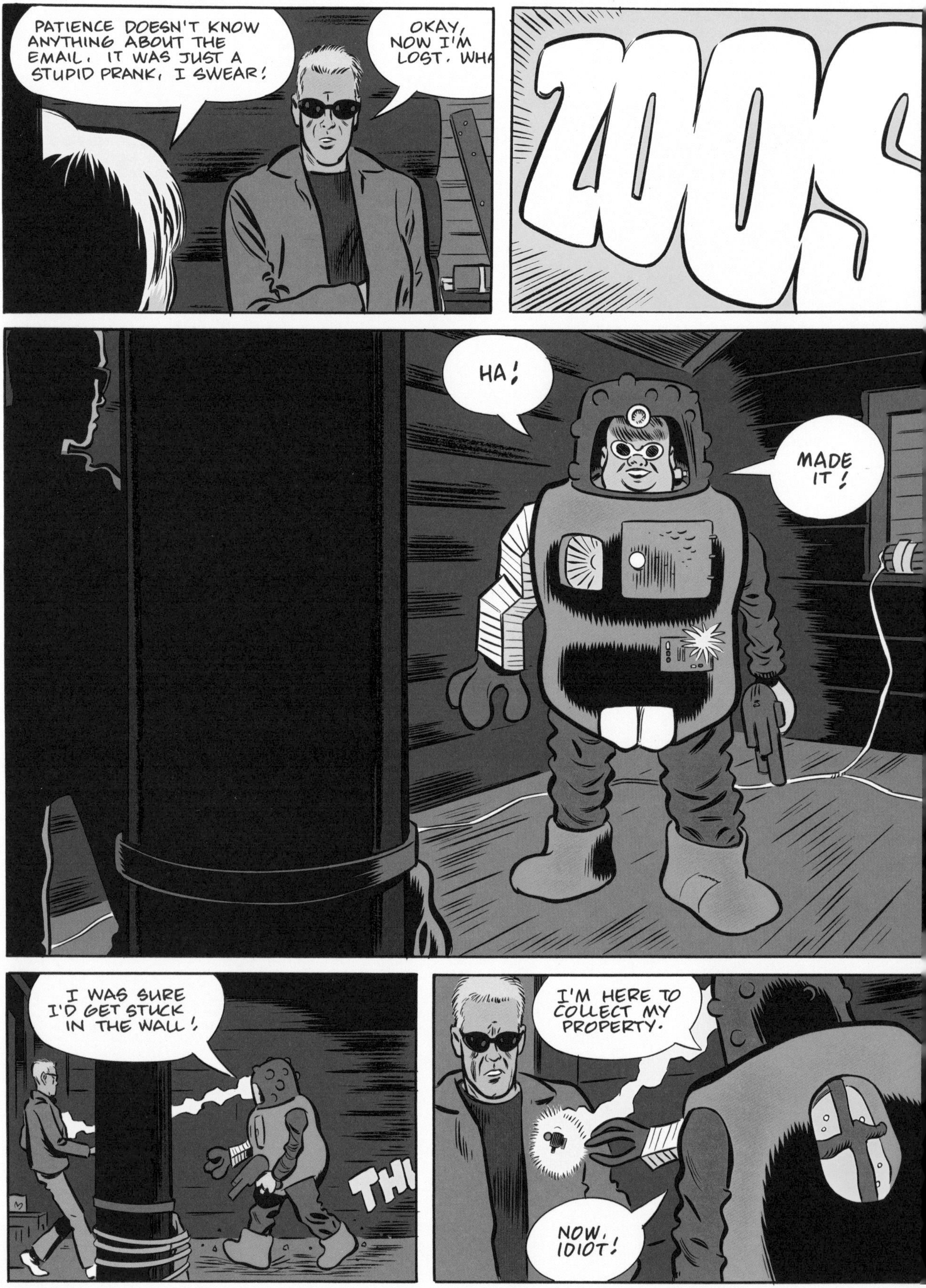
PATIENCE DOESN'T KNOW ANYTHING ABOUT THE EMAIL, IT WAS JUST A STUPID PRANK, I SWEAR!
OKAY, NOW I'M LOST. WHA
HA!
MADE IT!
I WAS SURE I'D GET STUCK IN THE WALL!
THU
I'M HERE TO COLLECT MY PROPERTY.
NOW, IDIOT!

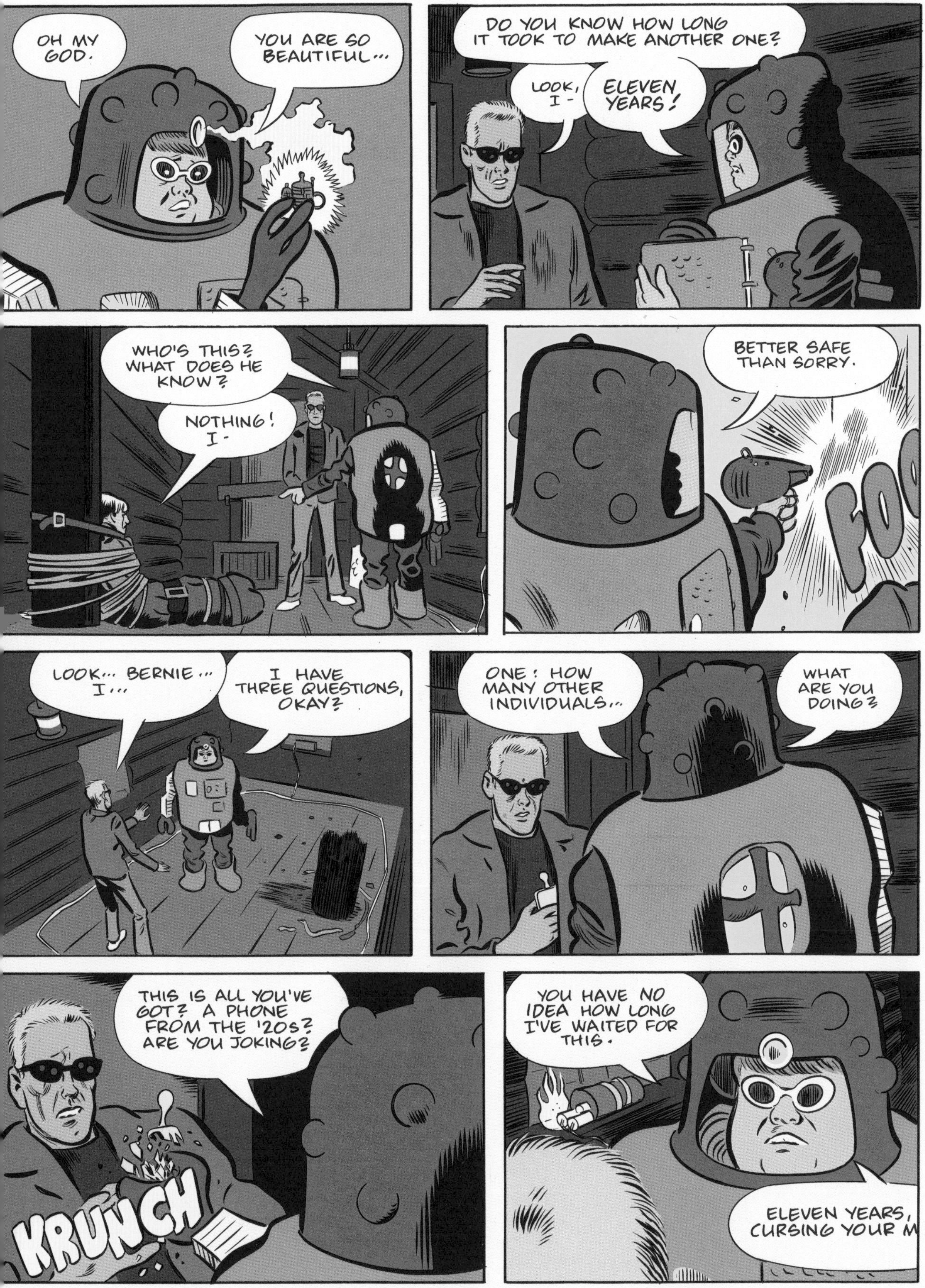
OH MY GOD.
YOU ARE SO BEAUTIFUL...
DO YOU KNOW HOW LONG IT TOOK TO MAKE ANOTHER ONE?
LOOK, I -
ELEVEN YEARS!
WHO'S THIS? WHAT DOES HE KNOW?
NOTHING! I -
BETTER SAFE THAN SORRY.
LOOK... BERNIE... I...
I HAVE THREE QUESTIONS, OKAY?
ONE: HOW MANY OTHER INDIVIDUALS...
WHAT ARE YOU DOING?
THIS IS ALL YOU'VE GOT? A PHONE FROM THE '20S? ARE YOU JOKING?
KRUNCH
YOU HAVE NO IDEA HOW LONG I'VE WAITED FOR THIS.
ELEVEN YEARS, CURSING YOUR M

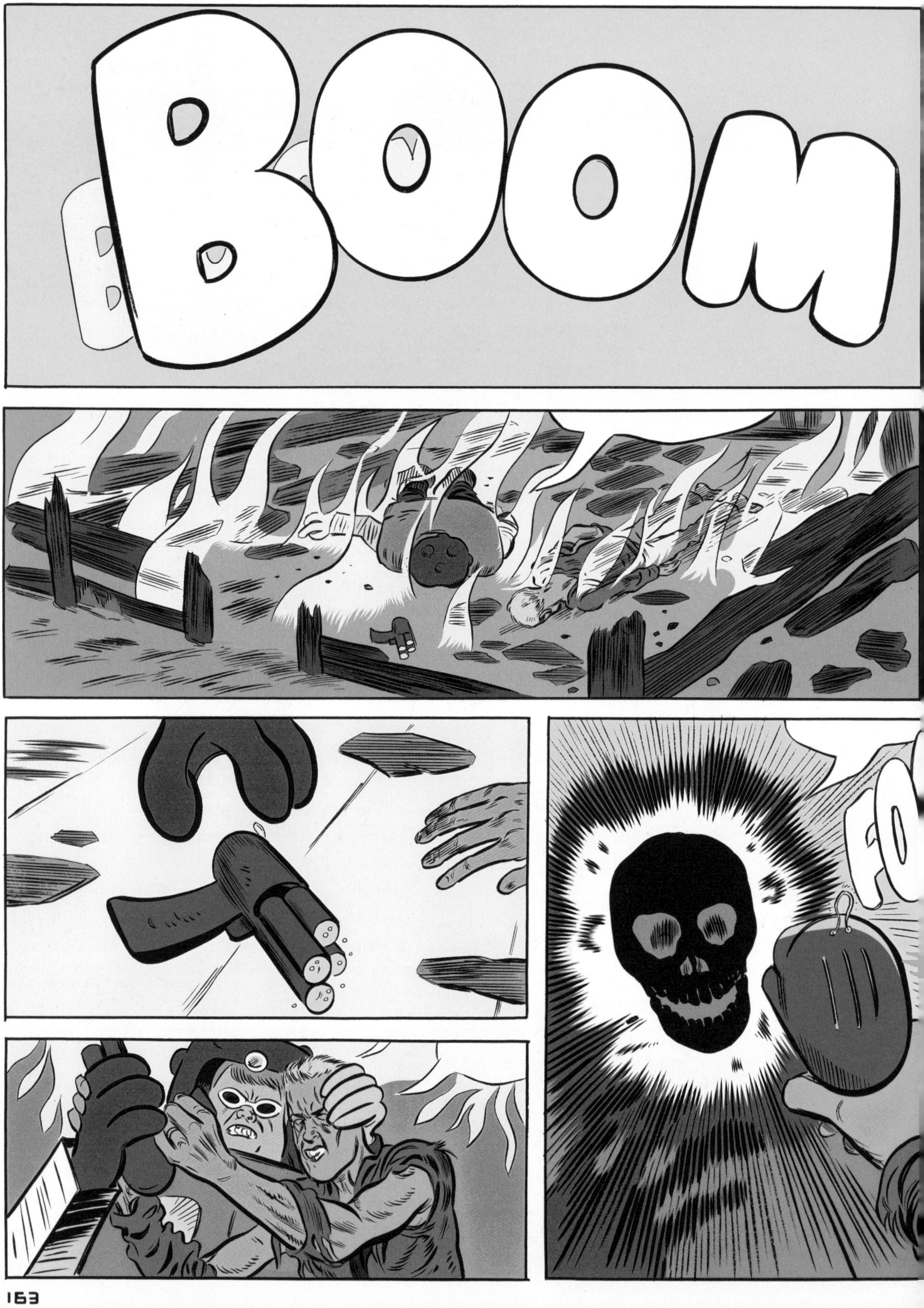
BOOM

AND JUST LIKE THAT, IT'S ALL GONE. A BIG HEAP OF ASHES.

PRETTY FUCKING HILARIOUS WHEN YOU THINK ABOUT IT.

BERNIE'S TRACKING GIZMO MUST HAVE TAKEN HIM TO THE LAST PLACE THE DEVICE EXISTED. FUCKING FAT DUMBASS SHOULD HAVE THOUGHT THAT THROUGH.

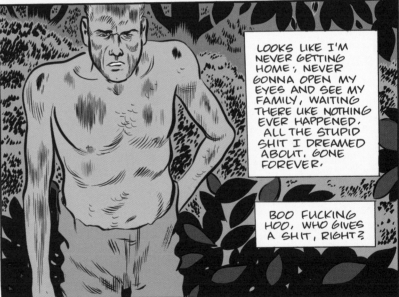

LOOKS LIKE I'M NEVER GETTING HOME, NEVER GONNA OPEN MY EYES AND SEE MY FAMILY, WAITING THERE LIKE NOTHING EVER HAPPENED. ALL THE STUPID SHIT I DREAMED ABOUT. GONE FOREVER.

BOO FUCKING HOO, WHO GIVES A SHIT, RIGHT?

I JUST NEED TO FINISH OUT THE DAY, SIT OUTSIDE THAT MOTEL ROOM LIKE A FUCKING LION UNTIL ZERO HOUR HAS COME AND GONE. I'LL WORRY ABOUT THE REST OF IT TOMORROW...

GODDAMMIT BERNIE YOU FUCKING MOTHE

164

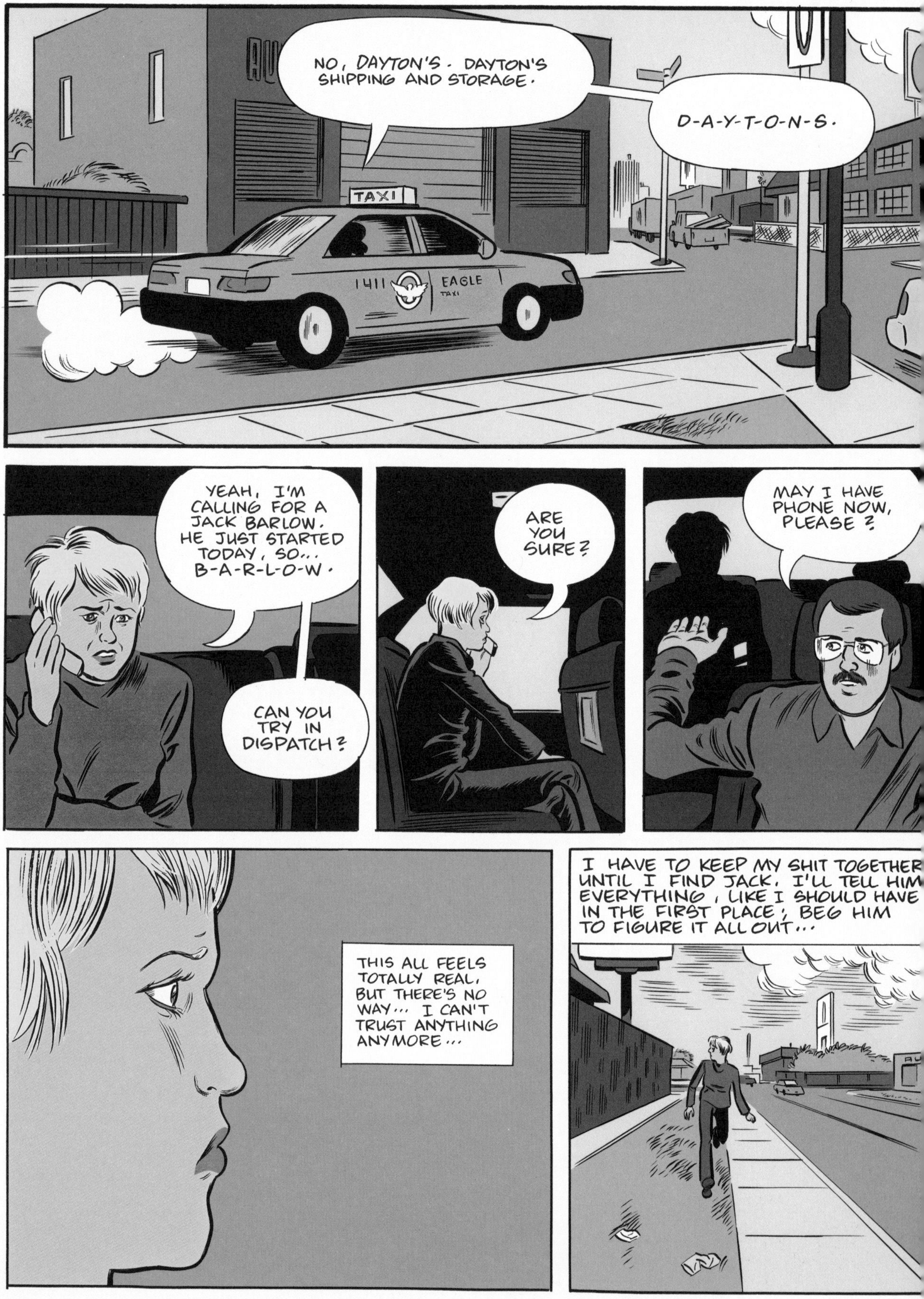
NO, DAYTON'S. DAYTON'S SHIPPING AND STORAGE.
D-A-Y-T-O-N-S.
TAXI
1411 EAGLE TAXI
YEAH, I'M CALLING FOR A JACK BARLOW. HE JUST STARTED TODAY, SO... B-A-R-L-O-W.
CAN YOU TRY IN DISPATCH?
ARE YOU SURE?
MAY I HAVE PHONE NOW, PLEASE?
THIS ALL FEELS TOTALLY REAL, BUT THERE'S NO WAY... I CAN'T TRUST ANYTHING ANYMORE...
I HAVE TO KEEP MY SHIT TOGETHER UNTIL I FIND JACK. I'LL TELL HIM EVERYTHING, LIKE I SHOULD HAVE IN THE FIRST PLACE; BEG HIM TO FIGURE IT ALL OUT...

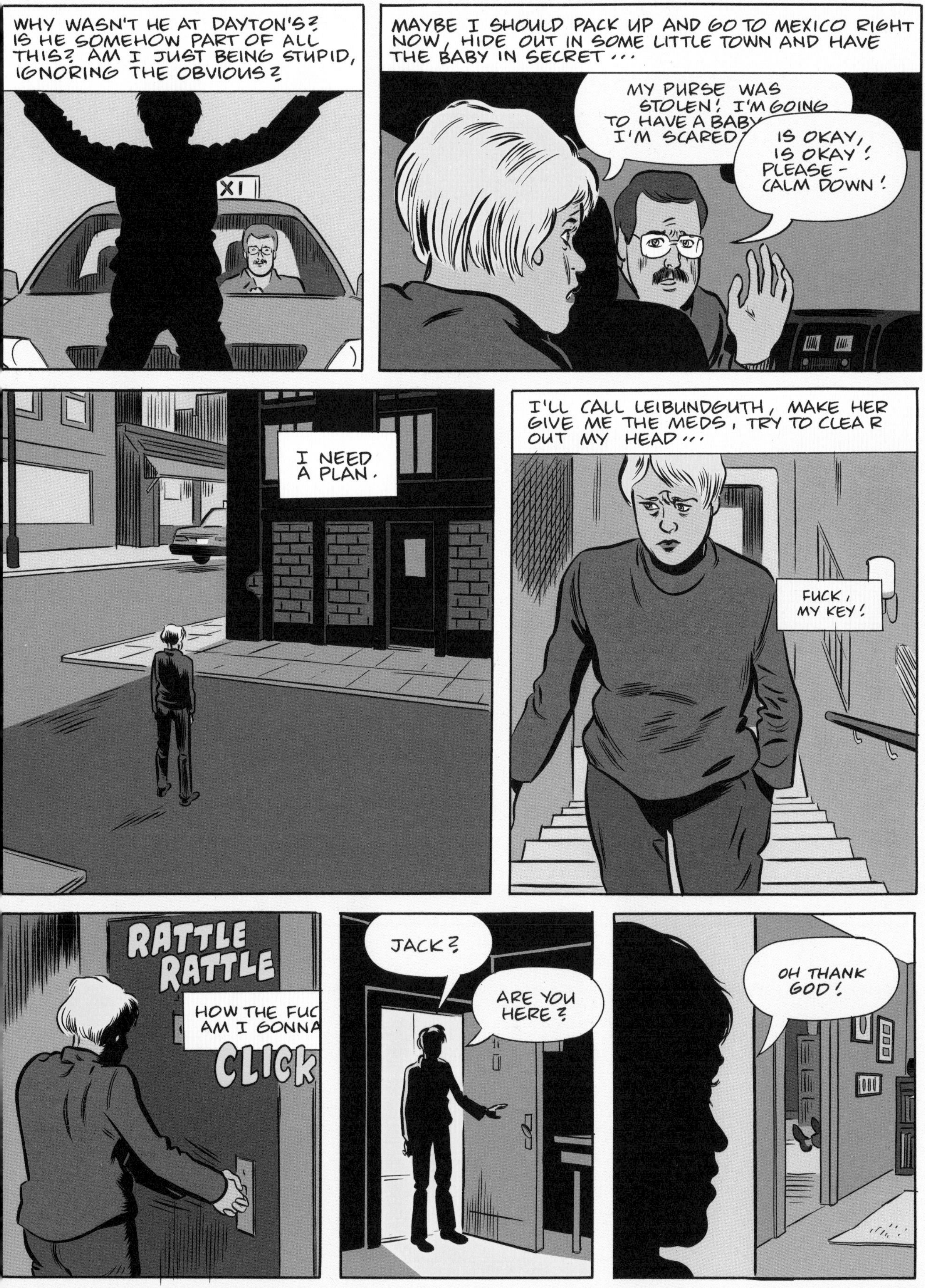

WHY WASN'T HE AT DAYTON'S? IS HE SOMEHOW PART OF ALL THIS? AM I JUST BEING STUPID, IGNORING THE OBVIOUS?
MAYBE I SHOULD PACK UP AND GO TO MEXICO RIGHT NOW, HIDE OUT IN SOME LITTLE TOWN AND HAVE THE BABY IN SECRET...
MY PURSE WAS STOLEN! I'M GOING TO HAVE A BABY I'M SCARED!
IS OKAY, IS OKAY! PLEASE - CALM DOWN!
I NEED A PLAN.
I'LL CALL LEIBUNDGUTH, MAKE HER GIVE ME THE MEDS, TRY TO CLEAR OUT MY HEAD...
FUCK, MY KEY!
RATTLE RATTLE
HOW THE FUC AM I GONNA
CLICK
JACK?
ARE YOU HERE?
OH THANK GOD!

HELLO, PATIENCE.

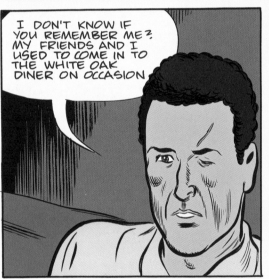

I DON'T KNOW IF YOU REMEMBER ME? MY FRIENDS AND I USED TO COME IN TO THE WHITE OAK DINER ON OCCASION.

WHERE'S JACK? WHERE'S MY HUSBAND?

EXCUSE ME...

YES, HOLD ON - I'VE GOT HER RIGHT HERE.

PATIENCE! YOU LOOK RADIANT! CONGRATULATIONS, THAT'S WONDERFUL NEWS!

WHAT IS THIS? HA

SHH!

LET ME GET RIGHT TO THE POINT, PATIENCE. I'VE JUST RECEIVED A VERY TROUBLING EMAIL FROM A FRIEND OF YOURS CONCERNING AN OLD VIDEOTAPE.

NOW, WHILE I CERTAINLY HAVE NO RECOLLECTION OF THE INCIDENT HE DESCRIBES I'D LIKE TO

GET THE FUCK OUT OF HERE!

SINCE A STORY LIKE THIS COULD PROVE DISTRACTING TO MESSAGE AS I MOVE FORWARD

I SAID FUCK OFF!

THIS IS SERIOUS, PATIENCE. BETTER LISTEN CLOSELY TO W

YOU M

OTHERFUCKE

CRASH

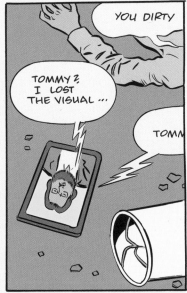

YOU DIRTY

TOMMY? I LOST THE VISUAL...

TOMM

DIE, MO

KRA

OKAY, PATIENCE— SETTLE DOWN...

THINK ABOUT THE BABY...

GET T FUC

THAT'S RIGHT, BITCH!

I'LL KILL YOU...

YEAH? YOU'LL KILL ME?

THIS IS NO HALLUCINATION.

THE WAY THE LAMP FELT WHEN IT HIT HIS SKULL, THE HOLLOW, COCONUT SOUND; THAT WAS FUCKING REAL.

BUT NOW IT'S ALL DANCING SHADOWS, DISTANT SCREAMS IN THE DARKNESS,

INTENSE FLASHES

PATIENCE!

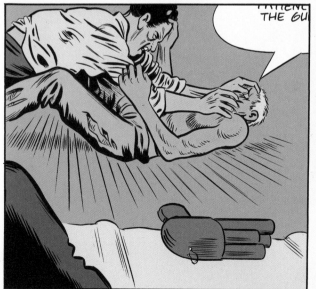

PATIENC THE GU

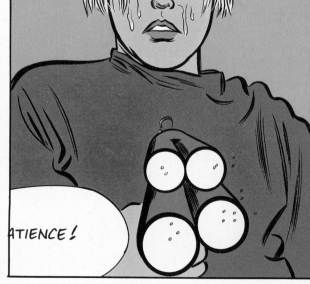

ATIENCE!

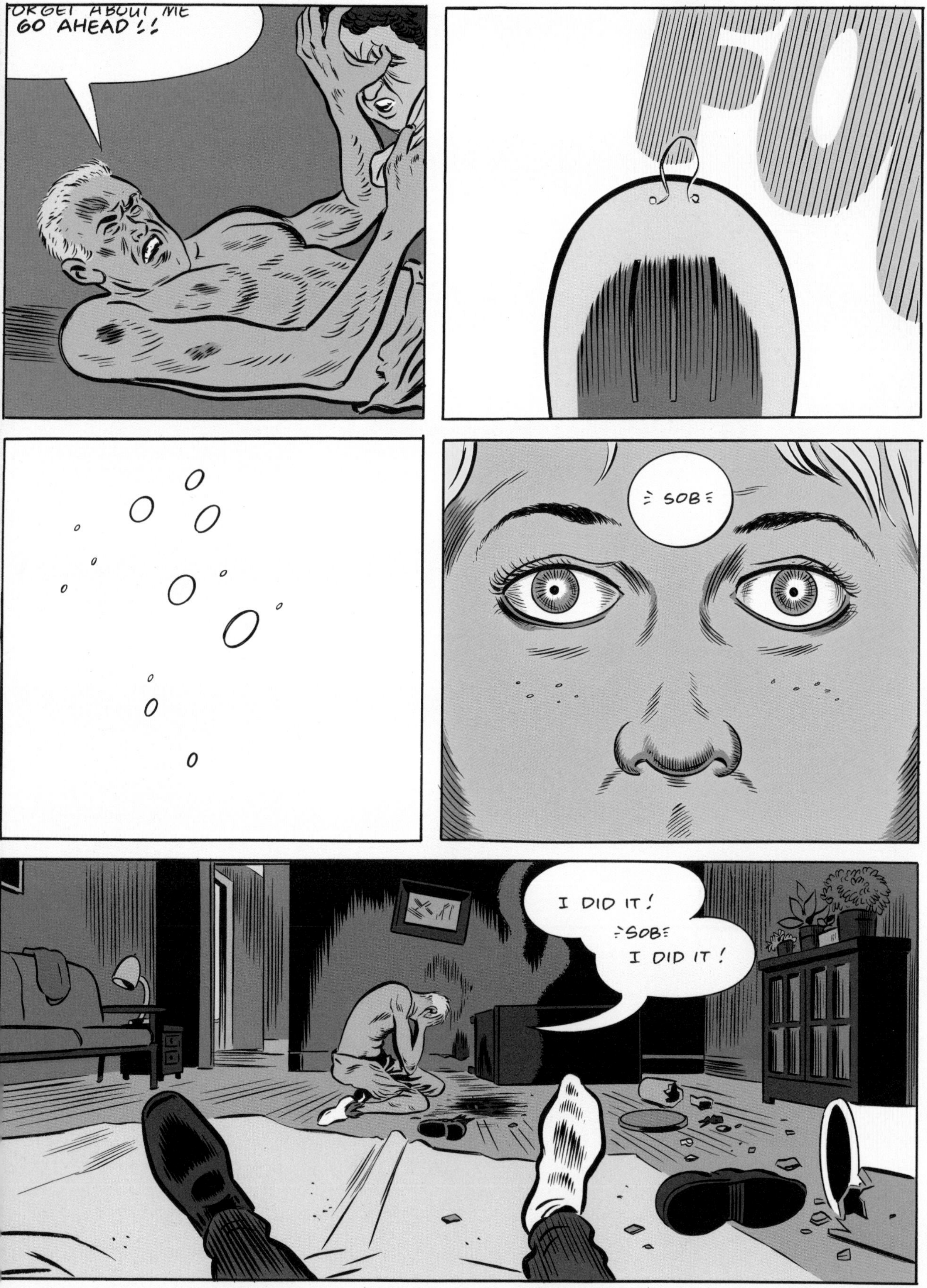
FORGET ABOUT ME
GO AHEAD!!
SOB
I DID IT!
SOB
I DID IT!

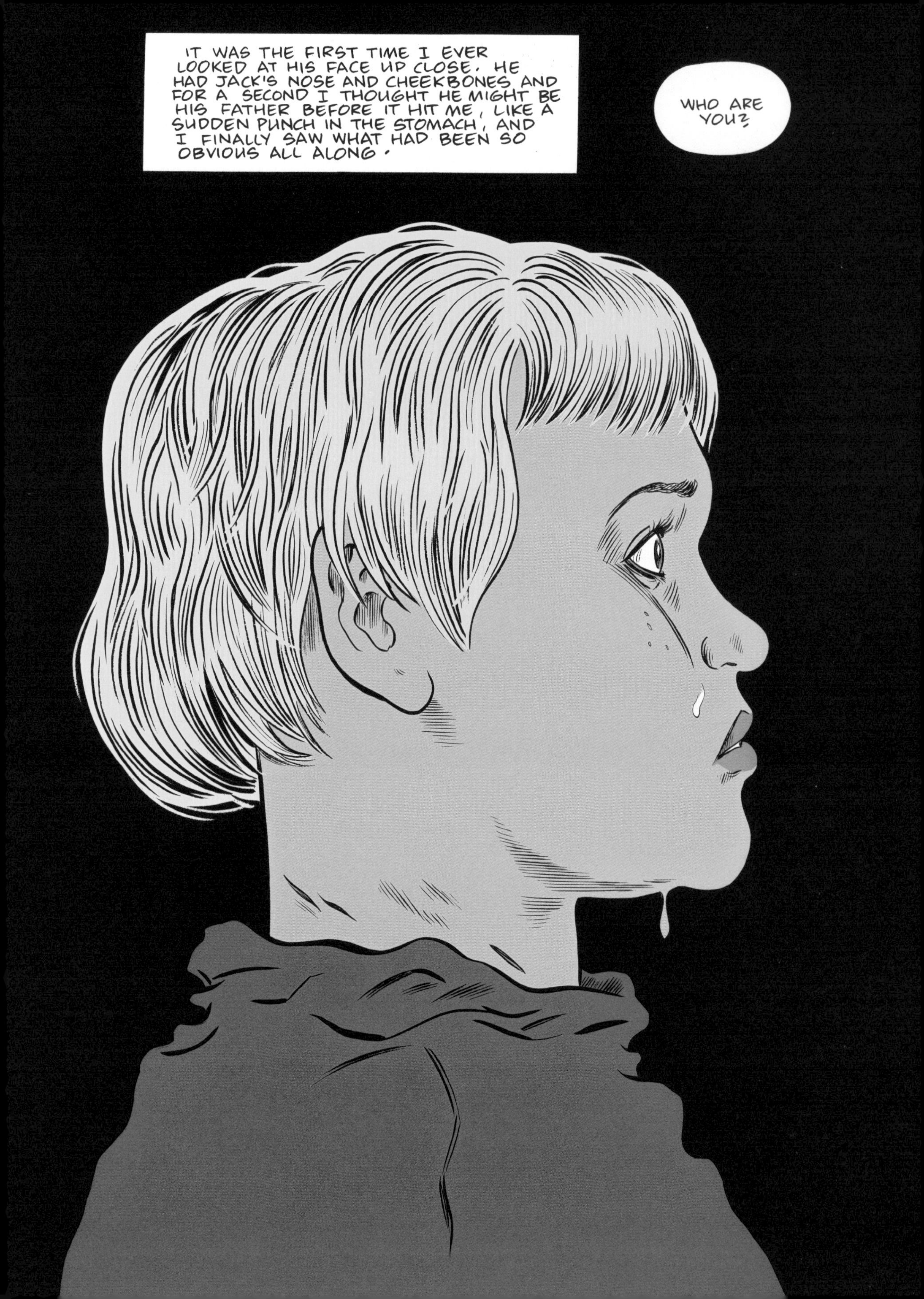
IT WAS THE FIRST TIME I EVER LOOKED AT HIS FACE UP CLOSE. HE HAD JACK'S NOSE AND CHEEKBONES AND FOR A SECOND I THOUGHT HE MIGHT BE HIS FATHER BEFORE IT HIT ME, LIKE A SUDDEN PUNCH IN THE STOMACH, AND I FINALLY SAW WHAT HAD BEEN SO OBVIOUS ALL ALONG.
WHO ARE YOU?

SHE DIDN'T KNOW. SHE REALLY DIDN'T KNOW. AND SO I TOLD HER, SIMPLE AND DIRECT, AND FOR THE FIRST TIME IN ALL OUR YEARS TOGETHER SHE LOOKED BACK AT ME WITH CLEAR, UNTROUBLED EYES.

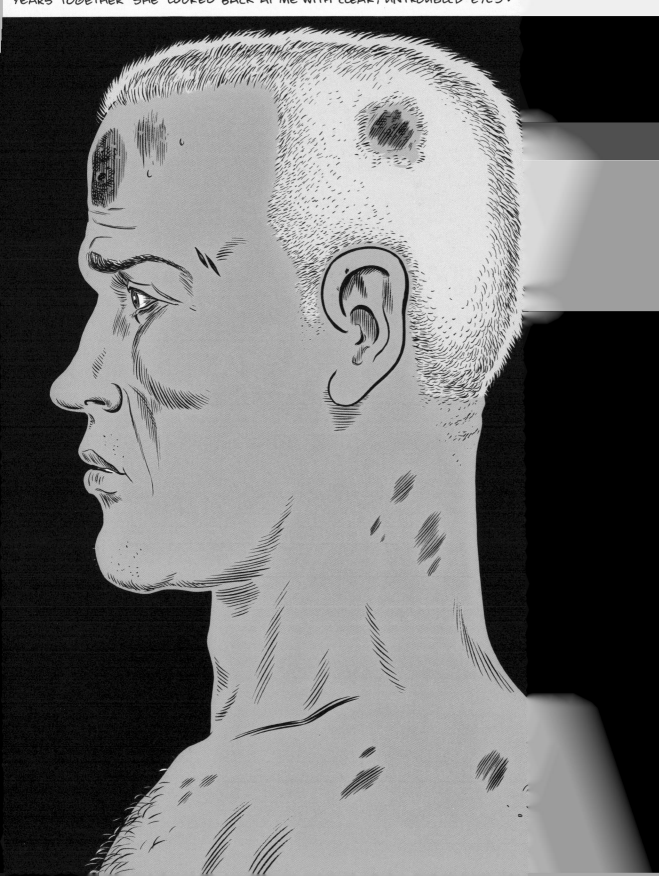

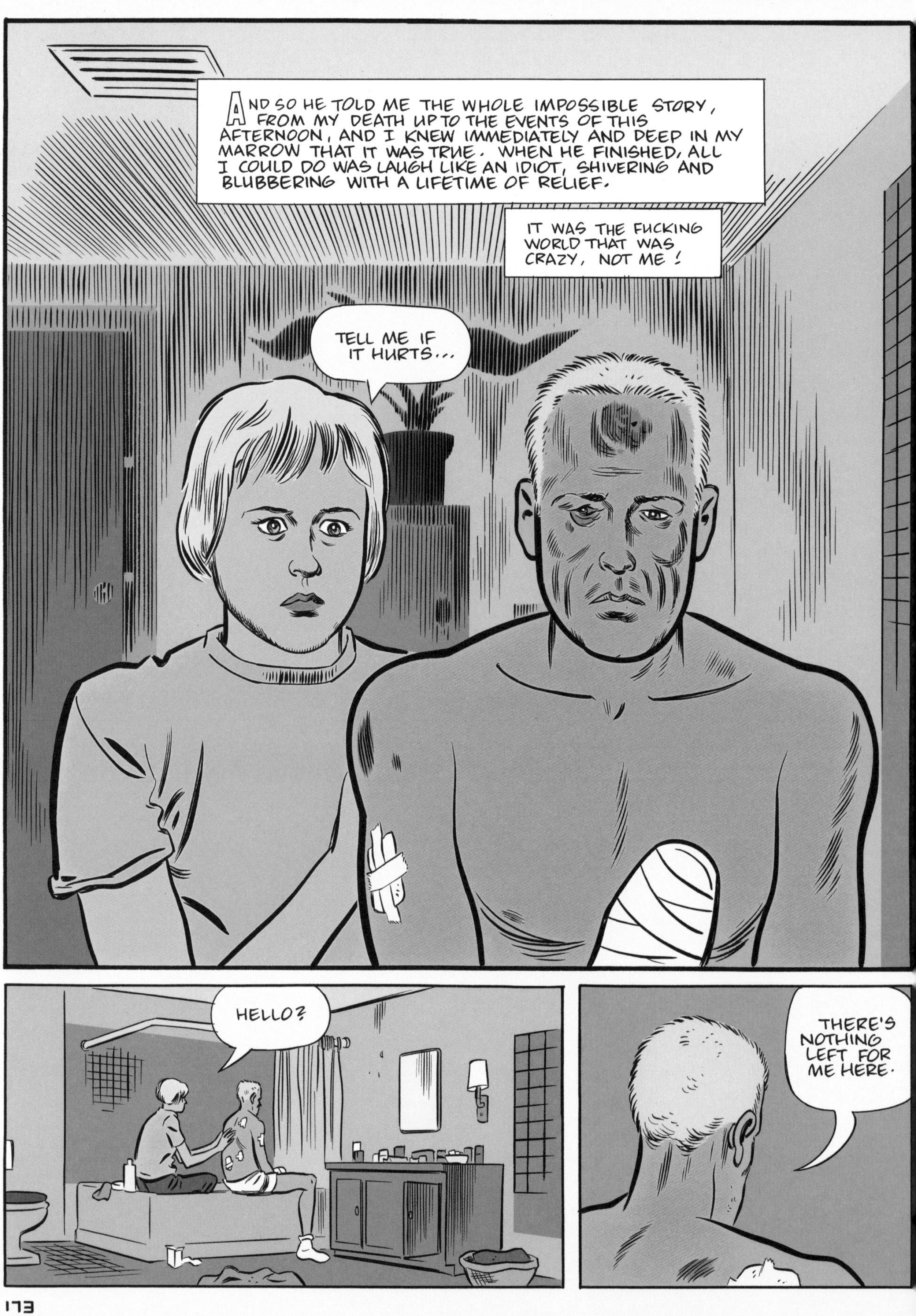
AND SO HE TOLD ME THE WHOLE IMPOSSIBLE STORY, FROM MY DEATH UP TO THE EVENTS OF THIS AFTERNOON, AND I KNEW IMMEDIATELY AND DEEP IN MY MARROW THAT IT WAS TRUE. WHEN HE FINISHED, ALL I COULD DO WAS LAUGH LIKE AN IDIOT, SHIVERING AND BLUBBERING WITH A LIFETIME OF RELIEF.
IT WAS THE FUCKING WORLD THAT WAS CRAZY, NOT ME!
TELL ME IF IT HURTS...
HELLO?
THERE'S NOTHING LEFT FOR ME HERE.

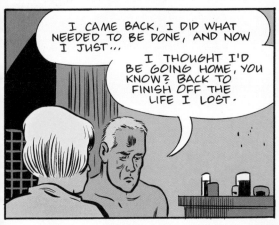

I CAME BACK, I DID WHAT NEEDED TO BE DONE, AND NOW I JUST...

I THOUGHT I'D BE GOING HOME, YOU KNOW? BACK TO FINISH OFF THE LIFE I LOST.

I GUESS I DID IT ALL FOR HIM.

BUT HE AND YOU... YOU'RE LIKE A...

A WORST-CASE SCENARIO?

HA! NO.

LISTEN TO ME, PATIENCE: WE'RE FINALLY FREE. THIS IS A WHOLE NEW THING. YOU CAN CHOOSE ANY LIFE YOU WANT!

I'M THE ONE WHO WENT THROUGH HELL AND TORMENT FOR YOU, I KNOW THINGS HE'LL NEVER BEGIN TO UNDERSTAND. WE COULD BE LONG GONE BEFORE HE EVER COMES THROUGH THAT DOOR!

YOU COULD HAVE DONE ANYTHING - CHANGED HISTORY, SAVED LIVES...

ALL I EVER THOUGHT ABOUT WAS YOU, YOU AND THE BABY.

YOU HAVE TO MAKE A CHOICE. YOU HAVE TO CLEAR YOUR MIND AND TELL ME WHAT YOU TRULY FE—

SHH!

I NEED A MOMENT OF SILENCE.

174

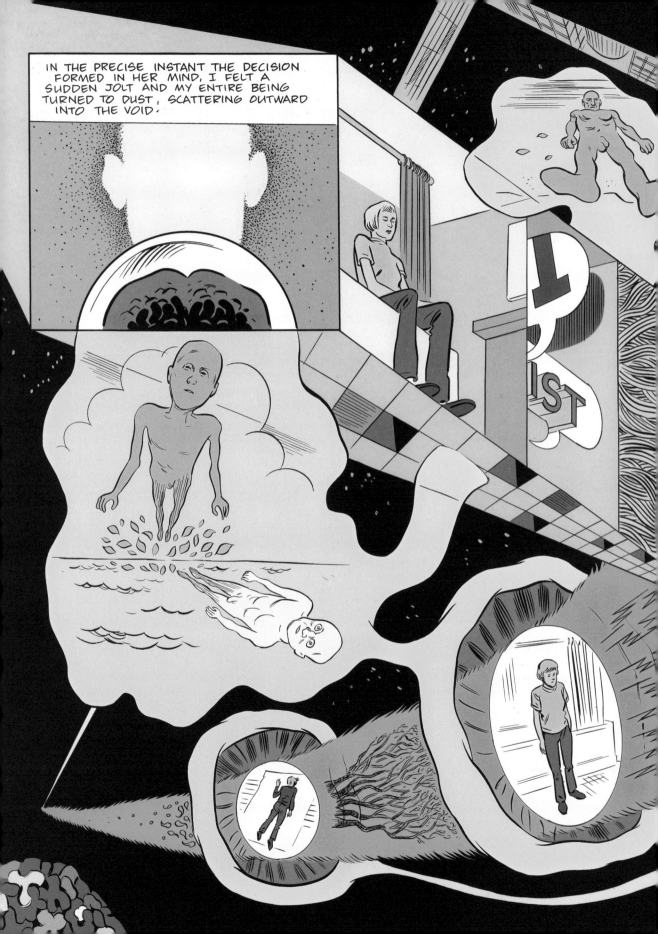

IN THE PRECISE INSTANT THE DECISION FORMED IN HER MIND, I FELT A SUDDEN JOLT AND MY ENTIRE BEING TURNED TO DUST, SCATTERING OUTWARD INTO THE VOID.

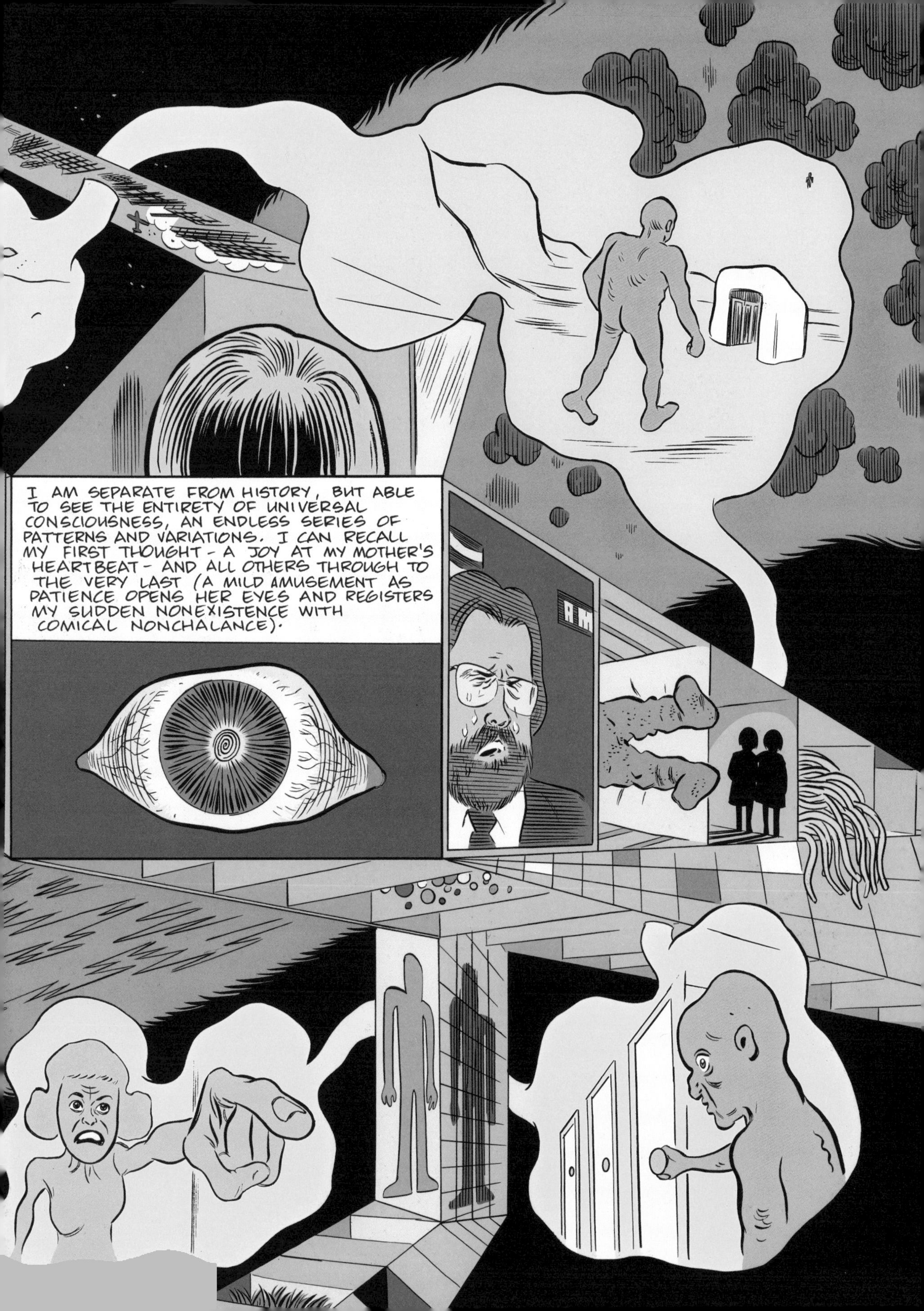
I AM SEPARATE FROM HISTORY, BUT ABLE TO SEE THE ENTIRETY OF UNIVERSAL CONSCIOUSNESS, AN ENDLESS SERIES OF PATTERNS AND VARIATIONS. I CAN RECALL MY FIRST THOUGHT - A JOY AT MY MOTHER'S HEARTBEAT - AND ALL OTHERS THROUGH TO THE VERY LAST (A MILD AMUSEMENT AS PATIENCE OPENS HER EYES AND REGISTERS MY SUDDEN NONEXISTENCE WITH COMICAL NONCHALANCE).
AM

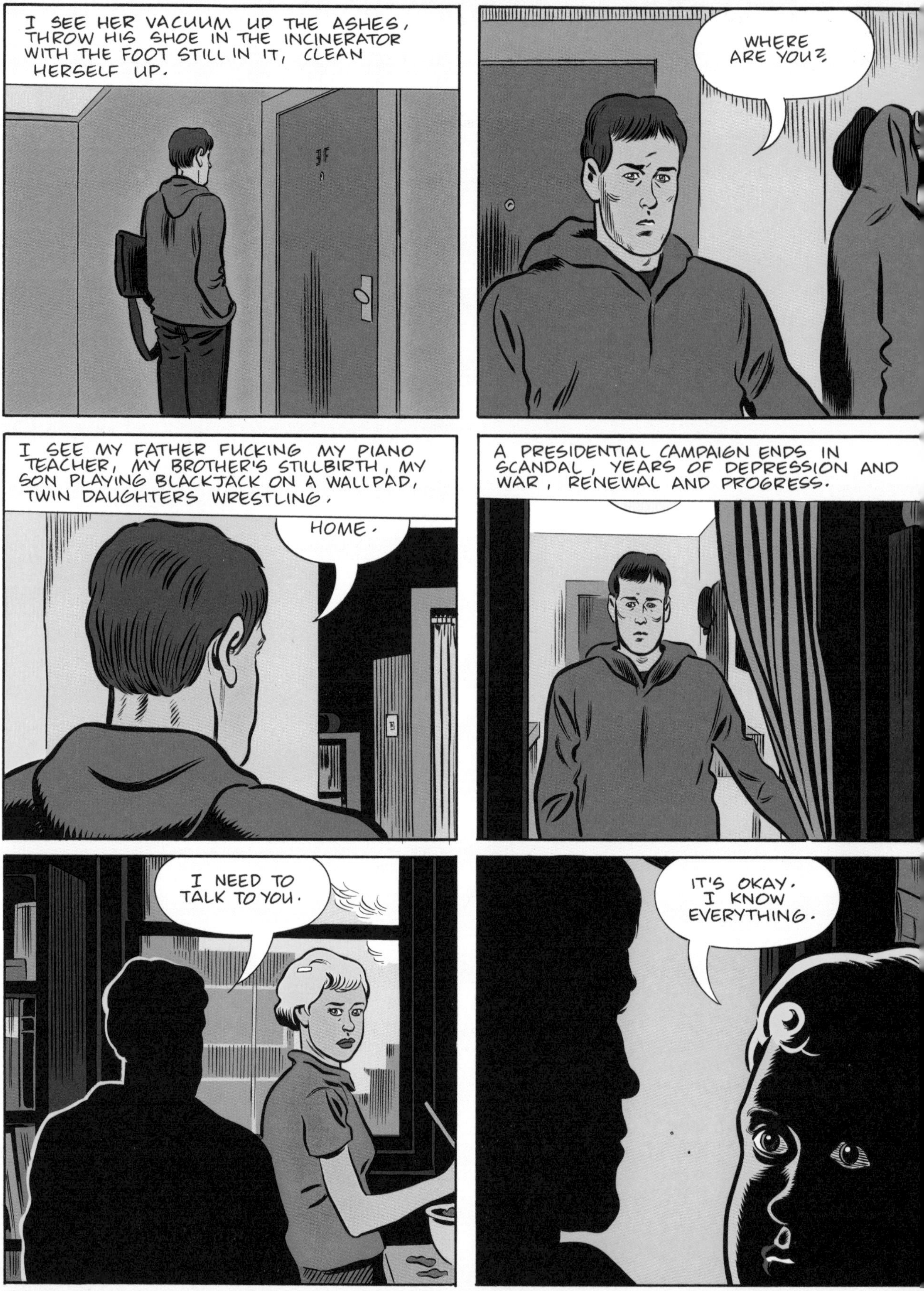

I SEE HER VACUUM UP THE ASHES, THROW HIS SHOE IN THE INCINERATOR WITH THE FOOT STILL IN IT, CLEAN HERSELF UP.
3F
WHERE ARE YOU?
I SEE MY FATHER FUCKING MY PIANO TEACHER, MY BROTHER'S STILLBIRTH, MY SON PLAYING BLACKJACK ON A WALLPAD, TWIN DAUGHTERS WRESTLING.
HOME.
A PRESIDENTIAL CAMPAIGN ENDS IN SCANDAL, YEARS OF DEPRESSION AND WAR, RENEWAL AND PROGRESS.
I NEED TO TALK TO YOU.
IT'S OKAY. I KNOW EVERYTHING.

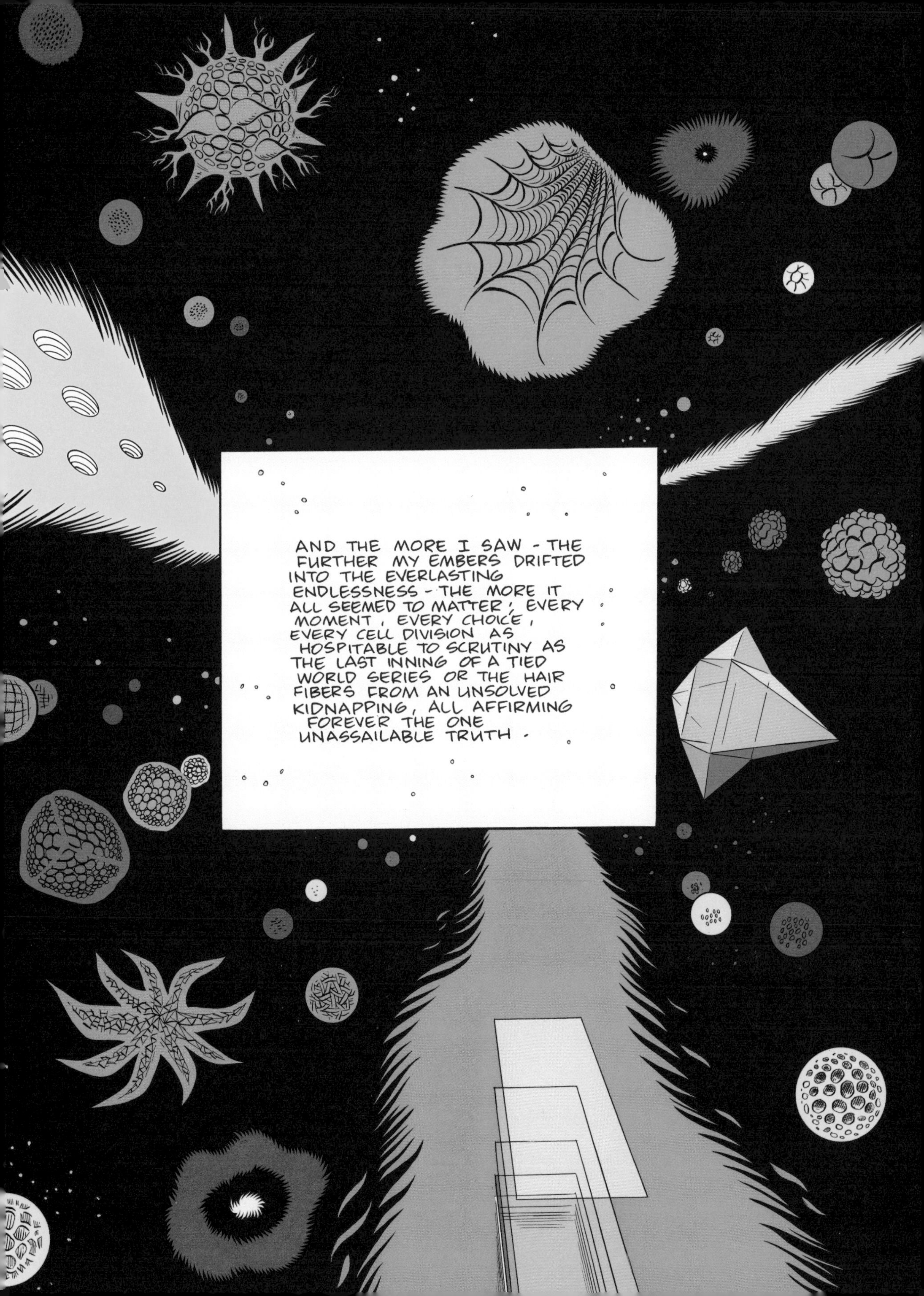
AND THE MORE I SAW - THE FURTHER MY EMBERS DRIFTED INTO THE EVERLASTING ENDLESSNESS - THE MORE IT ALL SEEMED TO MATTER; EVERY MOMENT, EVERY CHOICE, EVERY CELL DIVISION AS HOSPITABLE TO SCRUTINY AS THE LAST INNING OF A TIED WORLD SERIES OR THE HAIR FIBERS FROM AN UNSOLVED KIDNAPPING, ALL AFFIRMING FOREVER THE ONE UNASSAILABLE TRUTH.

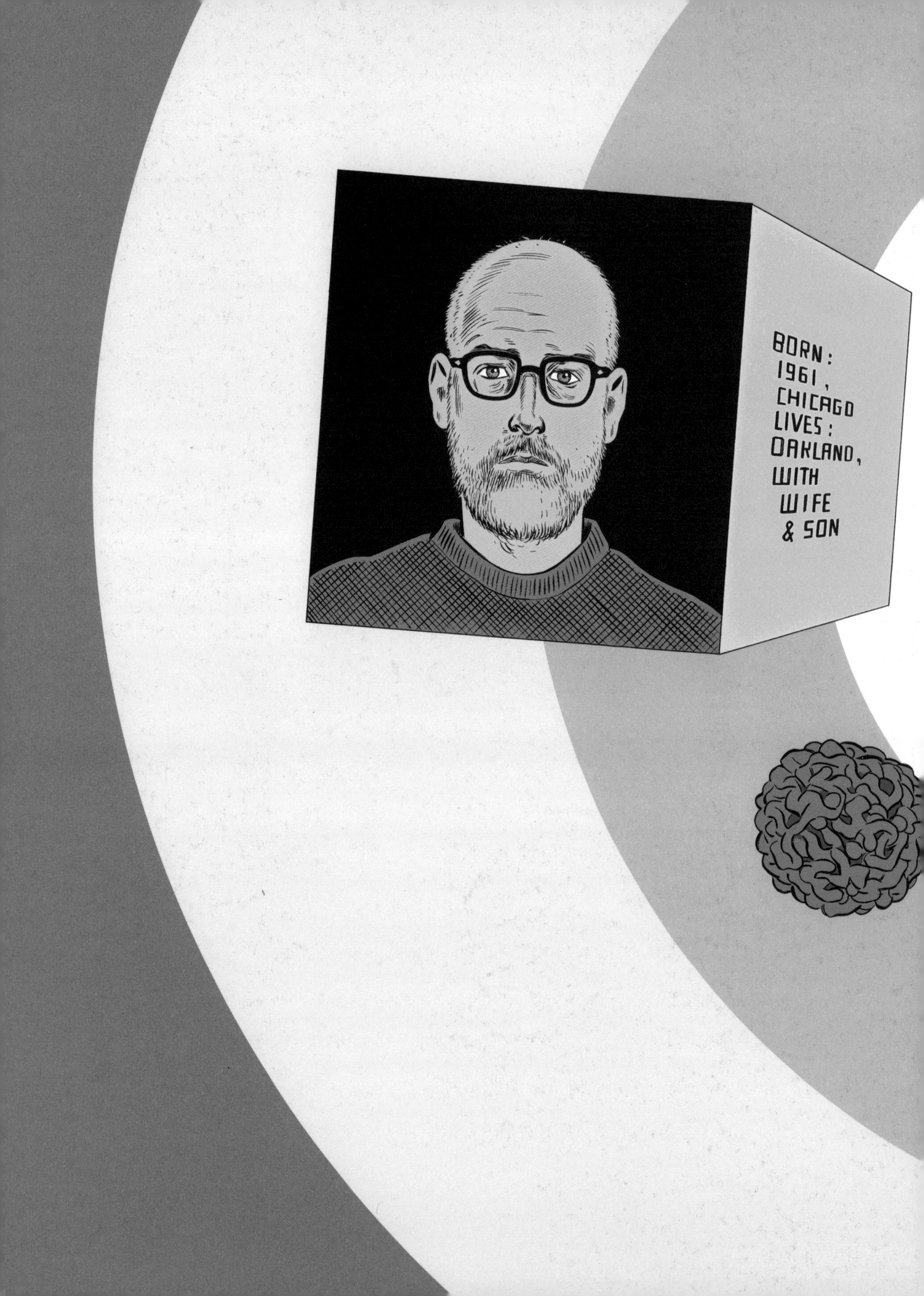
BORN: 1961, CHICAGO
LIVES: OAKLAND, WITH WIFE & SON

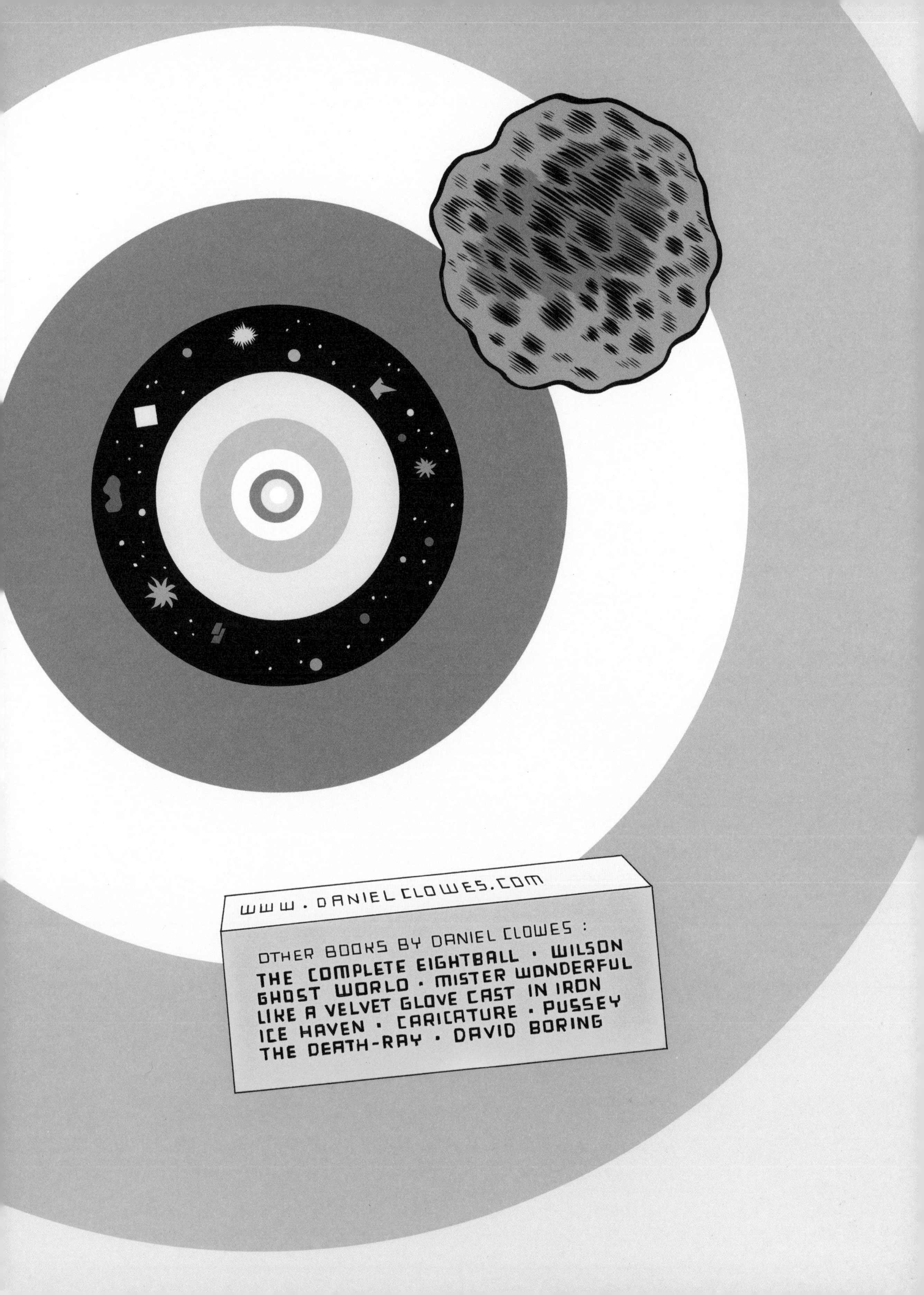
WWW . DANIEL CLOWES.COM
OTHER BOOKS BY DANIEL CLOWES :
THE COMPLETE EIGHTBALL · WILSON
GHOST WORLD · MISTER WONDERFUL
LIKE A VELVET GLOVE CAST IN IRON
ICE HAVEN · CARICATURE · PUSSEY
THE DEATH-RAY · DAVID BORING

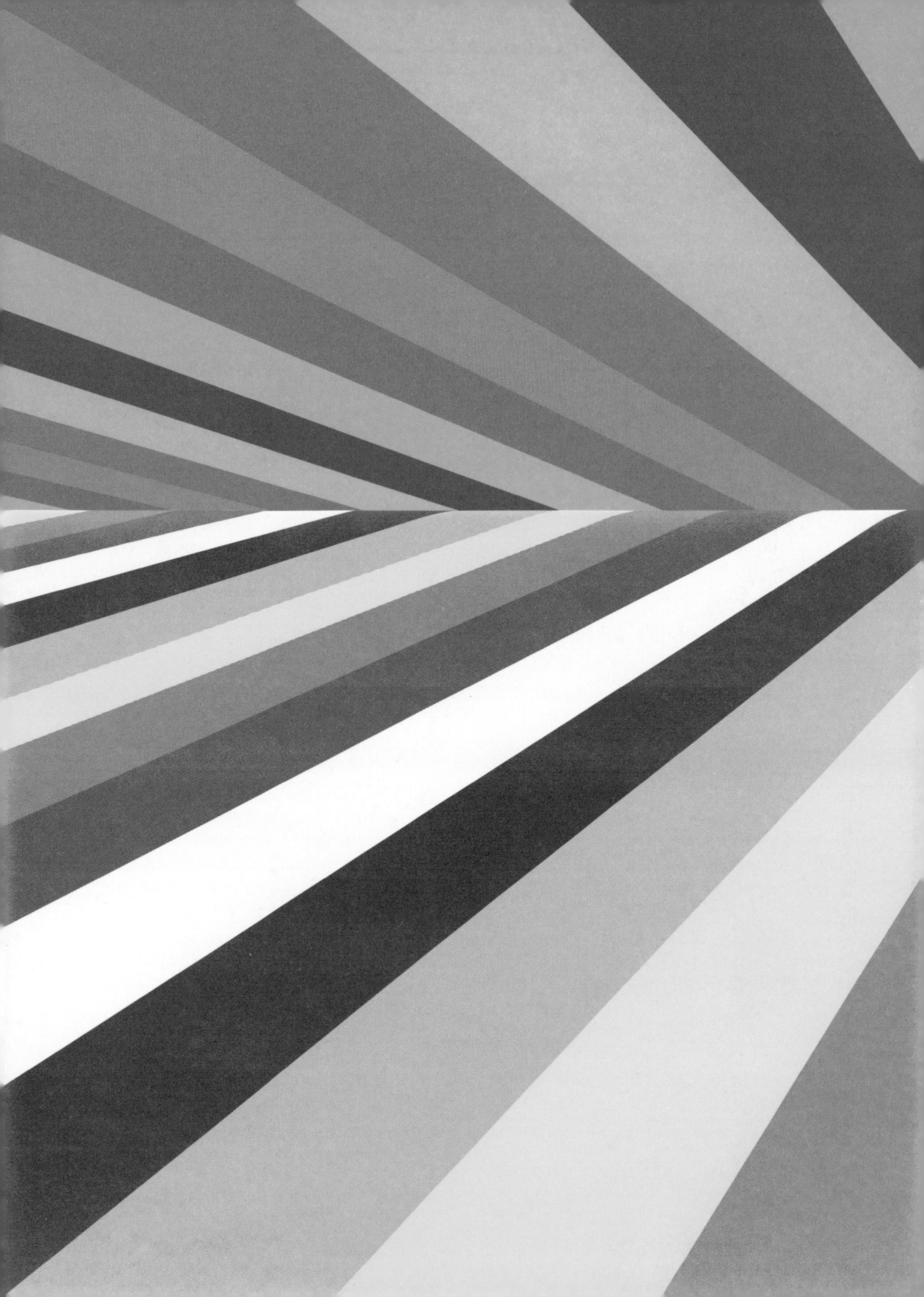